SABRES
over MiG ALLEY

SABRES over MiG ALLEY

The F-86 and the

Battle for Air Superiority

in Korea

Kenneth P. Werrell

Naval Institute Press

Annapolis, Maryland

Naval Institute Press
291 Wood Road
Annapolis, MD 21402

Library of Congress Cataloging-in-Publication Data

Werrell, Kenneth P.
  Sabres over mig alley : the f-86 and the battle for air superiority in
Korea / Kenneth P. Werrell.
    p. cm.
  Includes bibliographical references and index.
  ISBN 1-59114-933-9 (alk. paper)
  1. Korean War, 1950–1953—Aerial operations, American.   2. Sabre (Jet
fighter planes)—History.   3. Airplanes, Military—United States—History.
  4. Fighter pilots—United States—History.   I. Title.

DS920.2.U5W47   2005
951.904'248—dc22   2005007347

Printed in the United States of America on acid-free paper ∞

12 11 10 09 08 07 06 05   9 8 7 6 5 4 3 2
First printing

To Jeanne

Contents

Acknowledgments

This effort was inspired by those USAF pilots who flew F-86s at Lowery Air Force Base in the mid-1950s, especially those who had flown in the Korean War and awed a seventeen-year-old cadet at the Air Force Academy. These included Raymond Barton, Charles Gabriel, and William Yancey. I attempted to write this story there and then, but the academic system at that time would not allow it. So here, almost a half century later, is that account.

My sincere appreciation and thanks are extended to the great number of people who assisted in making this project a success. As the citations reveal, most of the research effort was conducted at the USAF Historical Research Agency, where Joe Caver, Archie Difanti, Dan Haulman, and Forrest Marion were notable for their help. At the Air Force Materiel Command, Bill Elliott lent valuable assistance, as did Doug Lantry at the Air Force Museum, Von Hardesty at the Air and Space Museum, Tim Nenninger at the National Archives, Tom Lubbesmeyer and Mike Lombardi at Boeing, and Wilson Sullivan and John Daly at the Federal Records Center in St. Louis. Thanks are also due to Sharon Sellers MacDonald for making sixty of her father's letters available to me.

Sixty former Sabre pilots made a great contribution to this study. They were very cooperative in describing their experiences and in answering my numerous questions in a candid manner. Their contribution broadened what otherwise would be a multi-archival study and deepened it into areas thus far neglected.

The reference librarians at the Air University and Radford University made my task much easier, as did the interlibrary loan librarians. Special thanks are also due Mark Gatlin at the Naval Institute Press for encouraging this project and pushing it along. Jennifer Till and my competent and patient copy editor, John Geldmacher, were also instrumental in getting this project into print.

But most of all, this book could not have been possible without the effort, encouragement, and support of my wife, Jeanne.

SABRES
over MiG ALLEY

MANCHURIA

• Mukden

Vladivostok
UNION OF SOVIET
SOCIALIST REPUBLICS

*Sui-ho
Reservoir*

KOREA

MiG Alley

*Chong-Chong
River*

Antung
Sinuiju

Sinanju

Korea Bay

⊛ P'yongyang

SEA

OF

JAPAN

Cho-Do

**Front Line
1951-1953**

38°
Paengnyong-Do

Kaesong

CHINA

Kimpo (K-14)
4th Fighter
Interceptor Wing

⊛ Seoul

38°

Suwon (K-13)
51st Fighter
Interceptor Wing

YELLOW

SEA

KOREA

Korea   Strait

JAPAN

Area of Operations
Korea, 1951-1953

0   100

Nautical Miles

Introduction

On the morning of 8 November 1950, Communist MiG-15 jets engaged a USAF air strike over the Yalu River near the city of Sinuiju. One of the MiGs dove in front of 1st Lt. Russell J. Brown, who was flying the number two (wingman) position in a flight of four F-80s. Although the American jets could neither out-climb nor out-run the MiGs, they could out-dive them. The heavier American plane quickly overhauled the Soviet fighter, and Brown held down the trigger. The USAF credited him with a kill, officially (and tersely) noting that, "During the encounter, Lt. Brown scored hits on an enemy MiG-15 that was seen to go down and explode."[1] This was the first jet-versus-jet combat and, according to American sources, the first jet downed by another jet.

The next day two MiGs bounced an RB-29 near Sinuiju. The aircraft's tail gunner, Sgt. Harry Lavene, returned the enemy's fire and claimed a MiG; the bomber was badly damaged and crash-landed in Japan, killing five of the crew.[2] Two days later MiGs downed a B-29. On 14 November B-29 gunner S.Sgt. Richard Fisher received credit for destroying a MiG.[3]

MiGs also tangled with Navy aircraft operating in the area. On 9 November MiGs engaged a formation of prop attack aircraft, escorted by jet-powered Panthers (F9F). During the ensuing battle Lt. Cdr. William Amen got on a MiG's tail, peppered it with 20 mm projectiles, and pursued it down to the deck. Amen's wingman saw the Soviet aircraft hit the ground. A week later, on 18 November, Ens. F. C. Weber destroyed a MiG; and Lt. Cdr. William Lamb and Lt. R. E. Parker shared credit for downing another.[4]

On 17 December 1950, a flight* of four F-86s (Sabres) led by Lt. Col. Bruce Hinton, commander of the 336th Fighter Squadron, took off from Kimpo airfield.[5] Hinton's formation, in an attempt to deceive the Communists, masqueraded as F-80s by using their radio call signs, air speeds, and altitudes. As the four F-86s headed in a northeasterly direction at twenty-five thousand feet, the number two man spotted four unidentified aircraft at eighteen thousand feet. The Americans quickly identified the aircraft as hostiles, and Hinton led the flight in a dive on the MiGs. The F-86s pulled 5 "g"s and out-turned the Soviet fighters, which dropped their tanks, began to dive, and then resumed a climb. The Sabres dove at full throttle, attaining a speed above the aircraft's Mach 0.95 red line speed, and closed the distance to their prey.

The Communist formation then spread apart, and the last man broke left, pursued by the second American element. Simultaneously, Hinton and his wingman pursued the other three MiGs. Hinton fired on the number two aircraft and observed hits on the aircraft's wing and fuselage. That fighter turned left and cycled his speed brakes as his aircraft began to smoke. Hinton closed to within eight hundred to one thousand feet as he bounced around in the MiG's jet wash. The American pilot fired a long burst and observed flame coming from the fighter's tailpipe and smoke from its fuselage. He fired another long burst and saw "long violent flames enveloping [the] entire aircraft, which then slowed down terrifically."[6] To avoid overshooting the Red fighter, Hinton extended his speed brakes and throttled back as he fired into the damaged aircraft, which continued to burn as it began to shed pieces. The second USAF element observed a "MiG spinning slowly and awkwardly at three thousand to five hundred feet, going down smoking." Although no one observed a crash or explosion, the Air Force concluded that Hinton had downed the MiG, achieving the first of more than eight hundred victory credits awarded to F-86 pilots in the Korean War.[7]

Thus began the titanic struggle between MiG and Sabre that would markedly shape the air war and, to a lesser degree, the entire Korean conflict.

The Korean War was a shock for Americans. The most powerful nation in the world, armed not only with conventional forces but also with atomic bombs and long-range bombers, was thwarted by the combined opposition of a second- and a third-rate military power. While the United States and

*Two aircraft flying together comprise an element; two or more elements flying together make up a flight.

United Nations (UN) achieved their initial objective, thwarting a direct invasion of the South, they failed to accomplish their later goal of unifying the entire Korean peninsula. Instead, the UN found itself in a grueling war of attrition with the most populous nation in the world. In sharp contrast to the total victory gained in 1945, the best the United States and UN could achieve after three years of fighting was a stalemate. Communist China emerged as a world power as it dealt a blow to the American psyche and pride. And the issue in Korea was not resolved. Fifty years after the end of the conflict, Korea remains divided, with American troops stationed there to counter the military threat that still exists on the peninsula.

The Korean War has become "the forgotten war" and stands in sharp negative contrast to World War II. The Korean War is not remembered for victory, glory, and accomplishment; it is instead remembered for allied frustration (certainly after the first six months), courage, and stamina. Trench warfare returned to the battlefield. In that respect, the Korean War seemed a throwback, not to the last war, but the one before the last.

If the ground forces were re-fighting World War I, the aviators were breaking new ground. In terms of victories and losses, the Korean War would become the largest air-to-air war of the jet era.[8] The North American F-86 Sabre, the primary MiG slayer in the war, would become the most successful air-to-air jet fighter of all time.[9] However, the aviators were not merely demonstrating their skill and the latest in aviation technology; they played an important role not only in how the war was fought but also how it turned out.

We should not overemphasize the glory and romance, the excitement and drama, of the air-to-air battle. Although the F-86 flew more sorties than the other USAF fighters engaged in the war (F-51, F-80, and F-84), the Sabre logged the lowest number of combat flying hours, aircraft lost, and casualties. The Sabres' victory was significant because it gave the United Nations air superiority. That air superiority was a powerful UN advantage in this conflict, allowing the airmen to provide close air support and interdiction for ground troops and preventing the Communist air arm from engaging in offensive actions. (A minor exception was the night nuisance raids by the aptly named "Bed Check Charlie.")

American air power enacted a heavy toll upon enemy forces and helped prevent UN ground forces from being overrun. Without air power, the result might have been different; certainly the cost would have been higher. Similar to the RAF's victory in the famous Battle of Britain, the American victory in the skies over northwestern Korea known as "MiG Alley" determined how a large part of the rest of the war was fought. Air superiority allowed UN air power to be effective.

During the first four months of the war, the UN airmen had things their own way. Then, in November 1950, the Communists introduced the MiG-15 and threatened UN air superiority. The USAF countered with small numbers of F-86s, the best American fighter of the day. Fighting against great odds, far from their bases and hampered by political restrictions, the Sabres successfully battled the MiGs.

It is clear that the Americans got the better of the fight in terms of victories and losses, despite some dispute about numbers engaged and downed. More important than this argument is the fact that the American success over MiG Alley not only kept Communist aircraft off the backs of UN ground forces, but also allowed UN air power to operate almost anywhere, except close to the Yalu River, without enemy aerial opposition. The battle over MiG Alley was a clear-cut UN victory, one of the few glorious UN military feats of the war. Just as the aviators of World War I fought and symbolized a different war than the one fought on the ground, so too did the pilots that flew the Sabres over MiG Alley. This is their story.

ONE

F-86 Design and Development

In mid-1944 the Army Air Forces (AAF) developed a requirement for a single-place, medium-range, high-altitude day fighter that would serve as both an escort fighter and fighter-bomber. The AAF released the proposal to the aircraft industry in October that same year. Late the following month, North American Aviation started design studies, and they submitted four designs to the airmen in early 1945. After selecting a design, the AAF awarded the company a contract in May to build three copies of an aircraft designated XP-86. The next month the airmen approved a mock-up of the fighter.[1] The AAF approved the design mock-up in June 1945.[2]

The design was of a straight-wing aircraft that borrowed from North American Aviation's concurrent work on the FJ-1 Fury that it was developing for the Navy. The FJ-1 and XP-86 had the same general lines, bubble canopy, J35 engine, armament, and wing. The fighter's straight wing was based on North American's legendary P-51 wing and would mount four speed brakes that actuated above and below the wing, reminiscent of the original P-51 (A-36) design that had wing-mounted dive brakes. Deleting the Navy-specific equipment decreased the AAF aircraft's design take-off gross weight by about half a ton to a design gross weight of 11,500 pounds and a maximum weight of 14,000 pounds. The designers also slimmed and lengthened the Fury's bulky fuselage and shifted some of the fuel to the wing. A General Electric J35 engine that could develop 4,000 pounds of thrust powered the fighter. The FJ-1 could achieve a maximum speed of 547 mph; the XP-86 had an estimated top speed of 582 mph.[3]

North American understood that the project had problems. First, studies indicated the design would have essentially the same performance as its rivals, the XP-80 and XP-84. The company realized that, because these two competing fighters were further along in their development, the XP-86 design would probably be canceled. Perhaps more importantly, it could not meet the AAF's top-speed requirement of 600 mph. North American met the challenge and came up with a dramatic change that would greatly improve the aircraft's appearance and performance: the swept-back wing configuration.[4]

Swept-wing and Slats

The swept-wing concept predated the North American design by a decade. For some time, the Germans had known that sweeping back the wing would facilitate higher speeds. At the 1935 Volta Scientific Conference on high-speed flight, Adolph Busemann delivered a paper discussing how swept-back wings would lessen drag at high speeds, enabling supersonic flight. The Germans quickly realized the importance of this concept, declaring it classified the next year and applying for a patent. A 1940 German report discussed the advantages of swept wings operating at high speeds (Mach 0.9); as early as 1941, the Germans conducted wind tunnel tests on the concept. Meanwhile the rest of the world virtually ignored this idea, and the Germans took the lead in the fields of jet propulsion and high-speed flight.[5]

The two principal German non-propeller fighters that entered combat during World War II featured swept-back wings, although neither adopted the swept-back wing for speed.[6] The Germans had a number of other designs on the drawing board that also employed swept-back wings. In contrast, the jet-powered aircraft flown by the Anglo-Americans during this period had straight wings.

The Americans knew the advantages of swept-back wings.[7] In mid-1944 the AAF conducted wind tunnel tests of swept-back wings, and by early the next year Bob Jones at National Advisory Committee for Aeronautics (NACA) had developed a theory about swept wings. At the same time, the American military recognized the German advantages in a number of aeronautic areas and therefore systematically gathered up German documents, aircraft, and personnel at war's end.[8] In 1945, the Technical Intelligence Survey team made German test data and interrogations of captured Germans available to North American. Larry Greene, a project aerodynamicist, who was competent in technical German, along with Dale Meyers and Harrison Storms, the chief technical engineer, worked late into the night for a week reviewing the material. They also studied copies of scientific papers at the Cal Tech library investigating the subject, and their assessment encouraged North American to set up an aerodynamics performance group, under the leadership of Jack Daniels, to calculate the performance of the swept-back wings. They were astonished at the improvement in performance.

By this time, however, North American was far along with the straight-wing design; in fact, they had begun construction. As a consequence, there was resistance to incorporating the new wing into the XP-86. Storms took the findings to Ed Horkey, chief aerodynamicist, who was thrilled by the results. But when he in turn took the news to his boss, Joe Greer, he met a roadblock. Greer thought it was horrible that the concept could not be used because the process was too far along. Storms, or Horkey, went over Greer's head to Greer's boss, Larry Waite, head of the technical section. He, too, thought it was too late to make a big change, remarking, "Get rid of it; bury it!" Storms was not dissuaded and instead went across the hall to Ed Schmued, head of advanced design (and designer of the P-51), who reacted "like a match dropped into a barrel of sky rockets." He took the material to the heads of the company, Dutch Kindleberger and Lee Atwood. They in turn enthusiastically discussed the findings with the AAF engineering department in Dayton, Ohio, which gave verbal approval to go forward with the new wing. When the word got back to California, Ray Rice, vice president and chief engineer, was angry that he had not been consulted, an oversight that was quite embarrassing for Storms and Horkey. Nevertheless, Rice authorized wind tunnel testing of swept-wings in late August 1945.[9] At this same time (the precise chronology is not clear), Ed Horkey went to the NACA to test the proposed North American airfoil.

North American built a .23-scale swept-wing model in two weeks and by mid-September had it in a wind tunnel. These tests indicated the benefits of the concept. The testers also applied a bent piece of metal around the leading edge to represent partial span slats, suggesting how performance could be improved at low speeds. North American used the extensive data the Germans had amassed for their proposed fully-swept Me 262 wing, coupled it with a North American laminar flow air foil, and extensively tested it in the wind tunnel. The company adopted the swept-back wing. The aircraft retained the straight empennage for a time, but by mid-October 1946, North American also swept back the empennage. This change slightly altered the aircraft's dimensions.

Another consideration in the wing design was the aspect ratio (the ratio of the span [wing length] to chord [wing width]). North American began with the 5:1 aspect ratio wing, and tested both it and also one with 6:1 ratio. That the latter had obvious performance advantages over the former, especially greater range, encouraged North American to change the baseline wing design to a 6:1 aspect ratio in October 1945. However, the higher aspect-ratio wing had stability problems, vicious pitch up tendencies that the design team was unable to solve. Therefore, in March 1946, the design changed back to the 5:1 layout.[10]

Rice discussed the swept-wing with Gen. Bill Craigie, who was in charge of research and development at Wright Field. Although the change would add six months to the development time, the Air Force gave its formal approval to the swept-wing modification on 1 November 1945.[11] The engineers calculated that the swept wing increased the critical Mach number of the wing (the speed at which the wing encountered supersonic flow) from Mach 0.8 with the straight wing (the same as the P-80) to Mach 0.9. This added 70 mph to the fighter's top speed and thus enabled it (in theory) to exceed the AAF high-speed requirement.[12] The decision to redo the aircraft's wing also improved the fighter's looks, giving it the elegant lines for which it is renowned. The F-86 was a good-looking airplane and would strongly support the old pilot saying, "if it don't look good, it won't fly good."[13] Better stated, "This bold decision to adopt the swept-wing changed the Sabre from a mediocre fighter into a great one."[14]

Along with the wing change, North American also lengthened and strengthened the fuselage, moved the engine back about 2.3 feet to accommodate more fuel and to deal with center-of-gravity issues, enlarged the cockpit to make room for an ejection seat, and changed the engine from the J35 to the J47.[15]

The swept-wing brought with it problems: with this configuration the fighter was less stable at high angles of attack and had a higher stall speed than the straight-wing design. To deal with these problems the Germans had used automatically operating leading-edge slats on the Me 262. Although there was some resistance at North American to "Germanize our design," the infamous "not-invented-here" mindset, the slats' merits won out. North American tested full-span leading-edge slats on a wind tunnel model in September.[16] Wind-tunnel tests with the 5:1 aspect-ratio wing yielded positive results, but testing 150 different slat configurations with the 6:1 aspect-ratio wing did not, pushing North American to adopt the lower aspect-ratio wing. Meanwhile, the

AAF shipped to North American the Me 262 wing (with slats) that would provide the basis for the fighter's slat system.[17]

In fact, the first seven aircraft built used the German design. American engineers went on to modify the system. At low air speeds, the slats automatically extended forward and downward on a curved track, increasing the wing's area and camber, producing more lift, stability, and control at low air speeds. The slats automatically closed at higher air speeds as aerodynamic forces pushed the slats snug with the wing contour, decreasing drag. The pilot then locked the four moveable slats into place to preclude asymmetric deployment in maneuvering. When the pilot unlocked the slats, they automatically deployed as the aerodynamic forces decreased at lower air speeds. To ensure the slats were operable for takeoffs and landings, the designers interconnected the slat locks and landing gear so that the slats were unlocked when the gear was extended. North American used the slat locks on the first 159 fighters, and then removed them in early 1949 when it incorporated a modified slat system into the fighter.[18]

First Flight

On 8 August 1947, North American rolled out the first XP-86. The fighter then went through taxi tests at the adjacent Mines Field (now Los Angeles International Airport) before the company disassembled the aircraft and trucked it to the Muroc test facility (now Edwards Air Force Base).[19] Now theory and design would give way to practice.

North American chose George "Wheaties" Welch as the chief test pilot for the P-86 project.[20] Unlike most AAF aviators, he was a son of privilege: his father was a senior research chemist with Dupont, and the family knew the Duponts personally. Welch graduated from a private secondary school and attended Purdue for several years before joining the Army aviation cadet program. He won his wings and commission in January 1941 and was posted to Hawaii. Francis Gabreski, of whom we will hear more later, was one of his fellow pilots there and described Welch as a rich kid, a real hell-raiser, but an excellent fighter pilot. Welch proved the latter when he gained everlasting glory as one of six AAF pilots at Pearl Harbor who got airborne and downed Japanese aircraft on 7 December 1941, getting the most kills: four Japanese aircraft on three sorties. Although nominated for the Medal of Honor by AAF chief Henry "Hap" Arnold, whose endorsement normally would have ensured that award, for unknown reasons he was instead awarded the Distinguished Service Cross.[21] Welch went on to complete three combat tours, becoming a triple ace (sixteen credits) against the Japanese.

After 348 combat missions and a bout with malaria, Welch left the service in 1944. With Arnold's recommendation, he joined North American in July of that year and became the chief test pilot of their Inglewood (Los Angeles) plant. Welch was to become the civilian pilot most closely associated with the F-86. Because he was independent and a loner capable of playing the prima donna role to the point of rudeness, he did not receive the publicity, acclaim, or credit that other test pilots received—and that he well deserved.[22]

On 1 October 1947, Welch took the XP-86 up for its initial flight and had to recycle the landing gear to get an "up and locked" indication on the nose gear. Having accomplished each of the test items as planned, he prepared to land thirty minutes later. Again, the nose wheel malfunctioned, failing to lock in the extended position. Welch recycled the gear a number of times, tried a 3 "g" maneuver, and used the emergency gear extension system, all without success. The nose wheel would not extend completely and was hanging at a 45-degree angle. The North American team on the ground radioed Welch that it was up to him to either bring the aircraft down without the nose wheel or to abandon the aircraft. Welch elected to land the fighter, but on the dry lakebed instead of the runway. He made a smooth approach with the nose high, touched down on the main gear, and held the nose wheel off the ground as long as possible. As the speed decreased and the nose began to drop, at the very last moment before touchdown, the nose gear snapped forward and locked. Welch radioed: "Lucky! Lucky!"[23] Flight number one was complete, despite some anxious moments. Welch logged fifty minutes of flying time.[24]

The design problem was two-fold: the aircraft's hydraulic cylinder was smaller than specified, and the nose gear retracted rearward and extended forward against the slipstream, an arrangement that was mandated by the aircraft's air duct design. Thus, a relatively simple and well-tried system—the landing gear and particularly the nose gear—almost led to disaster on the first flight and continued to dog the fighter early in its lifetime.[25]

Breaking the Sound Barrier

Welch was one of the first pilots to exceed the speed of sound. Clearly, this was a major feat, perhaps not so well appreciated today when military aircraft and the commercial Concorde have regularly flown at supersonic speeds. Five decades ago, however, the media wrote of a "sound barrier." The death of Geoffrey DeHaviland, son of the British aviation pioneer and owner of the British aircraft firm, along with a popular film of 1946 led to the mystique and anticipated perils of supersonic flight.

The official story is that Capt. Charles "Chuck" Yeager was the first to break the sound barrier on 14 October 1947 in the rocket-powered Bell X-1. This has been highly publicized and burned into the public imagination by the photogenic and likeable Yeager, and most especially by the book and movie, *The Right Stuff*. The USAF acknowledges that the F-86 broke the sound barrier, albeit in a dive, in April 1948. (The Air Force made this disclosure after an excited British pilot, Roland Beaumont, gave details over an open microphone that appeared in the June 1948 *Aviation Week*.)

As in most cases, there is more to the story. There was a competition for bragging rights over who would be the first to exceed the speed of sound. The Secretary of the Air Force, Stuart Symington, and Bell (builder of the X-1) wanted the glory, as well as the accomplishment, to justify the expensive X-1 project. North American had the potential to ruin the show and was warned by Symington not to do so. Nevertheless, North American obtained the use of highly accurate NACA speed tracking equipment, which was in place for Yeager's flight, to monitor some of Welch's early flights at Muroc. The device showed that Welch flew faster than Mach 1 in October or November 1947, either two days or a month after Yeager's feat.[26]

Some go further, claiming Welch was the first to go supersonic. Horkey implies Welch may have done so, since he was flying the same flight patterns prior to 14 October as he did when NACA registered his supersonic dive.[27] Al Blackburn, a former North American test pilot, goes beyond this. He relates that, prior to the XP-86's initial flight, Welch had asked one of the regulars (Millie Palmer) at Pancho Barnes's famous "Fly In" bar just outside the field to be alert for "a sharp boom like a clap of thunder" and to write down the time and the reaction of others to the event. On the first flight, Welch put the XP-86 into a 40-degree dive from thirty-five thousand feet aimed at Poncho's bar, and at twenty-nine thousand feet encountered slight wing roll and then the airspeed indicator jumped from 350 kts to 410 kts. As he pulled level at twenty-five thousand feet, he encountered the effect again. Palmer reported a "baboom." The noise and the airspeed jump are consistent with supersonic speed. Welch repeated the feat on 14 October, only fifteen minutes before Yeager's famous flight.[28]

So what? Clearly there is a difference between level supersonic flight, as the X-1 demonstrated, and supersonic flight in a dive. Certainly Yeager's achievement remains historic. On the other hand, there is a major difference between accomplishing the feat with a rocket-powered test aircraft carried to altitude by another craft and capable of only a few minutes of powered flight, and doing so in sustained flight or in an operational aircraft.[29] In any event, the Sabre was the first combat fighter to fly supersonic. The X-1 had its moment in history; the F-86's was yet to come.

North American turned the first test plane over to the USAF in November 1948, after almost ninety-eight flying hours. It served at Wright-Patterson Air Force Base for two and a half years before returning to Edwards Air Force Base (formerly Muroc) in April 1951. In May 1952, it was transferred to Kirtland Air Force Base. According to most secondary sources, the aircraft was wrecked in September 1952. Air Force records, however, indicate that the aircraft was tested to destruction at Kirtland AFB in September 1952. North America flew, built, and tested two other XP-86s.[30]

Development Issues

The F-86 evolved as it was tested. One major change was to replace the J35 with the J47 engine. The first thirty-three planes (F-86A-1) were powered by the J47-GE-1, an engine that developed 4,850 pounds of thrust (21 percent more than the J35), which of course improved performance. Top speed increased from 618 mph at fourteen thousand feet with the J35 to 677 mph at sea level with the J47. By May 1950 the F-86 was powered by J47-GE-7 and GE-13, which had a rating of 5,200 pounds of thrust.[31] North American also changed the windshield. The company installed a curved, bulletproof glass for the forward cockpit panel in the first F-86s. However, as this introduced an error into the gunsight, the company changed to a "V" shaped front glass in the F-86A-5.[32]

One of the unique features of the original F-86 design was gun doors that covered the muzzles of the six 0.50-caliber machine guns. These smoothed out the fuselage, cut drag, and created a more aesthetically pleasing design. When the pilot pulled the trigger the doors opened in 1/20 of a second and closed when it was released. While there was little gain in top speed, cruising speed and range improved. However, there were problems. The doors occasionally failed to operate and were shot off. They also cut the airflow to the guns, reducing cooling of the barrels, shortening barrel life, and causing "cook-offs," ammunition that was inadvertently fired due to excessive heat. Additionally, there were also maintenance complications, since the doors required considerable adjustment and tightening of the fasteners. The USAF tested open gun ports in the summer of 1949 and concluded they were superior to the gun doors. This change was quickly made.[33]

Another much more important change was the placement of the speed brakes. Such devices were not necessary for propeller-powered aircraft, because changing the pitch of the propeller (blade angle) could rapidly slow down the aircraft. Only in specialized operations such as dive-bombing were other devices needed to slow an aircraft; hence, the origin of dive brakes. Jet-powered airframes were much more streamlined than their predecessors although extended landing gear and flaps slowed the aircraft. The original F-86 design called for wing-mounted speed brakes; however, these were deleted in September due to a change in the wing design. They were replaced by three hydraulically actuated devices mounted on the fuselage aft of the wing's trailing edge, two on the side and one underneath. Wind-tunnel tests indicated problems, so they were rendered inoperative in the XP-86. (There is no evidence that they were ever employed during flight.) North American later changed the arrangement to two side speed brakes that increased the aircraft's drag by a factor of 2.5.[34]

The new aircraft was a winner. Although the production model was slightly heavier (about 350 pounds) than test models, its new engine (J47-GE-1) was much more powerful than the J35 it replaced. The USAF was quick to show off its new aircraft. The world aircraft speed record, confirmed by the precise rules of the Federation Aeronautique Internationale (FAI), had first exceeded 600 mph in November 1945 when an RAF Meteor clocked 606 mph. An RAF Meteor raised it to 616 mph in September 1946. The AAF broke this record with a modified P-80 in June 1947 (623 mph); the navy in turn broke that record twice with a Douglas D-558 Skystreak in August 1947 (the higher at 651 mph). At the September 1948 Cleveland National Air Races, the USAF attempted to set a world speed record with an unmodified production model F-86. Maj. Robert Johnson of the flight test division at Wright-Patterson AFB flew a Sabre under the precise FAI rules: two runs in each direction (to negate any tail wind) at a precise altitude (below 165 feet, to preclude building up speed in a dive) over a 3 km course and recorded by camera. Before a crowd of eighty thousand, Johnson flew the course three times in each direction, at an average speed of 670 mph. This was not accepted as a new record, however, because the cameras recorded only three of the runs. Ten days later, Johnson fared better when he flew six courses in another F-86 at Muroc. The FAI certified the average speed of 671 mph as a world record, which stood for three years until it was broken by an F-86D at 699 mph in November 1952.[35]

In February 1949 the 94th Fighter Squadron, the renowned "hat-in-the-ring" squadron and the unit of Eddie Rickenbacker, America's top ace in World War I, became the first USAF unit to receive the new fighter. It was part of the illustrious 1st Fighter Group, stationed at March Air Force Base. While the First would not see action in Korea, it did have an influence on the history of the F-86, for it named the fighter. In February, officers of the First examined seventy-eight names submitted by the group's men in a naming contest, and selected "Sabre" (with the distinctive British spelling). Unfortunately, we do not know the author of what became the aircraft's common name as of March 1949.[36]

TWO

Efforts to Improve Performance

A merican airmen recognized that the MiG-15 had a number of performance advantages over the F-86 due to its equivalent engine power and lighter weight. To increase the fighter's flying performance, they pushed to reduce weight, increase engine power, and lessen drag. To improve fighting performance, the airmen attempted to increase the lethality of the Sabre's armament.

Weight Reduction

Clearly the MiG was lighter and smaller than the F-86. Obviously, if the Sabre's weight could be reduced, its performance would improve; the question was: what to remove? A complication was that even if weight reductions could be achieved by removing equipment or subsystems, the size and weight of the existing airframe could not be changed. North American proposed a scheme that would reduce the fighter's weight by 2,800 pounds; however, as this called for a virtual redesign of the aircraft, this concept was dropped. Another factor that made the Sabre larger and heavier than the MiG was its designed range: the F-86 carried 17 percent more fuel internally than the MiG, which had been designed as a short-range interceptor. Certainly, the Air Force did not want to reduce range; if anything, it wanted to increase it. In the end, the North American fighter may have carried too much equipment, which made it heavier than the MiG; but the MiG probably carried too little equipment, which resulted in a better flying machine but not a better fighting machine.[1]

Increased Engine Power

In October 1951 Col. Benjamin Preston, Commander of the 4th Fighter Group, filed an unsatisfactory report on the F-86E's General Electric J47-13 engine. He wanted more power, recommending an engine with a minimum of 6,500 to 7,000 pounds of thrust. The USAF did have a better, but not much better, engine. The F-86F used the more powerful J47-GE-27 engine, which produced 770 more pounds of thrust (15 percent greater) than the J47-GE-13 used in the F-86A and F-86E. (Empty weight of the F-86F increased 4 percent, eating up some of that advantage.)[2]

The airmen wanted more power; however, the development of a bigger engine would take time. Therefore, on 11 January 1952, Gen. Earle Partridge, former commander of Fifth Air Force and now commander of Air Research and Development Command, gave priority to the task of improving Sabre performance.

The airmen were even willing to sacrifice engine life for this performance improvement unless it caused "an unsupportable burden on supply and maintenance." During the war, Wright Air Development Center (WADC) initiated and tested five projects to increase engine power: over-temperature, water-alcohol injection, solid rocket booster, pre-turbine injection, and liquid rocket booster.[3]

Engine Over-temperature

The airmen realized that running the engine at higher temperatures would increase thrust but would also lessen engine life. It was relatively easy to affect the higher temperatures by inserting segments (called "rats" and "mice" in the field[4]) into the tailpipe, reducing the exhaust nozzle area. In addition, they placed a detent on the throttle control beyond which the engine operated at higher than normal rpm in the over-temperature range. The airmen attached a timer to record the duration of over-temperature operations, which they wanted to limit to one-minute cycles to get the maximum life out of the turbine blades. Tests of the concept demonstrated increased thrust, averaging 27 percent between fifteen thousand and forty-five thousand feet, with a maximum increase of almost 30 percent at thirty-five thousand feet. Consequently, performance markedly improved. Nevertheless, the system met considerable resistance at GE and WADC because of shortened engine life and supply and maintenance issues. The USAF canceled the project prior to September 1952.[5]

Water-Alcohol Injection

The water-alcohol injection program got its start in late 1951, when discussions began between General Electric and the Power Plant Laboratory at Wright Air Development Center. The idea was to increase engine power by increasing both the fluid weight flow passing through the engine as well as the exhaust gas temperature. Water would satisfy the first requirement but would sharply reduce the exhaust gas temperature, thereby nullifying any benefit. Adding alcohol to the water would accomplish both objectives.

The Air Force planned to test the concept in a B-45, but delays with the aircraft prompted the airmen to switch the tests directly to an F-86 in April 1952. The USAF ran flight tests with an F-86A between June and early October 1952 and with an F-86F between late October and late January 1953. Although the results were encouraging, two problems emerged. First, there were breakdowns of the injection pump. More serious were flameouts in climbs at high altitude. Although adjustment to the mixture solved the problem, it also reduced the augmentation gain.

The testers concluded that the water-alcohol injection could increase engine thrust by 20 percent at twenty thousand feet to 30 percent at forty thousand feet. If performance above forty thousand feet was desired, the mixture had to be adjusted to prevent the flameout problem, thereby reducing the gain to 15 percent at twenty thousand feet and 20 percent at forty thousand feet. The downside was that the water-alcohol injection reduced the life of normal combustion system components on the J47-27 engine to two hours. There was also the problem of where to store the mixture; trading fuel for mixture would reduce the fighter's range, obviously not a viable solution when range was already a problem. Another difficulty was the realization that the device could not be tested for combat until late summer or fall 1953.[6]

Pre-Turbine Injection

The Air Force came up with a relatively lightweight and simple means to boost engine power called pre-turbine injection (PTI). PTI injected fuel into the engine forward of the turbine wheel and then burned it aft of the turbine wheel. The system also used a variable tailpipe nozzle that adjusted up to 15 percent of the area of the exhaust. This arrangement, in essence a very short afterburner, was necessary because of the space limitations on the F-86 and the requirement for minimal modifications.[7] PTI flight tests began in 1953 and indicated an increase of 40 percent in thrust. Although this gave the F-86 much better performance, the price was considerable wear on the engine, as turbine blades burned up after one hour of operations, and turbine wheels after three.[8] There were also problems with the nozzle binding. Nevertheless, one of the testers "concluded that the increase in performance of the F-86F due to PTI installation is of such a magnitude as to warrant further exploration of the system."[9] This was not to be, for despite considerable testing, PTI was not used; instead U.S. aircraft were (later) fitted with afterburners.

Solid Rocket Booster

Another proposal to increase power was using solid fuel rocket boosters, with the misnamed JATO (jet assisted takeoff) bottles. In the summer of 1952, the Air Force flight-tested an arrangement that consisted of three rocket bottles mounted in an insulated compartment in the aircraft's aft fuselage, directly below the speed brakes. Each unit produced one thousand pounds of thrust and could be fired individually in sequence (for thirty-eight seconds, increasing speed 15 kts) or simultaneously (for fourteen seconds, increasing speed 20 kts) at forty thousand feet.[10]

The USAF sent the rockets to the theater in August 1952 and installed them on six F-86Fs in the 334th Fighter Squadron, some with and some without the new leading edge. The rocket-equipped Sabres flew 136 combat missions and engaged in sixteen dogfights, during which they destroyed six MiGs. However, the rockets were only helpful in two of the credits, because one of these victories was accomplished without the rocket assist; and in three other kills the circumstances did not require the rocket boost. Aside from the fact that they were only minimally helpful, the rocket units added extra weight (600 pounds full and 450 pounds empty) and reduced maneuverability. On two occasions this loss of maneuverability prevented the F-86s from engaging the MiGs. In addition, the Air Force lost two of the modified F-86s. It should be noted that the test was not a fair comparison with standard F-86s: the tests employed highly experienced pilots who were given lead positions. Both of these factors enhanced the chances of success. In addition, the installation moved the center of gravity aft, creating a longitudinal instability problem that caused stick reversal (the aircraft moving in the opposite direction of that intended) under high "g" conditions and porpoising. Although maintenance problems were minimal, the airmen determined that the rocket-equipped aircraft required a turnaround time of three hours, compared with the normal one-half hour. The pilots emphasized the critical importance of timing in firing the rockets, the short duration of added power, and the betrayal of their position by the smoke trail. In brief, the pilots believed the rockets were of little value. Fifth Air Force received authorization to terminate the project in late November 1952.[11]

Liquid Rocket Booster

The Air Force also worked with a liquid fuel rocket booster that could be shut down and restarted. A study in early 1952 investigated an engine with thrust between one thousand and five thousand pounds, firing between 24 and 120 seconds. However, the installation would add weight and drag and thus reduce both speed and range when not operating. The study concluded that a small rocket motor of one thousand pounds thrust and 120 second duration was best suited for combat but went on to note that afterburning was a far superior approach.[12]

Nevertheless, the liquid rocket boost program continued, but slowly. It was not until January 1953 that the Air Force contracted with Aerojet to design, develop, test, and deliver a rocket of thirty-five hundred pound thrust (minimum), with a duration of 108 seconds, and capable of six starts. The Aerojet engine was not tested until fall 1956. Four years later, the Air Force tested a Rocketdyne rocket engine. None of these engines went into service on an F-86.[13]

Operation GunVal

The Sabre's six .50-caliber machine guns, used so successfully during World War II, proved inadequate during the Korean War.[14] Although some pilots liked this arrangement (the six guns provided redundancy, were a known quantity, were reliable, and had a high rate of fire that gave a shotgun effect), the Sabre's guns did not get the same results over MiG Alley as AAF fighters had in World War II. There were twice as many multiple kills per sortie in World War II as in Korea. (A number of pilots in the earlier war scored three or more kills on a single sortie while only one Korean War pilot scored more than two credits.) Whereas in World War II fighter combat over Europe 71 percent of the total Eighth and Fifteenth Air Forces' air-to-air claims were assessed as destroyed, that figure was 44 percent in Korea.[15] Numerous American pilots "fired out" (fired their entire load of ammunition) without achieving a kill. Evgeny Pepelyaev, the top Soviet ace of the Korean War with twenty-three credits, dismissed the American .50s as being like mere peas and told of MiGs returning to base with forty or fifty hits.[16]

A number of factors account for this reduced effectiveness. Jet aircraft were less vulnerable than their prop predecessors: their engines were simpler; they lacked the large prop; and their airframes were more rugged to endure the higher speeds and altitudes of their expanded flight envelope. The MiG-15 was a small, simple, rugged aircraft that carried no fuel in its wings. As a result, it had few vulnerable areas.[17] Jet fuel was less volatile than the high octane gas used in piston-powered aircraft, and the .50 API-ammunition (armor-piercing incendiary), which had proved to be so devastating in World War II, did not have oxygen to burn above thirty-five thousand feet, where most of jet combat took place. (Fighter combat in World War II took place at lower altitudes.) In short, armament had not kept pace with the expanded nature of jet fighter air combat.[18]

A May 1951 RAF report of their tests of the F-86A rated it as having superior all-around performance compared to any British jet, but the testers noted armament as the Sabre's most serious limitation. An initial USAF report from Korea in January 1951 stated that the "fire power of the F-86 is not sufficiently destructive."[19] Almost all American leaders and fighter pilots who discussed the F-86's armament wanted more firepower. As one report in August 1951 put it, "The F-86 pilots universally would like a heavier caliber gun so that when a hit is made, a sure kill results."[20]

The call for better armament came quickly from the field, but the Air Force response was slow. Within weeks of the first engagement between MiG and Sabre, Far East Air Forces (FEAF) forwarded a requirement for heavier armament, followed in March with a request for USAF trials of a 20 mm cannon on the F-86. In mid-June 1951, Headquarters USAF pushed for 20 mm guns in fighters at the earliest possible time. By the end of October 1952, the USAF had fired seven hundred thousand rounds in various tests, one-tenth of these from F-86s in a project code-named GunVal.[21]

The USAF had developed the T-160 20 mm gun (later known as the M39) from a German design. During World War II, Mauser built a five-chamber revolver-type weapon with a very high rate of fire. After the war, the concept was taken up in Britain, Switzerland, and the United States. After work by the Illinois Institute of Technology and the Springfield (Mass.) Arsenal, Ford became involved in 1950 and completed the gun in June 1951.[22]

The 20 mm T-160 was a much more powerful gun than the F-86's .50-caliber M-3. The 20 mm projectile was almost two and a half times heavier, and its muzzle velocity was 15 percent greater, giving it a shorter time of flight, flatter trajectory, longer range, and greater impact. It also had a 50 percent higher rate of fire. USAF tests showed that the .50 was more accurate at ranges below six hundred yards, while the 20 mm was more accurate beyond that range. Therefore, it had a greater kill potential than the .50.[23]

There were, of course, negatives. The 20 mm gun was heavier and larger than the .50, so the USAF replaced the six .50s with four 20 mm guns, which meant that the two packages fired the same number of projectiles (about one hundred per second). Because the 20 mm ammunition was also larger and heavier than the .50s, only 460 rounds were carried, compared with 1,600 rounds of .50s, giving a total firing time of 4.6 seconds versus 16 seconds. The 20 mm armament hurt aircraft performance because of extra weight and increased deceleration due to the guns' greater recoil.[24] Pilots in the theater were disturbed by this loss of flying performance and believed that it was "unwise to weigh a possible advantage with a known penalty."[25] Another factor was that the F-86's fire control system limited the guns and made the two installations essentially the same.[26]

The USAF mounted four T-160s in four F-86Es and six F-86Fs. In March 1952, North American's George Welch tested the guns between ten thousand to twenty-five thousand feet off of Catalina Island without a problem. After further tests at Edwards Air Force Base, the Air Force sent eight aircraft to the 335th Fighter Squadron. Along the way the airmen painted two additional gun ports on the GunVal aircraft so that they looked like the other Sabres with which they would fly.[27]

During combat tests between mid-January and the end of April 1953, the GunVal fighters flew 284 combat sorties, during which their pilots sighted 139 MiGs, fired at 41, and claimed hits on 21, 6 of which were claimed as destroyed. Proportionally, this record exceeded that of the standard F-86s; but this was not an equivalent situation because these pilots flew at times and positions that gave them a better chance of success. More significantly, they were very experienced; among them were seven Korean War aces who flew ninety-six GunVal missions. The pilots who flew the GunVal aircraft averaged almost 2,900 flying hours each—2,100 hours in fighters—and were credited with fifty-eight victories in the Korean War and twenty-nine in World War II.[28]

The GunVal aircraft encountered two problems. The first involved the reliability of the guns. The airmen fired ninety-eight thousand rounds of ammunition during the tests, with 210 jams, approximately twelve times the malfunction rate of the .50s. (In fairness, the 20 mm was a brand-new gun while the .50 had been in service for some years and had fired millions of rounds.) As might be expected, the jam rate declined through the course of the tests, from 3.4 per one thousand rounds for the first thirty-two thousand rounds fired to 1.2 for the last fourteen thousand.[29]

A more serious problem was engine stalls. Excessive gun gases caused twenty compressor stalls on 363 sorties, six of these in combat, causing the loss of two aircraft. What was not a problem below twenty-five thousand feet stateside turned out to be a severe problem above that altitude over Korea. Air Force engineers determined that the four 20 mm guns expelled four times the amount of gas as did the six .50s.[30] The airmen took a number of steps to solve the problem. Engineers at Wright-Patterson AFB proposed blast deflectors, but these failed in Korea. The airmen welded shut doors that bled air from the gun compartments into the engine intake duct and drilled holes in the gun-bay doors to vent the gases. The airmen also installed a selector switch that permitted the pilot to either fire two or all four guns. Firing only two guns at a time reduced gun gasses and gave the pilot twice the duration of fire. But this did not completely solve the problem. North American engineer Paul Peterson designed a horseshoe-shaped clip mounted in the gun panel port that broke up the gasses.[31]

The commander of the Air Proving Ground Command (APGC), Maj. Gen. Patrick Timberlake, concluded in an August 1953 report on GunVal that the project was unsuitable for combat due to the limited quantity of ammunition carried and the engine compressor stall problems. Although the Air Force persisted with the project, an April 1954 test report noted that the stall problems continued. It concluded that the available fire control systems limited the effectiveness of the 20 mm installation and allowed the .50s to achieve essentially the same results. In brief, the 20 mm installation did not provide the "desired degree of improvement over the M-3 [.50-caliber]."[32] But the Air Force had already made this decision. The T-160, now known as the M39, would arm the next air superiority version of the Sabre, the F-86H.[33]

Changes in Models

It is true that many of the concepts the USAF tried did not work out, at least in time to see service in the Korean War. Besides technical barriers, there were problems with getting new ideas through the bureaucracy and, of course, time constraints. The Air Force did improve the F-86 over the years, sometimes in small ways, other times more dramatically. The USAF designated these major changes by adding a suffix to the F-86 designation; in this case, the daylight air superiority F-86A evolved into the F-86E and F-86F.[34] (The Air Force also instituted changes within each suffix letter series known as block changes, usually in sequence of fives, e.g., F-86F-1, F-5.)

The F-86A

North American built 554 F-86As. It first flew in May 1948 and entered service in February 1949; the last was accepted in December 1950. The manufacturer mounted Mk 18 (optical, computing) gunsights into all but the last 24 F-86As. The builder put the A-1CM with a radar ranging device (AN/APG-5C or more commonly the AN/APG-30) from then on and retrofitted the rest of the series. The first 33 Sabres (the entire F-86A-1 block) had flush gun doors that opened when the guns fired and closed when they stopped, but these were removed for practical reasons, despite the loss of aesthetics and performance. The A-5 series also replaced the curved windshield with a "V" shaped one. North American moved the canopy jettison-release handle from the bottom forward cockpit panel to the right handgrip. The Air Force made other changes partway through the A-5 block, the most important of which was to reconfigure the wing slats to open and close at lower air speeds. This modification also allowed the builder to remove the slat locks (one less task for the pilot) and the stick shaker from the aircraft. Another improvement was to change the fuel flow meter reading from gallons to pounds and, later in the block, adding a totalizer that gave the pounds of fuel remaining.[35] The accurate Sabre fuel gauge proved very important in combat over MiG Alley.

The F-86E

North American built 456 F-86Es. This variant first flew in September 1950 and went into service in May 1951. The F-86E-1 weighed 460 pounds more than the F-86A-5 but was powered by the same J47-GE-13. The main difference between the two aircraft was a new and much more effective flight control system. The "E" replaced the conventional, hydraulically boosted aileron and elevator control surfaces with a system of full-powered hydraulics. In addition, the entire horizontal stabilizer moved, not just the elevator. NACA had tested the all-flying tail starting in 1943 and incorporated it into the Bell X-1; North American began testing the concept on the F-86A in mid-1949. Test pilots reported that the flying tail system was far superior to conventional controls above Mach .85. The "E" was a good gun platform throughout its speed range (up to Mach 1) and had positive control above 500 kts where the "A" had only marginal control. The result of these changes to the control system was to make the already fine handling Sabre a much better flying machine at a small cost in performance due to the additional weight. Another change was to switch the flaps from a hydraulic system to an electrical one.[36] The new flight control system was one of three major changes to the F-86 that greatly improved its fighting capability.

The F-86F

The USAF intended the "F" model to be a fighter-bomber, featuring three major changes to the F-86E: a more powerful engine, larger drop tanks, and improved armament (four 20 mm guns). The USAF planned to add the new guns and engine at the earliest possible point in production, but Headquarters Air Force revised this notion in late May 1951. The F-86F first flew in March 1952 and went into service a few months later. It weighed the same as the last blocks of the "E" series but was powered by the more powerful J47-GE-27 engine, which produced 12 percent greater thrust than did the J47-GE-13. The second major change was to use larger drop tanks. The first seventy-nine F-86Fs used 120-gallon drop tanks, as did the earlier F-86s; however succeeding F-86Fs could use either 120- or 200-gallon tanks. The USAF also added another pair of pylons to the existing two, enabling the F-86F-25 and F-86F-30 aircraft to carry four drops tanks or, more commonly when flying as a fighter-bomber, two drop tanks and two bombs. The 20 mm guns had some developmental problems and did not see service until the F-86H arrived after the Korean War.[37] The increased power was a major factor in improving the performance of the F-86F. However, even more important was the installation of a new wing.

The third major improvement to F-86s was a wing modification. The existing wing with the automatic leading edge slats made the Sabre relatively docile at lower air speeds but penalized the fighter's performance at higher altitudes and speeds. In 1951 North American experimented with an F-86E fitted with a larger wing without slats. It appears that North American originated the idea, most likely spurred on by their chief test pilot George Welch. In any event, at the end of the year, John Meyer (former commander of the 4th Fighter Group who had downed twenty-four German aircraft in World War II and two MiGs in Korea) flew the modified aircraft and was very much impressed; he therefore endorsed it with enthusiasm. Tests at Wright-Patterson and Edwards were also positive. Fifth Air Force learned of the work and in April requested combat testing.

The new wing was modified in two major ways. First it was slightly larger, six inches at the fuselage and three inches at the tip (hence the name "6-3" wing), increasing the wing area from 288 square feet to 302 square feet. Second, the slats were deleted. The problem of "tip stalling" that gave the aircraft a tendency to roll as it approached the stall was addressed by adding a small wing fence (five inches tall and extending sixteen inches from the leading edge) to each upper wing.[38]

The 51st Fighter Interceptor Wing received the first aircraft fitted with the 6-3 wing. In late August 1952 the unit reported on tests with the three modified Sabres (a fourth was wrecked in a crash landing) that flew for thirty-four hours, albeit without encountering MiGs. The pilots noted the improved performance: increased level speed (4 to 6 kts), dive speed (up to Mach 1.05), ceiling (four thousand feet), rate of climb (three hundred feet per minute), and range. The aircraft also turned tighter especially above Mach .85. There were no adverse handling problems.[39] On the other hand, higher stall speeds forced an increase in approach, landing, and touchdown speeds (about 10 to 14 kts), and reduced drag necessitated a flatter approach. This called for more attention in the landing phase, but as one pilot put it so well, "Since the air war is not won in the traffic pattern these characteristics cause little concern."[40] Because the modification was cheap, simple, and effective, it was quickly adopted.[41] In September, Fifth Air Force requested kits to retrofit all of its F-86E and F-86F aircraft. The change was also instituted on the production line in the midst of the F-86F-25 and -30 blocks.[42]

The F-86F, with its more powerful engine and fitted with the 6-3 wing, was equivalent—and in some respects superior to—its opposition. So, although much effort was expended for the few modifications enacted, the net result improved the F-86's flying and fighting performance.[43]

Gunsight

One of the major advantages American pilots had over their Communist adversaries was better auxiliary equipment. This included flight helmets, "g" suits, and better cockpit defrosting, but probably the most significant of these advantages was a superior gunsight. (The Communists validated the importance of these devices by making special efforts to capture and analyze American "g" suits and gunsights.)[44]

Hitting a target that is maneuvering in three dimensions from an aircraft that is likewise moving in three dimensions is a difficult feat. A number of factors must be satisfied to score hits. One element is range. Two aspects are important. Since machine-gun bullets and cannon shells are limited to a finite distance, it is futile to fire them beyond a certain range. Moreover, since the projectiles follow a parabolic rather than straight-line trajectory, the gunner, except for short-range shots, has to compensate for bullet fall. A second element is deflection. Unless the attacker and target are flying in trail formation, the pursuer has to maneuver to fire his guns ahead of a turning target. The gunsight is the device to aid the fighter pilot in solving these problems.

Fighter gunsights used through the late 1930s were of the "ring and bead" type. This type consisted of a small bead at the muzzle and concentric rings near the breach to aid the pilot in aiming ahead of his maneuvering target. Because the system was very crude, only an experienced (or lucky) pilot could score hits that required deflection. As a result, the majority of kills were either stern attacks or those achieved at relatively short ranges.

The reflector sight was a major improvement over the ring and bead type. The pilot set the span of his target's wings into the sight, which used lights and mirrors to project (or reflect, thus the term "reflector sight") a center dot and circle on a transparent glass screen set on the top of the instrument panel. With a hand control on the throttle, the pilot adjusted the size of the circle so that it encompassed the target, thereby allowing the sight to calculate the range. This solved part of the gunnery problem.

The Germans first used the reflector sight during aerial combat in 1918. At the onset of World War II, all the major air forces either had reflector sights in their fighters or were installing them. But the breakthrough came when the reflector sight was mated with a gyroscope and a calculator that allowed the device to indicate where the pilot had to fire. The British began development of calculating sights in 1939, and they were the first, in 1944, to field them in both a turret and fighter version. The American copies were designated K-14 (USAAF) and Mark (Mk) 18 (U.S. Navy).[45]

The new gunsights met resistance from the fighter pilots. It was mounted directly in front of the pilot, creating a definite hazard to the pilot's face on crash landings. Secondly, the pilot had to track the target for a second or so for the gyros to be effective. Perhaps most of all, it was new and different to pilots already familiar with existing equipment. However, the results could not to be denied. A Spitfire unit equipped with fixed sights scored kills in 26 percent of its combats, while another unit with the new sight claimed victory credits in 50 percent of its encounters. Another source states that pilots using the new sight scored hits five times greater, and kills three times greater, than pilots using existing sights. One reason for this success was that the sight achieved hits at greater ranges (as far as six hundred yards) and deflection angles (some over 50 degrees) than the older sight. The computing sight made average and inexperienced pilots good shots, especially when deflection was needed, whereas only a few pilots were able to master the older equipment.[46]

The next innovation linked radar to the gunsight. The British experimented with a radar-directed tail gun and installed it into a few Lancasters in 1944. In February 1943 the AAF had started a similar project for the B-24 but later fitted the equipment (APG-15) on the night-bombing variant of the Boeing Superfortress (B-29B). It performed well in tests but was a disappointment in combat.[47]

During the war, the AAF also developed a radar gunsight for fighters that was credited to Col. Leigh Davis and Dr. Stark Draper of MIT. The AAF conducted tests of the A-1 radar gunsight fitted in a P-38 against a banner towed by a B-26, and later with an F-84, and achieved excellent results.[48] Nevertheless, North American fitted the initial Sabres (F-86As) with its modification of the tried and true Mk 18 gunsight. (There is no explanation why they picked the Navy gunsight over its AAF sibling, the K-14.) The Mk 18 had a number of limitations. It was designed to operate against slower moving, propeller-powered aircraft and had problems with excessive vibration (from the firing of guns). After a few months of combat, 4th Fighter Interceptor Wing personnel complained of the sight's inaccessibility and the poor operation of the range control system, concluding that this "seriously hampered the effectiveness of the sight under combat conditions."[49] In short order, the USAF began to replace the Mk 18 with another gunsight.[50]

In March 1951, the USAF started to fit the F-86 with the A-1C sight, complete with automatic radar ranging. North American fitted the radar into the nose above the intake, giving the Sabre its "pouting upper lip" appearance. Gen. George Stratemeyer ordered the retrofit of the entire F-86 fleet with the new equipment, but the process was slow. By mid-June the USAF had modified seventy-six F-86As and estimated it would have four hundred completed by January 1952.[51]

The new sight—more correctly the additional radar rangefinder (APG-30)—improved accuracy at long ranges, allowing hits out to a range between twenty-five hundred to three thousand feet at the outer limits of the .50-caliber guns. The pilots needed the equipment because they consistently underestimated range and deflection—as have pilots throughout history. A 1952 USAF report made clear that, "despite popular opinion to the contrary, the bulk of the firing in combat is conducted at ranges and angles of in excess of 1,500 feet [range] and 10 degrees [deflection]."[52]

The new gunsight gave the American pilots a great advantage—that is, when it worked. Unfortunately, a combination of inadequate supply of parts, lack of test equipment, and—perhaps most of all—poor training of both pilots and maintenance crews led to malfunctions. A problem with the power supply caused inaccurate tracking. The sight proved fragile, especially in hard landings with the gunsight uncaged. The equipment also required extensive maintenance, prompting the Fifth Air Force director of operations to state that it was too difficult to maintain. In addition, the system had problems such as breaking radar lock at low angles off or extreme close range and having no way to check its accuracy while airborne. It performed erratically in clouds (due to moisture) and below six thousand feet (due to ground clutter). It was little wonder, then, that pilots came to distrust the system and some saw it as a useless 205 pounds of extra weight.[53] In brief, the USAF had fielded the system prematurely.

Despite all these problems, the USAF did not take clear action until the spring of 1952. In March a team of Air Force and company technicians was sent to the theater to work out the supply and maintenance issues, as well as replace the radar rangefinder with a new unit. Project Jay Bird finished up in July after retrofitting 159 F-86s.[54] Besides improving the gunsight's reliability, they did make one significant modification.

Jay Bird added a feature that addressed the gunsight's oversensitivity at long range. The original sight worked well at long ranges against non-maneuvering bombers but not against maneuvering fighters. The USAF's APGC developed a device that became known as the Jenkins Limiter that reduced the sensitivity at long range, greatly increasing the tracking ability at these distances. The Jenkins Limiter also gave the pilot a visual indication that the target was within range and that the gunsight was working. As one official document put it, it was successful "from the very first."[55]

At the same time, supply and maintenance issues caused major concerns. Fifth Air Force revised a number of supply and maintenance policies. For example, units were required to have a fifteen-day stock level at operating units. Critical items of radar and test equipment were to be hand carried to the theater in order to arrive in a timely manner. By April these issues had been resolved, and Headquarters Fifth Air Force described the in-commission rate of the A-1CM/APG-30 systems as excellent.[56]

In October 1952 the USAF began to replace the A-1CM with the A-4 sight. The A-4 was a redesigned and improved A-1 that eliminated or reduced the A-1's problems and, from the outset, was judged to be more reliable than its predecessor. Nevertheless, there were residual problems with the system's inverters and with spare parts.[57]

Unfortunately by this time the radar ranging gunsight had earned a poor reputation. Returning pilots complained about the gunsight's unreliability, high maintenance requirements, and excess weight; and some suggested that it was too sophisticated for the theater and that the simpler K-14 gunsight would be an improvement. In response to a Headquarters USAF query of 11 July 1952 regarding the A-1CM gunsight, the Fifth Air Force Headquarters staff talked with five experienced pilots who had scored victories over Korea. They wanted the automatic features of the A-1CM system and saw this sight as superior to the Mk 18. They correctly noted that, while superior pilots could do well with manually ranging sights, these pilots were the exception, not the rule. (One of the shortcomings of many USAF studies was the use of a highly experienced test pilot, rather than the average combat pilot, as a tester.) The pilots also concluded that the low number of deflection shots had more to do with the deficiencies of the armament than of the sighting system. Therefore, they recommended that the A-1CM be retained, provided that immediate efforts to improve reliability and maintenance were implemented. They further noted that the radar equipment's weight increase of 205 pounds was insignificant relative to its advantages.[58]

Despite this information from FEAF and firing statistics assembled by the APGC, the chief of staff of the USAF, Hoyt Vandenberg, was not satisfied. This came to a head in the summer of 1952 when fourteen Korean War aces meet with him and "vigorously" recommended that the radar gunsight be removed from the F-86. They assured their chief of the extremely high percentage of kills at short range during a stern chase and the need for 100 percent reliability. Further, they complained about the 205 pounds of extra weight in a complex and unreliable gunsight that was carried only for the "rather remote chance of a long range, high deflection kill."[59] Typical of this attitude was a comment attributed to World War II ace (28 aerial credits) Francis Gabreski (who also downed 6.5 in Korea) that: "I just stick a piece of chewing gun on my windscreen and use that as a sight."[60] The tendency of the older pilots to dislike and distrust the new equipment is understandable considering their lack of training with the radar ranging gunsight system, their success with the tried and true older gunsight, and—most of all—their experience of problems with the new one. On 8 September, Vandenberg directed that both the APGC and FEAF compare the radar ranging A-1C sight with the manual ranging Mk 18 series in fighter-versus-fighter combat conditions.[61]

The APGC used two methods to fulfill its assignment. First, it conducted flying tests with three F-86Es equipped with K-14 sights and three F-86Es equipped with the J-2 fire control system.[62] The Air Force assigned five Korean War aces, one Korean War veteran who was also a World War II ace, and two proving ground pilots to the tests. They flew 307 gun camera passes on a towed banner, 191 of which were used in the study.[63] This was the best the testers could do, but the results were questionable, since the target was non-maneuvering, slow, and had to be approached at angles greater than 15 degrees. The test report admitted that these conditions were "not realistic or comparable to fighter vs. fighter combat."[64]

The testers noted that the K-14 weighed 205 pounds less than the radar ranging, fire control systems. However, because center of gravity considerations would require ballast to offset the weight of the K-14 in the nose, weight reduction could only be realized in future designs.[65] The tests showed that the two sight systems achieved comparable results at short ranges, but the J-2 did much better at ranges in excess of twelve hundred feet. The pilots concluded that the A-4 was superior to the K-14 but that "the APG-30, despite the JAY-BIRD fixes, is still not suitable for use in the F-86E due to its unreliability, limited performance at low altitudes, inadequacy against jet fighter targets, erratic performance in the presence of clouds, excessive maintenance and personnel requirements, etc."[66] They recommended that the APG-30 be deleted and the A-4 sight be used with manual ranging. Furthermore, they recommended an intensive effort be made to improve the APG-30 radar and that a new radar should be designed to improve maintenance and reliability.[67]

The APGC evaluators also reviewed Korean War gun camera film.[68] They observed that World War II experience demonstrated that pilots grossly underestimated both range and angles off in engagements. They posited that the belief that fighter-to-fighter dogfights consisted of short range, minimum angle combat was reinforced "in the pilot's mind by the experience in non-combat maneuvers and training, and in the non-flying public's mind by films released for public consumption, showing close-in, highly effective attacks on enemy aircraft."[69] The selected film was of better pictures of targets (necessarily at shorter ranges) in which hits or damage could be seen. In fact, however, actual combat was at "considerably longer ranges" than indicated by either the APGC flying tests or selected Korean War gun camera film. Whereas 50 percent of the APGC test "firing" was at fifteen hundred feet and the selected film showed a range of sixteen hundred feet, the unselected (or unedited) film indicated an average range of three thousand feet. The evaluators divided the unselected film into three categories: pilots who scored two or more kills, those who scored one-half to two kills, and those who had no credits. They discovered that even the second group, which fired at shorter ranges than the other two, fired at longer ranges than that found in the APGC tests or unselected film. The tests indicated that the A-4 sight used in a manual mode was only 71 percent as effective as the complete J-2 system, and that the K-14 was 90 percent as effective as the A-4 in the manual mode and thus only 64 percent as effective as the J-2 system.[70]

Patrick Timberlake, the APGC commanding general, signed the overall report. He concurred with the comments on the APG-30's reliability and maintenance problems but did not agree with the recommendation that it be removed from the F-86, for he noted the majority of the firing was done at long ranges with high angles off. Under these conditions, kill probability with the J-2 system using radar ranging was twice that of either the A-4 or K-14 using manual ranging. Therefore he recommended that the APG-30 be retained but efforts should be intensified to improve its reliability.[71]

As might be expected, FEAF's response was less elaborate and elegant than that of the APGC. Three days after Vandenberg's cable, Fifth Air Force held a seminar at its headquarters with nine officers, seven of whom had downed twenty-six aircraft on 707 missions by that time.[72] Their conclusions did not vary from those put forth by FEAF in July. One view held in the the-ater, at least at the command level, was that the fourteen aces who influenced the chief of staff were probably not well-trained in the use of the radar rang-ing gunsight and had served in Korea when the gunsight reliability problem was at its worst. Those who had some training with the sight or familiarity with radar were less critical of it and saw its value.[73] The FEAF seminar par-ticipants wanted all the automatic features of the A-1CM gunsight. Again, they mentioned that while superior pilots could do well with the Mk 18 man-ual ranging gunsight, such pilots were the exception and that the low deflec-tion shots were a deficiency of armament not of the sights. The pilots reported that Project Jay Bird and the Jenkins Limiter had increased gunsight reliability and efficiency "immeasurably." In brief, they wanted to retain the A-1CM sight, redesign it to ease maintenance, and reduce the numbers of technical personnel. They also believed that pilots should get comprehensive training in the use of the gunsight.[74]

In the end, the USAF retained both the radar rangefinder and its prob-lems. For despite the Project Jay Bird, the gunsight's reliability continued to dog the Sabre units. Between 1 January and 15 March 1953, the 4th Fighter Wing experienced malfunctions of the fire control system on 10 percent of its 2,860 sorties, despite the fact that the unit discovered and corrected 845 mal-functions on the ground. On the GunVal tests in 1953, in what we can assume were pampered aircraft compared to the other F-86s in Korea, gun-sights failed on 8 percent of the missions. During the last months of the war (3 March through 27 July 1953) the ranging radar malfunctioned on 17 per-cent of the sorties. The older A-1CM had slightly fewer malfunctions than did the newer A-4. The aircraft equipped with the range limiter suffered mal-functions on 12.5 percent of the sorties while those without this equipment had a higher rate of 23.2 percent. (Perhaps the greater attention given to the new equipment accounts for the anomaly of additional and newer equipment combined with the same older equipment having better reliability than the same gunsight with less equipment.)[75]

Despite these difficulties, the radar ranging, computing gunsight gave American pilots an advantage over their foes, who used a sight equivalent to the World War II K-14. The poor marksmanship of the MiG pilots could be attributed to armament ill suited for fighter-to-fighter combat, inadequate training, and an outdated gunsight. John Meyer, the Fourth's initial group commander in Korea, believed the gunsight gave good shooters a 25 percent advantage. Statistical analysis indicated that pilots using computing sights fired at longer ranges and fired 18 percent fewer shots per burst than those using fixed sights. Most importantly, gun camera film showed greater hit probability for the computing sights beyond three hundred feet. (A September 1952 study indicated that computing sights were 1.3 times as efficient as fixed sights.) The value of the range limiter was validated by figures that showed that while pilots scored hits in 42 percent of the bursts fired below the limiter setting, they scored only 18 percent in which the bursts were beyond the setting.[76]

THREE

Maintenance

Unappreciated but Vital

F-86s in the Korean theater numbered less than a hundred until the second half of 1951 and then gradually increased to 352 in July 1953. By the end of the war, there were two wings of Sabres committed to air superiority (4th and 51st) and two wings to fighter-bomber duties (8th and 18th). Sheer numbers in the theater did not equate with the number of aircraft in combat; aircraft reliability, serviceability, supply, and ground support determined how many aircraft on the ramp made it into the air. One measure of aircraft reliability was the in-commission rate, or the percentage of aircraft on hand that were ready to fly. The F-86 averaged a 59 percent in-commission rate of fighters on hand during the war, almost the same as its two jet stable mates, the F-80 and F-84.[1]

Compared to the other two fighters, a greater percentage of Sabres were out of commission due to a shortage of parts. Some of these problems were caused by inefficient management and were easily solved. For example, in early 1952 the 4th Wing had a number of aircraft grounded because of a lack of replacement engines. The problem was that engines removed from the aircraft could not be shipped to Japan for overhaul because there was a lack of engine dollies, and the unit could only get replacement engines when a pulled engine was turned in, on a one-for-one replacement basis. When the 4th Group's new commander, Walker Mahurin, took over in March 1952, there were eighteen engines waiting for dollies. He scouted around the base and found a dozen dollies in various places, as well as another half dozen still in packing crates.[2]

Were there any differences between the maintenance of the various F-86 units? For the ten months that we have comparable figures, the 4th had a higher in-commission rate in all except one month and a slightly higher average overall in-commission rate compared to the 51st.[3] There was an intense rivalry between the two units, as might be expected from these young, aggressive fighter pilots who thirsted for promotion, bragging rights, and pride. One aspect of this was that the 4th posted a highly experienced supply sergeant to Japan who worked alongside the parts people there and personally tracked down parts requisitions from the 4th. He also put similar requisitions from the 51st at the bottom of the in basket. Another 4th tactic was more direct. Occasionally, fighters from the 51st short of fuel would land at the 4th base, because it was the closest U.S. airfield to MiG Alley. The 4th would use this opportunity to substitute their unusable parts for usable ones on these aircraft. This makes for a good story, but the fact is that the 51st had a lower percentage of aircraft out of commission for lack of parts than did the 4th in seven of ten months for which comparable figures exist. The 4th did beat down this rate from an average of 4.8 percent in the last half of 1952 to under 2 percent in May and June 1953.[4]

What of the Sabre's various subsystems? While there were problems with the radar ranging gunsight, the F-86's armament performed well. The Sabre's tried and true .50-caliber machine guns ran up an impressive record and proved to be very reliable, reasonably accurate, and fairly lethal. During the course of the war, the 4th fired almost 25 million rounds of .50-caliber ammunition, averaging approximately 6,000 rounds per malfunction. Since the F-86 mounted six .50-caliber USAF machine guns and could carry a maximum ammunition load of 1,800 rounds, it is clear that gun stoppages were never a major problem. During the last half of 1952, the USAF attributed 60 percent of the gun failures to personnel.

Not all this ammunition was fired in combat. For example, only 37 percent of the ammunition expended by the 336th Fighter Squadron during the last half of 1952 and 79 percent in the first half of 1953 was in combat.[5]

There was one dramatic incident regarding the armament that ended in disaster for the Americans. On 20 May 1951, Capt. Max Weill (336FS) was leading a flight of four F-86s that engaged some MiG-15s. "At the beginning of the second burst," Weill recalled, "I heard an explosion and saw several wild rounds of ammunition from the nose of my aircraft. Wild rounds were traveling 90 degrees to my line of flight."[6] The readings on his Mach meter, air speed indicator, and oxygen supply fell to zero, forcing Weill to break off the combat and return home. On his landing roll, he found he had no brakes because the hydraulics had been damaged, so he retracted the landing gear to stop the aircraft, slid off the runway, and totaled the fighter.

Three other fighters sustained similar damage. Capt. Milton Nelson (335FS) was leading a two-ship element when he engaged a MiG-15, which he destroyed. As he was returning to base, Nelson's wingman noted a large hole on the Sabre's left fuselage. Upon landing, his landing gear functioned properly although the indicator did not indicate that the nose wheel was down and locked. The left brake failed, however, due to damage to the hydraulic system; and Nelson attempted to ground loop the fighter to stop. Instead the fighter ran off the runway and was assessed to be beyond economic repair.[7]

Capt. James Roberts (335FS) had a similar, albeit less damaging, experience. As he fired three bursts at a MiG, he noted a large yellow flash just forward of the left side of the cockpit. He landed safely and found a large, jagged hole just forward of the lower left gun barrel.[8] Inspection of the blast tubes of all aircraft found a fourth aircraft with internal blisters on two guns.

The accident board found that the Sabre's ammunition (M-23 incendiary), which had a higher muzzle velocity than the standard M-8 ammunition, combined with inadequate cooling time between bursts, had exploded in the guns' blast tubes (four guns in Nelson's fighter, three guns in Weill's, and one in Roberts's). This was the first time the 4th had used the M-23 rounds and, understandably, the last. The incident had cost two F-86s.[9]

Other subsystems proved more difficult. The only evidence we have on the cause for aborts at the F-86 wing level covers the 4th Fighter Group over a seven month period, during which 24 percent of the aborts were caused by landing gear problems, 23 percent by engine problems, and 15 percent by radio problems. More extensive coverage from the 334th squadron supports these findings. The problems with the landing gear came as no surprise to those familiar with the F-86. One author explained that "the operation of the F-86 landing gear is dependent upon a multitude of micro switches, most of which are exposed to water and dirt splashed into the wheel wells . . . [that are] very difficult to check and can only be checked properly on a jacked-up aircraft."[10] The conditions on the Korean airfields was certainly much more primitive than those of the Sabres' American bases.

This study found that a small number of pilots had a disproportionate number of aborts. Of the group's seventy pilots who had aborts, a dozen (17 percent) had three or more aborts that accounted for 36 percent of the total aborts. One pilot had six, another five, and two had four aborts. But before blaming the pilots for the problem, note that a few aircraft had a disproportionate number of aborts. In fact, one third of the aborting aircraft had three or more aborts and accounted for two-thirds of the total aborts. One F-86 had five aborts and five others had four each. The pilot with six aborts (336FS) had three of these in the same aircraft on three different days, all caused by landing gear. All four aborts of another pilot (334FS) were caused by the landing gear in two different aircraft on four different days in June. Another pilot (336FS) aborted three times in two different aircraft, all due to inoperative radios. However, the pilot with five aborts (334FS) did so in five different aircraft, all to different causes. The study also noted that the F-86A had a much higher abort rate than did the F-86E, accounting for 45 percent of the aborts in the 336th although it comprised only 25 percent of the unit's assigned aircraft. Because the "A" model aircraft were older and probably had accumulated more flying hours than the "E" model fighters, its greater maintenance is understandable.[11]

The F-86 Sabre experienced three major mechanical problems during the Korean War. These difficulties were quite different: one was very sophisticated; the second, routine; and the third, simple. The cutting-edge radar-ranging gunsight and the old and well-known landing gear have already been discussed. The third problem came from an even simpler device, the jettisonable, external fuel tanks known simply as "drop tanks."

Range is one of the important elements of aircraft performance. While it is especially important for bombers and transports, fighter designers consider range after other performance aspects such as speed, ceiling, rate of climb, maneuverability, firepower, and acceleration. It is not that range is unimportant but that other aspects are more important in air-to-air combat. In short, to achieve greater range meant sacrificing other performance elements that are more important for fighter success.

Airmen understood the value of range early on and thought in terms of multi-place aircraft for escort duties. By the end of the 1920s, however, American airmen discussed the use of drop tanks to extend the range of fighters and tested a number of aircraft with droppable tanks.[12] American airmen considered drop tanks only for ferry duties because of concerns of safety and reliability. In 1939 the Chief of the Air Corps banned tactical aircraft from using such tanks. In any event, top U.S. airmen questioned the effectiveness of fighters in war and believed instead that bombardment aviation "may be capable of effectively accomplishing its assigned mission without [fighter] support."[13] This led to the dogma taught at the top American air school of the day, the Air Corps Tactical School, that high-speed, heavily-armed bombers flying in tight formations, at high altitude, and without fighter escort could successfully defend themselves and attack critical enemy targets. The one American pre-war effort to develop an escort for American bombers was the abortive, twin-engine Bell FM-1.[14] In fairness, it was not just Americans who went down this false path; aircraft designers worldwide believed that single-engine fighters would never be capable of long-range operations. The Germans went furthest, developing and mass-producing the twin-engine Me 110 for the escort role. While it performed well in a number of other ways, it failed as an escort because it could not stand up to single engine fighters.

Despite its major emphasis on bombers as its chief weapon and fighters designed as interceptors, in 1940 the Air Corps began to develop longer-range fighters. The air leaders realized that American fighters required longer ferry ranges if they were going to serve in European combat. In May 1941, Lockheed responded to an Air Force Materiel Command request with plans for 120-gallon tanks that would hang on bomb shackles. In September, the airmen modified the requirement by adding high-altitude escort duty as a fighter function. This change complicated matters, since it would require a boost pump to pressurize the tanks at operating altitudes. Nevertheless, by April 1942, Lockheed tested the tanks and used them to ferry P-38s across the Atlantic in mid-1942.[15]

World War II indicated that American fighters required greater range to close with and combat the enemy. Range can present major problems for the offensive fighter arm, as the *Luftwaffe* found out over Britain in 1940 and the AAF over Germany in 1943. The American airmen were slow in recognizing the need for escort fighters, and the ultimate solution (drop tanks) was hampered by managerial and technical difficulties: leaks, pressurization, shackles, jettison characteristics, and manufacturing. During the war, American fighters greatly expanded their escort radius of action: the P-47 increasing in a clean condition (without tanks) from 175 miles to 475 miles using two 150-gallon tanks; the P-38 to 585 miles with two 108-gallon tanks; and the P-51 from 475 miles in a clean configuration to 850 miles with two 108-gallon tanks.[16]

The AAF built more range into later versions of the P-47 and P-51. Efforts to develop other aircraft for this long-range escort role (the convoy defender YB-40, a heavily armed B-17) failed in action while the composite P-75 and twin-engine P-61 just could not perform as required. The twin-fuselage (from the P-51), twin-engine P-82 had the range and performance but arrived too late for combat.[17]

During the Korean War, American airmen had a number of problems with the F-86's drop tanks. The war found the USAF unprepared for the large number of tanks required and their staggering cost. There were also technical problems with tanks either not releasing or damaging the fighter as they departed. This is surprising because the Air Force had considerable experience in World War II with drop tanks. In addition, the introduction of jets magnified the range problem because they were notorious fuel guzzlers. Therefore, the USAF neglect of the fighter range problem and drop tank solution is difficult to explain and even more difficult to excuse. In any event, drop tanks proved to be a considerable and continuing problem for the Sabre units.

The crunch came when the USAF decided that one F-86 Wing (the 4th) was inadequate to maintain air superiority and thus re-equipped the 51st Wing with the North American fighter. Drop tanks were already in short supply during the last half of 1951, so doubling the number of F-86 units pushed the situation to critical. Stateside production could not keep up with the new requirements. The Air Materiel Command history for the first half of 1952 noted that "The major item of tactical deficiency was the droppable fuel tank, for which requirements had jumped 500 percent in four months because of the increase in air opposition and the extraordinary fuel needs of the F-84 and F-86 jets."[18] In January 1952 the number of F-86 drop tanks in the field fell to a three-day supply (for all-out combat), triggering drastic measures.

One response to the shortage of tanks was to fly the F-86s with only one tank, beginning toward the end of January 1952. This reduced the Sabre's range and endurance, cutting the coverage of MiG Alley and increasing the number of fighters returning home in a critical fuel state. Although such operations were feasible, they required changes for takeoffs. The pilots had to adjust the aileron and rudder trim and make additional use of brakes and nose wheel steering until they established sufficient rudder control. One exchange pilot noted that, while practical, "formation take-offs with single tanks hung on different sides tended . . . to be exciting."[19]

Another effort to relieve this critical situation was to airlift drop tanks to the theater. Between 21 January and 4 February 1952, C-124s delivered twelve hundred tanks, a ten-day supply. In addition, by February 1952, every ship arriving at Yokohama carried some tanks. Nevertheless, the 4th was forced to limit the number of sorties it flew in February. It was not until May that the shortage of tanks was met. The problem returned in January 1953, however, when the 4th reported that its supply of drop tanks was "critically low." Matters only grew worse when the USAF converted two existing fighter units to the F-86F fighter-bomber. In March the 4th used 3,531 tanks, the most it ever had used up to this point, and at the end of the month had 1,243 tanks on hand, about a ten-day supply.[20]

The original Sabre drop tanks had been designed by the North American engineers for ferry duty and were to be reused. Because of this and their high expense, the USAF authorized few spare tanks to the F-86 units. North American designed the shackle as part of the tank rather than part of the aircraft. This design was more streamlined than if the shackles were mounted on the airframe; however, it also meant that every time a tank was dropped, so too was a shackle. As one Fifth Air Force document explained, "these features caused expensive manufacturing processes and made the tank a luxury item."[21]

Certainly the tanks were expensive, but they were necessary if UN aircraft were to operate over northern Korea. North American built both 120- and 200-gallon tanks. The first worked well but the second created a number of problems, such as damaging the aircraft after release and causing the aircraft to porpoise in flight. However, the greatest disadvantage of the North American tanks was their cost.[22]

Shipping the tanks was another problem because the bulky tanks took up much valuable shipping space and had to endure the rigors of the trans-Pacific journey. They were sent to the theater in three ways: completely assembled, partially assembled (fins, pylons, and fairings packed as loose items), and completely knocked down ("nested"). Tanks were sometimes damaged in shipping; one report stated that "a large percentage" was damaged even in shipping crates. One problem was that the crates were designed to be lifted by forklift trucks operating from a smooth concrete or asphalt surface. In Korea, however, the operating surface was likely to be muddy or dusty, depending upon the season, and the handlers used truck cranes that employed a steel cable wrapped around four to ten of the tank crates at a time. The crates were not designed for such treatment and suffered damage as a result.[23]

Readying the tanks for operations took some effort, not only because of damage to the tanks but oftentimes also because of measures taken to protect the unassembled tanks. Tanks shipped in knockdown condition were coated with oil (oil fogged) to inhibit rust. As these tanks were transported in the open, the oil collected sand, dirt, and grit, which had to be removed before assembly. A shortage of solvents in Korea forced the airmen to use labor-intensive steam cleaning, which required between six to nine man-hours to clean each tank.

It took additional time to assemble the tanks. To complicate matters, the tanks of the six different manufacturers were not interchangeable and required modification (termed "excessive" by Fifth Air Force) to fit the F-86. Perhaps the worst case of non-standardization was the Ingersoll tanks that used two sway braces in contrast to the other manufacturers that used one. The USAF experienced what it termed "considerable trouble" with the two-sway-brace installation in the second half of 1950, yet Ingersoll turned out at least fourteen thousand such tanks. It was not until March 1953 that the Air Force stopped delivery of the two-sway-brace Ingersoll tanks. The non-standardization and quality control problems can be attributed to inadequate USAF direction and supervision.

The demand for labor forced the Americans to rely on Korean help. This was a problem because "much of this Korean labor was totally inexperienced in the act of mechanics—many did not know the uses of pliers or screwdrivers."[24] This sounds like American impatience, arrogance, and hyperbole, but it nevertheless indicates there was a problem. Each wing set up a tank farm for the assembly of the tanks, manned by fifty or more men. This unanticipated labor demand forced the Air Force to use all available help, including cooks and other kitchen staff. As with other maintenance in Korea, most was done in the open under difficult conditions. Clearly the USAF needed standardized tanks requiring simple field assembly, but the effort to speed production pushed the Air Force in another direction.[25]

Unfortunately, these are not all of the difficulties the airmen encountered with drop tanks. Two operational problems emerged. First of all, some tanks did not properly release from the fighter. The F-86 pilots jettisoned the external tanks when they spotted enemy aircraft in preparation for combat, and if a tank or tanks did not release from the aircraft, Air Force policy dictated that fighter head for home. It was not so much that a stuck tank caused asymmetrical flight, something that could be overcome with some trim and some care, but that the hung tank would cut performance. Because the F-86 was at best equivalent to the MiG-15 in performance, any degradation was most unwanted. To make matters worse, USAF policy stated that an aborting fighter would be escorted home; therefore, one hung tank meant two less Sabres in action. The release problem diminished with time but was never completely resolved. In June 1951, the 4th reported that between 5 and 10 percent of the tanks experienced release problems. By the end of the year, that number was below 1 percent. For the remainder of the war, the failure rate hovered just over 1 percent.[26]

The airmen concluded that the principal cause of the release problem was the shackles. Because these were part of the drop tank and thus built by each manufacturer, it is little wonder that there were problems. The 4th dipped the shackles into a compound and incorporated a gun-heating element on each shackle to prevent icing from binding the mechanism. The next month the 4th reported "the problems of tip tanks failing to release has almost been eliminated by the adjustment of the tank shackles and the use of Dow Corning compound as packing for tank release shackles." But this did not end the problem. In the first half of 1953, the 51st reported that shackles caused 90 percent of the failures of the Borg Warner tanks.[27] A July 1953 report stated that "in almost every case reported [of the failure of a tank to release], the failure occurred in the tank shackle and not in the aircraft manual- or electrical-release system."[28]

The second major operational problem was that all too frequently the released drop tanks flew back into, and damaged, the fighter. Some of the tanks slid forward and rode down the right wing's leading edge, shearing off the pitot tube and knocking out the air speed indicator. (These damaged F-86s could land by flying on the wing of another fighter with a functioning air speed indicator.) Other errant tanks damaged the flaps or empennage. Even before the Sabre entered the war, the USAF experienced problems with drop tanks damaging the fighter, so this problem was no surprise to the airmen.[29] Because this seemed to be caused by the fuel hose binding and the connections, the airmen lubricated the fittings, deleted hose clamps, and checked that the attaching bolts were properly torqued. The airmen instituted procedures that also seemed to help the situation. They found that if the air speed was above Mach 0.82 and there were some positive "g" forces when the tanks were released, separation went well.[30] The 51st came up with another solution, adding a small (2.5 inch) airfoil (spoiler) on the tank to aerodynamically force the tank down and away from the fighter upon tank release. During the twelve-week period prior to the first use of the airfoil, the unit suffered damage on 0.86 percent of tank releases; in the twelve-week period afterward, the damage rate was cut in half. This worked well with the tanks fitted with one sway brace but in fact increased the problem with those using two sway braces.[31] After a respite, Royal Heater tanks caused the problem to recur in the 4th in February 1953. In the first half of 1953, 63 percent of the 4th's aborts were due to tank problems. In April 1953, the 51st recorded 0.76 percent damaged from tanks.[32]

A third problem with the drop tanks was cost. Astonishingly, drop tanks accounted for half of the operating costs of the Sabre units.[33] Because the orig-

inal North American tanks cost $850 each, the USAF sought cheaper alterna-
tives. By July 1952 competition induced North American to slash its price to
$386 per tank. Beechcraft tanks cost $587 each. By November 1952, tanks
manufactured by Pastuchin and Ingersoll cost approximately $300 each. The
least expensive were Japanese-built tanks: American-made tanks sold for an
average cost of $457, including transportation; Japanese tanks could be deliv-
ered at half that, an average cost of $223. Although the percentage of operat-
ing costs attributed to drop tanks remained high, between 45 and 50 percent
from November 1952 through May 1953, the average cost per drop tank gradually declined to around $300 for the period February through April 1953.[34]

Although the Japanese tanks proved to be much cheaper than American-
built tanks, the airmen were slow in getting them into action. The 4th Fighter
Interceptor Wing did not test them until February 1952, and the Fifth Air
Force did not authorize their use until August. Compared with American-
built tanks (specifically North American and Beech), Japanese tanks were
cheaper but carried less fuel and had greater drag, requiring the F-86s to carry
5 percent more power to reach the same air speed. They were taken out of service for a time but then used again in 1953. While the 120-gallon Japanese
tanks proved very satisfactory, the 110-gallon tank built by Kawasaki did not. In
April 1953 one F-86 unit suffered 2.6 percent damage from the 1,014
Japanese-built 110-gallon tanks that were dropped, compared with 0.22 percent from the other 3,610 tanks dropped that were built by other manufacturers. The 4th discontinued use of these Japanese tanks in June, an action
endorsed by an Air Force study group the next month.[35]

This same study also recommended discontinuing the use of tanks built
by Royal Heater. These tanks caused the USAF considerable difficulties and
more than their fair share of damage. Nevertheless, the airmen were forced to
use them because of operational requirements. The airmen went so far as to
name the damage from the Royal Heater tanks as one of two factors that were
largely responsible for the declining efficiency of the 51st Fighter Wing in
February 1953 because the unit's victory-to-loss ratio fell from 26:1 in January
to 6:1 in February. Finally, in the first half of 1953, the Air Force was able to
discontinue or limit the use of the Royal Heater drop tanks.[36]

The USAF made a number of other efforts with drop tanks. The early
Sabres (F-86A-1 through early production of the A-5) could carry two 206.5-
gallon tanks. Then the manufacturer reduced this capability, apparently
because these tanks caused buffeting at higher speeds that restricted operations
to below Mach 0.8. North American replaced these tanks with two 120-gallon

tanks. Later, the company increased the Sabre's drop tank capability by fitting F-86Fs with either two 200-gallon tanks or two 120-gallon tanks. The company fitted the F-86F-25 (and subsequent aircraft) with four pylons that could carry four tanks (two 120-gallon and two 200-gallon) or a combination of tanks, bombs, or rockets. The manufacturer tested the larger tanks in the first half of 1952, using new pylons with leading edges that were cambered inward, allowing higher speeds. In December 1952, the 51st began testing the 200-gallon tank. These tanks increased the F-86's radius of action from 330 to 465 miles but also exhibited "undesirable flight characteristics."[37]

The USAF attempted to obtain a "standard contour fuel tank" for all of its aircraft. This certainly made sense in terms of logistics and lowering overall costs as opposed to having tanks that only fit one type of aircraft. After some resistance, four manufacturers agreed; as of mid-August 1952, however, the Air Force was convinced that North American was absolutely against such a program. This project had no impact on the war in Korea.[38]

There were other efforts to extend the F-86's range. In early 1951, the USAF tested aerial refueling on a T-33, F-84, and F-86. The airmen flew four flights in an F-86A in March using a drogue system from a KB-29 tanker and a 3.5-foot probe on an F-86 120-gallon external fuel tank. This configuration encountered problems because it placed the fighter's empennage in the tanker's turbulence, making longitudinal control "very difficult" and causing the drogue to bob. As a result, contact in the F-86 was more of a problem than with the other two aircraft. Maintaining contact required care. The testers concluded that aerial refueling with this arrangement was feasible but difficult.[39] Then, in the summer of 1953, Wright-Patterson AFB considered the use of a 200-gallon tank for in-flight refueling of the F-86F. The airmen concluded that although it was possible, requiring effort similar to formation flying, it "will require additional effort on the part of the pilot to maintain position due to the poor stability and control characteristics of the F-86F."[40] The Air Force later fitted an F-86E with tanks modified with refueling probes, but there is no record of any in-flight testing. The Air Force also conducted tests with a boom-equipped KB-29 and a Sabre fitted with a refueling receptacle just forward of the canopy. Photos document this effort, but, alas, there is no indication of when it took place. The USAF did not equip production Sabres with aerial refueling equipment, for by this time the F-100 with a fixed probe was about to enter service.[41] Since then, all USAF fighters have air-to-air refueling capability.

FOUR

F-86 Flying Safety

lying is not a risk-free activity, and military flying is even more dangerous. Since the first fatal army aircraft accident in September 1908, aviators have made great strides that have lessened, but not eliminated,
both risks and accidents. The late 1940s and early 1950s were a critical time
for the airmen, as the transition from prop power to jet power was neither easy
nor cheap.

The premier U.S. fighter of this period was the F-86 Sabre. It is a classic:
beautiful in looks, impressive in performance, and well regarded, if not loved,
by its pilots and aviation enthusiasts. It was a great success in service, especially
in combat, and the USAF employed more F-86s than any other jet fighter in
its history. It did, however, encounter problems, accidents, and casualties.

Props to Jet

The transformation of the Air Force from propeller-powered aircraft to jets was
a challenge. Besides greater performance, jet-powered aircraft had a number
of advantages. Although tricycle landing gear was novel to most pilots and
posed the possibility of dragging the tail on landing, it had an overall positive
affect because it eliminated ground loops and gave the pilot better visibility
during ground operations.[1] Torque-less jet power simplified flying. Jet engines
were less complex than prop engines and propellers; for example, jets had only
a throttle while propeller aircraft had throttle, mixture, and prop controls.

Initially, jet-powered fighters proved more dangerous than piston-powered fighters. The major accident rates of the prop-powered P-51 (later F-51) from World War II to August 1953 exceeded that of the jet-powered P-80 (later F-80) in only one year.[2] Performance of the P-80 was higher, as were takeoff, approach, and landing speeds.[3] Higher speeds not only gave the pilots less time to react but also caused the altimeter to lag, giving the pilot erroneous altitude information.[4] Jet engines were new to Air Force pilots and ground crews. One of the most dangerous aspects of jet power was that it took jet engines some time to deliver increased power (to "spool up"), unlike prop engines that delivered power almost at once.[5] Another peril was that jamming the throttle too rapidly forward could cause a jet engine to "flame out" (stall) and lose all power. F-86 pilots were warned to "accelerate *very* slowly (ten to twenty seconds from 'IDLE' to full open) at high altitudes in order to minimize [the] possibility of acceleration flame-out."[6] A unique problem of jet engines was their tendency to suck up debris on the ground and damage their internal parts.[7]

In addition to a higher accident rate, jet power brought other changes: new equipment. Because "crash helmets," later tactfully called "flight helmets," were slow to enter the system, pilots were forced to do without or use expedients such as football-type headgear borrowed from the Army's tank drivers.[8] The use of "g" suits was less of a problem, as the Army Air Forces (AAF) had used them during World War II to increase pilot tolerance to high-acceleration maneuvers (high gravity ["g"] forces).

Ejection

Escape from a crippled jet fighter in flight was more difficult than from a prop-powered fighter because of the increased speeds, "g" forces, and altitudes. Not only was there a problem getting out of the cockpit because of increased "g" loads on the pilot and air loads on the canopy, but there was also difficulty clearing the tail. The Germans led the way in improvements with a patent for an ejection seat in 1939 and experiments with seats propelled by compressed air, springs, and gunpowder. The first emergency seat ejection was made from an He 280 in January 1943. By war's end the *Luftwaffe* had fitted a number of both prop and non-prop aircraft types with ejection seats, and reportedly more than sixty pilots used the device.[9] The Allies took the German invention and developed it. The first American emergency use of the ejection seat was made from an F2H-1 in 1949.[10]

Although the seats worked well, the pilots distrusted them at first. Some understandably feared sitting atop a seat powered by a 37 mm cannon charge, and they flew with the device deactivated. As with standard bailouts, aircraft attitude, altitude, and speed played a major role in determining results. Ejection below two thousand feet was found to be "extremely hazardous." A study in May 1951 noted that seven of nine USAF pilots killed in forty-two ejections had ejected too low. It found that the Sabre had the lowest fatality rate of the three USAF jet fighters (F-80, F-84, and F-86).[11] A 1956 study of Canadian experience reinforced these conclusions, reporting that the F-86 had the lowest fatality rate (7 percent) of the three jet types they flew.[12] In over six hundred major USAF F-86 accidents prior to August 1953, pilots bailed out eighty-five times, thirteen (15 percent) with fatal results.[13] This was better than the Air Force average during 1949–53, when 23 percent of USAF ejections proved lethal.

USAF experience demonstrated that it was safer to eject than to stick with the aircraft and crash land. One study found that while 11 percent of all jet fighter bailouts were fatal, 20 percent of the crash landings proved lethal. (However, pilots might have little choice if, for example, the seat malfunctioned or if the aircraft were too low to eject.) Although the Sabre had a better ejection record than its rivals, it had a worse record in crash landing: 11 percent of F-80 and F-84 crash landings were lethal, compared with 21 percent of F-86.[14]

The F-86's superior ejection performance is somewhat surprising. Initially, the Sabre's ejection seat was not recommended for exit in all circumstances. The 1948 flight manual instructed the pilot in low-speed bailouts (speeds not specified) to jettison the canopy and then roll the aircraft over, release the safety belt, and push clear of the aircraft. It went on to note that: "As seat ejection subjects the pilot to extremely high forces, this method of exit [ejection seat] should be used only when normal bail-out is impossible (at extremely high speeds or when [the] airplane is uncontrollable)."[15] No wonder pilots distrusted the system and some deactivated the ejection seat! In addition, in the early F-86A models the canopy jettison handle was mounted on the lower forward cockpit panel between the pilot's legs forcing the pilot to reach forward and extend his arm to activate the canopy jettison, not an easy task if the aircraft was violently maneuvering or experiencing heavy "g" loads. Furthermore, the ejection seat was only armed when the canopy was jettisoned. This system was changed in the F-86A-5 so that the pilot could jettison the canopy by raising the right seat handle. In mid-1951, North American proposed a system that would permit the pilot to eject through a closed canopy and fitted twenty aircraft with the system, but the USAF disapproved the change. It was not until 1953 that the seat could be fired through the canopy. (This was a last resort maneuver. Of twenty-six ejections through the canopy, 42 percent proved fatal compared with the USAF ejection fatality rate of 17 percent.)[16] Another potential problem was that the F-86 ejection canopy had the tendency to "dish down," and therefore the pilot's manual warned the pilot to "keep head and body as low as possible."[17]

A 1951 study revealed that, relative to the F-80 and F-84, the Sabre had less difficulty with the canopy. The F-86 suffered only two canopy failures in flight, compared with fifteen in the F-80 and eleven in the F-84. However, in late March 1953, Fifth Air Force F-86Fs experienced four inadvertent canopy departures.[18]

Capt. Richard Barr (94FS) was the first man to abandon an F-86 when he was blown out of the aircraft following a midair collision in June 1949. Two months later, 2nd Lt. Robert Farley (71FS) made the first ejection from a Sabre. With no aileron boost, one drop tank that would not jettison, and in an inverted spiral, he punched out at about 500 mph at one thousand feet. The shock of the parachute opening tore off his shoes, watch, and dog tags. Nevertheless, like Captain Barr, he survived the ordeal, albeit with major injuries.[19] He was certainly lucky to have survived such a high-speed, low-altitude bailout, one that would certainly have proved fatal without an ejection seat.

Training

Training was crucial to flying safety. During World War II, the AAF produced approximately 200,000 pilots, 40 percent of whom flew single engine aircraft.[20] The availability of so many pilots, along with the drastic draw-down in the military after the end of the war, led the AAF to stop all pilot training until October 1946. Since the classes that followed were not as large as those during the war, the majority of USAF fighter pilots on active duty in the early 1950s had trained prior to 1946. In the period from July 1949 to June 1950, 62 percent of the USAF's 1,100 jet fighter pilots had earned their wings prior to 1946. At first glance, this did not seem to be a problem: these men had earned their wings when young, and, with their flying experience, they should have been able to easily transition to jet aircraft. However, the introduction of the jet modified the conventional wisdom that experienced pilots (measured in total flying time) were safer than inexperienced ones. Although pilots with 1,000 to 2,000 total flying hours were safer in jet fighters than those with less total flying time, pilots flying their first 100 jet hours—even those who had flown many hours in prop aircraft—had the highest rate of jet accidents. Put another way, pilots with less than 300 hours total flying time had 1.5 times more accidents than the entire group while pilots with less than 100 jet hours had a rate almost 3 times that of the entire group. A later study covering January 1951 through June 1953 found that pilots with less than 150 jet flying hours accounted for 45 percent of the jet accidents.

During the period July 1949 until June 1950, the 290 pilots who earned their wings in 1949 comprised 25 percent of the fighter pilots, flew 27 percent of the jet time, and yet accounted for 37 percent of the jet accidents. Their major accident rate was more than double the USAF average.[21] The class of 49C that graduated in September 1949 was a particular problem. Between 1 December 1949 and the end of April 1950, six of sixteen fatal F-80 accidents and three of eight fatal F-84 accidents, (although neither of two F-86 fatal accidents) involved graduates of 49C.[22] Five of the fatal F-80 accidents were in the Far East, prompting the commander of Fifth Air Force, Gen. Earle Partridge, to restrict pilots from that class from operational flying until they were reevaluated. Partridge's command gave these pilots a training program that included twenty hours flying in the T-6 and T-33 before they were returned to operations.[23]

An early 1950 report indicated that the accident problem arose from three causes: a lack of accelerated testing and development of solutions before the fighter aircraft were produced in quantity, inadequate training, and a lack of pilot indoctrination in the new aircraft.[24] In support of the third conclusion, the report cited the case of the 33rd Fighter Group. It converted from flying F-84s to flying F-86s and within a five-day period had lost one pilot and one aircraft and damaged two aircraft.[25] Perhaps the 1st Fighter Group, the first unit to transition to the F-86, would have been a better example. It received F-86s in February 1949 and suffered its first major accident in April. During its first quarter of operations, from April through June 1949, it suffered five major accidents, including two fatalities and three total wrecks. Five more major accidents, including two write-offs, occurred in its second quarter, and two major accidents followed during the last quarter of the year.[26]

The report blamed neither Air Training Command nor the tactical units for the inadequate training. It diplomatically explained, "the phrase 'inadequate training' must be considered to be due to several factors, chief among which are the urgency of international affairs, the reduced budget of the Air Force, and the state of the arts."[27] A later report was more blunt, noting the "inept flying on the part of pilots recently graduated from the Air Force flying schools."[28] The report indicated that new pilots were not getting enough fighter flying time; the F-51 was an unsuitable aircraft for jet fighter training; instrument and night flying training were inadequate; and the curriculum was lacking certain important elements, such as the characteristics and limitations of jet aircraft, gunnery, rocketry, and bombing. In brief, "graduates therefore are not proficient fighter pilots."[29] This report went on to criticize the lack of standardized USAF flight instruments, specifically the attitude gyro and airspeed indicator. These instruments were located in different positions on the instrument panel of the various jet fighters, and the trainees were using three different types of attitude indicators. In addition, some jet fighters and trainers were using airspeed indicators graduated in miles per hour while others were using knots per hour.[30] Clearly this was a poor situation for flight training and inexperienced pilots.

Early on, the airmen realized that special training was required to transition to jet-powered aircraft and began planning such a program in January 1946. The program used P-80s, which were easy to service. Nevertheless, maintenance proved a problem because of a shortage of maintenance personnel experienced in servicing jet aircraft.[31]

Another major problem with USAF training was the absence of a two-seat jet trainer. New pilots flew only prop-powered aircraft in training, and from day one, the jet fighter pilot trainee had to fly solo with an instructor flying in an accompanying aircraft. This arrangement worked well when there were no problems but could prove hazardous, and sometimes fatal, if there were difficulties. In fact, sixteen pilots were involved in a major accident during their first F-86 flight. (One of these accidents was fatal and another three resulted in destroyed Sabres.)[32] In mid-1947, Lockheed lengthened the fuselage of an F-80 by three feet to accommodate a second pilot in tandem. The two-seat trainer first flew in March 1948, initially designated as the F-80C; it was redesignated T-33A in May 1949 and went into service at Williams Air Force Base in June 1949. The T-bird greatly enhanced pilot training and was used to train many pilots throughout the world.[33]

The Korean War forced changes within the Air Force, which was already in turmoil as it transitioned from prop to jet aircraft. The war's demand for large numbers of pilots was met by increasing the graduation rate of the training schools by lowering standards, reassigning pilots from desk jobs, and recalling reserve pilots to active duty. The result was an influx of what an Air Training Command historian called "notoriously unqualified" individuals going through jet training. Many of the recalled reservists had been out of the cockpit since the end of World War II, and a considerable number of those in the regular air force had been in administrative jobs for years.[34] A retraining program in the F-80 began at Nellis Air Force Base in mid-July 1950 but was discontinued in January 1951. There is no explanation for this action, although by the end of June 1951, the USAF had two jet fighter schools, labeled "fighter-bomber/escort," based at Luke and Nellis Air Force Bases, where students flew F-51s, F-80s, and F-84s. It was not until the end of 1951 that the USAF established a training program for the F-86 day fighter; and by 1953 there was a program for both the F-86 day fighters and fighter-bombers at Nellis.[35]

For all of the shortcomings and criticisms of the USAF pilot training program, one fact should be emphasized: it produced pilots far better trained than their foes. For when these men were called upon to perform in combat, they did so in a spectacular fashion. During the Korean War, Sabre pilots ran up high scores against MiG-15s, despite an at best equivalent aircraft, superior numbers of Communist fighters, and the location of the combat. The major American advantage in the air-to-air battle was the skill, training, aggressiveness, and experience of the Sabre pilots.

F-86 Problems

Like all new aircraft, the F-86 had early problems; fortunately, none were serious or long lasting. Chronologically, the first involved the landing gear. This is surprising because that system was neither new nor exotic. North American test pilot George Welch had difficulties with the gear on the fighter's first flight in October 1947, and four of the Sabre's first five major accidents involved the nose gear. As late as November 1950, the Air Force complained of an excessive number of accidents involving the nose gear. The problems with the system included an undersized hydraulic cylinder, weak nose gear trunnion, faulty cylinder rod, and gear vulnerability during ground-towing operations (a towing wedge was required, but sometimes was not used).[36] If the pilot retracted the landing gear at too high a speed, it could slam back into the aircraft and damage the piston rod. Almost 10 percent of the F-86 major accidents through July 1953 were connected with the landing gear, two-thirds of these with the nose gear. The Air Force worked out these problems in the succeeding Sabre models. Whereas 12 percent of the F-86A major accidents involved the landing gear, this figure fell to 5 percent for the F-86E and 7 percent for the F-86F.[37]

The F-86 also had troubles with its instruments. An early 1950 survey noted problems with the Sabre's airspeed indicator (reading 15 kts low at the aircraft's high speed limitation). Non-standardization of attitude indicators created a more serious problem. In early 1951, the 33rd Fighter Interceptor Wing was using four different types of attitude indicators, and, as late as August 1951, at least three different types. The danger was that two of the types gave opposite presentations, a situation that was confusing at best, and certainly hazardous at night or in emergency or weather conditions.[38]

From the earliest days of flying, one of the terrors was getting into a spin. For its part, the F-86 was noted to be an "honest aircraft," that is, it gave adequate warning of an approaching stall and potential spin.[39] Early on, North American pilots performed over one hundred spins in the Sabre. George Welch, the company's test pilot, wrote that neutralizing the controls would cause the rotation of a spin to stop within three quarters of a turn, permitting the pilot to pull out of a spin within five thousand feet.[40] This performance allowed the company to claim that it was difficult to keep the fighter in a spin, perhaps a commercial overstatement. Initially, the Air Force was somewhat more cautious. The 1948 pilot's manual prohibited spins. A few months later the revised manual gave spin recovery instructions, noting that recovery was normal and could be completed within one-quarter to one-half turn with the loss of approximately one thousand feet of altitude. An early 1954 report stated that recovery could be made in one-half to one and one-half turns with proper technique and in two to three turns with hands off.[41]

Despite the great admiration the pilots had (and have) for the F-86, certainly the early Sabres ("A" models) did have some difficulties. Lt. Col. Harrison Thyng, then Commander of the 33rd Fighter Interceptor Group and an ace fighter pilot with five kills in World War II and another five in Korea, noted in June 1950 that "the F-86 is a highly specialized jet aircraft. It cannot be handled and flown like a typical Air Force fighter plane, or even like the F-80 and F-84 jet."[42]

The F-86A-5 had difficulties with both its J47 engine and heavy stick forces in high-speed pullouts. As a result of the latter, one accident board found it unsuitable for air-to-ground gunnery. The commander of Nellis Air Force Base, where the Air Force conducted F-86 training, recommended that these aircraft be restricted from dive-bombing and high-angle strafing.[43] Almost two and a half years later, another commander at Nellis curtailed student flying of

F-86As in both air-to-air and air-to-ground firing. He noted that this model was known for its "violent snap roll tendency" in a high-speed stall.[44]

Another serious problem concerned the control stick. In January 1953, accident investigators reported that the separation of the stick grip from the control column caused a fatal accident in which the pilot flew into the ground at Nellis. A review of the incident records and an inspection of F-86s at the base revealed three other incidents involving separated stick grips and another four cases of loosened grips. The USAF noted that since 1 January 1952, there had been a dozen undetermined fatal accidents that might have been caused by the same problem.[45] (The one-year lapse between the first incident and the fatal accident in January 1953 indicates that the Air Force's system of quickly circulating hazard information was flawed.)

Engine failure was the greatest cause of F-86 accidents, accounting for 15 percent of the major accidents.[46] Some of these failures could not be further pinpointed because both rapid throttle movement (pilot induced) and system failure (materiel or maintenance failure) could cause flameouts. A case in point is the F-86 experience with the emergency fuel system. In addition to the standard fuel system, the Sabre was fitted with an emergency fuel regulator that could pump fuel to the engine in the event the main system regulator or switch failed. It could either be switched "on" to replace the normal regulator, or engaged in the "standby" position (on takeoff), in which case it would automatically take over fuel regulation if it sensed the fuel flow was not acting in accordance with the throttle position. Standard procedure directed the pilot to turn off the emergency fuel regulator after takeoff and use it only in the event of the failure of the main regulator. If the emergency fuel regulator was left "on" or inadvertently switched "on," it could, along with rapid throttle movement, call for too much fuel and cause an engine flameout.[47]

This safety device proved troublesome from the start because the first emergency fuel regulators were "sensitive to rapid throttle movement." In the year beginning March 1949, the 1st Fighter Wing suffered seventeen flameouts, fifteen with the older of two types of emergency fuel regulators. (One pilot survived two flameouts in one day; another, two flameouts in one month.) In early 1950, an accident board recommended that F-86s equipped with this device be restricted to flying below twenty-five thousand feet, and that fall, one engineering officer urged that these Sabres be used only as lead aircraft and flown only by experienced pilots. The USAF replaced the early emergency fuel regulator with another, yet this did not completely solve the problem.[48]

In September 1952 an accident board supported the USAF study that the device should be removed from the North American fighter. Two weeks later another accident board made the same recommendation and further coun-seled that the system should only be used when the primary system had failed. The engineering officer wrote, "This system might possibly cause more accidents than it prevents."[49] An accident board in February 1953 echoed these views. It went on to note that the Navy's version of the Sabre (FJ-2) had no emergency fuel system. Perhaps more persuasive was the state-ment by the commander of a training unit using the F-86: "Pilots forgetting to turn the stand-by switch off after take-off proved to be so destructive . . . [that] this Group was forced to abolish its use for take-off." Col. Clay Tice went on to state, "The emergency fuel regulator has been responsible for the destruction of far more aircraft at this base than it has saved. It is inconceiv-able that it has not been redesigned."[50] The next summer the authorities reported that malfunctioning emergency fuel regulators had caused five major accidents at Nellis. They wanted a new switch (with only a manual "on" and "off" position) that would satisfy their current standard operating procedure that the device was to be used only in the event of the failure of the main regulator. Tice again criticized the system: "The emergency fuel system in the F-86 aircraft has been unsatisfactory since the first models of the F-86 were delivered to the USAF. The system is still unchanged, although it has been repeatedly U.R.ed by using organizations."[51] Air Materiel Command recommended that the device not be used in a standby mode and only be engaged if the main fuel system failed.

Despite these criticisms, the system had its supporters, including the Fifth Air Force staff and Maj. Gen. Glenn Barcus, vice commander of Air Training Command, who did not agree to remove either the device or its automatic feature.[52] In the end, the system was retained without the "standby" feature, consisting only of "on," "off," and "test" positions.[53]

A further fuel control problem involved the main fuel pump. A 1954 report stated that 32 of 144 F-86F accidents (22 percent) were determined to be or suspected to be related to the fuel control system. It noted that the F-86F's engine (J47-GE-27) was "very susceptible to compressor stall." The report blamed the pilots for not following proscribed procedures.[54]

USAF accident statistics lump all F-86 accidents together, not distin-guishing between the various models. Three Sabre models served in the Korean War: the "A," "E," and "F."[55] By the end of the Korean War, the Air Force had received 554 "A"s, 396 "E"s, and 1,139 "F"s. By that time, two-thirds of the "A"s, one-third of the "E"s, and under one-tenth of the "F"s deliv-ered were involved in major accidents.[56]

An analysis of 637 major F-86 accidents through July 1953 reveals little difference in accidents of the various Sabre models. One significant difference involved ejections. Up through this time period, ninety-one pilots ejected from the Sabre. The "A" had the lowest percentage of parachute/ejection seat use in major accidents, half that of the "F." Perhaps more remarkably, only 5 percent of the pilots using parachutes in the F-86A were killed, compared to almost five times that rate in the "E" and five and a half times that in the "F." This may actually understate the differences because there were additional incidents involved with the latter two models where the pilot may have attempted egress.[57] A lower percentage of F-86A pilots were injured in major accidents than in the later model Sabres.

There were few differences between the models in regards to the causes of accidents. Problems with the landing gear markedly declined in the models that followed the F-86A. Engines were the most frequent and significant problem for each variant and accounted for thirteen fatal accidents.[58]

Prior to August 1953, there were twenty-one F-86 accidents involving two or more aircraft in which one or more fighters were destroyed. These multiple accidents involved forty-seven Sabres, wrecked forty-two fighters, and killed twenty-one pilots. As expected, the bulk of these were midair collisions.

Paradoxically, the three accidents involving three or more F-86s were not midair collisions. On 18 October 1950, the 335th Fighter Squadron (4th Fighter Group) lost three F-86s and two pilots when the leader let down through the clouds and flew into the Potomac River. Weather was the primary cause of another multiple Sabre accident on 31 January 1953. Seven F-86s (432FS) took off from Traux Field, Wisconsin, on a practice mission and ran into unexpected rapidly deteriorating weather. As a result, four Sabres were destroyed and two pilots killed. The third incident was somewhat different, involving a flight of four F-86Fs (67FBS) taking off on a combat mission in Korea. The leader crashed on takeoff, most likely due to an improper elevator trim setting. The number four man in the formation fell behind the other two Sabres as they began a return to base and disappeared. He was killed in an unexplained crash. The original number two man attempted to land but, clearly shaken by the events, aborted two landing attempts and on the third skidded off the rain-slick runway. He survived without injuries from the crash that destroyed his aircraft. The result was three fighters destroyed and two pilots killed.[59] This incident is set apart from other multiple accidents in that the three aircraft, even though they took off together, were destroyed by different causes.

The Big Picture

Since 1921, the first year in which army airmen kept comprehensive records, the flying accident rate has declined. This has not been a straight-line trend; the rate shot upward in 1941, when America began the buildup for World War II, and again in 1946, a result of the rapid demobilization following that conflict, before resuming its downward trend.[60] Even during the hectic expansion of the Korean War, the USAF's worldwide accident rates fell. In fact, in 1953 the flying accident rate was the lowest yet registered in terms of major accidents. Moreover, the fatal accident rate was only better in one year, 1939; and the rate of wrecked aircraft was only better in two other years, fiscal 1950 and calendar 1952, than those rates in 1953.[61]

These figures lump together all Air Force aircraft. As might be expected, there was a great difference in the accident rates for aircraft types. During World War II, the major accident rate for fighters was about three times the AAF average, over seven times that of transports, and almost five times that of four-engine bombers. Although all accident rates fell after the war, the gap between categories remained. There were also differences between specific aircraft within categories. During World War II, for example, the P-39's accident rate was over twice that of the P-51. The accident rates of jet fighters displayed similar characteristics: a higher incidence than other types of USAF aircraft, and a spread, albeit somewhat smaller, between specific fighter types.

The standard measure for flying safety is based on the number of incidents per one hundred thousand flying hours. On its face, this seems flawed. Fighter missions are shorter in duration than those of bombers or transports and are frequently at the edge of the performance envelope—clearly more dangerous than the straight and level operations of transports. There are other ways to compare the flying record of these aircraft.

An alternative to using flying hours would be to use landings as a measure. Between two-thirds and three-quarters of all major accidents occurred during taxi, takeoff, approach, go around, or landing, maneuvers that take approximately the same amount of time for all the aircraft. The remaining one-quarter to one-third of the accidents occurred in the air, where the flight time of the different types and models of aircraft vary.[62] Using landings as a basis, the spread of accident measures between the entire USAF and jet fighters widens. This measure also changes the relative position of the four fighters. Using landings as a measure, the F-86 replaced the F-51 as the safest fighter. (The F-51 had a considerably greater endurance than the jet fighters.)[63]

Another alternative method would be to compare the various fighters at comparable stages of their life cycle. This would account for the learning curve. If we stagger the chronology by comparing the accident rate at the same cumulative flying-hour intervals, the F-86 once again comes off best.[64] The learning curve can be seen because the major accident rates for all three fighters declined sharply between the one hundred thousand and five hundred thousand flying-hour mark, with the F-86 experiencing the largest drop.[65]

The superior flying safety record of the F-86 is not easy to explain. The F-86 was a more advanced aircraft than its peers, capable of a higher top speed and, more importantly from a flying safety point of view, higher takeoff, approach, and landing speeds than the other fighters. Its higher performance put additional strains on man and machine. The F-86 was designed shortly after the F-80 and at essentially the same time as the F-84. One possible explanation for the Sabre's superiority focuses on the way the three fighters were employed. The F-80 and F-84 were primarily used as fighter-bombers and thus carried heavier loads than did the F-86, which was initially fielded as an air defense fighter (interceptor) and primarily used in the Korean War as an air superiority fighter until 1953, when a fighter-bomber version went into action. Bombing and strafing runs took these aircraft close to the ground, where a small miscalculation or mechanical problem could easily cause an accident. The same incident at altitude, however, where most air-to-air training was conducted and where air-to-air battles began, gave some margin for recovery. The first operational jet fighter, the F-80 was extensively used in pilot training, both for those learning to fly and also for those who would fly the Shooting Star in combat. Through 1953, 38 percent of the fatalities in F-80s occurred in flight training units, compared with 25 percent of the F-86 fatalities.[66] It is possible that better pilots were attracted to or assigned to fly the F-86, or that pilots flying the Sabre were more careful. Or it could simply be that the F-86 was just a better aircraft.

Conclusion

Just about everyone familiar with the F-86 agrees it was a fine aircraft, and all use positive, if not superlative, words when speaking of it. It was the top aircraft of its day and was a better performing and safer fighter than either of its two USAF teammates, the F-80 or F-84. Having said this, it is true the Sabre had problems. It is also a fact that its safety record does not compare with Air

Force fighters that followed it. Even the much maligned F-100 and F-104 had superior safety records. Bringing the story up to date, comparing the Sabre's safety record with the F-15 (the Eagle), the safest fighter in USAF history, is astonishing. The Sabre had eighteen times the Eagle's major accident rate, eleven times its wrecked accident rate, and eleven times its fatal accident rate.[67] However, in its day, the Sabre was a standout in terms of flying performance, combat record, and safety.

Clearly the USAF has come a long way in terms of fighter performance and flying safety since the days when the F-86 ruled the skies. The progress since this period has been absolutely remarkable. Compared to a major accident rate of 24 per one hundred thousand flying hours in 1953, the lowest rate to that point, the major USAF accident rate has been less than 2 per one hundred thousand flying hours beginning in fiscal year 1983. Between fiscal year 1975 and fiscal year 2000, the rate averaged 1.92 major accidents per one hundred thousand flying hours.

A number of factors account for this progress: certainly, new and better equipment; probably improved training; and, perhaps most of all, a different attitude about flying safety. During the years prior to 1960, accidents were almost accepted—that is, they were considered a cost of flying. Although we lack documentary proof to support this assertion, there is anecdotal evidence. One former F-86 pilot recalled that checklists were not required during the 1950s, and that "most real fighter pilots did not carry a checklist with them." He went on to note that, "a lot of our accidents were [a result of] trying to prove our manhood."[68] During the Korean War, a World War II ace and an experienced pilot (over eighteen hundred flying hours), lied about having prior experience in the Sabre and asked for no help other than that of the crew chief to start the engine when he made his first flight. He crashed after logging eleven hours in the Sabre, according to another pilot, because he did not know how to use the fuel in the drop tanks.[69] There have been significant changes in the Air Force over the past half century, and nowhere are they more obvious than in the area of flying safety.

FIVE

Soviet Fighters and Development of the MiG-15

oviet fighters in the 1920s and 1930s were comparable to any in the world. In the mid-1930s, the Russians attained qualitative fighter superiority when they introduced the stubby, all-metal Polikarpov I-16, a low wing monoplane that featured retractable landing gear. In the Spanish Civil War, the Russian fighter did well at first, outperforming Nationalist's fighters, including the early models of the famous Bf 109B.[1] However, during the early years of World War II, the Germans achieved air superiority against the Soviets with better aircraft and better trained, and certainly more experienced, pilots. Nevertheless, the Russians withstood the German onslaught, enduring horrendous losses but eventually producing more aircraft than the Germans, thus defeating them.[2] To be clear, Russian air success in World War II was due more to superior numbers than to superior-quality aircraft or aircrew.

Soviet Jets

The advent of the jet age gave the Soviets a chance to reset the playing field. The Russians had both the incentive (a desire to challenge western superiority in aviation) and opportunity (occupying territory from which 85 percent of German aircraft were manufactured) to capitalize on this situation. They did this by shipping large quantities of German machinery, aircraft, and documents, as well as three thousand to six thousand aviation technicians to the

Soviet Union. They tested a number of German aircraft, and considered putting the Me 262 into production but decided against that course of action in December 1945.[3]

The Soviets tinkered with jet and rocket propulsion during the war, but—unlike the Americans, British, and Germans—they did not fly a jet-propelled aircraft during the conflict. In February 1945, the Soviets issued an order for a single-place jet fighter. Four design bureaus responded. On the same day in April 1946, two of these aircraft made their first flight, both powered by German engines. The Yakovlev bureau's Yak-15 was a modification of its successful piston-powered Yak-3 and was the first jet to enter service in the Red Air Force. The Yak-17 appeared in 1947. It differed from its predecessor mainly in employing tricycle landing gear, a slightly more powerful engine, and an enlarged tail fin. The Soviets built 280 Yak-15s and its trainer version (Yak-15U) and 430 Yak-17s.[4]

The second aircraft, the Mikoyan and Gurevich bureau's MiG-9 was designed from the outset to be jet powered. With 3,520 pounds of thrust versus 1,980 pounds in the Yak, it had a higher top speed (560 mph versus 502 mph). The Soviets built 550 of these fighters. In late summer 1946, the twin engine Su-9 and La-150 made their first flights; however, they proved less successful.[5]

While Soviet airframes compared well with western fighters, their most significant deficiency was inferior engines. The Russians had worked on jet propulsion beginning in the 1920s, focusing on turboprop engines and testing one of these before World War II. The Soviets also went into turbojet area, reportedly developing a 1,104-pound thrust engine (RD-1) that was three-quarters complete when the war began. It was shelved in the early years of the war, along with a 4,410-pound thrust engine also under development. The Soviets did not resume work on turbojets until 1944. Because German engines were proven and outperformed Soviet ones, they were used in the first Soviet jets.[6]

Nevertheless, Soviet jet engines were inferior to those employed in the West. Therefore, it was a monumental coup in September 1946 when the British agreed to sell the Soviets their best jet engine, the Rolls Royce Nene. (This action supported the comment by Lenin that capitalists would sell the rope to their hangman.) The Soviets quickly reverse engineered the power plant and had it coming off the production line in August 1947 designated as RD-45. The Soviets went on to build thirty-nine thousand of these engines, and the Chinese another eight-five hundred.[7] The Nene (RD-45F) could produce about five thousand pounds of thrust while its Soviet modification (VK-1A) was rated at six thousand pounds. These engines would power the best Soviet fighter, arguably the world's best fighter of the day, the MiG-15.[8]

The MiG-15

The design, development, and employment of the MiG-15 is a remarkable story because it illustrates how the Soviets, behind in aviation technology in the early 1940s, leaped to at least a position of equality, if not superiority, with the West by the end of that decade. Apparently impressed by the scenes of devastation caused by Anglo-American strategic bombing in areas it occupied, the Soviets sought an air defense fighter with which to combat U.S. long-range bombers. In March 1946, the Soviets established a specification for a high-altitude (over forty-six thousand feet), high-speed (over 620 mph) interceptor that would mount cannon armament, exhibit a high rate of climb, show good maneuverability above thirty-three thousand feet, and have an endurance of one hour. As with other Soviet equipment, the aircraft was to feature ease of maintenance. Three design bureaus (Lavochkin, Mikoyan, and Yakolev) submitted proposals.[9]

The Mikoyan designers considered a number of configurations before settling on their final design. The Soviets dropped a twin-engine version because of the shortage of engines. They also considered a twin-boom version, similar to the British Vampire, and a variable sweep design. The Russian design team had access to World War II German work, as did the Anglo-Americans; but, contrary to what some believe, the fighter was not a direct development of Kurt Tank's similarly configured World War II concept, the Ta 183. The Soviets also had information on American development, not only because of the openness of American society, but also as a result of their espionage. Secrecy characterized the police state to such an extent that there was no cooperation or interchange between the various Russian design bureaus, who knew more about Western designs than competing Soviet ones.[10]

The Mikoyan team built their design, originally known as I-310, around the Nene engine. The nose intake followed the pattern of earlier Soviet jets and, for that matter, American fighters (P-84 and P-86) under development at this time. The origin of the swept wing is unclear but probably can be attributed, as with the American development, to a combination of indigenous aerodynamic design and captured German research. In any case, the designers mounted a wing with a 35-degree sweep and two wing fences midway on the wing.[11]

The wings presented a problem. The lack of stiffness caused wing drop, which could make the fighter uncontrollable at high speeds. This was due to the structure of the wing and to poor quality control in manufacture that resulted in asymmetric wings and, consequently, unequal lift. Therefore, while the fighter's initial red line was Mach .92, it was restricted to Mach .88. To combat the problem, the manufacturer instituted tighter quality control and added individually fitted tabs ("knives") on the wings. According to one secondary source, the Soviets began efforts to cure this deficiency in September 1950. If so, this was a belated reaction to a major issue. In any event, the solution was hardly elegant but did help fix the problem.[12]

The designers also encountered difficulties with the jet exhaust. They therefore shortened the size of the exhaust nozzle and the fuselage length, enhancing the fighter's stubby appearance. The vertical tail appeared oversized in profile relative to the lines of the fuselage. The horizontal tail was affixed midway on the vertical tail as with other Soviet fighters of that period. The fighter's main landing gear extended outward from the fuselage and retracted into the wing. The designers equipped the machine with the standards of the day for jet fighters: an ejection seat and pressurized cabin. The Soviets added hydraulic speed brakes beginning with the third prototype.[13]

The original MiG-15 used mechanical controls, as had World War II propeller-driven aircraft. However, the higher speeds increased the loads on the control surfaces, forcing the designers to incorporate hydraulic-boosted ailerons on the twentieth fighter. Above Mach .86, aileron efficiency was poor; in addition, the rudder control reversed (depressing the right rudder moved the nose to the left). As a result, the fighter had poor roll control and relatively slow transition from one maneuver to another.[14] Clearly, the aircraft exhibited difficult characteristics at high speeds.

The MiG-15 was heavily armed to fulfill its air defense role. The designers considered a number of options before establishing the aircraft's armament. Installation of a 45 mm cannon was downsized to a 37 mm that was to be mounted in the inlet splitter in the nose. It would be complemented by other guns, initially two 12.7 mm, then one 23 mm, and finally two 23 mm cannons below it, the same configuration as in the MiG-9. Firing tests on the MiG-9 demonstrated that the engine ingested gun gases and occasionally flamed out. Therefore, the designers moved the 37 mm to the right side of the fuselage and the 23 mms to the left. All three cannon were mounted on a tray that could be easily accessed by hoist for quick service and rearming.[15]

This armament proved inadequate over Korea. It suffered from poor accuracy, due to the inadequate rigidity of the mounts and limited duration of fire; the 37 mm had a firing duration of 6 seconds and the 23 mm, 5.3 seconds. Combat in Korea demonstrated that this armament was successful in its intended task (anti-bomber engagements) but less so in fighter-versus-fighter combat.[16]

The MiG first flew in December 1947, only months after the F-86's maiden flight. The flight was planned for 1948, but the test pilot, Ramenskoye Yuganov, was short of money and took off on his own, despite the poor weather and lack of authorization, in order to earn the ten thousand ruble bonus for the initial flight. He flew two circuits around the field and landed. Because of his initiative in advancing the timing of the test, no important personages witnessed the event.[17]

The Soviets built three prototypes, which they began testing in May 1948; by the end of the year, they designated the fighter MiG-15. The testers noted that the aircraft had some handling problems. In a tight, high-speed turn it could quickly flick into a stall and spin. The fighter demonstrated poor spin characteristics due to its swept wing and high horizontal tail, easily going into a flat spin from which it was difficult to recover. The second prototype was destroyed and the test pilot killed in a spin.[18] This was a harbinger of later problems.

The Soviets judged the MiG against its rivals, the La-15 and Yak-30. The Lavochkin and Mikoyan fighters were similar in appearance, except for the La-15's high-mounted wing and the main landing gear that was housed in the fuselage. The Lavochkin was faster and more stable at speeds approaching Mach 1 than the MiG. However, the short wheel track of its main landing gear made cross-wind landing more difficult, and it was judged to be more complicated to build and maintain than its rival. The La-15 was built in small numbers (about five hundred) and served briefly as a ground support aircraft.[19] Less is known about the Yakovlev. Apparently, it was more agile than the MiG but slower and not as well armed. Thus the MiG became the Soviet's fighter of choice.[20]

The Soviets introduced the MiG-15 to the world at the July 1948 Tushino air show. The first aircraft went into service with Ivan Kozhedub's unit in February 1949. (Kozhedub was the top Soviet ace of World War II with sixty-two credits.) When the Korean War began, Soviet air defense forces had about 2,000 jet fighters; many, if not most, were MiG-15s. By comparison only 560 F-86s were delivered to the USAF by the end of that year.[21]

MiG-15bis

The Soviets pushed to improve the MiG-15. In 1949, they fitted the airframe with an upgraded Nene engine, designated VK-1, that produced approximately 20 percent more thrust than the RD-45F.[22] Therefore, although the fighter's weight increased marginally by 524 pounds, performance improved. The fighter, known as the MiG-15bis, increased top speed at low altitude from 651 mph to 667 mph, rate of climb at sea level from 8,285 fpm to 9,060 fpm, and service ceiling from 49,856 feet to 50,840 feet. The only diminution in performance was a 9 percent increase in landing roll.[23]

The new engine was the most significant change although the Soviets tried several other improvements. In September 1950, orders were signed to substitute two flexible 23 mm guns for the standard armament. Developed by B. Shpitlny OKB, the guns could elevate upward 11 degrees and downward 7 degrees, allowing the pilot to draw more lead on a maneuvering target. The Soviets tested the system in sixty-three flights in the summer of 1951. Although these tests demonstrated that the system improved tactical performance, the device was not fitted on production fighters for unstated reasons.[24]

The Soviets made a number of attempts to improve the fighter's poor rearward visibility. One effort was a periscope, tested in June 1952, but it proved unsuitable.[25] Three other changes did improve rearward vision. In September 1951, the Russians tested a new canopy that had less framing in the rear, thus providing the pilot with superior visibility. It went into production in 1952. The Soviets went further. In October 1952, the Russians fitted fifteen fighters engaged in the Korean War with rearward-looking radar, known as the Sirena radar homing and warning system. This worked well, encouraging the Soviets to equip all their MiGs with the device.[26] There is no indication it was ever used in the action. A third effort to alert MiG pilots to rearward attacks was to mount a radar detection device, a "fuzz buster," in the tail. It had a range of four to five miles and gave an audible "howl" when it picked up pulses from American radar-ranging radar. The Soviets tested ten units in May 1952 and, despite its occasional false warnings, installed it as standard equipment on Red fighters.[27]

The Soviets made other changes as well. In November 1952, they fitted an improved gunsight into the MiG that increased accuracy and was more suitable in highly maneuvering dogfights.[28] Another change that improved the MiG's tactical capability was to increase the size of the fighter's speed brakes. The MiG's original speed brakes had a triangular shape with an area of 5.2 square feet. This was not altogether adequate and gave the aircraft a pitch up tendency when employed. In 1952 the Soviets enlarged the speed brakes to 8.6 square feet. This change entered production in September 1952 and was retrofitted into fighters engaged in the Korean War.[29]

The MiG-15 would prove itself in combat over Korea. It completely outclassed the UN's prop and straight-winged jets and would outperform the F-86 almost to the end of the war. However, the MiG force was unable to wrest air superiority from the UN: that is the crux of this story and the stuff from which history and legends are made.

SIX

Korean War, Phase I

June through November 1950

The United States initially considered Korea to be of little strategic importance; American interest in the peninsula grew more by happenstance than by plan. However, at the end of World War II, Japan was of critical importance to U.S. interests, and Korea was too close geographically to ignore. With the Soviets poised to enter the Japanese colony, action to protect those interests had to be taken quickly. This led to the decision in 1945 to divide the country at the 38th parallel, with the Soviets disarming the Japanese forces north of that line, and American troops disarming those to the south of it. This division was to be temporary. As in Germany, however, the Cold War led to the formation of two mutually antagonistic governments: a militantly Communist government in the north and an authoritarian, although less organized, one in the south.

The American policy was "Europe first." In Washington, the dominant view was that Europe was more important to American interests and more threatened, a position hammered home by the recently concluded Berlin Blockade of 1949. Moreover, the United States thought the next Communist move in Asia would most likely be an invasion of what was then known as Formosa (now Taiwan). Most American military leaders considered South Korea indefensible.

The United States did not want to engage in a land war on the Asian continent. Despite increasing cold war tensions, it withdrew its troops in 1949, leaving only a military advisory team of less than five hundred personnel to help the South Koreans build a lightly armed force intended (at least by the

Americans) only to provide internal security. Washington feared that a better armed military might tempt the South Koreans to seek to unify the peninsula by force, as their president threatened. As a result, the Republic of Korea (RoK) was left with a mere constabulary: its army consisted of less than ninety-eight thousand troops; it had no tanks, no antitank capability, and no artillery heavier than 105 mm; and its aviation component consisted of three trainer and thirteen liaison aircraft.

In contrast, the Communists trained and equipped a conventional army in the north that numbered approximately 135,000 troops. About one-third of these had fought with the Chinese Communists during China's civil war and were well equipped with World War II Soviet artillery and about 150 T-34 tanks, as well as 132 Soviet prop-powered combat aircraft. Thus, the north had a tremendous military advantage, which was greatly enhanced by striking the first blow.[1]

Some lay blame for the conflict on a speech by Secretary of State Dean Acheson in January 1950 in which he excluded Korea from the sphere of U.S. interests. Even if this statement had never been made, however, the Communists would probably have attacked because of the weak American military position in South Korea and the fierce determination of North Korea to unify the peninsula as a Communist state. We now know that the North Korean leader, Kim Il Sung, made the decision to invade and maneuvered both the Soviets and the Chinese into supporting him, despite the lukewarm backing of the much more conservative Soviets and the reluctance of the Chinese, who were indeed planning to invade Formosa.

Early on 25 June 1950, the North Korean army crossed the 38th parallel and quickly crushed the South Korean Army.

Much to the surprise of just about all, the United States quickly and directly responded. On 26 June, Washington authorized U.S. air and sea forces to assist the South Koreans to stem the invasion. When these forces proved inadequate, President Harry Truman ordered U.S. ground troops in on 30 June. (He was able to do this under the UN flag, because the Soviets were boycotting the international body at the time.)[2]

Truman was an avid and serious student of history who had been in Washington when German and Japanese aggression plunged the United States into World War II. He and other key decision makers in Washington feared that the North Korean invasion was only the first Communist move, and he well remembered the disgraceful sellout of Czechoslovakia at the 1938 Munich Conference that did not preclude but only postponed World

War II. The ghosts of Munich haunted this generation of leaders. They believed that the United States and the "Free" World had to make a stand here or worse would ensue.

Much to the surprise of most Americans, the introduction of U.S. forces, hastily flown in and committed to action piecemeal, hardly slowed the Communist advance. By 5 August, the North Koreans had pushed the remnants of the RoK army and growing numbers of American forces into the southeastern corner of the peninsula around the port of Pusan, an area that became known as the "Pusan Perimeter." The situation was dire as the North Koreans were on the offensive and threatening to drive the UN forces into the sea. By 1 September, however, UN forces outnumbered the Communist forces 180,000 to 98,000 and had somewhat beaten them up, forcing them more and more frequently to impress South Koreans at gunpoint to fight for them. UN air attacks further battered the Communist army and supply lines.

Then, on 15 September, the UN launched an amphibious assault at Inchon, on the west coast of Korea near the South Korean capital of Seoul, hundreds of miles behind the front lines. Gen. Douglas MacArthur, the architect of this move, pushed this bold and risky operation over the objections of the American high command. It caught the Communists by surprise and was a smashing success. The UN followed the Inchon assault with an offensive from the Pusan Perimeter, the two UN forces linking up on 26 September. After some heavy fighting in Seoul, the war became a UN pursuit of the broken North Korean army. On 1 October, RoK troops crossed the 38th parallel, followed by other UN forces on 9 October. Truman met with MacArthur on Wake Island on 15 October, where the general told the president that the war would be over by Thanksgiving and that many of the western troops would be home for Christmas.

In response to Truman's questions, MacArthur rejected the notion that the Chinese would intervene in the war. Ten days later, the Chinese Army surprised and mauled UN forces in sharp fighting before pulling back as quickly and mysteriously as they had appeared. The UN commanders believed that this was merely a show of force. On 24 November MacArthur took the offensive but ran into a massive Chinese attack the next day that threw the stunned UN forces back in a costly rout. This was a huge intelligence and aerial reconnaissance failure. It also was a new war.

The retreat of the UN force from North Korea was a disaster and arguably the worst defeat in U.S. military history. The action is that much more remarkable because the UN force was clearly trounced even though it was not greatly outnumbered and had overwhelming superiority in armor, artillery, air, and sea power. When the year ended, the combatants faced one another along the 38th parallel.

A Chinese offensive early in January swept south of the 38th parallel, recaptured Seoul, and reached a point sixty miles southeast of the South Korean capital. As January 1951 closed, UN forces counterattacked and were able to again recapture Seoul. By the end of that month, the battle line was along the 38th parallel, a line that the UN forces pushed northward in the next weeks.

Then, after almost a year of mobile warfare that swept back and forth across the Korean peninsula, the war dramatically changed character. In late June, the Soviet ambassador to the UN called for negotiations; armistice talks began on 10 July 1951. Thus, over the next two years there was little movement in the battle lines, despite bitter fighting that resembled World War I trench warfare. The major fighting stopped just before midnight on 27 July 1953. In the interim both sides shed much blood, and the names of such engagements as the Punchbowl, Heartbreak Ridge, and Pork Chop Hill became notorious for high casualties and futility. The war ended close to where it had begun, with Korea divided between a fiercely Communist North and an anti-Communistic (and authoritarian) South. During the three-year war, the Communists military suffered 1.6 million casualties, and UN forces suffered about .5 million casualties. Three million South Korean civilians died, along with untold North Korean civilians. The United States lost 34,000 killed, over 10,000 missing, and 103,000 wounded.[3]

The war was not in vain, for the Communist invasion was thwarted, and South Korea gradually became a thriving economic power and a democracy. Meanwhile, North Korea declined economically as it built up a large conventional (and perhaps nuclear-armed) military. American troops remain in Korea to this day.

The North Korean air force had no opposition from the South Korean air force but in turn was no match for the American airmen. The USAF had about twelve hundred aircraft in the region at the beginning of the war, a figure that grew during the period of July to September to almost seventeen hundred UN aircraft.[4] The two air forces quickly came into conflict.

On the first day of the war, 25 June 1950, two North Korean fighters strafed the airfield at Kimpo (just outside of Seoul) and destroyed an American C-54 on the ground, and four other fighters strafed the Seoul airfield and damaged seven RoK aircraft. The first course of action for the Americans was to get U.S. civilians out of South Korea. That day Gen. Earle Partridge, commander of the USAF Fifth Air Force, ordered his units to prepare for an airlift of the estimated two thousand Americans in South Korea to Japan. Just before midnight, the American ambassador to South Korea, John Muccio, told MacArthur of his decision to evacuate the civilians by ship; MacArthur in turn ordered the USAF to provide air cover. That afternoon a Red fighter bounced two F-82s defending the ships but did not fire at them or the ships. Following orders, the Twin Mustang pilots took evasive action but did not engage the North Korean aircraft.

Although Muccio planned to use more ships, the rapid North Korean advance forced him to request air evacuation. On 27 June USAF transports evacuated 850 people to Japan escorted by F-80s, F-82s, and B-26s. Around noon, five Red fighters flew over Seoul heading for Kimpo. Five F-82s intercepted them and Maj. James Little, commander of the 339th Fighter All Weather Squadron (FAWS) who had claimed seven Japanese aircraft in World War II, fired the first U.S. shots of the war. But the Air Force credits 1st Lt. William Hudson of the 68th FAWS with the first American air-to-air victory of the war. In all, six F-80 and F-82 pilots downed seven North Korean aircraft that day, each getting one victory except for 1st Lt. Robert Wayne (35th FS) who bagged two IL-10s.[5]

The Air Force attempted to fly bombing strikes that night but was thwarted by weather. The next day, 28 June, however, the USAF launched two dozen B-26s on two missions, one against railroad yards and the other against road and rail traffic. One of the bombers hit by antiaircraft fire crashed at its home base, killing all aboard, while another got down safely but had to be junked. B-29s based on Okinawa also entered the war on 28 June, four hitting rail and road targets. The North Korean air force was also active, that afternoon strafing the Suwon airfield, twenty miles south of Seoul, damaging one B-26 and one F-82, and returning later to destroy a C-54 on the ground.

On 29 June nine B-29s hit the Kimpo airfield with excellent results. That day General MacArthur flew to Korea to get a first-hand view of the action and to meet with President Syngman Rhee of South Korea, Ambassador Muccio, and top American and South Korean officers. According to one account, during the conference in a Suwon schoolhouse, four North Korean fighters made a pass on the Suwon airfield. MacArthur and his officers watched as Mustangs downed all four of the enemy. (Another source states that the conference took place between two North Korean air attacks on the airfield.) The USAF claimed a total of fourteen aerial victories during the month. The constant and aggressive North Korean air attacks prompted MacArthur to authorize attacks on North Korean airfields. On 29 June the Americans attacked North Korea for the first time when eighteen B-26s hit an airfield near the capital, Pyongyang, destroying twenty-five aircraft on the ground.[6]

The United States deployed two additional B-29 groups to the theater and converted some of the fighter units from the F-80 to the F-51 in July. Although the World War II fighter was more vulnerable than the jet fighter, the Mustang had longer range and endurance and could better operate out of the shorter and rougher airstrips in South Korea. On 3 July the Royal Navy and the U.S. Navy entered the air war, attacking airfields in North Korea. During the first day's assault, F9F pilots downed two North Korean fighters. After the Joint Chiefs of Staff authorized a plan to attack eighteen strategic targets in the north, B-29s began bombing the few strategic targets in North Korea on 6 July when nine B-29s hit an oil refinery and chemical plant. Four days later four Communist fighters attacked an American infantry unit with bullets and bombs. On 27 July North Korean aircraft dropped a bomb on a USAF headquarters without causing any damage. These were the only cases of American troops being attacked by enemy aircraft during daylight in the Korean War.[7] On 12 July the North Korean air force had its best day of the war when it downed one B-26, one B-29, and one L-4 in aerial combat. The USAF fighter pilots claimed six Red aircraft destroyed in the air in July along with another nineteen on the ground. The Navy also battered the North Korean air force with two strikes on 18 July on an airfield near Pyongyang, and the next day launched two attacks on the airfields near the east coast that destroyed between thirty-two and forty-seven aircraft. The Navy hit other targets as well—the Wonsan refinery on 18 July and enemy troops for the first time on 22 July.[8]

B-29s were involved in three incidents in 1950 that had the potential to widen the war. On 27 July a Superfort got lost and flew well into Chinese territory. Russian fighters intercepted the American bomber but did not fire on it. About two months later (22 September) a B-29 bombed the marshalling yard at Antung, just north of the border. Antung was hit again on 13 November when one of more than one hundred bombs unloaded on the North Korean target of Sinuiju went astray.[9]

The American airmen achieved air superiority in the last half of July, reducing the North Korean air force to an estimated eighteen serviceable aircraft. During June and July the Air Force lost twenty-five aircraft to enemy action: four in air-to-air combat, twenty to ground fire, and one to an unknown cause.[10] The USAF fighter pilots claimed twenty North Korean aircraft destroyed in air-to-air combat and another nineteen destroyed on the ground. In addition the B-26s and B-29s destroyed other aircraft on the ground, and the Navy claimed two aircraft destroyed in the air and others destroyed on the airfield attacks. In August B-29s no longer required fighter escort and the Navy's aircraft carriers could operate closer to the Korean coast.[11]

August saw the critical fighting around the Pusan Perimeter. The North Korean advance made air support more difficult as it forced a number of the fighter units based in Korea to move back to Japan. The war showed that failing in air-to-air combat, the most effective methods to counter UN air power was antiaircraft artillery and capturing UN airfields. The Communist ground threat was so grave that on 16 August ninety-eight B-29s carpet-bombed a twenty-seven-square-mile area near UN lines. The Superforts dropped over 840 tons of bombs, but reconnaissance failed to detect any significant damage. On 18 September forty-two B-29s flew a similar mission against a two-square-mile area near Waegwan with better results. The four engine bombers then returned to hitting the few strategic targets in the north along with interdiction targets in the south. On 27 August two F-51s strayed across the Yalu River and shot up an airfield five miles inside China. There is no mention of the physical damage, but the Chinese vigorously protested.

Another significant event in August was the first USAF rescue of an American aircrew during the war. On 5 August an Air Force SA-16 amphibian plucked a Navy pilot out of the sea. A month later, on 4 September, saw the first USAF helicopter rescue of the war. An H-5 flown by Lt. Paul Van Boven picked up (now) Capt. Robert Wayne, the F-80 pilot who had downed two Il-10s on 27 June, from behind enemy lines.

There was little action against the North Korean air force after July, with no aerial claims and only five ground claims during August and no aerial claims and six ground claims in September. The Inchon invasion on 15 September and the breakout from the Pusan Perimeter a few days later turned the war around. As the UN ground forces swept northward, the Air Force continued to bomb strategic targets, but having eliminated the eighteen original strategic targets and about to occupy all of North Korea, the Joint Chiefs of Staff canceled such missions on the 27 September.[12]

Air power, land and carrier based, was critical in the defeat of the North Korean invasion. The USAF claimed that air attacks killed at least thirty-nine thousand North Korean troops and destroyed 76 percent of their tanks. In an August interdiction campaign the USAF dropped thirty-seven of forty-four targeted bridges. Interrogation reports indicated that air attacks accounted for 47 percent of North Korean personnel losses and 75 percent of tanks, 81 percent of trucks, and 72 percent of artillery destroyed. The official USAF history is more circumspect claiming that the airmen caused about the same number of enemy casualties as artillery, and "noticeably greater" equipment losses. Whatever the actual figures, air power probably tipped the balance in favor of the UN forces, which were untouched by enemy aircraft while their opponents were battered by air power. The UN ground commander, Lt. Gen. Walton Walker, declared: "I will gladly lay my cards right on the table and state that if it had not been for the air support that we received from the Fifth Air Force we would not have been able to stay in Korea."[13]

As the UN forces moved northward in October, the USAF deployed four fighter groups and two reconnaissance squadrons from Japan to Korea. With no more strategic targets to hit, the Air Force sent two B-29 groups back to the states. On 8 October two F-80 pilots got lost and shot up a Soviet airfield near Vladivostok. The Russians strenuously protested and the USAF court-martialed the two pilots (they were found not guilty) and removed the group commander, transferring him to Tokyo. Two Red aircraft attacked Inchon Harbor and Kimpo airfield on 14 October. UN ground troops continued their northern advance and entered the North Korean capital on 19 October. As already noted, the Chinese hit RoK forces on 26 October and American forces on 1 November and then withdrew.[14]

The war took a new course in November. For over three months the North Korean air force had not engaged the UN forces in aerial combat. Then, on the first day of the month, three Yak fighters tussled with an American strike over northwestern Korea. A B-26 claimed one (not acknowledged by the USAF) and F-51s claimed the other two. More ominous, later that day six MiG-15s fired on UN aircraft but did not register any damage. F-51s downed two Yak-9s on 2 November and two on 6 November. On 8 November an F-80 pilot claimed a MiG, and the next day a Navy F9F pilot claimed another. Navy F9Fs claimed two MiGs on 18 November. Both the Navy and Air Force attacked the Yalu River bridges with some effect despite restrictions levied on them to hit only the southern (North Korean) end of the bridges and fly bombing runs that did not overfly Chinese territory. Intense Red flak from both sides of the river, pontoon bridges, and the icing of the river rendered these attacks ineffective. The MiGs attacked the B-29s, downing a Superfort on 10 November. B-29 gunners also scored, claiming MiGs on 9 November and 14 November. More significant, the Chinese attacked in force on 25 November, which kicked the UN out of North Korea. The new war, and especially the introduction of the MiG-15, forced the USAF to respond.[15]

SEVEN

Air War Overview, 1950–53

J ust as Chinese intervention turned the entire ground war around, the introduction of the MiG-15 completely changed the air war. The Soviet jet was vastly superior to the prop-powered American fighters and clearly superior to the F-80s. Only the experience level of the U.S. pilots and corresponding inexperience of the Soviet pilots kept this situation from becoming a wholesale slaughter. The USAF took rapid measures to correct the problem.

Prior to the appearance of the MiG, American airmen were quickly and easily able to win air superiority with the numbers and aircraft they had in the theater. There were concerns, however, over the air defense needs of Japan in the event of a Soviet air attack. With this in mind, Lt. Gen. George Stratemeyer, commander of Far East Air Forces (FEAF), requested replacements in early September 1950 for fighter units he had sent to Korea. Air Force Headquarters denied the request, explaining that there were other commitments for the F-80s, mechanical problems with the F-84, and logistical problems and stateside air defense priorities for the F-86.[1] The initial American response to the appearance of the MiGs was mild. Gen. Hoyt Vandenberg, Chief of Staff of the Air Force, commented that the operations on 1 and 2 November indicated that "only token air forces [were] employed, conforming in general with [the] pattern [of the] ground forces." He concluded that there was "no evidence as yet of [a] major air threat to UN forces in [the] Far East."[2] Vandenberg wrote that in the event there was a buildup of jet fighters by the Communists, he would send F-84s to the theater. Within a week, the chief of staff took just such action. On 8 November, Stratemeyer received a message from Vandenberg that began: "In view of the changed military situation, particularly the resurgency [*sic*] of hostile air and [the] appearance of jets, I propose to deploy to FEAF on temporary duty one each F-84E and F-86A wings."[3]

The 27th Fighter Escort Wing was a Strategic Air Command unit that flew F-84Es. Despite its unit designation and the hopes of the Air Force, the F-84E (the Thunderjet) was no match for the MiG: during the course of the war its pilots claimed ten aerial victories while eighteen Thunderjets were lost to MiGs. As a result, the straight-winged Republic fighter went on to become the Air Force's primary fighter-bomber in the conflict, flying more combat sorties and dropping more bombs than any other USAF fighter-bomber. The Air Force listed 335 F-84s lost in the theater, 153 to enemy action.[4] Unloved but useful, the F-84 was one of the stalwarts of the air war. The star of the air war was, of course, the North American F-86 Sabre.

The 4th Fighter Wing: Initial Operations, December 1950

The USAF sent the 4th Fighter Interceptor Wing to the Korean War. (The USAF wing organization consisted of an aircraft unit, in this case the 4th Fighter Group, composed of the 334th, 335th, and 336th Fighter Squadrons and the various base and support units.) Formed in the summer of 1942, the 4th became one of the most famous and successful American fighter units of the war. It was initially manned in World War II by former members of the famous Eagle Squadrons and went on to destroy over one thousand German aircraft, more than any other American unit. After World War II, it flew P-80s until March 1949, when it received F-86As. That January, the unit's designation changed from "Fighter" to "Fighter Interceptor." There is no indication why it was selected to go to Korea.[5]

The USAF alerted the 4th for its deployment to the war on 9 November, giving it forty-eight hours to prepare for the movement. Four other F-86 units traded sixty of their newer aircraft for those in the 4th, which began flying fighters to the West Coast on 11 November. Given the highest Air Force priority, by 15 November the unit had two hundred airmen and forty-nine Sabres of the 334th and 335th squadrons at Naval Air Station San Diego for embarkation on the escort carrier *Cape Esperance*. The remainder of the wing's aircraft, twenty-six F-86s of the 336th, was carried as deck cargo aboard four tankers. The first tanker, carrying six F-86s, arrived in Japan the first week of December. Meanwhile, the carrier left the states on 29 November and arrived at Yokosuka on 13 December. The airmen ferried the fighters by barge from the port of entry to Kisarazu Air Base and then flew them to Johnson Air Base, located northwest of Tokyo, which became the 4th's Japanese base. That same day, the unit's group commander, Lt. Col. John Meyer, took an advanced detachment to Kimpo airfield outside of Seoul, known to the USAF as K-14.[6]

Although the unit got some F-86s quickly into action, the ocean voyage had not been flawless. To protect the fighters sent by tanker, the USAF "cocooned" the aircraft in a rubberized material. Unfortunately this was not done properly, resulting in salt corrosion to the magnesium trailing edges of the wings and control surfaces. This meant that many of the control surfaces and most of the wing trailing edges had to be replaced. The Sabres aboard the carrier were not "cocooned" but were periodically oiled and greased during the voyage. These aircraft also suffered corrosion damage, particularly those positioned on the forward part of the ship. Although most of this damage was minor, five fighters required replacement of part of their wing trailing edge. In addition, improper tie downs damaged the nose gear of some of the aircraft and later caused landing gear retraction problems. The dockworkers also dropped and damaged one fighter. These problems delayed the F-86's introduction into combat.[7]

The unit in Korea consisted mainly of personnel from the 336th Fighter Squadron that built up to squadron strength by 24 December. The Americans flew their first combat mission on 15 December. During the month, the unit put into the air one to four flights of Sabres (each flight consisting of four fighters flying in two elements in the tried and true "finger four" formation) which flew to the patrol area, about 220 miles from Kimpo, just below the contrail level, between twenty-seven thousand and thirty-five thousand feet. Initially, the Americans patrolled at relatively low air speeds to conserve fuel, but this put them at a disadvantage when they engaged the Russian fighters; therefore, they quickly increased their cruising speed. The average mission was about one and one-half hours in duration, about twenty to twenty-five minutes of which was spent in the patrol area. The Americans adopted a pattern by which four flights of four would arrive in the patrol area at five-minute intervals to extend the duration of the F-86 protection. The engagements usually began at high altitude and high speeds, exceeding the Sabre's Mach .95 redline. If the fight continued beyond one pass, both the air speed and altitude decreased. The high speeds just about prohibited deflection shooting so that the overwhelming majority of engagements consisted of getting on an opponent's tail and shooting up his tailpipe. As related above, on 17 December Lt. Col. Bruce Hinton earned a credit for downing a MiG, the first for the F-86s. On the morning of 22 December, eight or more MiGs bounced eight Sabres from out of the sun and "an enemy burst in the initial pass hit one friendly aircraft, which was last seen aflame and in a flat spin."[8] (Capt. Lawrence Bach, the only F-86 combat loss of the month, survived both the shoot down and captivity.) That afternoon, eight F-86s engaged fifteen or more MiGs and drew blood: six F-86 pilots each claimed one MiG destroyed. That is the USAF version. For their part, the Soviets claim they downed five F-86s and lost only one MiG that day (or three, according to another source), demonstrating the pattern of discrepancy between the American and Communist accounts that would continue throughout the war and frustrate students of the air war to this day. The F-86s were forced to move from K-14 on 2 January, due to the advancing Chinese ground offensive.[9]

The airmen encountered numerous problems in these initial operations. Starting the jet was difficult in the cold Korean weather. Maintenance personnel used new techniques that worked; however, these methods also damaged some of the engines. The airmen also found that the personal equipment, other than the flying helmet and "g" suit, were unsatisfactory. The bulky clothing made movement in the cockpit difficult and uncomfortable and rendered some of the switches hard to reach. Pilots reported that the "V" shaped windshield blocked out forward vision and caused distracting reflections on the canopy. On the other hand, they noted that the Sabre's guns operated well, which was attributed to the continual use of gun heaters in flight. Understandably, the main interest of the Sabre pilots was how their aircraft compared with their opponent's.[10]

It must be clearly recognized that comparisons in combat are very difficult and imprecise, and risk being inaccurate. Not only are such reports based on pilot perspectives but they also lump together a number of factors besides the technical qualities of the aircraft, such as pilot ability, training, doctrine, rules of engagement, and leadership, all of which impact on the performance of the aircraft in combat.

Nevertheless these assessments proved remarkably accurate, as confirmed shortly after the war when U.S. pilots systematically tested a MiG-15. These reports concluded that the two fighters were about equal in speed, with the F-86 having a slight edge at lower altitudes and the MiG at higher altitudes. The Russian fighter had the advantage of better climb and zoom performance at higher altitudes. The Sabre appeared to have the advantage in turning ability, at least up to thirty-seven thousand feet, the highest reported engagement altitude. The two fighters had about the same rate of roll. The USAF pilots noted three major problem areas. They desired longer range and endurance, although not at the cost of other flying performance. The Mark 18 gunsight was a sore point, having a number of inadequacies. The pilots also criticized the F-86's armament as "not sufficiently destructive," yet the Americans cited the armament and gunnery as a distinct advantage of the Sabre. In brief, the airmen attributed their success not to the superiority of their aircraft, but to better U.S. tactics, leadership, and pilot quality, along with the poor tactics and lack of aggressiveness of the MiG pilots.[11]

About six months later, the 4th again reported on its problems, confirming these views. This report again criticized the Sabre's armament as inadequate and observed that the Mk 18 gunsight had been designed for use against slower aircraft. It pushed for the radar ranging gunsight that had just arrived in the theater. Finally it noted the problem with drop tanks, a failure rate of 5 to 10 percent, compounded by the policy requiring the Sabres to operate in pairs; one hung drop tank meant two aborting fighters.[12]

A month after this report, Lieutenant Colonel Hinton wrote a follow-up to his January report that compared the F-86A with the MiG based on the 4th's operations between December 1950 and mid-July 1951. During that 160-day period the F-86 pilots were involved in over four hundred separate engagements and claimed forty-five MiGs destroyed, seven probably destroyed, and seventy-five damaged.[13] The Sabre showed a slight edge in turning ability whereas the MiG demonstrated superior climbing and zoom ability above twenty-five thousand feet as well as better acceleration. Hinton wrote that the Soviet fighter had better deceleration using only the throttle than the F-86, but the latter slowed quicker using speed brakes. The report observed that except for the most recent forty-five days, the MiG was hampered by its fire control system. It went on to note the great difference in the pilot skills of the MiG drivers, a matter often commented on by the American airmen. While about half the MiG pilots "performed with skill, precision and good judgment . . . [the remainder were] either unable to properly handle the MiG-15 or [were unable to] combine headwork with his skill to obtain the best performance in evading or attacking the F-86."[14] There seems to be general agreement on these views although other observations in the report are in dispute or in error. Hinton wrote that initially the MiG could outdive the Sabre, but when the fighters reached lower altitudes, the F-86 could slowly overtake the Red fighter. The American erroneously believed that the MiG could exceed Mach 1 in a dive. The airmen credited the MiG with equal control response at high speed and equal rate of roll with the F-86. The MiG appeared to have better spin recovery characteristics, being able to pull out at lower altitudes than the Sabre.[15]

Operations in 1951

The pullout of the 4th from K-14 in early 1951 ended Sabre operations over MiG Alley for the moment. The F-86s were out of action for two weeks, and then on 17 January they began flying primarily close air support and armed reconnaissance missions out of an airfield at Taegu (K-2). In comparison to 229 effective sorties flown in December and 207 in January, the unit flew but 1 effective sortie in February. It wasn't until 6 March that the 4th, using Suwon as a staging base, resumed operations over MiG Alley. After claiming seven MiGs in December, the Sabre pilots did not down another until 31 March when Flight Lt. J. A. O. Levesque (RCAF, attached to the 334FS) claimed a MiG. Suwon had little more than a concrete runway—no taxiways but lots of mud. Nevertheless, after the addition of some parking space and tents, the 334th moved into the base on 10 March. At the same time, the 336th moved to Taegu and staged out of Suwon for its combat missions. April was a better month for the Sabre pilots, during which they claimed fifteen MiGs destroyed without a combat loss. On 20 April Capt. James Jabara claimed his fifth and sixth victories, making him the first American ace of the war.[16]

Operations in March and April confirmed the view that only the Sabres could deal with the MiGs. FEAF notified Fifth Air Force on 26 February that as it was again able to escort B-29s in northwestern Korea, the bombers would resume their attacks on interdiction targets. On 1 March the USAF launched eighteen Superforts against these targets; but unforecast winds forced twenty-two F-80s to break off their escort early. Thus, when the bombers reached their target unescorted, they were easy game for nine MiG-15s. The Super-fort gunners claimed one fighter destroyed and two others damaged, but ten of the Boeing bombers were damaged, three so severely that they had to make emergency landings in Korea. (The Soviets claimed three B-29s and one F-80 destroyed without any MiG losses on that day.) While other bomber attacks in the month were less costly, it was primarily due to the unwilling-ness of the MiGs to attack. On 12 April forty-eight F-84s provided close escort for thirty-nine B-29s attacking the Yalu River bridges, with the F-86s flying high cover. The bombers broke up into three formations that spread out the Thunderjet escort. The Communists took advantage of the situation with at least fifty MiGs attacking the bombers. In the resulting battle the B-29s claimed to have destroyed ten MiGs (later credited with seven); the F-86s, four; and the F-84s, three probably destroyed. Three B-29s were lost and seven others were damaged in contrast to Soviet claims of ten Superforts and four Thunderjets destroyed. Nevertheless, the 8 percent bomber loss rate was too high to bear, forcing General Stratemeyer to withdraw the B-29s from daylight operations in northwestern Korea. The United States had lost air superiority over MiG Alley. While some might dispute this, since UN fighters and fighter-bombers could still operate there, those aircraft did not rival the bomb carrying capacity of the B-29s.[17]

The air leaders were apprehensive that the Communists might launch an air offensive in early 1951. The UN expected a Communist land offensive and the fluid ground battle might be affected by the reduction of UN air support, and certainly by Communist air attacks on UN ground forces. The Red fighter pilots were demonstrating increased proficiency. More ominous, since February aerial reconnaissance revealed the Communists were repairing their airfields in North Korea, and in early April the Reds appeared ready to move aircraft into these facilities. To counter such a move, Brig. Gen. James Briggs, commander of FEAF Bomber Command, came up with a plan to use small numbers of B-29s to neutralize the airfields just as they became operable and then continue with small attacks to harass and delay reconstruction. B-29 operations in small numbers close to the Yalu River might very well trigger a massive battle for control of the skies.[18]

As April began, the 4th had two of its three squadrons in Korea, stationed at Suwon and Taegu. This was less than optimal for the already outnumbered Sabre pilots. American engineers upgraded the facilities at Suwon allowing the third squadron to move in by 22 April.

Between 16 and 23 April, the USAF launched about a dozen Superforts a day against about nine airfields, postholing the airstrips with delayed action bombs. Light bombers attacked during both day and night to disrupt repair work. On one occasion Sabres returning from MiG Alley swooped down to strafe repair efforts. The MiGs did little to interfere with these operations. There was only one major air battle during this week when, on 22 April, three dozen MiGs flew across the Yalu to engage a dozen F-86s. The Sabres claimed four MiGs destroyed and another four damaged without a friendly loss. By the end of the month American photo interpreters concluded that all

Communist airfields in North Korean were unserviceable. Thus the Chinese ground offensive that kicked off on the night of 22 April did so in the face of UN air superiority over the front as well as over almost all of North Korea.[19]

The USAF did note the buildup of air power at the North Korean airfield at Sinuiju, just across the Yalu River from one of the main Chinese airfields and Communist MiG bases at Antung. Reconnaissance spotted 38 prop powered fighters and attack bombers in revetments along with support facilities. The UN launched 312 USAF and Marine aircraft against the airfield on the afternoon of 9 May. The attack employed both Sabres and Panthers as top cover, Shooting Stars to suppress AA, and Corsairs and Mustangs to pummel the airfield area with bombs, rockets, and napalm. Although 50 MiGs took off, only 18 made halfhearted passes. Therefore there was no major aerial battle with only two claims of damaged MiGs, one by an F-84 and another by an F-86 pilot, and one Thunderjet damaged. The attack was a rousing success.[20]

The Communists did not give up their efforts to contest UN air superiority. One innovative effort was to demolish buildings along a section of road within Pyongyang, the North Korean capital that yielded a runway 7,000 feet long and 375 feet wide. While the UN air forces could hit and put these large airfields out of commission, the smaller dirt strips for smaller aircraft were much more difficult to detect and attack. Although these airfields could only support small numbers of the lighter aircraft, it was from these airstrips that the Communists launched their nighttime heckling raids. When the weather cleared, the airmen struck the Red airfields with everything they had: B-29s, B-26s, and fighter-bombers during the day, and B-26s at night. The campaign began in mid-June and continued for a month. It came to an end after reconnaissance noted on 12 July that the Communists had stopped trying to repair their airfields.[21]

Although the air superiority effort was the Air Force's top priority, as it played out, the bulk of USAF effort in the Korean War was directed against Communist supply lines. During the Korean War, the USAF flew 48 percent of its sorties on interdiction missions, compared with 20 percent in close support, and 19 percent in counter air. The interdiction effort was at its height between 1 December 1950 and 1 April 1952, with an overall average of 58 percent of the sorties. The interdiction missions were the USAF's mostly costly, accounting for 51 percent of operational losses (749 in number) and 55 percent of losses to enemy action (415).[22]

The USAF did not have the tools to effectively wage an interdiction campaign, especially at night. Its principal aircraft for this mission was the World

War II Douglas B-26 (formerly A-26) Invader that lacked maneuverability and navigational equipment for low-level operations in the mountainous North Korean terrain. The interdiction crews had neither the equipment to detect enemy targets at night nor munitions any more accurate than the bombs and bullets that had been used in World War I. The airmen tried a variety of innovative technologies to pierce the night and to accurately hit enemy targets. B-29s dropped two types of guided bombs, the 1,000 pound Razon and 12,000 pound Tarzon, with mixed technical and limited tactical results. The Air Force also experimented with infrared detection devices on B-26s and dropped both roofing tacks and tetrahedrons from the venerable C-47 to puncture the truck tires, but with little success. The C-47s and other aircraft also dropped flares to allow attacks on night logistical traffic. Despite these efforts the airmen were unable to come up with effective tactics or technology to seriously impede Communist supply efforts.[23]

Probably more important to the eventual failure of the interdiction effort than American shortcomings were the actions taken by the Communists. The Communists had minimal supply requirements unless involved in full-scale combat operations. A Chinese division required only fifty tons of supplies a day, one-fifth of that of a comparable sized American formation, a tonnage that could be carried by two and a half railroad cars or twenty-five trucks. Unless the UN ground forces took the offensive, the Communist could control both their casualties and supply requirements. Poor weather and rugged terrain made night operations hazardous even without enemy opposition. As the Communists had abundant manpower to repair damage and build more bridges and bypasses, the interdiction campaign pitted Communist engineers and laborers against the UN airmen. The Communists took more active measures as well, increasing the number of antiaircraft guns by a factor of four during 1951, stringing cables across valleys, using deceptive lights to decoy the night bombers, and setting up flak traps. These not only knocked down UN aircraft but also forced them to fly higher and make only one pass, thus lessening accuracy. Ground defenses also diverted aircraft from strike to flak suppression; in October 1951, 20 percent of the fighter-bomber effort was so engaged.

Who won this competition? On the last day of May 1951 the airmen began an interdiction campaign they codenamed "Strangle." While initially the operation seemed to have positive results, by mid-June the front settled down and the Communists adapted to the attacks. FEAF concluded: "Operation Strangle was not successful due . . . to the flexibility of the Communist logistic system."[24] In late December, Fifth Air Force intelligence conceded that the Communist repair and building troops had "broken our railroad blockade of Pyongyang and [won] the use of all key rail arteries."[25] Clearly, the Communist troops suffered from the constant day and night attacks on their supply lines that extended over two hundred miles from the Chinese sanctuary to the front lines. In the end, the Communists were able to launch large ground offensives and make air operations over North Korea expensive. One measure of the failure of the air effort was that while in July 1951 the Chinese fired about 8,000 rounds of artillery, in May 1952 they were able to fire 102,000 rounds. The air war against Red supply lines continued, but despite considerable effort, constant losses, optimistic claims, and high hopes, it was never able to decisively affect the ground war.[26]

In mid-1951 both sides pushed the air superiority war. On the American side, the field commanders wanted more F-86s to meet the threat. In June, U.S. intelligence estimated the Communists had 445 MiG-15s in the theater compared with a total of 89 F-86s, with only two of three Sabre squadrons deployed in Korea. Air Force Chief Vandenberg was reluctant to send any more Sabres to the war because of the demands of homeland defense and probably because of the low North American production along with the needs of the European forces.[27] On 20 September he made clear to Gen. Otto Weyland, commander of FEAF, that there would be no additional F-86s for the war. A few months earlier in July, however, the Air Force ordered that the new F-86E be sent to Korea to replace the "A" model, and in August the new aircraft began to arrive, albeit in small numbers. (By October the F-86E was flying 40 percent of the 4th's combat sorties.)[28]

Although MiGs were seen as far south as Pyongyang in June, air-to-air action had been sparse for the Sabres, with nine credits in June, six in July, four in August, and seven in September. The Communists made their move in September, sending more MiGs across the Yalu and demonstrating better formations and tactics. When reconnaissance spotted construction of three jet fighter airfields in late September, it was clear the Communists were again attempting to contest air superiority. In response, the USAF dispatched B-29s to neutralize these installations. The first attack on 18 October caught the Reds by surprise, and they offered no aerial opposition. But when the B-29s attacked again on 21 October, the Communists downed one Superfort, and two days later downed three more along with an F-84. B-29 attacks on bridge targets later in the month also met fierce MiG resistance. As a result the Air Force suspended daylight attacks by B-29s at the end of the month. October

1951 was the worst month of the war for the USAF in the air-to-air battle when it lost fourteen aircraft to the MiGs, the highest number of losses in one month in the entire war, while claiming thirty-five MiGs (twenty-five by F-86s). The last quarter of 1951 saw three of the five highest monthly air-to-air losses of the war.[29]

The increased air battles and construction in North Korea were not the only signs of the Communist intent to contest air superiority. Intelligence noted the movement of both jet and prop-powered aircraft across the Yalu; the introduction of a new version of the MiG (MiGbis) with an upgraded engine and better performance; and, in early December, MiGs flying south of Seoul. Therefore the Air Force escalated its plan to convert an F-80 wing to F-86s scheduled for spring 1952. Vandenberg directed Air Defense Command to send seventy-five F-86s along with air and ground crews to Korea. The field commanders, however, had a different idea: Fifth Air Force commander Lt. Gen. Frank Everest proposed to send just the F-86s to the 51st Fighter Interceptor, which was then flying F-80s. Vandenberg met with Weyland in Tokyo and approved the conversion plan.[30]

To meet the Red bid and realizing that the 51st would not be in action for weeks, if not months, FEAF sent the 4th's third squadron from Japan to join its two sister squadrons in Korea. The 335th deployed to Kimpo on 2 November. During this month the MiGs had superior numbers and the initiative north of Pyongyang. Nevertheless the Sabres had another good month, claiming twenty-five kills for the loss of two F-86s in air-to-air combat. (A dozen of these victories were scored on 30 November when the Communist airmen made one of their few offensive actions of the war.) The Sabres destroyed another four MiGs on the ground at a North Korean airfield.[31]

The 51st Converts to Sabres

In December 1951 the 4th's Sabres were joined by those of the 51st. This unit had been formed a year before the United States entered World War II and had served in the China-Burma-India theater where it downed seventy-one Japanese aircraft. In February 1950 it was redesignated "Fighter Interceptor" and deployed to Japan in September. It flew over 17,500 sorties in F-80s, claiming two aerial victories while losing seventy-three aircraft, thirty to enemy action. Its last F-80 mission was on 19 November 1951. At the time of its transition to Sabres, it consisted of two squadrons, the 16th and 25th. A number of pilots who were flying with the 4th transferred to the new Sabre unit, including the 51st's wing and group commanders, Francis Gabreski and George Jones.[32]

The 51st initiated F-86 operations on 1 December and claimed five MiGs in that month. (1st Lt. Paul Roach got the first 51st victory on 2 December and added one more on 28 December. A transfer from the 334th Fighter Squadron, Roach had earned a half credit on 25 September.) In January 1952 the unit hit its stride as it notched twenty-seven victories while the veteran 4th had a mere five. Some of this success could be attributed to the fact that the 51st was flying the newer F-86Es while the 4th was flying a mixture of the older, well-used F-86As along with the E model. In May the USAF attached a third squadron to the unit. (The 39th had been flying F-51s in the 18th Fighter Bomber Wing.) In June the new squadron was the first to receive the new F-86F. The next month the 51st adopted its checkerboard tail markings, with the 16th's painted blue; the 25th's, red; and the 39th's, yellow. Initially the Sabres had three black stripes separated by two white stripes painted on their wing tips and tail. Early in 1952 this scheme was changed to wide yellow bands on the wing tips and fuselage. Apparently the 4th also painted the yellow band on the vertical tail, a practice not followed by the 51st.[33]

As to be expected from the highly competitive fighter pilots, there was a keen rivalry between the two units. Certainly this was fanned by the unit's flamboyant wing commander, Gabby Gabreski. But the rivalry was also fueled by those in the unit, according to the wing's historian, who believed that the fighter school at Nellis was funneling its best graduates to the 4th. In any case, the 51st believed, as recorded in its history, that while the 4th claimed 10 percent more kills, it had twice the losses of the 51st. This is not borne out by the documents. Comparing the two units beginning with the 51st's first claim on 2 December 1951 indicates 392 credits for the 4th versus 306 for the 51st or 28 percent more credits. During this same time period the 4th lost a total of seventy-nine aircraft (forty-four in air-to-air) compared with its rival's losses of sixty-nine (thirty-four in air-to-air) or a difference of 14.5 percent. However, if we compare air-to-air claims and air-to-air losses, the 4th had 28 percent higher credits and losses. In the period 1 January through 30 June 1953, the 4th flew more hours (12 percent) than the other Sabre outfit and had 15 major accidents compared with 21 for the 51st, which yielded a lower accident rate (67 major accidents per one hundred thousand flying hours) than for the 51st (105).[34] The 4th ended the war as the top scoring USAF fighter (56 percent of the total Air Force 893 claims) and the bulk of the aces. On its part, the 51st had the highest scoring ace, Joseph McConnell, and two pilots who would go on to greater fame, astronauts John Glenn and Edwin Aldrin.[35]

The fight for control of the skies heated up in late 1951. In addition to the slaughter of eleven prop-powered aircraft and one MiG on 30 November (without a loss), the Sabres scored thirteen other victories in the month. December was also a good month for the F-86s, as they downed thirty Red aircraft. They got fourteen of these in one day (13 December), all but one by the guns of the 4th. This was the highest one-day toll the F-86s would enact during the war, although it was later tied. In exchange, the USAF lost two F-86s on the 13 December and a dozen Sabres during November and December, eight in air-to-air combat.

At the same time the F-86s were running up this score, the units had to deal with a lowering of pilot quality. Most of the original highly experienced pilots were rotating out of the war, having flown the required one hundred missions. In their place, the units received a mixture of brand-new pilots out of flight school and others whose flying experience was in multiengine aircraft.[36] The 4th complained that it was an "almost impossible task to take a pilot who flew transport or heavy bombers in World War II, who got out of the service and grew old mentally and fat physically for several years, recall that pilot, and expect him to fly a quick course in F-80s and become a replacement pilot for F-86 flying." Only a very few rare and unusual individuals could accomplish this feat, for "air to air fighter flying calls for a pilot with an aggressive, competitive mental attitude. He must be young mentally. Age, as measured in years, is not the criteria for selecting fighter pilots. As long as a pilot's reflexes and vision hold up and his physical machinery will continue to stand the pace, he can continue active fighter flying providing he started out in fighters."[37] This position contradicted Air Force policy that held that any Air Force pilot could fly any Air Force aircraft, a policy carried through the Vietnam War. Nevertheless, the Sabre pilots were able to post impressive victory totals and to increase the victory-to-loss ratio in the last months of the war.

The F-86E was introduced in late 1951. It was about six hundred pounds heavier than the "A" model but with the same engine, therefore losing some performance. It was an overall improvement, however, because its hydraulically powered control system and all-flying tail (the entire horizontal stabilizer moved, not just the elevators) gave it superior handling abilities, especially at high speeds and when pulling "g"s. So, while there is a dispute as to whether the Sabre or MiG had the faster rate of roll, the F-86 could transition more quickly from one direction to the other. The Sabre was considered a more stable gun platform than the MiG. The downside, the pilots noted, was that the aircraft's hydraulic systems were vulnerable because the main and emergency lines were located too close together in the tail.[38]

All accounts agreed that the MiG had superior rate of climb and ceiling (about five thousand feet) compared to the Sabre. The Americans believed that the F-86 was faster below twenty thousand feet while the MiG held that advantage above that altitude. The Russian fighter had superior acceleration, which gave it an initial advantage in dives, although the Sabre could (slowly) overhaul the MiG in sustained, high-speed (Mach .95 or higher) dives. At lower speeds the two were equivalent in dives. The American fighter had superior dive recovery while the Communist fighter had the advantage in a zoom climb. Prior to March 1952 the Americans believed that the Sabre could slightly out-turn the MiG below thirty thousand feet as well at high speeds (Mach .85 or higher), except at very high altitudes, while the MiG held an advantage in turning above thirty thousand feet. After that date, the MiG was judged to be equal, if not superior, to the F-86 in turning. The Sabre could decelerate faster than the MiG as its speed brakes were more effective, although slower to extend. After March 1952, the Americans believed the MiG was definitely superior to the F-86 above thirty-five thousand feet, marginally better between that altitude and twenty-five thousand feet, and equivalent below twenty thousand feet.

The Sabre's armament and gunsight were considered better than the MiG's for jet fighter-versus-fighter combat as they were superior at ranges below fifteen hundred feet and in the fast moving aerial combat that often required "snap shots." Nevertheless, an operations analyst summed up the situation in his April 1952 report with this chilling warning:

> In general, the F-86-E is a sound, "honest" airplane, well liked by its pilots, and whose record in Korea speaks for itself. On the other hand, the fact must be faced that it is fighting a specialized aircraft on its own ground and that the relative superiority of the present F-86-E pilot-plane-weapon "team" is not likely to continue forever. In point of fact, it is the considered opinion of most pilots that, given the present MiG-15 advantages of combat location, the rising proficiency of the MiG-15 "team" will eventually void our present superiority.[39]

Operations in 1952

The F-86s were engaged in two specific projects of note during the first half of 1952. The first was an attempt to extend the use of the F-86 from strictly an air superiority role to a ground support role. The fighter's gunsight enabled the pilot to fire bullets and rockets as well as to drop bombs, and each Sabre could deliver either sixteen rockets or two bombs.[40] The pressing requirements of air superiority, the limited number of Sabres, and the light bomb loads that the F-86s could deliver (it had only two pylons) restricted initial efforts to combat experiments. In January 1951 Sabres fired 162 rockets, 24 in February 1952, and then 60 rockets in December. In April 1952 the F-86s dropped six tons of napalm and the next month thirteen tons of bombs. This was not a very efficient use of the scarce Sabres and their pilots. That picture changed with the introduction of more F-86s—specifically, the conversion of two fighter-bomber units to the F-86s in early 1953—that gave the airmen essentially twice as many fighters as they had for the first two years of the war. Whereas the number of F-86s the USAF had in the field ("committed units") did not exceed 100 until December 1951 and did not exceed 160 until October 1952, the numbers rapidly rose to 297 in July 1953. In addition, the new F-86F-25 with four pylon positions permitted the Sabre to carry more stores.[41]

A second major USAF effort was directed against the North Korean hydroelectric industry. As truce negotiations dragged on, FEAF sought a way to use air power to pressure the Communists. In April 1952 the FEAF staff submitted a plan to attack high value targets in North Korea. Although such targets were few in number, the one target set that stood out was hydroelectric power. The Americans were aware of this target from the start of the war, although it was not on the original lists of eighteen strategic targets in North Korea because of economic (reconstruction), diplomatic (the Chinese used electricity generated there), and military (the difficulty of taking out the facilities) factors. The premier generator site was at Sui-ho, the largest generating facility in the Orient and the fourth largest in the world that supplied 90 percent of the power for North Korea and 10 percent of the power used in Manchuria. The May 1952 change of command with Gen. Mark Clark replacing Gen. Matthew Ridgway as commander of UN forces was more than a mere exchange of generals. Clark was less reluctant than Ridgway to attack these targets and in mid-June ordered the Air Force and Navy to attack all of the power targets except Sui-ho, which required permission from the Joint Chiefs of Staff. However, the chiefs added Sui-ho to the target list after getting the specific approval of President Truman. The American airmen would attack Sui-ho, located on the Yalu River within thirty miles of two of the main MiG airfields, and three other generating sites on the east coast. The largest of these attacks was a joint Air Force–Navy attack on Sui-ho, the first Navy attacks in MiG Alley since 1950.

In the early afternoon of 23 June under the cover of eighty-four F-86s and thirty-five F9Fs, thirty-five Navy Skyraiders from three carriers unloaded 85 tons of bombs on the generating facilities at the Sui-ho. Later in the afternoon seventy-nine F-84s and forty-five F-80s attacked with another 145 tons of bombs. The Communists met the air attacks with flak but not with fighters. In fact, the American air attacks flushed the MiGs that, instead of rising to defend Sui-ho facility, flew (or perhaps more accurately, fled) west into China. The massive American assault may have appeared as an attack on the Chinese airfields. As a result, only two attacking aircraft suffered minor damage. There were Air Force and Marine attacks on three other power targets as well. The four-day operation of 968 USAF and 546 Navy sorties, which cost two Navy aircraft whose pilots were rescued, rendered eleven of the thirteen plants unserviceable and knocked out over 90 percent of the potential North Korean power production. North Korea was blacked out for over two weeks, before it was able to restore perhaps 10 percent of its former electrical capacity.[42]

The Americans followed up these attacks on Communist power production with naval and B-29 strikes in July and a night B-29 attack on Sui-ho on 12 September 1952. For the latter attack, four B-29s with electronic countermeasures orbited to jam Communist radar while B-26s and Navy aircraft attacked searchlight and antiaircraft gun positions to aid the twenty-five four-engine bombers. Red fighters downed one Superfort, and AA damaged others. Months later, on 15 February, the USAF sent low-flying F-84s covered by F-86s against the target. These attacks caused political problems for the U.S. government. At home, congressmen were eager to know why these targets had not been hit sooner. Meanwhile, the Labor party in Britain called the attacks "provocative."[43]

The year 1952 proved to be a better year than 1951 for victory credits. Whereas the Sabres had claimed 122 MiGs, of a total of 175 USAF claims in 1951, the next year the F-86s score was 375 MiGs of USAF's 383 total claims. Further data dramatically underscore the improvement: while in 1951 there were only two months in which the Sabre claims exceeded 19 MiGs, in 1952 there were only two months of fewer than 20 kills.

The Sabres had three big days in 1952. On 1 April they claimed ten MiGs for the loss of one F-86. The airmen also did well on 4 July, covering an attack on the North Korean Military Academy. Here they claimed thirteen MiGs at the cost of two Sabres. A week later UN airmen launched a massive operation against the North Korean capital. American and British naval aviators joined Marine and Air Force airmen to put more than 1,200 aircraft over Pyongyang in the largest daily effort made to this point in the war. Losses were light: two Navy and one Air Force (F-84) aircraft. On 29 August UN airmen put 1,400 sorties over Pyongyang with good results. The Sabres posted another thirteen victories on 4 September, although this time four F-86s went down. In September the F-86s downed sixty-three MiGs, the highest monthly total to that time, at the cost of nine Sabres downed by MiGs.[44]

One boost to the American advantage came with the introduction of the F-86F into combat. With a more powerful engine and soon retrofitted with a higher performing wing (fixed leading edge, 6-3), this Sabre clearly lessened, if not eliminated, most of the MiG's flying advantages. The first "F" models went to the 51st's 39th Fighter Squadron in August 1952 and then to the 4th's 335th Fighter Squadron in October. (There is no mention of why these units were chosen.) The other four squadrons continued to fly the "A"s and "E"s until October, when all of the "A" models were taken out of action.

The 39th had just converted to Sabres in June but in short order became the highest scoring squadron in the 51st. The 335th, already the top-scoring unit in its group, maintained that position, ending the war as the highest scoring Sabre squadron. In the six months in which the 39th was the only squadron in the 51st that flew the F-86F, it claimed 46 percent of the unit's victories, while in the four months in which the 335th held a similar advantage in 4th, it accounted for 53 percent of the unit's victories. In the last five months of the war, all but one (the 39th) of the 4th's and 51st's six squadrons increased their victory-to-loss ratio. How much of this success was due to the F-86F is open to speculation, but surely it helped. Since the 335th claimed 42 percent of the 4th's victory credits in the four months prior to receiving the "F" and 54 percent after, the advantage may have been approximately 10 percent.[45]

In March 1953 the USAF distributed the "F" models to all six squadrons. The ever-increasing numbers of these aircraft along with complaints (and lowered morale) from the pilots in the excluded squadrons pushed this redistribution. Another aspect that rubbed salt into the wounds, at least in the 51st, was that because the F-86F could fly higher than the "A" and "E" models, the pilots of the 39th were put on a special diet to minimize gas and reduce discomfort at higher altitudes. They got better food—in the words of one of these pilots, "we ate like kings." So the 39th squadron got the best birds and the best chow—great for them, but not conducive to good morale for the rest of the unit.[46]

Operations in 1953

The F-86s did even better in 1953. The Sabres claimed 294 of the 298 USAF victories and scored 25 or more victories in each of last seven months of 1953. In May, they had three days in which they scored 10 or more victories and experienced no losses. The 57 claims and 1 loss in May gave the Sabres their best claims to loss ratio of the war. In June the Sabres scored the most victories in one month: 77 MiGs at the cost of 5 fighters lost to MiGs and 1 to friendly fire. On 30 May, they scored 14 victories without a loss to equal the record for victories in one day set on 13 December 1951. The ratio of F-86 claims of MiG-15s downed to F-86s lost in air-to-air combat skyrocketed in 1953: for the entire war, the ratio was 8.2 to 1; in 1953 that ratio was more than 13 to 1.[47]

Why did the Americans finish with such a flourish, not only increasing the number of kills, but also increasing the ratio of claims to losses? The introduction of the F-86F with the solid leading edge was certainly a factor. Another factor was that the Soviets phased out of the war, leaving the less-trained and inexperienced Chinese and North Korean pilots to face the Sabres. Finally, I believe the American pilots became bolder, realizing that the war was ending and that this would be their last shot at the glory of downing enemy aircraft.

One of the most effective air actions of the war was connected with the effort to pressure the Communists to come to terms at Panmunjom. Just as talks reached a break-off point in mid-May, General Clark proposed a number of measures, including hitting twenty previously untouched irrigation dams on the west coast of Korea, and he even mentioned air operations against targets in Manchuria and North China. President Eisenhower was willing to threaten the Communists with an expansion of the war, and in late May, Secretary of State John Foster Dulles told visiting Indian Prime Minister Nehru that the United States had decided to attack Communist bases in Manchuria if an honorable peace was not agreed to at Panmunjom. Some believe President Eisenhower implied he would consider using nuclear weapons.

On 13 May, F-84s hit the dam at Toksan, twenty miles north of Pyong-yang. The resulting flooding took out five square miles of rice fields and seven hundred buildings, inundating an airfield and miles of railroads and high-ways. Later attacks by fighter-bombers and B-29s did further damage and forced the North Koreans to lower the level of their reservoirs, thereby reduc-ing rice production. In June, the Communists agreed to the peace terms; in late July, the war ended.[48]

The last major air effort of the war was to deny the Communists the use of airfields in North Korea that could accommodate MiG-15s, that is, those with runways over three thousand feet long. (The armistice terms called for a freeze on the introduction of replacement aircraft after the truce went into effect.) The airmen attacked irrigation dams to flood some of these airstrips, but the Communists countered by lowering the level of the reservoirs. Stan-dard attacks did the job, and by late June all but one airfield had been neu-tralized. It again became a race between the Red engineers and laborers and the airmen. The airmen won, evidenced in pictures taken on 27 July, which indicated that all North Korean airfields were unsuitable for jet operations.[49]

EIGHT

Exploitation of Enemy Aircraft

When the Soviet MiG-15 appeared over North Korea in November 1950, the American airmen knew little about the aircraft beyond the fact that it clearly outperformed American jets and was similar in appearance to the F-86. There was a desperate need to learn the capabilities and advantages — but most especially the vulnerabilities — of this machine and the men who flew it. Without being overly dramatic, the fate of the battle for air superiority, if not the war, could well be influenced by such information.

Obtaining an intact MiG was extremely unlikely. In contrast to World War II, when the Allies obtained a number of German aircraft that landed or crashed in Britain, Sweden, Switzerland, or on the battlefield, obtaining an enemy plane in Korea was more difficult. The Soviet fighters were based just north of the Yalu River: this meant that, considering the fighter's short range and Soviet rules of engagement, few MiG-15s came close to the frontlines. In addition, because the UN had an efficient rescue service and control of the seas, Soviet pilots were forbidden to fly over water to prevent capture of the downed pilots.

If the MiGs would not come to the Americans, then the Americans would have to go to the MiGs. In early 1951, the commander of Fifth Air Force, Lt. Gen. Earle Partridge, told a visiting USAF general that his command would make every effort to salvage parts of a MiG-15.[1] The man in charge of the operation was WO Donald Nichols, one of those colorful, larger-than-life, bold, and outlandish characters that occasionally appear and add sparkle to tedious histories. (Partridge later wrote that Nichols was "the most amazing and unusual man among those with whom I was associated during my military service.")[2] A former motor pool sergeant, Nichols headed an intelligence unit in South Korea after World War II that engaged in the kind of clandestine operations that Hollywood celebrates. Described as a combination of "Lawrence of Arabia" and "Dirty Harry," he had direct contact with flag officers and the president of South Korea. The job also had its risks: Nichols survived three assassination attempts and there was one attempt to kidnap his son.[3]

The MiG salvage operation moved very fast. On 1 April Nichols began training his small group in parachute jumping, salvage of aircraft, and concealment in enemy territory. Personnel from Air Technical Intelligence Center, using an F-86 as a model, instructed his team about aircraft parts identification. The unit then practiced on a wrecked T-33 and jet engines, since the MiG's power plant was the priority intelligence target.[4] The unit's training was cut short when, within two weeks, a target of opportunity presented itself.

On 13 April 1951, Lt. Robert Prasccindo (25FS) spotted the wreckage of a MiG twelve miles south of the Chong Chong River and about twenty-five miles inland. The fighter unit forwarded the information up the chain of command, noting, "Wrecked plane definitely a swept wing fighter." The unit supplied the coordinates and added, "fuselage burned out but wing was left lying in clearing on wooded hill."[5] The report reached the Fifth Air Force Headquarters the next morning, prompting the immediate launch of a photographic reconnaissance aircraft. However, it failed to locate the wreck, as did two efforts the next day. The mission was about to be scrubbed when a Fifth Air Force intelligence officer returned from Far East Air Forces Headquarters with further incentive and orders. "Additional information confirms possibility of MIG crash. Get the pilot that made the original sightings to lead a photo plane to observed crash."[6] As a result, the airmen located the Soviet fighter.

Nichols and six Koreans left Seoul on an H-19 helicopter just before noon on 17 April for Paengnyong-do, an island behind enemy lines occupied by the UN. The helicopter, piloted by Capt. Joseph Cooper and Capt. Russell Winnegar, then flew on toward the wreck as F-51s strafed the area and fifty jets provided overhead cover. The helicopter landed in a barley field about two hundred meters from the crash site.[7]

Nichols writes that although the MiG was guarded, the Communists ran off after a brief exchange of fire.[8] The landing party found the MiG with its nose smashed but otherwise in good shape. While Nichols photographed the

MiG, his Korean crew removed turbine blades, skin samples, ammunition, and the combustion chamber. Then the Koreans used hand grenades to detach more pieces, including the exhaust pipe, another combustion chamber, and the horizontal stabilizer. At this point, the men spotted approximately twenty men coming up the hill. The team loaded the pieces aboard the H-19, with the stabilizer protruding out the open door. The salvage operation took about thirty-five minutes.

Cooper had difficulties getting the overloaded helicopter off the ground, needing a second downwind effort to clear a hill. The helicopter climbed to 5,500 feet and, about ten miles from the coast, encountered enemy fire that hit a rotor blade. Cooper put down near the coast and loaded some of the booty aboard Lt. Danny Miller's H-5 before landing for fuel at Cho-do, another UN–held island behind the front lines. The two choppers returned to Paengnyong-do where the pieces were put aboard an SA-16.[9]

The airmen shipped the parts to Wright-Patterson AFB for analysis. On 28 April 1951, Air Materiel Command wired their conclusions back to the theater. The engine was a scaled-up British Nene engine, about 15 percent larger in all areas, putting the engine into the 6,000-pound-thrust class. The analysts noted that the welding was good production quality and that the general workmanship was comparable to U.S. and British practices.[10]

The airmen were eager to get more information about the MiG. On 1 June 1951 a FEAF C-47 dropped fifteen Koreans behind Communist lines to salvage pieces of a downed MiG. As with most of these operations, all the Koreans were captured.[11] On 9 July 1951, a MiG crashed onto mud flats on the west coast of North Korea. A Royal Navy fighter pilot spotted the wreck, but neither a photoreconnaissance aircraft nor a boat could find it, hampered by the fact that the MiG was above the water line at low tide, but in nineteen feet of water at high tide. The wreck was located, and Donald Nichols was again called in to recover the pieces. He went to the U.S. Navy for help, but the Navy was reluctant to get involved.[12] The initial plan, conceived by Capt. W. L. M. Brown of the HMS *Cardigan Bay*, called for two junks to lash the MiG between them and sail away, but the U.S. Navy came up with a better solution: a landing craft (LSU-960) fitted with a crane.

On 20 July 1951, a flotilla of three Royal navy ships, one South Korean vessel, and the LSD-7, which was carrying the LSU-960, began the operation under air cover provided by a British carrier. Earlier in the day, a helicopter from the HMS *Glory* marked the position of the Soviet aircraft, which was 2.5 miles offshore at high tide, but uncovered at low tide. By the end of the day they had recovered the engine and tail but twice failed to get the wing aboard. During the night, the USS *Sicily* relieved the HMS *Glory*. Early the next morning, LSU-960 returned to its task as a shore party recovered aircraft pieces. By 0700 the salvage team was under fire, prompting suppression attacks by carrier aircraft. This drove the Communist troops off, but artillery fire continued. The UN force recovered both the wing and fuselage, and by 0900 was at sea. Despite warnings of MiG-15s heading toward the navy force and a reported submarine contact, there was no further action. The flotilla put into Inchon on 23 July, and the parts were put aboard a C-119 bound for Wright-Patterson Air Force Base.[13]

This success did not stop the UN quest for information about the MiG. In October 1951 there were three unsuccessful attempts to salvage a MiG that had crashed on a beach on the west coast of North Korea.[14] In the end, the airmen got what they wanted the easy way: Communists pilots delivered flyable aircraft.

Defecting MiG Pilots and a MiG to Keep

On 5 March 1953, Polish Lt. Franciszek Jarecki crash-landed a MiG-15 on the Danish island of Bornholm. Although the Danes returned the aircraft on 22 May, the western (NATO) allies took advantage of the two and a half months to completely disassemble, examine, and then reassemble the MiG and even conduct firing tests of the fighter's armament. While interrogation of the pilot was considered of marginal value, because he was so inexperienced, the aircraft provided valuable information. USAF intelligence calculated that the fighter's top speed was Mach .92 and that there was an improvement in Russian manufacturing tolerances, since shims were no longer needed. Workmanship was reported as utilitarian—first class where necessary, but not when unnecessary. The airmen concluded that the layout was simple but effective, designed for easy construction, and the engine workmanship was comparable to U.S. standards.[15]

A few months after the end of the war, a surprising and important incident took place. On the morning of 21 September 1953, American airmen at Kimpo were surprised when a swept-wing fighter landed the wrong way (against the traffic), barely avoiding an F-86 landing in the proper direction. The fighter taxied off the runway and, ignoring a ground crewman who gave hand signals, shut down. The pilot emerged from the cockpit with his hands raised high; he was a North Korean, the airplane a MiG-15.

Twenty-one year old No Kum-Sok had flown three hundred combat missions and claimed he defected because he "was sick and tired of the Red deceit."[16] Americans swarmed over the aircraft, and in short order American F-86s and Australian Meteors were airborne to defend this precious prize. The airmen should have been better prepared for this situation, because the previous April the UN offered political asylum and $100,000 to the first Communist pilot who defected with a MiG, and made this known by dropping over a million leaflets and radio broadcasts.[17] While the Americans hoped that this would net a fighter, they also believed it might shake up the defensive and suspicious Communist leadership. In fact the defector was unaware of the offer.

The next day, the USAF removed the fighter's wings and shipped it to Okinawa aboard a C-124 transport. Also dispatched from Korea were F-86s flown by seasoned pilots while the USAF flew in some of its top test pilots for flight tests. Despite poor weather on Okinawa, the tests began on 28 September. Five pilots flew the MiG on eleven flights over Okinawa in a one-week series of tests. Gen. Albert Boyd, commander of Wright Air Development Center, was one of those who piloted the MiG, along with two pilots he picked, H. E. "Tom" Collins from the Ohio base and Charles "Chuck" Yeager from Edwards AFB. Two other pilots, Maj. J. S. Fallon from the Air Proving Ground Command and Lt. Col. Eugene Summerich of the 4th Fighter Interceptor Wing, also flew the Communist fighter.

In a 1960 interview that was reprinted in Yeager's autobiography, Boyd claims that Collins won a coin toss to make the first flight; Yeager would fly second and Boyd, third. That makes a good story but, according to Collins, Boyd decided to allow Collins to make the first flight, remarking that "Yeager has had his share of firsts."[18] There are other discrepancies in the MiG testing story. Yeager wrote that the pilot couldn't turn on the fighter's emergency fuel pump because it would blow off the tail section of the MiG. Defector No claims he doesn't recall telling Yeager that, but then equivocates. A Soviet MiG-15 pilot calls this warning pure nonsense. Common sense would also urge some skepticism regarding Yeager's statement.[19] However, both Collins and Yeager write that the fighter gave no stall warning, while official USAF reports use the adjectives "insufficient" and "poor" regarding stall warning.[20] Stalls led to spins, for which the MiG-15 was notorious. No writes that spins were dangerous because spin recovery was difficult, and if recovery was not successful in three rotations, pilots were instructed to eject from the fighter.

Spins were more common in the MiG than in the Sabre and more likely to be disastrous due to the poorer training of Communist pilots as well as the characteristics of the aircraft. For these and other reasons, Yeager referred to the MiG-15 as a "quirky aircraft that killed a lot of its pilots" and a "flying booby trap."[21]

Collins relates that he spent eighteen to twenty hours studying the MiG cockpit. He was assisted by No and a translator on the wing and used ink and tape to label the Russian language instruments. The Americans encountered other difficulties. For example, the Soviet radios were incompatible with American radios, and the technicians could not come up with a quick fix. Hence, there was no aircraft-to-aircraft radio communication during these tests. Collins also experienced oxygen problems in the MiG. Boyd, as quoted by Yeager, maintains that the deprivation resulted because Collins's oxygen requirements were higher than those of Yeager, who took the fighter higher than fifty-five thousand feet. Collins writes that the MiG's oxygen system was faulty and had to be repaired, after which it worked satisfactorily for all the pilots.[22]

The tests pushed the Soviet fighter to its maximum air speed. The MiG was redlined at Mach .92, and a red warning light illuminated upon reaching that speed. Collins experienced heavy buffeting above Mach .92 and pitch-up at about Mach .95.[23] Yeager talked with Collins and proposed to climb to a maximum altitude (fifty-five thousand feet), roll inverted, and then pull through to about 45 degrees and depend on the fighter's pitch-up tendency to pull the aircraft vertical. Yeager asked Boyd to authorize a full-throttle, vertical dive from a high altitude to see exactly how fast the fighter could fly. He got Boyd's okay and flew the mission as he and Collins had discussed. The F-86 pilot flying formation with the MiG had to retard his throttle and extend his speed brakes slightly to stay with Yeager. As the MiG approached its maximum speed, it began to experience severe buffeting and at Mach .98 lost all aileron control. That is as fast as the machine would go. In the thicker air at eighteen thousand feet Yeager began to get some control and at twelve thousand began to pull out of the dive. The MiG was flying straight and level at three thousand feet.[24] The testing confirmed what the Americans already knew—the Soviet fighter had a number of superior qualities. It outpaced the F-86 in acceleration, rate of climb, and ceiling. The fighter's speed brakes were quite effective. American pilots who flew the MiG called it a "beautiful flying machine" and commented that it was light on the controls. But there were also numerous deficiencies. The airmen concluded that the MiG's field of vision was average, except to the rear where the horizontal stabilizer, mounted halfway between the top of the tail and the fuselage, made rear vision extremely limited. The MiG-15 had poor control at high speeds and no control above Mach .93. It also had a low rate of roll and poor stall characteristics. Compared to the Sabre, the MiG was poorly equipped, having an outmoded optical gunsight, no provision for a "g" suit, and inadequate cockpit heating and defrosting. The necessity to constantly adjust the defroster as the aircraft climbed kept the pilot busy. An October 1953 report concluded that, while the MiG-15 was good for anti-bomber work (its original mission), it was an inferior air-to-air fighter because of its handling problems and speed limitations. Perhaps the most important conclusion was that the flight tests confirmed wartime U.S. intelligence estimates. The North Korean defector summed it all up by comparing the F-86 to a Cadillac and MiG-15 to a Chevrolet.[25]

The MiG was later tested by the USAF at both Wright-Patterson and Eglin, and by the Navy at Patuxent River Naval Air Station. In April 1956, an RAF pilot made a hard landing that badly damaged the MiG's nose wheel. In October 1957 the fighter was given to the Air Force Museum where it is currently on display.[26]

Exploitation of F-86s

The Communists also wanted to exploit enemy aircraft. American airmen suspected the worst, reporting numerous incidents of U.S. aircraft acting in a hostile manner. In December 1951 intelligence noted the fifth incident of hostile F-80s, and three more F-80 incidents occurred in 1952, along with two involving hostile F-84s. There are no such reports in 1953, but there were four reports of hostile F-86s in 1952. There is no information from the Communist side concerning these incidents, which leads this writer to conclude that these reports were caused by either misidentification of Communist aircraft or incidents of friendly fire ("blue on blue").[27]

One reason for disbelief of Communist combat use of American aircraft is that such equipment had so much more value for intelligence purposes. Probably their greatest interest was in F-86 auxiliary equipment: the radar-ranging gunsight and the "g" suit. In one ambitious effort to capture a Sabre and pilot, the Soviets organized a special unit that arrived in China in March or April 1951 with nine (or twelve or fifteen, depending on the source) crack pilots, albeit test pilots, not combat pilots. The Russian airmen in the field were dubious about the idea and irritated by the arrogance of the test pilots. This idea from a far-removed bureaucrat failed and cost the Reds two or three aircraft before the team left empty-handed in October.[28]

More successful was Communist recovery of downed F-86s. The first was ditched on a mud flat at the mouth of the Chong-chong River on 6 October 1951. Evgeny Pepelyaev, the top Russian scorer of the Korean War with twenty-three credits, hit (from 130 meters with one 37-mm shell) the F-86A directly behind the cockpit and damaged both the engine and ejection seat, forcing 2nd Lt. Bill N. Garrett (336FS) to crash-land. Despite enemy ground fire, he was rescued by an SA-16.[29] UN airmen unsuccessfully attempted to destroy the Sabre. That night the Communists dragged the F-86 away, camouflaged it, and the next day cut off the wings for transportation. Low clouds gave the recovery operation some cover. The Reds drove their precious cargo by night, hiding in tunnels while it was daylight, and one night surviving a B-26 rocket attack. Pepelyaev and his pilots had a chance to sit in the F-86 cockpit before it was shipped to Russia and were impressed by the Sabre's excellent visibility.[30] They concluded that it had a well-laid-out cockpit, and that the F-86 was like a luxury car compared with the MiG-15, which was more like an average car (echoing the Cadillac-Chevrolet comparison). The second F-86 recovered by the Communists was the F-86E flown by World War II ace Col. Walker M. Mahurin (4FG), who was shot down by Red anti-aircraft guns on 13 May 1952.[31]

The Soviets obtained valuable information from the Sabres. Russian technicians filed their report on the first downed aircraft in late May 1952. The Soviets showed an interest in the ailerons, speed brakes, slotted flaps and leading edge slats. They noted that the Sabre was larger and heavier than the MiG, with a lower-power engine, and thus would have slightly lower top speed and markedly inferior rate of climb. The Russians considered building the F-86 in quantity in May 1952 and even put some resources into this project before thinking better of it.[32] The Soviets learned much from the first Sabre taken to Russia, including details about the control system, air conditioning system, radar gunsight, electrical system, and aluminum alloys, as well as production and assembly techniques. There is no record of the F-86 flying in Russia, and as one writer concludes, "its ultimate fate is unknown."[33] In 1993 a Russian who had worked in the MiG design bureau confirmed that an F-86 had been disassembled and copied. He went on to state that when this task was completed, the aircraft was destroyed or recycled.[34]

Captured F-86 Pilots Taken to the Soviet Union

There are some who believe that the Communists also took F-86 pilots to Russia for interrogation and did not repatriate them after the war. During the course of the Korean War, the Defense Department listed over 13,000 Americans as missing in action. In early 1954, DoD adjusted this number to just under 3,000, of whom 349 were USAF personnel.[35] However, another more recent list puts the total number of missing in action at 4,200.[36] In any event, the belief that the Soviets took a number of captured F-86 pilots to Russia persists to this day.

Understandably, the Soviets focused intelligence efforts on USAF F-86s because it was the most modern fighter in the U.S. and Western inventories. It is also possible that Stalin saw USAF POWs as potential hostages. However, the Communists returned 220 USAF crewmembers after the war's end, including 28 F-86 pilots, seemingly nullifying this speculation. In any event, the Soviets had seventy people in the field searching for downed American aircrews.[37]

Knowledgeable individuals have stated publicly that American POWs were taken to the Soviet Union and never released. As recently as 1996, two congressmen claimed that the Communists retained American POWs after the war. Representative Owen Pickett stated "the evidence that U.S. Korean War POWs were held in North Korea, China, and the former Soviet Union is irrefutable."[38] One DoD witness at the June 1996 House hearing testified that there was "significant evidence" that the Soviets took U.S. POWs to Russia.[39] An Army intelligence officer "emphatically" testified to a senate hearing that based on hundreds of intelligence reports from agents, defectors, Communist prisoners of war, civilians, and repatriated U.S. POWs, American prisoners had been taken to the Soviet Union.[40] A DoD paper written in 1993 concluded that "the Soviets transferred several hundred U.S. Korean War POWs to the USSR and did not repatriate them."[41] It went on to state "the range of eyewitness testimony as to the presence of U.S. Korean War POWs in the GULAG is so broad and convincing that we cannot dismiss it."[42] Another author writes, "the documents on American POWs from Soviet military archives, taken together with the testimony of Soviet veterans of Korea and now-declassified papers from U.S. archives, clearly point to Soviet complicity in the disappearance and probable death of dozens, if not hundreds, of those POWs who were not repatriated."[43] On the other hand, a director of POW/MIA affairs strongly held that there was not a shred of evidence to support the case of F-86 pilots being transferred to the Soviet Union.[44]

What is the evidence? One piece is the assertion that of fifty-six F-86 pilots shot down over enemy territory, only sixteen POWs or bodies were returned, while another nine (another source says eleven) were presumed to have died. The remaining cases represent the highest rate of bodies or individuals not recovered from all types of USAF aircraft lost in Korea.[45] There are also a number of witnesses who provided testimony to this position. There are reports that at least one F-86 pilot accompanied the recovered F-86 that was sent to the Mikoyan and Sukhoi design bureaus.[46] Information from nineteen human intelligence sources and at least six interviews with North Korean defectors led another DoD analyst to conclude that the North Koreans held a group of defectors as well as ten to fifteen POWs.[47] A Soviet Air Force commander claimed that he transported a group of F-86 pilots out of Korea to Siberia during the war.[48] A Czech defector stated that American prisoners from both Korea and Vietnam were exploited for technical information and medical experiments.[49] Two members of the Soviet intelligence service and a former Soviet railroad worker claimed to have observed several trainloads of American POWs being transferred from Chinese to Soviet custody and shipped to Russia between November 1951 and April 1952. A captured North Korean general revealed that the U.S. POWs had been sent to the Soviet Union.[50] But perhaps the most starling (or bizarre) story comes from a 1996 interview of a Soviet who claims to have seen a captured F-86 pilot in late spring 1953. He went on to describe the pilot in some detail and state that he later became an instructor at the Monino Air Force Academy in Moscow in the mid-1950s.[51]

Where does this leave us? There is no clear evidence, no "smoking gun," no specific document, photograph, or American POW to indicate that any American prisoner was held back after the conclusion of the war. Surely some of the support offered for this allegation can be dismissed. However, the number of such stories by a variety of witnesses does leave open the possibility that captured F-86 pilots were taken to the Soviet Union where they remained. Until western investigators have open access to Chinese and Soviet archives, this issue cannot be adequately explained.

NINE

Friendly Islands and Rescue Service

D uring the northern advance to the Yalu River in 1950, UN forces took control of numerous islands off both coasts of North Korea. A year later the Communists initiated concerted action against these positions, retaking half of them by the end of November. The Americans responded slowly to the Red offensive, deploying air and sea power and stationing a regiment of RoK marines on five of the islands in late 1951. By the end of 1952, the Air Force listed thirty-four islands under friendly control, fourteen of which it recommended for rescue purposes. At this point, the USAF had 9 officers and 150 airmen stationed on five islands off the west coast of Korea.[1] The UN used these islands as listening posts, staging areas for raids and intelligence operations, radio relay stations, direction-finding stations, navigation beacons, radar sites, and bases for air-sea rescue services.

The importance of these positions to the UN increased as the war bogged down into a stalemate. In mid-February 1952, Fifth Air Force put early warning radar into operation on Cho-do, which was 40 miles north of the 38th parallel, 125 miles behind the front, and about 5 miles from the mainland. It could detect aircraft taking off and landing at the Chinese airfields near the Yalu when the aircraft climbed to altitude, but the radar had no coverage below ten thousand feet over China. Radio intercepts assisted in this early warning duty. In May 1952, Fifth Air Force directed that a small tactical control center be added, and lightweight equipment was airlifted to the island within weeks. In short order, operators on Cho-do began vectoring Sabres against MiGs.[2]

Intelligence

One function of the islands was to serve as a listening post for radio intelligence. America reorganized its intelligence services and communications intelligence (COMINT) prior to the Korean War, just as it reconfigured its armed forces. This led to the creation in 1949 of the Central Intelligence Agency (CIA) and the Armed Forces Security Agency (AFSA). The USAF, newly created in 1947, converted what had been a portion of Army COMINT dedicated to Army Air Force's (AAF) use to the Air Force Security Service.

The reorganization, however, could not overcome serious problems. In contrast to the great code-breaking successes of World War II, when the Allies could read both German and Japanese messages, the condition of American communications intelligence during the early years of the Cold War was dismal. One significant problem was lean budgets. Another major blow fell when the Soviets, having learned through an agent inside AFSA of U.S. penetrations of their ciphers, shut out American intelligence efforts. This resulted in a virtual blackout of information just before the Korean War in what some official intelligence historians have called "perhaps the most significant intelligence loss in U.S. history."[3] Because they had limited resources and focused primarily on the Soviet Union, intelligence agencies gave little or no attention to North Korea, except in connection with the Soviets.

In any event, radio intelligence gave no hint of the 25 June 1950 invasion, a failure that was only exceeded by the failure to warn of the Chinese intervention later that year. At the beginning of the war, AFSA had 3 individuals assigned to North Korean analysis, 2 half-time cryptanalysts and 1 linguist. Staffing increased to 87 by March 1953. In contrast, AFSA had 83 analysts assigned to China duties at the outset of the war, and that number was doubled to 156 by February 1951. Operations were also hampered by shortages of equipment, much of which was outmoded; inadequate numbers of linguists; and, in the field, by difficult terrain.[4]

The USAF had only two mobile units in 1950. The one in the Far East focused on the Soviet Union rather than Asia because American intelligence believed that the Soviets were more likely than the Chinese to intervene in Korea, since the Chinese were concentrating on a planned invasion of Taiwan. Although that unit quickly switched from monitoring early warning of war to tactical support, progress was slow. It was not until mid-September 1950 that the Americans began round-the-clock surveillance of Chinese communications, and not until December that U.S. personnel began to work on breaking Chinese codes and ciphers. It took the Army's signals intelligence (SIGINT) unit until January 1951 to begin traffic analysis and until June 1951 to begin issuing daily traffic analysis reports.

The Air Force organized one SIGINT unit in late July 1950. USAF personnel in Seoul quickly made use of a South Korean COMINT unit because there were few Korean speakers in the U.S. military and even a shortage of Korean-American language dictionaries. The Americans provided the Koreans with U.S. rations, pay subsidies, and supplies—in one case medical care for a Korean officer—in exchange for Korean interception and translation work and, later, cryptologic efforts. It was not until mid-1951 that the Army Language School was able to provide Korean linguists in any number to the forces; even then, the shortage of Korean linguists continued to be a problem. The intelligence services later had similar difficulties in providing Chinese speakers, primarily because few were conversant in the Mandarin dialect used by the Chinese Communist radio operators. This situation forced the Army to employ Chinese Nationalist linguists, seventy-five of them by March 1951. Russian speakers were also in short supply.[5]

COMINT provided valuable information to the UN airmen. The operators intercepted Communist instructions to the MiG pilots and funneled that information in nearly real time to American pilots, using radar plots as a cover. The efficiency of this service improved when the USAF established a listening site on Paengnyong-do, an island behind enemy lines, in mid-1951. Its success and the Chinese shift from high frequency, longer range Morse code communications to very high frequency, shorter range voice communications led the Air Force to beef up the detachment on Paengnyong-do and establish another site on Cho-do in spring 1952.

In January 1951, the USAF used a C-47 to collect Communist radio signals on twelve missions and to drop agents behind Communist lines. In February 1953, the USAF installed COMINT equipment and one operator aboard a C-47, which flew about twenty miles behind enemy lines, serving as a radio relay aircraft. This intelligence was automatically relayed to a ground station on Cho-do and then passed on to the GCI (ground control intercept) site next door. While there is some confusion as to exactly what transpired, the aircraft apparently flew twenty-six missions by mid-March 1953. Beginning in December 1952, RB-50G aircraft equipped with electronic gear and manned by a Chinese or Russian linguist who listened for Communist ground-to-air communications were mixed in with the B-29 bomber formations. In April 1953, the USAF flew RB-50Gs over

North Korea and orbited over the Yellow Sea for five hours as they collected COMINT.[6]

Air Successes

Two incidents dramatically brought together the elements of friendly islands and radio intercepts. At 0900 on 19 June 1951, the Americans intercepted a message from Beijing to a Chinese air unit ordering prop-powered Il-10s to attack Sinmi-do, a relatively large island under UN control located about forty miles southeast of the mouth of the Yalu River. These air attacks were to support a Communist ground assault against Korean forces on the island. The message was quickly decoded, and the information rapidly passed through the Air Force chain of command. The next day, a flight of F-51s spotted and then engaged eight of the Communist bombers, destroying two and damaging three others. The battle escalated as another flight of Mustangs battled six Yak-9 fighters and downed one. In short order, MiG-15s appeared and engaged a third flight of F-51s and its F-86 cover. In the ensuing battle, four MiGs were damaged and one F-51 destroyed.[7]

Four months later, the Sabre pilots had even greater success. In late October 1951, the Communists issued orders to take over UN occupied islands close to the mouth of the Yalu. The most significant of these was Taehwa-do, an island defended by twelve hundred troops and located forty miles southeast of the mouth of the Yalu and sixty miles north of Cho-do. On the night of 5 November, the Reds attacked the adjacent island of Ka-do. To support their attack, nine twin-tail, twin-engine, prop-powered Tu-2s, escorted by sixteen prop-driven La-11 fighters covered by MiG-15s, attacked Taehwa-do early the next morning. On 14 November, the Reds used Yak fighters to strafe UN forces on Ka-do and quickly captured the island. The next day the Communists hit Taehwa-do in a daylight assault by eleven bombers and then began launching almost nightly bombing raids of both islands. The attack was devastating, killing 60 UN troops and wounding another 122. Just before midnight on 29 November, Communist forces landed on Taehwa-do; an hour and half later, six bombers attacked UN positions. On the afternoon of 30 November, the Communists launched another air assault consisting of Tu-2s, escorted by La-9s and MiG-15s, toward the island.[8] It was the same pattern that had worked before, but this time the Red airmen would meet airborne opposition.

The American airmen had prior knowledge of the attack, and on the morning of 30 November, pilots of the 4th Fighter Group were briefed that their mission was to intercept and destroy a group of Tu-2s escorted by La-9s and MiG-15s. The best pilots in the Sabre unit manned all available aircraft. Col. Ben Preston, the group commander, led the thirty-one F-86s and employed unusual tactics. Instead of climbing slowly in loose formation from their base to the Yalu River, as they normally did to save fuel, the Americans flew east of their normal route behind the North Korean mountains, staying low and maintaining radio silence to shield their approach from the Communists. Their efforts were rewarded; they achieved both surprise and success.[9]

Near the Yalu, the Sabres climbed to altitude, headed west, and took up a combat formation. They spotted the twelve Tu-2s flying at about 180 kts fifty miles from Taehwa-do closely escorted by sixteen La-9s at eight thousand feet.[10] However, the Red plan went slightly askew because the Red bombers arrived at the rendezvous five minutes early, throwing off the timing of the planned MiG cover. Preston led the charge, diving on the bomber formation with F-86s from the 334th and 336th fighter squadrons while the Sabres from the 335th remained at altitude to deal with the expected arrival of the MiGs. In short order, Preston radioed Maj. Winton Marshall, leader of the 335th Sabres on this mission, "Bones, come on down and get 'em."[11] Sabres fired, bombers burned, fighters maneuvered, and crews bailed out during the chaotic dogfight. "Everybody was going wild," one F-86 pilot observed. "Planes were just missing each other, and bullets were literally flying in all directions from both sides. The sky must have been chock-full of lead. Planes were smoking, there were splashes below, and radio fight talk was intense. It was the damnedest violent action I ever saw—kill-or-be-killed destruction."[12] Another American pilot later wrote, "There were parachutes absolutely everywhere, like a mass airdrop of the 82nd Airborne."[13] It was a slaughter: the prop-powered aircraft did not have a chance against the Sabres. According to American accounts, the remaining damaged bombers turned for home before reaching Taehwa-do, dropping their bombs short, according to Chinese accounts. Meanwhile, eighteen of the approximately fifty MiG-15s aloft during the encounter engaged the Sabres. The MiGs could not prevent the debacle and for their efforts lost one fighter to the F-86s.

Two American pilots became the fifth and sixth American aces of the war in the action that day: Maj. George Davis (334FS) claimed four aircraft, three Tu-2s and one MiG; and Maj. Winton ("Bones") Marshall (335FS), a Tu-2 and an La-9. Davis's four kills on one mission established a Korean War record.[14] Davis's accomplishment pointed out both the vulnerability of the prop-powered bombers and his excellent marksmanship: he did not exhaust his ammunition, firing only twelve thousand rounds even though he employed the older, less sophisticated Mk 18 gunsight.[15] As usual, the two sides differ over the results of the action: the Chinese admit losing four Tu-2s, two La-11s, and one MiG-15, while the USAF credited the 4th's pilots with destroying eight bombers, three prop-powered fighters, and a MiG-15. This was the highest score the USAF had racked up in the war thus far, exceeded only four times.[16] Whatever the true number of losses, this was the last daytime Communist bombing effort. The Reds planned assaults on UN airfields in South Korea on two occasions in 1952 but, fearing reprisals, did not launch them.

Although one Chinese pilot claimed to have destroyed a Sabre, none was lost on this mission.[17] The Communists did damage four F-86s in the battle and gave at least two Sabre pilots close calls. Capt. Ray Barton (334FS), flying as an element leader, made a classic gunnery pass on the Red bombers but missed his target. He then came around again, closed onto the tail of a Tu-2, fired a long burst, observed strikes over the entire aircraft, and watched the bomber explode. As he chandelled to make a third run, he looked to his rear and saw a jet following him that he assumed was his wingman, John Burke.

Barton flew through what was left of the Chinese bomber formation without scoring any hits and was headed for home when an orange fireball passed over the top of his canopy. The jet behind him was not a Sabre; it was a MiG![18] Barton turned as hard as he could, circled, and outmaneuvered his attacker, who broke off his attack. Then four MiGs, followed a bit later by two others, attacked Barton. The F-86 pilot was able to shake off his pursuers by climbing into the sun. Now at ten thousand feet he headed south and passed over Taehwa-do, where two more MiGs bounced him. Barton maneuvered desperately while radioing for help. Fortunately, George Davis heard his call and, although already short of fuel and south of Taehwa-do, flew to the rescue. Davis spotted a MiG at three thousand feet and smoked him. After seeing the MiG crash into the sea, Davis joined up with Barton and the two headed for home, Barton with one credit, and Davis, with four victories in the engagement, now an ace. The USAF awarded Davis the Silver Star for his actions.[19]

"Bones" Marshall was another Sabre pilot who almost didn't make it home. After scoring two victories, he was observing the dogfight when his wingman, John Honoker, called "break hard." Marshall lost consciousness as shells from an La-9 attacking head-on tore through the Sabre's canopy and hit the armored headrest. Honoker latched onto the Red fighter, covered it with hits, and watched it explode and fall in three sections into the sea. Mean-while, Marshall was in trouble, wounded in the head, neck, and hands, and his aircraft was damaged. Marshall's helmet was split open, forcing him to hold his oxygen mask to his face. Cold and injured, he managed to fly his Sabre back to base. But the saga was not over, for in the landing pattern he was forced to go around to allow another F-86 to land first. This was George Davis, who—landing without power—had the right-of-way over Marshall's plane, which was only damaged. Marshall landed safely, flew again, and rose to flag rank in the Air Force.[20]

Communist Air Attacks

The Communists continued to press the UN forces on the islands. In early December, UN forces evacuated two hundred partisans from Taehwa-do after the Chinese landed on the island. The Reds were well aware of the activities on Cho-do and attacked it with both artillery and aircraft. On 5 September 1952, three Communist guns on the mainland fired about 100 to 120 shells at the island, injuring six civilians but no UN personnel. One Royal navy and three U.S. Navy ships responded, as did UN aircraft.[21] Shortly after midnight on 13 October 1952, Cho-do radar observed six aircraft headed toward the island. About half an hour later a USAF crash boat spotted four aircraft orbiting north of the island at about one thousand feet. From the sound of the engines, their low air speed of 80–85 kts, whistling sounds consistent with guy wires on a biplane, and light bomb load, the USAF concluded the attackers were probably PO-2 biplanes. The Red aircraft made seven separate bomb runs to deliver fourteen bombs. Two American antiaircraft gunners were wounded and four Korean civilians were killed and five wounded in a nearby village.[22] The Communists launched a similar attack on Paengnyong-do on 12 November without any physical military effect. Two weeks later, on 26 November, Cho-do radar tracked six aircraft, which attacked in two waves of three aircraft. U.S. forces observed explosions from about four to five bombs from the first wave and six from the second, none of which caused any casualties or damage. There were further air attacks on 5 and 10 December.[23] By this time the UN had beefed up the defenses of the islands with more antiaircraft guns and some searchlights.

The airmen also attempted to intercept the raiders with night fighters. The major problem was that the fabric-covered Communist aircraft gave faint radar returns, were small, and flew slow and low. The airmen called these aircraft, "Bed Check Charlie." The Soviets had used these tactics during World War II against the Germans, who noted that the attacks "caused considerable discomfiture and not a few losses."[24] USAF F-94 night fighters established radar contacts a half dozen times, as did a Marine F4U on one occasion, but all without success. Finally, a Marine F3D Skynight downed one of the night raiders on 10 December 1952. The Communist air attacks on the islands stopped for a number of months; but then, shortly after midnight on 15 April 1953, they returned to Cho-do, killing two antiaircraft gunners and destroying one gun. On 6 May, Cho-do gunners may have destroyed an attacking aircraft, although no wreckage was found to confirm that claim. The airmen were increasingly frustrated by these attacks and tried all sorts of efforts to foil them: Marine ADs, B-26s, armed T-6s, flare-dropping transports along with the F-94s, and revised rules of engagement for antiaircraft guns. Although the USAF credited the F-94s with two kills, two were lost in the low-speed, low-altitude, night engagements.

The nighttime heckling raids extended beyond the islands and scored successes. On 17 June 1951, a Communist raider bombed the Kimpo airfield, home of the 4th Fighter Interceptor Wing, destroying one F-86 and damaging two others. Two years later the attacks were still hitting installations in South Korea. Two were notable, one that jarred the mansion of the RoK President on 15/16 June 1953 and another the next night that destroyed five million gallons of fuel at Inchon. The most successful defensive effort was turned in by Navy Lt. Guy Bordelon, borrowed from the carrier *Princeton*, who claimed five of the night raiders during June and July 1953 in his F4U and became the only American ace of the war who did not fly an F-86. In addition to the two USAF and five Navy credits, the Marines claimed four of the night raiders.[25]

Air Sea Rescue

The two islands also served as a base and position for rescue operations. Prior to World War II, the Germans pioneered in this area and the *Luftwaffe* was thus the best prepared of the warring air forces when air operations took place over water. In contrast, the British got a late start, not coordinating RAF and Royal Navy rescue operations until August 1940. In a similar manner, the AAF was late in preparing for rescue operations. In Western Europe, the

Americans initially depended on the British for rescue services and only began their own air sea rescue service through the Eighth Air Force in May 1944. British and Americans, mostly the British, rescued 36 percent of almost 4,600 Eighth Air Force airmen who were reported to have ditched or bailed out over water. A much greater percentage of AAF operations against the Japanese were over water. In the B-29 campaign, the AAF rescued 42 to 48 percent of about 1,424 men, in 129 aircraft, who went down at sea. In the entire war, approximately 5,000 AAF aircrew were rescued. In March 1946, the AAF established Air Rescue Service and the next month assigned it to Air Transport Command.[26]

When the Korean War erupted, the USAF had two rescue units stationed in the Far East, the Second Air Rescue Squadron, based on the Philippines and later at Okinawa, and the Third Air Rescue Squadron, on Japan. The USAF had organized the latter in February 1944 for operations in the Pacific theater, where it made 220 saves. Within a month, the Air Force dispatched rescue L-5 single engine liaison aircraft and H-5 helicopters to Korea and then, late in July, sent four SA-16 amphibians to the Third. In March 1951, two test YH-19s manned by Air Proving Ground Command personnel arrived in the theater. These two helicopter types and the SA-16 were the rescue workhorses of our story.

Grumman designed the twin-engine, prop-powered SA-16, the Albatross, for the Navy. It first flew in October 1947, and the manufacturer delivered 297 to the Air Force. The Albatross carried a crew of as many as seven, as well as six passengers. It could fly 3,220 statute miles and as long as twenty-three hours; fitted with Jet Assisted Takeoff (JATO) bottles and reversible propellers, it could take off and land in short distances.

The Sikorsky H-5 made its maiden flight in August 1943. Manned by a crew of two, it could lift two others in external litters. It was limited in flying performance, with a top air speed of 106 mph and designed maximum range of 360 statute miles although the USAF put its effective radius at a mere 85 miles.

Sikorsky's H-19 had a gross weight of 7,900 pounds, compared with the H-5's 4,800 pounds. First flying in November 1949, it had a three-man crew and could carry up to ten others. The H-19 had a maximum speed of 112 mph and a 360-statute mile range, although the USAF put the radius at 120 miles. In addition to its improved performance, it brought a significant innovation to rescue operations: a one-hundred-foot cable with a sling that was powered by a hydraulic motor. With it, rescues could be accomplished without setting down.[27]

During the Korean War, Air Force rescue units recovered 170 of 1,690 USAF aircrew who went down in enemy territory. Helicopters accounted for 102 men, or 60 percent, of those rescued; SA-16s, for 66, or 39 percent; and liaison aircraft, the remaining 2 men. The Air Force also rescued 84 other UN airmen, in all bringing out 996 UN servicemen from enemy territory. Because of the excellent rescue services available, the pilots' chances of rescue were good, despite the fact that they lacked survival training, if—and of course this was a big if—they could make it to the sea. For the UN had not only air, but also sea, superiority.[28]

In November 1951, the USAF ordered that three SA-16s be kept in commission at Seoul. That fall, SA-16s would orbit north of Cho-do when the UN launched air attacks against positions in northwest Korea. But the winter weather hindered the amphibious rescue aircraft (it could not operate in seas with waves greater than five feet and had problems with icing), so the Air Force began to use helicopters in December. Because the USAF did not initially consider Cho-do secure, the USAF dispatched two H-5s from Paengnyong-do to the island for daytime alerts in good weather. The USAF later established a detachment of two helicopters there in January 1952. The next month the rescue unit began to convert from the smaller, more limited H-5s to the larger H-19s. Eventually the Air Force stationed two choppers on Cho-do and a third on Paengnyong-do. The USAF also stationed a number of crash boats at these islands along with the aircraft.[29] This small force proved very effective.

Cho-do was an excellent rescue position, located halfway between the Yalu River and friendly airfields in South Korea. In many ways it served the same function for the F-86s in Korea as Iwo Jima had served for the B-29s during World War II, except that the jet fighters could not land at Cho-do. However, at least three landed on the beach at Paengnyong-do, about thirty-five miles south of Cho-do, and returned to their Korean bases after refueling.[30]

The Sabre, flying at high speed for combat purposes, had limited endurance and the American fighter pilots attempted to get every moment they could in MiG Alley. Fortunately for the pilots, the F-86 had a very good fuel counter. It was not uncommon for the Sabre pilots when returning to base to shut down their engines to conserve fuel and restart them as they neared the airfield. Dead stick (unpowered) landings were frequent; Harrison Thyng, commander of the 4th in 1951 and 1952, states that his unit averaged ten to twelve such landings a week but lost only one aircraft as a result. Two factors aided this technique. First, the F-86 was a very streamlined aircraft and could glide clean (landing gear and flaps up, speed brakes retracted) for an amazing distance, 70 nm (nautical miles) from thirty thousand feet in no-wind conditions. Usually a westerly wind, sometimes a stiff jet stream, extended that distance.[31] A number of pilots tell of running out of fuel, taxiing in after landing or shutting down after a mission with less than one hundred pounds of fuel remaining. On many occasions there was more than one fighter approaching the Korean airfield in an unpowered glide.

Some pilots, however, could not get all the way home because of lack of fuel, combat damage, or mechanical problems. During the course of the war, forty-two Sabre pilots were recovered from the sea or from behind enemy lines. SA-16s made about one third of these rescues; helicopters, most of the rest. The first of these occurred on 13 September 1951, when an SA-16 plucked 2nd Lt. Joseph Burke out of the Yellow Sea following his ejection after his engine blew up.[32] Sabre pilots had a much better chance of rescue than did other USAF airmen: in all, one out of four Sabre pilots was rescued, compared with one out of ten AF aircrew. The Sabre's higher operating altitude, coupled with the UN sea supremacy and the proximity of MiG Alley to the water, bolstered the Sabre pilot's chances of rescue. Other factors were the technology provided by the SA-16s and helicopters; bases that put the rescue aircraft within range of the downed pilots; an organization of rescue; and, perhaps most of all, rescue personnel willing to go into harm's way to truly operate in the spirit of the organization's motto: "That Others May Live."

Among the forty-two F-86 pilots rescued, sixteen had registered, or would register, victory claims. Nine had scored prior to their rescue mission (24 credits), nine scored on the day of the rescue (10.5 credits), and eight scored on succeeding missions (29 credits). Two, Frederick Blesse (334FS) and Joe McConnell (39FS), were already aces; and two more, Clifford Jolley (335FS) and Lonnie Moore (335FS), would go on to become aces. To put this into a broader perspective, the USAF lists a total of about 220 F-86s lost on both combat and non-combat missions in the Far East during the Korean War. The USAF put total Sabre pilot casualties at forty-seven killed, sixty-five missing, and six wounded.[33] The recovery of these pilots was quite an accomplishment.

It is not necessary to relate every rescue, but a few accounts are in order. Enemy fire damaged Lt. James Bonini's (16FS) Sabre on 8 August 1952. He made it to the vicinity of Cho-do and ejected. Within a minute and ten seconds, an SA-16 crew pulled him from the sea. This certainly was one of the fastest rescues on record.[34]

Joe McConnell had seven credits when he took off on 12 April 1953, leading a flight of four F-86s.[35] The Communists were up in force at that moment, and four MiGs engaged the four Sabres. McConnell chased the MiGs toward the Yalu and then maneuvered onto the tail of one and was just lining up to fire when another Communist fighter latched onto his tail. McConnell's wingman radioed "BREAK!" McConnell looked rearward, did not see the MiG that was low and behind him, and continued to pursue the MiG to his front. The Red fighter fired and hit McConnell's aircraft. The F-86 shuddered and slowed down. In McConnell's words, he looked back to see "the sky was full of MiGs." The American ace immediately executed a barrel roll, got behind his assailant, fired, and destroyed the MiG. (Prior to nailing McConnell, Semen Fedorets had scored his fifth victory, downing 1st Lt. Robert Niemann, 334FS.)[36]

McConnell's aircraft was emitting heavy smoke and, with a smashed radio and engine power at 50 to 70 percent, was in serious trouble. McConnell headed south as his number three man, 1st Lt. Harold Chitwood, notified Air Sea Rescue of the situation. He spotted a chopper heading north that turned around and paralleled the fighters' southward course. McConnell ejected and was pulled from the water in less than two minutes by an H-19 helicopter piloted by Bob Sullivan and Don Crabb. McConnell later told his sister, "I barely got wet."[37]

The Air Force released a photo to the public of an H-19 with rescue markings hovering above the water's surface with a man in a rescue hoist and a caption crediting Sullivan with McConnell's rescue. This photo was widely published, appearing within days in papers across the country. It also appeared in the USAF's official history of the Korean War with the caption "Capt. Joseph McConnell was picked up within minutes after bailing out of his damaged Sabre."[38] In fact, the helicopter that pulled the ace from the sea did not carry the rescue markings, as it was not from the rescue unit but a special operations outfit also using Cho-do as a base. This staged photo was probably a USAF attempt to celebrate the rescue abilities of the Air Force without exposing this clandestine unit.[39]

The rescue pilot, Bob Sullivan, relates that on 12 April two choppers were scrambled when they got a call that F-86s were heading south from MiG Alley with two in bad shape. One helicopter, piloted by Dick Kirkland from the rescue unit, and one from special operations flew north toward the fighters. First Lt. Norman Green (335FS) went into the sea north of the helicopters and was rescued by an SA-16 crew. Meanwhile, the F-86 pilots reported that McConnell had ejected just north of Cho-do and had a good chute. Sullivan saw McConnell's fighter go into the water about three miles west of his position and then spotted McConnell's chute just off to his right, three hundred to four hundred yards away. As he recalls, "The weather was great, the sea was fairly calm, and the rest is about a school book pick-up, maybe better!"[40] Sullivan directed the chopper's medic, Arthur Gillespie, to run out about twenty feet of cable and approached the downed pilot in a sideways, crab-like movement, so that he could keep him in sight through the side window. Gillespie quickly pulled the Sabre ace aboard the H-19. McConnell's first words to his rescuers after "thanks" were that he had a mission at 1530, and he asked Sullivan if he could make that, either a sign of bravado or his lack of concern over his recent experience. We may assume that Sullivan replied that he did not think McConnell would be back in time for that one.[41]

McConnell was back at his base that night. The next day McConnell made a low pass down the valley on Cho-do just as Sullivan was coming up it in the opposite direction. In Sullivan's words the "'86 pitched up off the valley floor, looking like it was moving at the speed of light."[42] Four days later McConnell scored his ninth victory and finished the war with sixteen credits as the top American ace of the Korean War.[43]

For all the praise the USAF Air Sea Rescue Service deserves, it was not 100 percent successful. One of its embarrassing moments was "one that got away," or perhaps more accurately, one that Air Force rescue services did not rescue. Col. Albert Schniz's story is an outstanding survival effort that reflects well on him, but not on the USAF. However, perhaps most of all, it again demonstrates the role luck and individual effort plays in human affairs.

Schniz downed four Zeroes in World War II and half of a MiG on thirty-eight missions in Korea. On 1 May 1952, the 51st Wing operations officer led a flight of F-86s into MiG Alley. Schniz's aircraft was hit in a dogfight, perhaps by friendlies, damaging the hydraulic controls and starting a fire in the tail pipe. For unexplained reasons, his attacker allowed him to slip away, but the Sabre was badly damaged and barely under control. Schniz could only adjust his altitude by changing engine power to create a porpoising action. He headed southward toward Cho-do, but knew he could not make it because he was losing altitude with each porpoising cycle. As he descended below 1,500 feet, he spied a large island below with a village at the north end and two apparently deserted reefs at the south end. He radioed his position to rescue forces and stated his intention to bail out over the south end of the island. He was told to spend the night there and wait for pickup the next day.

Schniz ejected at a low altitude (below one thousand feet) and barely survived. Although he had not had any escape, evasion, or survival training, the colonel had seen an escape and evasion training film only a week before and prepared to put what he had seen into practice. He hit the water about one hundred feet offshore, between the two reefs. After inflating his life preserver, the pilot attempted to apply a technique shown in the movie: using the partially inflated chute as a parasail to get him to dry land. This attempt almost killed him. Schniz got ensnarled in the parachute risers and the chute collapsed and began to sink, threatening to take him down with it. After a number of dunkings, he was able to inflate his one-man dinghy and get free of the chute. (He was very lucky not to have drowned, and to have gotten rid of the chute for, unlike other pilots, he did not carry a knife.) After a number of attempts, Schniz made it into the raft. He tried to use his survival radio, but it was inoperative. He then attempted to make it to shore, but he could not find any paddles, and his efforts to use his hands to propel the raft proved futile. The tide carried him out to sea. The exhausted pilot fell asleep and awoke seven hours later to the sound of breakers; the tide was now moving him shoreward. At this point, a low-flying USAF B-26 flew overhead, and Schniz attempted to light one of his flares, but it fizzled out. It took him five more hours to reach shore.

Schniz now began the land phase of his survival effort. A journalist who wrote of it was not too far afield when he titled his story, "Robinson Crusoe of MiG Alley." Although the downed pilot lacked matches, he did have a Zippo lighter that worked, allowing him to start a fire and dry his clothes. Pushing inland, Schniz found a small settlement of four houses in a clearing. After observing the huts for a time and circling them to ensure they were uninhabited, he entered and found them filthy and littered with debris, suggesting that UN troops had been there weeks earlier. Schniz also discovered a stream that provided water, which the pilot boiled before drinking. Scavaging around the area, he found a few ears of unharvested corn, a patch of dandelion greens, and a few spring onions. These provided his first meal in twenty-four hours.

The next day he pushed toward the village and, after observing it for three hours, found that it, too, was deserted. The next night, hearing a B-26 fly over the hut where he slept, Schniz fired his second and last flare, but the aircraft's crew apparently did not see it. The next day he constructed an "SOS" signal in a clearing, the first of a number of signals he built to attract the attention of UN airmen. That night, when another aircraft flew over, he lit the signal; it fizzled out. Schniz continued to explore and found some tools and a bag of dried beans. By this time, he was losing both weight and strength. After about two weeks, Schniz decided to move into the village where he found twenty-five bags of rice, a fresh-water well, and two drums of fuel. The next day he built a signal fire fueled by the diesel oil, which attracted a F-51. He waved wildly, but apparently the pilot mistook the bedraggled aviator for a Korean. On another occasion, Schniz spotted a junk sailing just off the beach, yelled at the one man aboard, and ran toward him waving his arms. The boat turned around and sailed off. He built more signals, this time "MAYDAY," the international distress signal, and signal fires. Although aircraft flew over the island, rescue did not follow. Schniz finally built a signal consisting of three rows with the letters "I M" "U S A F" "P" which he meant to signal, "I am a USAF pilot."

At this point, he almost made a fatal mistake. Schniz had found some trip flares; when a B-26 flew over the island, he attempted to fire the flares, which failed to ignite. As Schniz picked one up, it exploded in his face, burning, blinding, and deafening him. Fortunately, he recovered both his sight and hearing. Using boiling water, he sterilized some needles he had found and took shrapnel out of his injured hands.

After this scrape with disaster, events took a dramatic turn on the night of 9 June 1952. Around 0230 he was jarred awake by a bright light in his eyes. Someone grabbed him and he heard voices speaking in Korean. After one of his visitors saw his colonel's eagles he heard in broken English "American. American colonel." Schniz responded, "I surrender. I surrender." But the Koreans patted him on the back and shouted "OK, OK." They were friendly Korean partisans, sent onto Taehwa-do by Lt. James Mapp after he saw an F-51 go down nearby. A secondary account provides more detail but not necessarily more accuracy. It claims that a routine sea patrol saw Schniz's fire and investigated. It goes on to state that the downed pilot had reported his position in error, and thus the search for him was misdirected. Further, the rescue people had seen the activity on the island but concluded that since no airmen were reported down in that area, it was a Communist attempt to ambush a rescue effort. The Americans put together and launched a commando team to check the island out just as Schniz was found. In any event, after thirty-seven days, the F-86 pilot was back in friendly hands.[44]

An L-5 liaison aircraft brought Schniz back to the 51st's base at K-13, happy, rather thin, and bug bitten. One observer noted that "he looks and acts a little strange, as might be expected after what he has gone through, and still seems to be in a state of semi-shock."[45] The next night, he attended a drunken party to celebrate his safe return and the departure of Gabreski.

After talking to a number of individual officers about his ordeal, he addressed the entire group of about 150 officers for about an hour and a half. He ended by relating how, on more than one occasion, he was saved by breaks that he attributed to God. So this epic survival story ended successfully, marred by numerous mistakes and errors by the pilot and the USAF, but certainly a testament to Schniz's determination and luck.[46]

Not all of the F-86 experiences ended successfully. On 11 March 1952, MiGs damaged 1st Lt. John Arnold's (16FS) Sabre. Arnold headed for Cho-do but flamed out en route due to a lack of fuel. He attempted to make a dead-stick landing on a short emergency strip on the island but overshot, crashed, and died. Apparently, he did not bailout over the island because he could not swim. Arnold was one of at least four Sabre pilots killed attempting to reach Cho-do.[47]

Other failed rescues demand attention. On 3 February 1952, enemy fire damaged 1st Lt. Charles Spath's (334FS) F-86. Spath made a successful bailout and radioed that he had broken his leg and was unable to walk. A nearby force of guerrillas heard the transmission and was able to move the downed aviator before the Communists arrived. Fifth Air Force intelligence personnel planned to pick up the Sabre pilot with a rescue H-19 helicopter. It took several weeks to plan the operation due to the danger presented by the Reds, the distant location, and high altitude of the area.

Capt. Gail Poulton was assigned the mission and noted a number of inconsistencies in the situation that raised his concern that the mission had been compromised. On 22 May 1952, Poulton approached the pickup point and talked with Spath. When asked how many people were with him, Spath answered that he did not know. This increased Poulton's suspicions, and he then asked several more questions that Spath answered with ambiguous replies. At this point, Poulton laid out the situation: "We are here to pick you up, if everything down there is OK. You are giving me uncooperative, and unclear answers, . . . I have leveled off and discontinued my approach . . . and we'll abort this rescue attempt if you don't answer my questions fully . . . in the next 15 seconds." Spath responded "you can chalk me off for saying this, but get the hell out of here; it's a trap." Spath died in captivity a few weeks later.

On 27 March 1953, another H-19 attempted a pickup of a downed F-86 pilot, most likely squadron leader Graham Hulse, an RAF exchange pilot who was believed to be either evading capture or with friendly guerrillas. Hulse, who already had 1.5 credits, shared another MiG with his wingman when he was downed on 13 March 1953. After damaging a MiG, Hulse overshot his target, who proceeded to shoot off Hulse's wing. The location was

only twenty-six miles from Antung, China, one of the deepest helicopter penetrations of Red territory during the war. Escorted by a rescue SA-16, a special
operations chopper that was piloted by Capt. Frank Westerman and Lt.
Robert Sullivan did not find the pilot but did encounter a number of well-
armed hostiles in the designated area.[48] This probably was a Communist trap
because the Communists used downed American airmen to lure in and capture rescue helicopters, as they apparently did to one or two navy choppers on
2 and 8 February 1952. Interrogations of Communist prisoners in the first
half of 1952 revealed that the Reds trained fourteen men to lure UN helicopters with cloth and hand signals.[49]

The islands clearly were an asset to UN forces and the F-86 pilots in particular. Cho-do and Paengnyong-do provided radar and radio intercept coverage that aided the airmen in the air battle. Most of all, these islands were
very valuable in getting F-86 pilots home, either directly through radar services and radio relays or indirectly by rescue operations.

The Sabre started out as a straight-winged aircraft as this North American model illustrates. *Boeing Company Archives*

North American trucked the XP-86 from Los Angeles to Muroc Field. It arrived for its flight tests on 10 September and made its maiden, 50-minute flight on 1 October 1947. *Boeing Company Archives*

George Welch (on left) was the chief test pilot associated with the F-86; Francis Gabreski (on right) commanded the 51st Fighter Group and downed 6.5 MiGs in Korea. Welch had 16 credits and Gabreski 28 in World War II. They both were at Pearl Harbor on 7 December 1941, where Welch downed 4 Japanese aircraft. *Boeing Company Archives*

Aircraft number 597 was the first of three experimental XF-86s built and tested by North American. They flew it for 98 hours before turning it over to the Air Force in December 1948. Note the wing slats and the lack of armament. *Boeing Company Archives*

The Air Force combat tested 20-mm cannon on the F-86 in a project codenamed GunVal. While the tests went well in the United States, firing the guns at high altitude in combat over Korea caused the engine to stall, resulting in the loss of two aircraft. *Boeing Company Archives*

North American tested aerial refueling with a hose system and, as shown here, a flying boom from a KB 29. *Boeing Company Archives*

The USAF used both aircraft carriers and merchant ships to transport Sabres to Japan. *HRA*

More Sabres were lost to accidents than to MiGs. Capt. Clifford Thompson crashed on 7 September 1951 after his engine failed as he attempted a go-around. He suffered minor injuries; the Sabre was wrecked. *HRA*

51st Fighter Group F-86 taking off in June 1953. *HRA*

The checkerboard tail pattern indicates aircraft of the 51st Fighter Group in this photo from October 1952. *NARA*

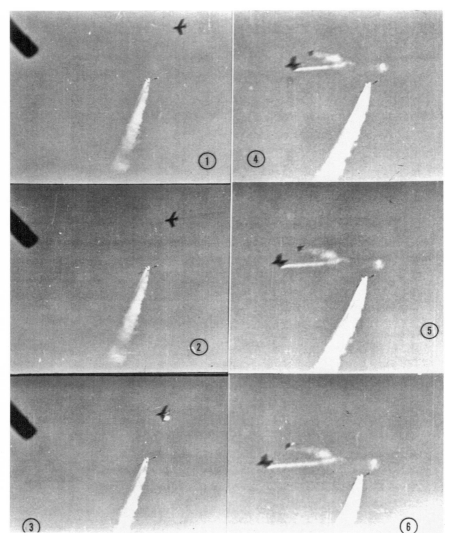

After damaging a MiG, the Sabre overshot his smoking victim. The MiG then fired on the F-86 and scored a hit that blew off the Sabre's wing (frames 4 through 6). The wingman, whose gun camera took these pictures, then dispatched the Communist fighter. *NARA*

Maj. Gen. Albert Boyd (on right), commander of Wright Air Development Center, was one of five USAF pilots who flew the defecting MiG-15 during the initial American tests over Okinawa. Note the MiG's USAF markings, wing fence, and high horizontal stabilizer. *USAF*

MiG taking off with an F-86 chase aircraft in background. The USAF ran extensive tests on the defecting North Korean MiG-15. *HRA*

The photo shows B-26s flying over Cho-do toward North Korea (seen in the background). This island, well behind Communist lines and just off the coast of North Korea, provided intelligence and rescue services and served as a base for guerrilla and agent activities. *HRA*

Five F-86As of the 4th Fighter Group in mid-1951. Note the extended wing slats. *HRA*

Capt. Dolph Overton set a record by downing five MiGs in four days. But when the ace admitted crossing the Yalu to accomplish this feat, he was sent back to the States under a dark cloud. *HRA*

Capt. Joseph McConnell was the leading American ace of the war, with sixteen credits. Midway in his tour, he survived a bailout into the Yellow Sea. *USAF*

Capt. Joseph McConnell, America's top ace of the Korean War, looks on as President Dwight Eisenhower shakes hands with Capt. Manuel Fernandez, the number three ace. *National Museum of the USAF*

Maj. James Jabara (on left) had 6 credits and was flying his second tour when Capt. Manuel Fernandez (on right) downed his fifth and sixth MiG on 18 February 1953. Jabara ran his score up to 15, the second highest, and Fernandez to 14.5, the third highest. *NARA*

Clockwise from lower left are some of the aces of the 4th Fighter Group: Maj. Winton Marshall (6.5 credits), Col. Benjamin Preston (group commander, 4 credits), Maj. George Davis (14 credits), Maj. Richard Creighton (5 credits), Col. Harrison Thyng (5 credits), and Capt. Kenneth Chandler (1 credit). Davis, who was killed in action, had downed seven Japanese aircraft; Thyng, five aircraft; and Creighton, two German aircraft in World War II. *HRA*

These six 335th Squadron (4FG) pilots scored at least one victory during August 1952. Standing from left to right: Maj. Edward Ballinger (1 credit), Maj. Frederick Bleese (10 total credits), Maj. Richard Ayersman (2 credits), and Capt. Leonard Lilley (7 credits). Kneeling left to right: Lt. Charles Cleveland (4 credits), Lt. Gene Rogge (1 credit). *HRA*

Five of the eleven American aces with 10 or more victories. From left to right: Capt. Lonnie Moore (11 credits), Col. Vermont Garrison (10 credits), Col. James Johnson (10 credits), Capt. Ralph Parr (10 credits), and Maj. James Jabara (15 credits). Jabara was the first ace of the war and ended the conflict as the second highest scoring American ace. Parr downed the last Communist aircraft in the war. *NARA*

This 4th Fighter Group F-86E sustained battle damage on 24 June 1952 and was written off. *HRA*

Maj. John Bolt was the only non-USAF jet ace of the War. The Marine claimed six Japanese aircraft in World War II and six Communist jets in the Korean War. *Department of Defense*

Lt. Simpson Evans (on left) was one of the few naval aviators who flew F-86s in Korea. The USAF credited him with one MiG destroyed. Air Force Lt. Col. Bruce Hinton (center) scored the first Sabre victory. He went on to claim one more. Lt. Paul Bryce is on the right. *NARA*

Maj. John Glenn, shown here after his first victory, was another Marine who flew F-86s in Korea. He claimed three MiGs over a ten-day period in July 1953 and probably would have been an ace had the war not ended first. *USMC*

Maj. Thomas Sellers was a Marine exchange pilot who flew with the 4th Fighter Group. Just days before the war ended, he downed two MiGs, but in turn was shot down and killed. *Sharon Sellers McDonald*

The USAF credited Maj. Felix Asla with four MiGs destroyed before he was killed in combat. *HRA*

Nine of the twenty-five pilots who were aces at the time attended a conference in Washington in early 1953. Seated on floor, left to right: Col. Francis Gabreski (6.5 credits), Lt. Iven Kincheloe (5 credits), Maj. William Wescott (5 credits), Lt. James Kasler (6 credits), Maj. William Whisner (5.5 credits). Second row left to right: Lt. Col. John England, Capt. Robert Latshaw (5 credits), Capt. Ralph Gibson (5 credits), Gen. Nathan Twining (Vice Chief of Staff), Secretary of the Air Force Harold Talbott, Gen. Hoyt Vandenberg (Chief of Staff), Capt. Frederick Blesse (10 credits), Col. John Meyer (2 credits), Col. Harrison Thyng (5 credits). Standing left to right: Col. Donald Rodawald and Col. Clay Tice. *NARA*

Lt. Dayton Ragland was one of the few African-American pilots who flew F-86s in combat in Korea. He was the only black USAF pilot to claim a victory. He survived Korean captivity but was killed in action in Vietnam. *HRA*

Lt. Col. Glenn Eagleston's Sabre was badly damaged in a dogfight in June 1951. The port guns absorbed the impact of one of three cannon hits and protected the pilot. *HRA*

F-86F in flight. *USAF*

The F-86D's prominent nose housed a radar antenna that gave it a distinctive appearance. Instead of guns, it was armed with twenty-four 2.75-inch unguided rockets housed in a retractable tray. *U.S. Naval Institute Photo Archive*

More FJ-3 s were built than any other of the naval versions, 47 percent of the 1,148 Furies manufactured. It served with both the Navy and Marine Corps, operating from both land and carrier bases. Note the refueling probe near the right wing tip. *Boeing Company Archives*

TEN

Sensitive and Controversial Matters

D espite the passage of a half century, a number of issues concerning the air war over MiG Alley remain sensitive or in dispute. We have adequate material from the UN point of view on most of these; however, we lack detailed materials from the Communist side. The implosion of the Soviet Union did not bring forth the hoped-for access to Communist documents; thus far, much of the material that has emerged from the Communist side obscures rather than answers questions.

Friendly Fire

One of the dark and unspoken elements of combat is that of fratricide, or "friendly fire." Only in the past two or three decades has the subject come into the light, not only because of the passage of time but also because a significant number of allied casualties were sustained in this manner in the first Gulf War. It was, and is, a sensitive issue.

During the Korean War, there were a number of "friendly fire" incidents, and unlike in the first Gulf War, a number of these were air-to-air examples.[1] At first glance, this seems improbable. When the two contesting fighters are parked next to one another, they are readily identifiable. The MiG is smaller with a wing mounted midway on its stubby fuselage and the horizontal tail midway on its vertical tail. In contrast, the Sabre is larger and sleeker with a low mounted wing and tail. But the two fighters did not engage in combat parked next to one another. Both employed nose intakes and swept wings and tails and, at a distance and at high speeds and high altitudes, the two were remarkably similar in appearance. In addition, the high stress and high "g" loads that the pilots were under made misidentification understandable. As one Sabre pilot wrote in his diary, "It's an easy mistake to [misidentify], since the F-86 and the MiG-15 look so damned much alike. You have to get up pretty close before you can distinguish the obvious differences."[2]

Psychological factors help explain some of the instances of "friendly fire." Clearly some American pilots thirsted for a MiG kill. Terms like "MiG Fever" or "MiG Madness" describe the attitude of some F-86 pilots. Sometimes the pilots, in the heat of the moment, saw what they wanted to see: an enemy aircraft ripe for the picking. Because the Sabre lacked airborne radar, the pilots had to use eyesight and recognition skills to spot and then identify both friend and foe, just as their predecessors did in World Wars I and II.[3] It is little wonder, then, that there were cases of mistaken identity.

A number of F-86 pilots report initiating attacks on other F-86s. One way that Bruno Giordano (334FS) identified MiGs was by the distinctive spaced puffs from their three slow-firing cannons, unlike the steady stream of smoke from the Sabre's much faster firing six .50s. Near the end of the war, Giordano was leading a flight of four fighters on a clear day when he spotted a dogfight ahead and below him. After dropping his tanks, he zeroed in on a swept-wing fighter that was firing with "very distinctive intermittent 'puffs.'" Giordano closed and was about to fire when he noted the yellow identification stripes on the wings, a Wing Sabre! He later learned that this was a test (GunVal) Sabre armed with four 20 mm cannon.[4]

Some also tell of being fired on by friends, and a few admit to firing on other F-86s. Hal Fischer (39FS) writes that his group commander "had a visual problem and a great desire for shooting down MiGs; [therefore] he was dangerous to have anywhere in the six o'clock position."[5] One day, the eager colonel spotted two jets heading south across the Yalu and swung in to attack. He fired on Lt. Sam Darby and his wingman, despite Darby's calls over the radio. Fortunately, the lieutenant outturned the colonel. On the ground, Darby confronted his attacker, who profusely apologized. The colonel's gun camera film was immediately destroyed. This was not the only such incident.[6] Yet, there are no reports of .50-caliber machine gun damage on returning Sabres, and "friendly fire" was not mentioned in the official records.[7]

Despite this lack of official recognition, Sabres were indeed downed by "friendly fire." The exact numbers will never be known because some pilots honestly believed their kills were MiGs and reported them as such. Other incidents were concealed. On 22 June 1951, a senior officer from 4th Group headquarters shot down 1st Lt. Howard Miller (336FS). The shooter's gun camera film clearly showed the F-86's identification stripes. The shooter was immediately transferred out of the unit.[8] On 2 April 1952, 1st Lt. Joe Cannon (25FS) was shot down by another F-86. The unlucky American pilot was rescued south of Cho-do by a helicopter.[9] Col. Al Schniz (51FGp) was flying his thirty-eighth mission on 1 May 1952 when he was downed, probably by a fellow F-86 pilot.[10]

Flight Officer Andy MacKenzie (RCAF) was posted to the 51st Group as an exchange pilot. In World War II, he had downed 8.5 *Luftwaffe* aircraft and been shot down twice by flak, once by American gunners. On 5 December 1952, he was flying his fifth Sabre mission as a wingman when the formation spotted contrails and then two MiGs flying underneath the F-86s. The Canadian decided to pounce on the MiGs; as he did, he tried to radio his decision to his leader, but radio interference intervened. Thus, MacKenzie became separated from his formation, and as he dove through the remaining American formation, he was fired upon; in his words "all hell broke loose." The machine gun bullets hit the canopy, and tore up the instrument panel, shredding pieces of the right wing as well as the fuselage and knocking out the hydraulic system. MacKenzie ejected, was captured, and survived his prison ordeal.[11]

In early 1953, a senior officer on the 4th Group staff shot down and killed an F-86 pilot, probably the same incident Robert Windoffer (4FGp) describes.[12] Windoffer was leading a flight of four on 26 January 1953 when he engaged four MiGs. As he got behind the last of these, he observed gunfire passing over his canopy. He called a left break and pulled 6 or 7 "g"s. Windoffer rolled out of the break, but his wingman, 2nd Lt. Bill Stauffer, did not and had two F-86s in pursuit. Windoffer radioed for the Sabres to break off their attack. He also called to Stauffer several times to bail out before he hit the ground. The shooter's gun camera film clearly captured the incident; he was sent home.[13]

The most famous, or infamous, example of "friendly fire" involved James Jabara (334FS), who ended the war as the USAF's second leading ace. He flew two tours and was an aggressive pilot. As one fellow pilot described him, "Jabara was an excitable street fighter who would fearlessly wade into a fray."[14] He was eager to run up his score and known not to see too well, and thus wanted wingmen with sharp eyes, who could stick with him through tight maneuvers. First Lt. Richard Frailey fit the bill and had flown on Jabara's wing.

Ironically, Frailey was flying Jabara's aircraft as the number four man in another formation on 15 June 1953 on his sixty-fifth combat mission. Frailey's formation saw another flight of F-86s and turned toward them. Led by Jabara, that flight mistook Frailey's formation, which was crossing the Yalu in a southerly direction, for MiGs and attacked. Jabara's gun camera film showed him opening fire at three thousand feet and firing nine bursts, with the last three hitting the Sabre, despite Frailey's radio call, according to one source: "Jabara you're shooting at me." Jabara's bullets hit the left wing, canopy, instrument panel, and engine. Recovering from a dive, with a smoking engine only putting out 78 percent power, Frailey got the fatally damaged F-86 over the Yellow Sea before he was forced to eject. He had difficulty getting out of the seat and was just able to deploy the parachute before his feet hit the water. He then got tangled up in parachute and shroud lines. Although his life preserver wouldn't keep him afloat because a .50-caliber bullet that passed between his arm and chest had penetrated it, he was able to get into his one-man life raft. Frailey then saw a USAF SA-16 amphibian taxiing toward him. Despite fire from Communist shore artillery, the rescue team got him aboard the two-engine aircraft and lifted off quickly using rocket assist.

Jabara was apologetic and contrite for the rest of his tour. According to this same account, Frailey flew nine more combat missions and downed one more MiG. Another pilot states that the USAF attempted to keep the story secret and shipped home Frailey, not the shooter.[15]

As might be expected, the Communists also had "friendly fire" problems. Part of the difficulty came from a lack of coordination between Soviet, Chinese, and North Korean units. Cecil Foster noted a MiG firing on another in December 1952. Walker "Bud" Mahurin writes that, according to U.S. radar operators, MiGs downed three of their comrades in another incident. As related elsewhere, one U.S. claim involved one MiG destroying another.[16]

Reluctant Warriors

Some would also rather forget the existence of F-86 pilots who were reluctant to fight. Some of these were recalled pilots who now were older, married, and perhaps wiser than they were when they won their wings and fought as, or thought of themselves as, eager fighter pilots in World War II. Others were brand new pilots who found the reality of aerial combat less appealing than the anticipation. Some of these men, known as "nervous Nellies," would fly north of the battle line to get mission credit and then abort the mission. Others got into the battle area but then avoided combat. Even more seriously, at least two downed Sabre pilots note that they were shot down because their wingmen abandoned them in the midst of action.[17]

Some reserve majors and lieutenant colonels who had no previous fighter experience but who were assigned to the fighters were a problem; Francis Gabreski (51st wing commander) asserts that this was "a very serious problem." Gabby did not pull any punches, writing that, "In many instances senior officers made very poor wingmen; they had no desire to be fighter pilots, showed no enthusiasm for their work, and a few generated a fear of combat to the point that they were dangerous as a member of the combat team, and certainly they could never act as an example or an inspiration to the young 2nd Lieutenants."[18] Bud Mahurin writes that, while 18 percent of pilots could be depended on to mix it up with the enemy, 70 percent would fly into the combat zone, but not see the enemy or fire a shot. The remaining 12 percent "would inevitably develop some sort of mechanical, mental, or physical difficulty sufficient to cause them to turn back home." While these numbers are certainly arguable, and the implied criticism of the 70 percent seems harsh, if not unfair, some pilots did not live up to expectations of fighter pilots. As one pilot who flew 95 missions and earned 1.5 victory credits wrote, "The fact I did not make ace was some what alleviated by the fact that I did walk away unscratched. At least I had put myself in harm's way, and I didn't disgrace myself. I was a fighter pilot."[19]

Numbers

According to the common view of the war over MiG Alley, vast swarms of MiGs battled far fewer numbers of Sabres. This, of course, makes the American victory in the air superiority battle and the high American victory-to-loss ratio in air-to-air combat that much more amazing. During the first year of that battle from December 1950 until December 1951, the USAF fielded one wing of F-86s, the 4th, with a strength in the theater averaging less than fifty fighters. Then in December 1951 the 51st Fighter Interceptor Wing transitioned from F-80s to F-86s and joined the air superiority battle. The two units operated an average of 127 to 165 F-86s throughout 1952. In early 1953 two more units, the 8th and 18th Fighter Bomber Wings, transitioned to Sabres, albeit with fighter-bomber versions having the primary role of ground support. The numbers in the four wings gradually increased from an average of 163 early in the year to a peak of 297 in July 1953.[20]

American intelligence put the average number of Communist jets in Manchuria in July 1951 at 410, rising to 640 by March 1952. The airmen believed these numbers continued to increase to 830 in January 1953 and 985 by June 1953.[21] Unless these intelligence figures are off, or there were major differences in the readiness rates or rate of sorties per aircraft per day of the two opposing air forces, the Americans were fighting at a numerical disadvantage of perhaps as high as 8:1 in 1951 and over 3:1 at the war's end. This disparity in numbers seems to bear out the conventional wisdom that the Communists had overwhelming numerical superiority.

That being said, a better gauge of the respective numbers is the number of sorties each air force generated. The F-86s flew almost 85,000 combat sorties in the war. The bulk of these were in the air-superiority role: 68,000 were characterized as "counter air-offensive" and another 5,000 as "counter air-defensive."[22] In comparison, information from the Communists indicates that they flew 86,000 to 90,000 sorties, all but 3,000 during the day, hardly overwhelming numbers.[23] More to the point, the two forces did not always meet. For example, Sabre pilots observed MiGs on 60 percent of the days after 1 July 1951. During this time period, the American pilots flew 69,000 sorties and spotted 42,000 MiGs. Of course, not all these sightings resulted in combat. The Sabres only engaged 16,000 of these MiGs in about 12,000 F-86 sorties and claimed 736 destroyed. Therefore, based on the best information we have at the present, primarily American, the combat ratio—that is, the numbers actually engaged—was about 4 MiGs to 3 Sabres.[24]

Crossing the Yalu

One of the most controversial aspects of the Korean War was the Chinese sanctuary: American fighters were forbidden to attack the enemy over China. Fighting for less than total victory with less than full intensity was foreign to Americans. It irritated American military and civilians alike and made this war frustrating and, to some degree, unpopular. The American penchant was to fight to win or not fight at all, an issue that would reemerge during the Vietnam War. This policy was particularly difficult for a nation that had just fought a successful total war and to those men who either fought in that war or were raised in that era.

There were good reasons for the policy. American decision makers believed that Europe was more important to U.S. national interest than was the Far East. Some thought that the Korean War was a diversion, a clever Communist feint to divert attention from Europe, to suck in and tie down U.S. and western military forces in a land war against endless masses of Asians, allowing an easy Communist takeover of Western Europe. Our allies in Western Europe clearly felt this way. While a quick, victorious war against a minor power such as North Korea was understandable, acceptable, and worthwhile, a long intense conflict in Asia with a major power was not. To engage the most populous nation in the world backed by the number two world power on the ground in far-off northeast Asia seemed, at best, questionable.

To the men flying and fighting under these circumstances, it was a matter of life or death. We have known for some time that individuals crossed the border; but we didn't know that so many Sabre pilots did so—and that leaders at the group, wing, and air force level knew of this, did nothing about it, and even encouraged it. How did this come to pass?

Aside from a few inadvertent violations of Chinese and Russian territory, the issue of sanctuary did not become a problem until Chinese troops intervened in the war on 25 October 1950. A week later, the MiG-15s first engaged USAF F-51s. They would climb to altitude over China and then swoop down on UN aircraft, or they would make hit and run attacks and gain shelter in Communist territory. The introduction of a superior aircraft operating from protected bases presented a new problem to the airmen. The decision makers did not know how far the Reds were willing to go with their intervention and feared that they would attack the vulnerable UN air bases and possibly nullify the one clear and vital UN advantage, air power. Because some believed that Chinese intervention might be the beginning of an attack on Europe, the Joint Chiefs of Staff (JCS) placed U.S. forces worldwide on alert. The 6 December message stated: "The JCS considers that the current situation in Korea has greatly increased the possibility of general war."[25]

Hot Pursuit

The airmen quickly responded to the MiG challenge. The day after the first Soviet jet fighter appeared in action, Gen. Earle Partridge, commander of Fifth Air Force, sent his superior, Gen. George Stratemeyer, commander of Far East Air Forces, a message that read, "Request clearance for our fighters to pursue enemy aircraft across North Korean border to determine location of bases and to destroy such aircraft."[26] Stratemeyer immediately requested that the overall commander, Gen. Douglas MacArthur, grant authorization "for UN aircraft to pursue enemy aircraft across the NK border to destroy them in the air or on the ground."[27] That same day (3 November 1950), Stratemeyer discussed the matter with MacArthur, and the five star general told the airman that he would not act on the request until he had more information that the Chinese were actually engaged in strength against the UN forces. According to Stratemeyer, MacArthur said, "I want to muddle over this a bit longer."[28]

In short order, MacArthur agreed with his subordinates on the subject and pressed the JCS on the problem on 7 November. The joint chiefs, the State Department, and the president also favored a policy of "hot pursuit." The theory of pursuing a malefactor wherever the chase might lead was not a new concept to western nations. The JCS apparently intended to allow pursuit a short distance into China, six to eight miles according to one source, and two to three minutes according to another.[29] At this point, Secretary of Defense George Marshall, asked Secretary of State Dean Acheson, to inform American allies that the United States was contemplating hot pursuit. Instead, Acheson instructed American diplomats to obtain the views of the allies on the subject. It is not clear whether this significant change was a result of a miscommunication between the two departments, Acheson's interpretation of the request, or a skillful ploy by someone in the State Department to derail the policy. The diplomats contacted six of the allies, who gave a "strongly negative response" because they believed that such a policy was unwise, "dangerous and not desirable."[30] As a result, the United States never adopted a policy of hot pursuit; the official policy was to respect the borders of both China and the Soviet Union.

In practice, the airmen believed, or certainly acted, as if a policy of hot pursuit was in force. There was, however, some difference of opinion as to exactly when this policy was in effect, and a belief that the policy varied over time.[31] As might be expected, the perceived policy of hot pursuit was stretched to its limits. It was a small step between hot pursuit and wholesale violation of the Chinese–North Korean border.

Crossing the Yalu, Seeking MiGs

UN aircraft flew numerous missions into China and the Soviet Union during the Korean War, some authorized at a high level, others authorized or condoned by USAF officials at a lower level in the theater, and some clearly unauthorized. In the first category were a number of reconnaissance missions flown by RB-45s, RF-80s, and RF-86s to gather photographic intelligence over China and Russia. These began almost immediately, with an RF-80 overflying Vladivostok during the first weeks of the war.[32] The primary interest, however, was the MiG airfields in China, which, at least during the last year of the war, were observed on a weekly basis. F-86s escorted some of these flights. According to one reconnaissance pilot, "invariably" MiGs would jump the American formation. On one such mission in May 1953 near Mukden, Mele Vojvodich, a reconnaissance pilot, flew wing as James Jabara downed two MiGs.[33] We presently have only sketchy information on these overflights. The project was not declassified until almost fifty years after the event, and because of its very high classification, few documents have survived. Nevertheless, indications are that scores of these flights took place during the war.[34]

There may have been a few other missions on which the fighters were authorized to cross the river. Bruce Hinton recalls an escort mission around June 1951 in which B-29s were to bomb Yalu bridges at Antung. Hinton was briefed to take four Sabres north of the river and set up a patrol line, not to initiate a fight but only to respond to a MiG attack. As he recalls, "There I was with four F-86s in the actual midst of MiGs all around us, many of them descending into the pattern in the Antung area, while others were climbing out from takeoff, and all of them flying by with no regard for our obvious USAF markings. Needless to say, not one made a hostile movement, or I am absolutely sure all of us would have made ace on that mission."[35] Dolph Overton tells of a similar mission when the Sabre pilots were briefed to cross the Yalu and circle the airfields and attack any MiGs that took off. Much to the chagrin of the Americans, not one took off.[36] Another mission that apparently authorized F-86 flights into China was to provide fighter cover for an F-84 strike on the Suiho dams. The Sabre pilots were briefed to enter China thirty minutes before the fighter-bombers, fly low and fast, and discourage the enemy fighters. This they did much too well because, much to their disappointment, they encountered no MiGs.[37]

The bulk of the flights into China, however, fell into a black area: clearly unauthorized. Despite the official policy, individuals and small groups of pilots took it upon themselves to cross the border. Why? To paraphrase the famous 1950s bank robber Willie Sutton, that's where the MiGs were. And therein lay the fame, glory, and the essence of being a hot fighter pilot: killing MiGs.

For all their aggressiveness, one thing the U.S. pilots would not do was strafe the MiGs on the ground north of the Yalu. Perhaps the courts-martial of the two unlucky F-80 pilots who got lost and mistakenly shot up a Soviet airfield in 1950 was the reason. In any event, MiGs on the ground were off limits and were not attacked—most of the time. Bud Mahurin recalls that he was intrigued to read a 51st Fighter Interceptor Wing mission summary that claimed thirty-seven aircraft destroyed on the ground since there were no flyable Communist aircraft on the ground in North Korea. When the 4th Group intelligence officer couldn't find the airfield mentioned in the report, Mahurin attempted to talk to the 51st's wing commander about this claim, but Francis Gabreski was reluctant to explain it and would say only that the report was accurate. A few days later the claim was deleted. Mahurin later learned that the 51st had mistakenly beaten up a Chinese airfield twenty miles north of the Yalu and, to cover their incursion, had made up a name for the airfield.[38]

While the F-86 pilots would not shoot at MiGs on the ground, the Soviet fighters did not have to be very far off the ground before being engaged. The Communists confirm the border crossing and attacks on their airfields. As early as April 1951, American aircraft were spotted in China, and in 1952 and early 1953, the cross-border attacks were almost daily occurrences. One Soviet stated that the F-86s "blockaded" the Russian bases. The first Soviet MiG commander in the war, Georgii Lobov, writes that, "the Americans were constantly crossing the border."[39] In the first six months of 1952, the Sixty-fourth IAK's lost twenty-six aircraft over their own airfields. That September, half of MiG losses were over their own fields. The Chinese note that on 13 and 15 May 1952 they lost five fighters and two pilots due to airfield attacks.[40]

Gabreski, for example, chased a MiG over the main runway at Antung, at top speed and minimum altitude through a cloud of flak, before downing the Soviet fighter. He then pulled up and executed a victory roll along with his wingman, as the latter recounts.[41] Others buzzed the Communist airfields. James Hagerstrom claims he went over Antung at an altitude of ten to fifteen feet at Mach .9.[42] Harrison Thyng ordered an RAF exchange pilot, Paddy Nichols, to make a low-level, high-speed pass to "boom" the Antung airfield to attract the MiGs. Thyng later chased a Red fighter across that field, blowing it up and scattering pieces down the runway. After some other action, Thyng and Nichols "blasted back across Antung, throttles wide open, on the deck, dodging the flak."[43]

Frederick Blesse was circling a Chinese airfield, with orders to keep the MiGs on the ground but not to attack them on the ground, when he saw a group of MiGs taxiing out to take off. He descended to eight thousand feet and then, timing his dive as the first two MiGs began their take-off roll, swooped down on them. He was about a mile behind the pair when they both throttled back, bellowing blue smoke as they stomped on their brakes, and ran off the runway, collapsing their nose gear. Not only were the two MiGs destroyed without firing a shot, the remaining MiGs turned around and shut down for the day. Mission accomplished.[44]

Robinson Risner was flying a screen for a bombing mission that carried him over China when he got into a tussle with four MiGs. The extended engagement at low altitude carried him between two hangars on a Chinese air base about thirty-five miles across the border. The MiG crashed alongside the runway.[45] It was little wonder then that some of the Sabre gun camera film showed not only MiG-15s with their landing gear extended but also pictures of runways and parked MiGs. Understandably, this film was destroyed along with other film that indicated the F-86s were operating north of the Yalu.[46]

Gen. Frank Everest, commander of the Fifth Air Force, told Gabreski and Mahurin that he had orders not to violate the border, and then went on to say that he knew that the JCS approved of hot pursuit even though he did not have that in writing. Apparently, he and the JCS believed the Soviets were not upset with the situation because although both Communist countries protested, they did not do so strongly. The two colonels took this to mean that Everest would wink at any border violation.[47]

In early 1952, Everest called in the 4th and 51st group commanders after he saw, through the wonder of radar, one pilot, Al Morman, twice circle Mukden! The general stormed into the room, displayed anger, and chewed out the two commanders for violating the border and orders, and threatened them with a court-martial. He said he had learned American pilots were violating the border, something that he could neither tolerate nor condone. Everest stalked out of the room and slammed the door. But then he poked his head back into the room and said, "And furthermore, if you are going to violate the Manchurian border, for God's sake turn off the damn IFF set."[48]

It did not take long for Mahurin to act. After one mission, he asked about five pilots to stay after the debriefing and then told them they had to find a way to stop the MiGs. He asked if anyone was interested in crossing the Yalu; all five said yes. Mahurin assigned a Communist airfield to each.[49] Gabreski and Mahurin led four others on what was probably the first deliberate, unauthorized crossing of the border. They flew out over the Yellow Sea, turned off their IFF, and went low to avoid tracking by friendly radar. Other pilots joined this operation.

Charles Cleveland had just arrived on the 4th's base and was walking to the officer's club when an official sedan pulled up and he was told by the colonels inside to hop into the back seat. As the vehicle drove away, Cleveland heard Thyng and Mahurin discuss crossing the Yalu. After flying a number of missions as a wingman, during which he never got to fire his guns, Cleveland was advanced to leader. On one mission, he watched from 38,000 feet as a flight of four MiGs entered their landing pattern. He dove and got into firing position as one MiG was about 150 feet off the runway and at 120 kts. Cleveland fired and registered some hits as he flew at 600 kts through the Communist flak. Six MiGs lifted off in pursuit of the marauding Sabre, and in the engagement that followed over the Yellow Sea, Cleveland got close, fired, and got some hits. A MiG pilot bailed out, and Cleveland earned one of his four credits.[50]

A number of the F-86 leaders, including squadron, group, and wing commanders, flew north of the Yalu. Michael DeArmond recalls that the 4th Fighter Interceptor Wing commander, Col. Harrison Thyng, briefed his pilots that there would be a court-martial for those who violated the Chinese border. On that very mission, Thyng led a flight of four Sabres deep into China, almost to Mukden, where he destroyed a MiG. After landing, Thyng asked his wingman where he had downed the Communist fighter. DeArmond answered, "somewhere around the mouth of the Yalu." To which Thyng responded, "Son you have a bright future in the Air Force."[51] As another Sabre pilot who rose to flag grade summarized later, "There were a lot of airplanes shot down in Korea by guys who . . . [did] not necessarily play by the rules."[52]

The Communist side commented little on these airfield attacks except to acknowledge that they occurred. It is not difficult to conclude, however, that these aggressive American tactics coupled with MiG losses over their own territory and bases had a devastating impact on Communist morale. These actions certainly had a major influence on the attitude of new and inexperienced Sabre and MiG pilots. Nothing was safe, even north of the Yalu, from the aggressive American pilots. And this psychological superiority was clearly an advantage for the F-86s in the battle for the skies.

It is impossible to know how many pilots violated the border and how many MiGs were downed in China. For years, the widespread belief was that few crossed the river. In fact, a prominent aviation author recently wrote that there were "a few inadvertent excursions across the Yalu River by wandering U.S. airmen."[53] Wrong. Apparently "many" would be a more accurate estimate. A majority of the aces crossed the Yalu, perhaps as many as twenty-five of the thirty-nine and probably nine of the eleven aces who scored ten or more credits.[54] There were, of course, some pilots who did not violate Chinese air space. Cecil Foster, who claimed nine victories, writes that he did not cross the river. Hinton states he only crossed the river when so briefed. Other pilots would only penetrate into China when they were flying the wing of their leader but not on their own initiative.[55]

Despite this violation of direct orders, which became common knowledge among the Sabre pilots, few were punished. Following the downing of the 16th Fighter Squadron commander Edwin Heller deep in Chinese territory the 16th was grounded for a week.[56] Three aces also suffered for crossing the Yalu. The top U.S. ace of the war, Joe McConnell, crossed a number of times and was grounded for a brief time for his actions. However, the 51st Wing Commander John Mitchell made McConnell's superior officer lift the grounding after two weeks.[57] Another ace, Lonnie Moore, attended a briefing around March 1953 and returned to say Gen. Glenn Barcus "says screw the Yalu." If true, the word did not get down to Moore's immediate superiors, one of whom told his troops not to violate the border, for he intended to make an example of the first pilot who did. In June, Moore got caught and was sent home.[58] The most drastic punishment occurred in January 1953 to a young, eager, successful fighter pilot who had just become an ace, Dolph Overton.

Dolph Overton, Ace and Scapegoat

Dolph Overton was born in Andrews, South Carolina, in April 1927. He demonstrated an early and sustained interest in aviation, flying with his father as a boy, soloing at age sixteen, and reading everything he could on the World War I aces. Overton began college at The Citadel when he was sixteen but dropped out at seventeen to enlist in the Navy during World War II. He hoped to get into the Navy's flying training program, but because the war was winding down, he did not. The Navy discharged Overton, who then earned an appointment to West Point. He graduated in 1949 and was one of ninety-two in his class to join the Air Force. After earning his wings the next year and sharing a room with another future ace, Iven Kincheloe, he was assigned to the 31st Fighter Group, commanded by World War II ace David Schilling (22.5 credits).

His career hit a bump when he had a major accident in an F-84 as he tried to set a record of the shortest time in the traffic pattern on his third

flight. Schilling told him he would be a second lieutenant until he said different and gave Overton a variety of extra assignments. Overton flew F-84s both
stateside and in England before volunteering to join the fight in Korea. He
arrived there with considerable experience in the Thunderjet, more flying
time, in his words, "than the rest of the squadron put together." This is not
entirely hyperbole because this was a National Guard unit that had little experience with jets. Therefore, he was made a flight leader and assistant squadron
operations officer in short order. He flew 102 F-84 combat missions in his year
tour and then volunteered for a second tour in Korea flying F-86s.[59]

Overton joined the 51st Fighter Group and flew forty missions without
posting a kill claim. He overcame any foreboding or premonition by sitting in
the chapel, not praying or asking for guidance, but just sitting alone until he
"was normal again." Overton didn't think he was superstitious, but he began
growing a mustache that he did not shave off until he flew his last mission. He
reversed the view that thirteen was an unlucky number; instead, he considered
a lucky number any number with three in it or that could be divided by three.

Overton was above all a smart and serious professional. He visited the
American radar site on Cho-do and saw where the Communist aircraft
landed, how long they stayed airborne (about thirty-four to thirty-five minutes), and how they made their let downs to the airfield. Using this information and notification from Cho-do radar that the Communist fighters were
taking off, Overton knew where, how, and when the MiGs would commence
their landing approach. Overton waited in place, flying a racetrack pattern
with minimum maneuvering (when the aircraft turned the sun could cause a
glint that would warn the enemy), attempting to get between the sun and the
MiGs. He hoped that with his IFF turned off, the Red radar operators would
think his aircraft was just another MiG getting ready to land.

Then everything came together. He writes that "Forty-four times I flew,
studying, practicing, training and making mistakes and had quite a few MiG
encounters with some probable damage to several of them. Finally, near the
end of January 1953 . . . they started to fly in big groups every day and flew
exactly according to the previously described predictions." As the Communist
fighters flew by, Overton slid in behind them and shot them down. All of his
kills were parallel intercepts, non-deflection shots from close range without
using the radar ranging feature of the Sabre's gunsight; all of his kills were
north of the Yalu. The entire process might take fifteen minutes during
which he could not take his eyes off his prey and had to depend on his wingman to cover his rear. Overton expressed his surprise at how easy this was,

writing, "It worked, and I was amazed they never seemed to see us or recognize us until too late."[60]

Overton downed five planes in four days (21–24 January 1953), setting a record. The fifth and last claim was on his forty-ninth mission. The next morning Overton was called into the Wing Commander's office where a Colonel from Fifth Air Force, David C. Jones, later USAF Chief of Staff, asked him one question: "Were you over the river yesterday?" The new ace answered, "Yes sir." And that was all. The next day the wing commander Col. John Mitchell told Overton that he was grounded and being sent home.[61] He made clear that he was not going home a hero, and his squadron was grounded for ten days. Overton would get none of the decorations that he had earned, including those from his F-84 tour that had not yet been awarded. Gen. Glenn Barcus had twice pinned a Distinguished Flying Cross on Overton, but the decorations had not been formally written up. In addition, he was getting a terrible efficiency report "elaborating on my inability to follow orders." Overton noted the radical change in policy. No one had been punished for crossing the river and there had been no new policy about watching the border or warning to stay out of China. Overton also observed that on the day in question, he was flying as the number four man, or as he put it: "I know that it flows down hill, but it seemed to me that this was a long way down." To rub further salt in the wounds, Overton knew that the wing commander had flown across the river and had condoned such flights.

Overton was not alone in thinking he was being treated unfairly. According to Iven Kincheloe, Gabreski told Jones that the 51st crossed the river because the MiGs outnumbered the Sabres ten to one and that was the only way the Americans could maintain air superiority. Gabreski asked the colonel if General Ridgway had had any problem with enemy aircraft at the front. Rising to the occasion, he suggested that the colonel or his general fly up to the Yalu any day in a T-33 to check for violations and take down aircraft buzz numbers! Possibly his most provocative comment was to suggest that if Fifth Air Force wanted "to kick ass," they should start with his.

Overton took off his captain's bars (his spot promotion only applied in the position for which it was granted) and returned home without decorations and without official recognition of his five victories. Probably as part of the effort to punish Overton, the military delayed official recognition of his victory credits until December 1953, almost a full year after the event. These were the last claims blessed by the USAF process, which usually took a month or so. Before the year was over, Overton resigned his commission. Twenty-five years later, the USAF awarded Overton his medals.[62]

What prompted the USAF to punish Overton for an offense so many others had committed and which was condoned by so many in the chain of command? Apparently, two incidents that involved Overton were responsible. The shoot-down of 16th Fighter Squadron commander Edwin Heller was one. It was not that he was downed and captured but the fact that he landed deep within China, 150 miles according to one account, 60 miles according to another.[63] The second was a remarkable piece of bad luck. Apparently Swiss observers to the truce talks at Panmunjon were traveling through Manchuria when they spotted a dogfight well north of the Yalu River. Their complaints prompted the investigation that snared Overton.[64]

Appraisal

Clearly there was a lot more crossing of the Yalu River and violation of the Chinese sanctuary than previously known. A good number of American pilots flew north, giving the Communist airmen much less a sanctuary than generally acknowledged. This gave the American side a degree of initiative that may have been necessary to offset the numerical disadvantages under which they fought. It is also clear that success in air-to-air combat depends a great deal on being aggressive, as certainly many American fighter pilots were. In brief then, violation of the official orders played a role in the American success in the battle for air superiority.

There is, however, another side of the story. Was the overall risk taken worth this benefit? The F-86 excursions could have resulted in an international incident or pushed the Communists to widen the war. The fact that the Communists also restrained their actions is mostly overlooked by westerners. The MiGs did not fly over water or near the front lines.[65] They could have attacked UN airfields in Korea or Japan, or employed submarines to attack ships not only off of Korea but also off of Japan. Should the violation of the border by individual pilots, including some of the commanding officers, which was condoned by the chain of command, be regarded as "military necessity," or perhaps better put, "tactical necessity," or something else? Was it a case of a lack of discipline by glory-seeking fighter pilots? As one former Sabre pilot saw it, "the F-86 missions flown into China served no purpose other than to provide an opportunity for the possible personal glorification of a handful of foolish and celebrity-hungry pilots."[66] Or, was it the rivalry between the Sabre units that drove this situation? Another element of this story is that with Sabres trolling and fighting in China, other American aircraft operating in North Korea had less cover. Was the goal of the F-86s to shoot down MiGs, wherever they might be, or was the goal to protect UN aircraft? Could the Sabres adequately or effectively protect UN aircraft in North Korea while they were in China?[67]

Claims, United States (mostly) and Communist

The USAF Korean War victory credits are based solely on the Far East Air Forces General Orders. A Fifth Air Force Regulation dated May 1952 established the criteria for destroyed credits, listing four possible conditions: (1) The enemy aircraft was observed by a second party (in the air or on the ground) to strike the ground; (2) a second observer or gun camera film showed the aircraft disintegrating, losing a major component necessary for flight, "persistent fire in the engine or tail section," or the pilot bailing out; (3) witnesses observing the aircraft "in such a position that known limitations or circumstances would preclude possible recovery"; or (4) the aircraft was seen to explode or burn on the ground. The USAF apparently used a more liberal policy during the Korean War than the stated one used during World War II.[68]

The USAF claims system includes more information than just the number of credits. In addition to basic information identifying the pilot and the time and location of the engagement, it usually consisted of a three-sentence summary of the dogfight mentioning the pilot's position in the formation, numbers, who attacked whom, and how it concluded. Analysis of this data allows us to quantify what we have to this point only guessed or assumed.[69]

Shooter Position

It has long been known that pilots flying in the lead position scored most of the MiG kills; to be precise, pilots flying as lead registered 82 percent of the total MiG claims, a percentage that varied little over the course of the war.[70] This predominance of leaders shooting was about the same in the two F-86 units. As most would expect, the men who finished as aces scored most of their kills as leads, 93 percent compared with 75 percent of those pilots who scored but did not tally five kills.[71]

Wingmen were taught that their first and last function was to protect their leader, who was the shooter. One pilot made this very clear, telling his wingmen that *he* would shoot them down if they varied from this concept. What, then, were the exceptions that allowed wingmen to score? Of the 138 victories claimed by wingmen, 13 were noted to be defending "friendlies," mostly their leaders while another 22 continued attacks initiated by their leaders who either exhausted their ammunition or were out of position. In a few cases, MiGs just flew in front of the wingmen, or so they reported. But the majority of the wingmen who scored had simple notations of having "attacked" the MiGs.

Aggressor

It is also widely accepted that American pilots were much more aggressive than Communist pilots, and it is commonly believed that many, if not most, of the MiGs shot down were of poorly trained, inexperienced MiG pilots. While U.S. data cannot quantify this last issue, we do have data on who initiated engagements during which American pilots were awarded credit for the destruction of MiGs. The data reveal that U.S. pilots had the initiative in 86 percent of the overall claims. This ratio varied little by unit or whether or not the shooter became, or was, an ace.[72] The percentage of kills claimed by U.S. pilots having the initiative steadily increased over the course of the conflict, from 80 percent in the first quarter of credits to 89 percent in the last.

MiG Claims by Cause

MiG credits were awarded based on pilot reports verified by other pilots or by gun camera film. Apparently some claims were confirmed by other intelligence sources, that is, radio intercepts; but none of this data is currently available.[73] Pilots assert that the F-86 gun cameras were unreliable, and even when the equipment worked, it too often produced poor quality images. In addition, some pilots complained that the credit system standards declined over time.[74] The reports do not indicate on what evidence the claim is based. With this in mind, 3 percent of the overall kill claims were attributed to explosions and disintegration of the MiGs, 46 percent to the MiG pilot abandoning his aircraft, and 35 percent to the observed crash of the Communist fighter. Reports on the remaining 16 percent "other" category do not mention any of the previous evidence (explosion/disintegration, bailout, or crash) but instead usually describe the F-86 pilot closing on the MiG, firing, scoring hits, and then ending with something like "the MiG was last observed diving straight down."

Over the course of the war, there was a decided difference in the cause for claims between the two F-86 units. The two Sabre units registered about the same percentage of MiGs seen to crash, but the 4th reported a greater percentage of MiG pilots to bail out and MiGs to explode than did the 51st while the 51st claimed more in the "other" category. There was a similar spread between the aces and the non-aces who claimed victories. The aces had a higher percentage of claims based on MiGs exploding/disintegrating and pilots bailing out—the same percentage of MiGs seen to crash—but a lower rate of "other" claims. Sixteen of the thirty-nine Sabre aces had no "other" claims, thirteen had one, and seven aces had one-quarter or more of their MiG claims in this category. Four of Dolph Overton's 5 credits were in this category, perhaps understandably, because all were earned north of the Yalu River. Also, 4 of Pete Fernandez's 14.5 credits were also of this nature.

Exchange Pilots

A number of pilots from the Marines, Navy, and Commonwealth countries flew F-86s in combat—at least five Navy, fourteen Marine, seven RAF, and fifteen RCAF pilots. They undoubtedly were the "cream of the crop" because other services and countries most certainly sent their best to this prestigious and important assignment. Most, if not all, flew shorter tours than the one hundred missions normally flown by USAF pilots. Nevertheless, two Navy, eleven Marine, five RAF, and six RCAF pilots scored victories. One Marine pilot, John Bolt, became an ace. Comparing the aces, including Bolt, with the exchange pilots, again including Bolt, there is no difference in what position they flew when they scored. However, while the aces had the initiative in 88 percent of their claims, and the non-ace USAF pilots the initiative in 85 percent, the exchange pilots had the initiative in only 68 percent of their claims. The exchange pilots had a lesser percentage of "other" claims, a far greater percentage of claims based on MiGs observed to crash, and a lesser number of MiG pilots seen to bail out than both the USAF aces and non-aces.

MiGs Downed Without a Shot

Some authors have commented on the number of MiGs that were destroyed without a shot fired. This is attributed to a tricky aircraft or poorly trained, low-morale, inexperienced pilots flying under dangerous conditions. An analysis shortly after the war noted that the MiG spins were not due to structural problems because American observers had seen some of the Communist pilots conduct "brilliant flying maneuvers." It went on to note, however, that when the Soviet fighter stalled, it quickly snapped into a flat spin. The Americans attributed this to "critical longitudinal stability" due to the MiG's wing sweep, wing tip bending, and the position of the horizontal tail.[75] Postwar American tests of a MiG-15 revealed that the MiG had virtually no stall warning and would snap into a spin, clearly dangerous characteristics for inexperienced pilots.[76]

Wartime USAF studies noted fifty-six cases of MiG spins in 1952 through April 1953. While fifteen of these pilots recovered, ten others ejected and twenty-five crashed; the fate of the six remaining pilots is unknown. The authors characterized nine of the spins as successful in evading the Sabres while thirty-nine were classified as appearing to be accidental. In eight cases the MiGs were hit by F-86 bullets, in eight cases they were fired on but not damaged, and in thirty-nine cases they were not fired on. The analysts observed that in 1952, only two out of the thirty-two pilots were reported to have recovered, whereas in the first four months of 1953 MiG pilots recovered in thirteen of the twenty-four cases of spins. The difference in recovery rates probably indicated better trained and more experienced pilots. The Americans saw lack of pilot training and experience as the Soviets' major shortcoming, for "with the exception of stability, in the present tactical situation the MIG as an aerodynamic entity equals or outperforms the F-86 in every respect."[77]

Six percent of F-86 pilots' MiG claims were earned without firing a shot. The credit system allowed the pilot who spotted the spinners to claim the victory, prompting discussion and dispute as to whether the leader and wingman should share such credits.[78] The 4th accounted for thirty-one of these, and during the period when the 51st also flew Sabres, the 4th had twenty-eight no-shot victories compared with the 51st's seventeen. The exchange pilots scored 10 percent of their claims in this manner, in contrast to the aces, who registered 4.4 percent of their claims, while the other USAF pilots claimed 6.9 percent of their totals.[79] The numbers of these claims markedly increased in the last half of the war, from eight such cases recorded in the first quarter of the credits and seven in the second (both 3.6 percent) to thirteen in the third quarter (6.6 percent) and twenty in the final quarter (10.2 percent). So, contrary to the assumption that improved spin recovery rate at the end of the war was related to greater training and experience, these figures indicate continuing Communist problems with training, experience, or morale.

U.S. Claims

Claims are one of the most controversial aspects of air warfare. The combatants proclaim victory (claim/kill) numbers that invariably differ and are higher than losses admitted by their foe. This has been true in all air conflicts. Investigation of one period in World War II indicates that both Germans and Americans overestimated their victory credits by a factor of about 2.4.[80] During the Korean War, the United States claimed 840 MiGs destroyed compared to 600 admitted by the Communists while the Reds claimed about 800 F-86s destroyed in contrast to U.S. admissions of fewer than 100 Sabres in air-to-air combat.[81]

There are at least three factors involved in this overestimation of victories. First and foremost, aerial combat is a high-stress, fast-moving situation with much happening at once. Gun cameras did not always work, and even if they did, they only operated when the guns were fired. Sabre pilots had limited endurance in MiG Alley, where most of the engagements took place, and even less if they crossed the Yalu River. Short endurance and the hostile environment gave few opportunities to follow the damaged prey to its demise. Distracted, busy, and stressed participants do not make the best witnesses.

A second factor was deliberately false claims. There was considerable pressure on individuals and units to score victories. Downing enemy fighters was the epitome of success for fighter pilots and brought attention, decoration, promotion, and fame for the individual, especially if the pilot scored five or more victories to be acknowledged as an ace. There clearly was a rivalry between the F-86 units that pushed unit leaders and their pilots. And there is always a tendency in any organization to "please the boss." In some cases this rivalry pushed the claims board to optimistically evaluate claims and, in some cases, upgrade claims. Considering these difficult circumstances and serious temptations, it is therefore noteworthy that there were not greater discrepancies between American claims and Communist admission of losses. A few F-86 pilots admit that there were some dubious claims. Two pilots recall there were rumors that some high-ranking pilots from headquarters exaggerated their claims; in the words of one, some ranking officers "were sometimes overeager to enhance their accomplishments." Another tells of a senior officer bullying a claims board to confirm a kill.[82]

Finally, American intelligence officers had no opportunity to seek out and find the remains of enemy aircraft destroyed in fights over enemy territory or over the ocean. Unlike World War II, no enemy pilots or enemy records were captured. Consequently, the claims posted remain uncertain. Nevertheless, F-86 pilots believe that the claims system worked fairly well, considering these problems.

Communist Claims

The situation was somewhat different for the Communist pilots. Certainly the first two factors noted above applied to them. But in the third area they had a clear advantage. Because all the air-to-air action took place over Red-held territory or offshore, the Communists had the opportunity to inspect downed aircraft and to interrogate captured pilots; thus, their claims were arguably more accurate. However, Communists leaders and pilots faced a unique fourth issue. History and accuracy have never had high priority under the Communist system; indeed, history was manipulated and falsified on a regular basis to serve the state. The strict, if not draconian, system under Stalin may have produced statistics that would please, or certainly not displease, those higher in the chain of command. While both American and Communist pilots faced the temptations of "cooking the books" for personal advancement, the Communist pilot also faced very harsh penalties for failure, or perceived failure.

For their part, Communist claims of air-to-air victories range between 1,000 to 1,600 UN aircraft. The most frequent number in the secondary literature for Soviet claims is 1,106, of which 651 are F-86s.[83] The most detailed and seemingly most authoritative document on claims from the Soviets, however, puts the number at 986 USAF aircraft, of which 595 were Sabres, plus 30 other UN aircraft.[84] To these numbers must be added the claims of the Chinese and North Korean air forces. A recent scholarly work put the Chinese claims at 330, of which 211 were F-86s,[85] although most sources use a figure of 271 aircraft for both Chinese and North Korean claims.[86]

The Russians list over fifty MiG pilots as aces, two with twenty or more kills, compared with the forty American aces.[87] The top American ace claimed sixteen victories. One Soviet ace, Evgeny Pepelyaev, credited in various sources with nineteen, twenty, or twenty-three UN aircraft, admits, "I am absolutely certain of only six of my kills, and I saw just two of those actually crash."[88] There is a massive discrepancy between Communist claims and the losses admitted by the American airmen.

The USAF, which suffered the overwhelming bulk of combat losses in the war, admitted losing 1,466 aircraft to operational causes. The USAF considered 139 aircraft to have been lost in air-to-air action, with an additional 305 listed as unknown or missing. The figures for the F-86 were 78 lost in air-to-air combat and 26 in the unknown or missing category. Even if these categories are combined, they represent an overclaiming of F-86s by the Communists by a factor of over eight.[89]

ELEVEN

Top Guns

The Five Leading F-86 Aces

Those pilots that flew fighters and earned victory credits stand out in the minds of both the public and their peers. Among those pilots, the aces and, understandably, the higher scorers among them attract the most attention. The French initiated the concept of the "ace" during World War I, awarding that accolade to any pilot who achieved five aerial victories. The leading scorer of that war was Germany's Manfred von Richtoven, with 80 credits, while the top American ace was Eddie Rickenbacker, with 26. The top ace of World War II was another German, Erich Hartman, with a score of 352. The leading American ace of World War II was Richard Bong, with a total of 40.

A relatively small number of fighter pilots accounted for a disproportional share of the victory credits. During World War II, the Army Air Forces (AAF) credited 7,306 fighter pilots with 15,799 aerial victories. Just over 9 percent of those were aces, who claimed 34 percent of the total victories.[1] The same was true in Korea. Of the one thousand or so pilots flying the F-86 during the Korean conflict, the USAF credited 355 pilots with 756.5 victories.[2] Thirty-nine achieved ace status by downing 305.5 enemy aircraft or, in percentage terms, 11 percent of those who got credits. Four percent of the pilots that flew Sabres in the Korean War accounted for 40 percent of the victories. The five highest scoring pilots claimed 13 or more victories and downed 72.5 enemy aircraft, or 10 percent of F-86 pilot claims.

One of the largely ignored aspects of the ace story is that along with their accomplishments and resulting fame came a higher risk of death. This relationship probably results from the fact that those pilots who excel in shooting down enemy aircraft are more aggressive, confidant, and daring than the average pilot. All of these traits lead to more risk taking. Of the top seventeen AAF World War II aces, eight died in combat or accidents: four in action, three in aircraft accidents, and one in an auto accident.[3] This was even truer of the top aces of the Korean War, where four of the top five American Korean War aces came to an untimely end. One was lost in action, two died in aircraft accidents, and the fourth was killed in a car accident. "Boots" Blesse, a double ace, put it this way, "Nobody's telling you [fighter combat is] just as safe and easy as sitting in a rocking chair back home. You pay your money and take your chances. If you know what you're doing, and don't play the odds too close, the chance are pretty good you'll come out with something worthwhile."[4]

One counter-intuitive element of the air war over MiG Alley was the age of the American pilots. War is fought by the young, but because the Korean War followed close behind World War II, a good number of pilots served in both. As the official Air Force historian wrote, "Many Sabre pilots were 'old men' by usual standards for fighter pilots, but jet combat in Korea demonstrated that a pilot's physical age was much less important than his experience and sound judgment."[5] In early 1952, the average age of the pilots in the 4th Group was 29, while that of the aces was 30.5 years. Two-thirds of those who downed MiGs by March 1953 were over 28 years old, but about the same proportion without credits were less than twenty-five years old. The average age of the top five U.S. aces when they scored their first Korean War victory was 30.1 years of age.[6] Why? One reason was that the older pilots had seniority and thus were more likely to be flying as leaders, where most of the shooting was done.

Another factor was experience. Of the 355 pilots who scored victories in the Korean War, 56 had also posted credits in World War II. Seven earned ace status in both World War II and Korea; 14 other World War II aces added less than five credits in the Korean War, and 5 Korean War aces had fewer than five credits in World War II.[7] All 5 of the top Korean War aces had served in the big war, and the 3 who saw combat as fighter pilots had earned victory credits in that war. Undoubtedly there were others who had flown and downed enemy aircraft in World War II who also flew in the Korean War without adding to their victory totals.

There are two other aspects that should not be overlooked: luck and opportunity. Certainly those who scored had more than their fair share of flying and shooting skill, daring, and confidence. Yet there were other important elements, such as the position they flew (wingman or leader) and just plain luck. If the Red fighters did not come up, there would be no dogfights, and no chance for victories, for it takes a willing, or unwary, adversary to engage in an aerial battle.

Joe McConnell: Top American Ace of the Korean War

Joe McConnell was born in New Hampshire in January 1922. He enlisted in the Army at eighteen and went into the Medical Corps. It took him two years to get into the AAF, where he volunteered for pilot school and, according to one account, flunked out and then trained as a navigator. McConnell earned his wings in October 1944, and flew combat missions in B-24s over Europe. He decided to stay in the service, reapplied for pilot training, and was accepted in the program in 1947. In February of the next year pinned on pilot's wings.[8]

McConnell was stationed in Alaska when the Korean War broke out. He volunteered to serve in the war and was told he was too old. Following his Alaskan tour, the Air Force transferred the eager fighter pilot to George AFB in California where he flew F-86s.[9] In mid-1952 the USAF sent him to Korea and in September assigned him to the 16th Fighter Squadron in the 51st Fighter Group. He achieved no aerial victories with that unit. In January, he was reassigned as a flight commander in the 39th Fighter Squadron where things quickly changed for the better. McConnell got his first credit on 14 January 1953 and his fifth a month later (16 February) to become the twenty-seventh U.S. ace of the war. He later survived a shoot down and rescue on 12 April.

Less than two weeks later, McConnell joined a very elite group when he shot down his tenth MiG. Only eleven of the thirty-nine F-86 aces in the Korean War would be credited with ten or more aerial victories.[10] At this point (24 April 1953) the top scoring American pilots were George Davis with fourteen victories, followed by Royal Baker with thirteen, and Pete Fernandez with eleven; all three flew with the 4th. During the next three weeks, McConnell hit a dry spell while Fernandez added 2.5 credits. But in less than a week, McConnell downed six MiGs while Fernandez got only one more. Gen. Glenn Barcus, commander of Far East Air Forces, reportedly said, "I want that man [McConnell] on his way back home to the USA before you hear the period at the end of this sentence."[11] The USAF pulled both pilots out of action, leaving McConnell as the leading American scorer of the war, with 16 MiGs, and Fernandez with 14.5. McConnell had flown 106 missions.[12]

McConnell finished his combat career in a blaze of glory, for his last day (18 May 1953) was his best day in combat. The ace was leading a six-ship formation that the 51st was using at the time (which lasted only briefly as it proved unwieldy). Maintenance problems quickly unraveled the formation, as one fighter aborted on the takeoff roll; his wingman stayed behind as well. Later, the number three man could not release his drop tanks, so both he and his wingman headed for home, leaving McConnell and his wingman, Dean Abbott, in the combat area. Cho-do radar alerted the pair that the MiGs were up; shortly after reaching the Yalu, the Americans spotted them and followed two across the river.[13] The F-86s trailed the pair of MiGs by a half-mile but could not close the gap. McConnell than pulled up his nose and fired a short burst. This surprised Adams because both actions would slow the Sabre, and the possibility of scoring hits at this distance were small. But if the MiG was hit or the pilot saw tracers, he might turn and give the pursuers an opportunity to close the gap. In this case, McConnell's shots lit up the MiG's tail; however, this became moot as three MiG flights engaged the Sabre element from both sides. McConnell counted twenty-eight MiGs, and noted that there probably were a lot more. The ace broke hard into one flight, during which Adams ended up in front of McConnell and one of the MiGs. The ace quickly rolled in behind the Red fighter to protect his wingman, fired, and "really clobbered him." The MiG pilot ejected. The dogfight continued, with Adams again finding himself in front of both a MiG and McConnell. McConnell half rolled, got into position behind the MiG, and shot him off his wingman's tail.[14]

McConnell's wartime report, of course, differs in places from his wingman's postwar recollection and leaves out some of these details, notably crossing the Yalu. The ace's rendition does not include shooting either MiG off the tail of his wingman and instead notes that the second MiG had gotten behind McConnell, at least momentarily. At one point, after flying through the MiG's smoke, McConnell feared an impending collision as "the [MiG] pilot looked up at me and pulled up into me as though to ram me. I pushed forward violently to avoid hitting him."[15] The MiG then snapped over and spun into the ground. This was the only time McConnell got two MiGs on one mission.[16] He was now a triple ace.

During the engagement, Adams called out, "My God, there must be thirty of them!" McConnell responded "Yeah, and we've got 'em all to ourselves."[17]

The 51st was monitoring the radio and, according to Adams, this remark "gained Mac a lot of notoriety." The two Americans were on the defensive and maneuvered to work their way southward. McConnell recalls, "I really kicked that Sabre around just dodging those balls of fire, faintly hearing the thumping cannon on the MiG behind me and not even wondering whether the next one would be the last one I would hear. . . . I was too busy to be scared."[18] Besides exploiting the nimble Sabre, the overwhelming number of MiGs may have aided the Americans because the Red fighters got in each other's way. Nevertheless, the Communist pilots could have run the American pilots out of fuel, if not for their policy of not pursuing the F-86s over water. The MiG pilots were more disciplined in not breaking their policy of not flying over water than the Americans were in observing their policy of not flying north of the Yalu. Although low on fuel, the two 51st fighters "limped back and landed on fumes."[19]

Although he had bagged two MiGs and now was the leading American ace of the war, McConnell flew that afternoon. The MiGs tried to decoy McConnell into a trap, but their timing was off, and the Americans turned the tables. McConnell engaged one, got hits, and the MiG began to smoke. The Communist pilot bailed out.[20] This brought McConnell's total for the day to three. It was McConnell's last combat mission and raised his score to sixteen, the most any American pilot would register during the war. It was also a great day for the American pilots, who downed eleven MiGs, all by the 51st. There were no USAF losses.[21]

McConnell, somewhat unusual for a fighter pilot, was a modest individual. He explained his success by noting, "It's just a case of getting up there when they're around. Sometimes you can go for days without finding a MiG."[22] He didn't consider himself a hero, stating that the troops on the ground were the heroes. For himself, he wrote, "I'm just a lucky jet jockey with a good plane and a lot of good training."[23] He went further to explain his record: "It's the teamwork out here that counts; the lone wolf stuff is out. I may get credit for a MiG, but it's the team that does it . . . not myself alone."[24] McConnell authored an article that began with the self-deprecating lines, "I'm just a guy doing a job. I'm just another guy in spite of this triple jet-ace title with which I've been tagged."[25]

McConnell was an aggressive pilot who took risks. On one day McConnell and his wingman, Dean Abbott, were orbiting Cho-do as spares when McConnell's hydraulic system failed. There was a back up system, but because stick forces would become extremely high if that system failed, the policy was to immediately return home. However, Cho-do radar radioed that numerous MiG formations were over Mukden, 120 miles northwest of the Yalu. McConnell did not hesitate to pursue the MiGs although it meant violating two policies: one concerning the hydraulic system, and the other respecting Chinese air space. As it turned out, the MiGs had landed by the time the pair of Sabres reached Mukden. McConnell then made not one but two complete circuits over the city before heading back to base.[26]

A number of his fellow pilots claim that McConnell took chances and even turned away from MiGs to lure them in, implying that this is what led to his shoot down in April.[27] In his eagerness for combat and MiG kills, he violated policies and certainly put himself and his wingmen in peril. According to another ace, he also flew with his parachute straps disconnected to permit him more latitude to move around in the cockpit and look for enemy aircraft.[28] Like most fighter pilots and all aces, McConnell had self confidence. One former Sabre pilot, Tuel Houston, recalls a conversation with McConnell before shipping over to Korea in which Houston mentioned that he would consider his tour a success if he downed one MiG. McConnell replied, "I wouldn't even want to go if I didn't know I was going to make ace. I *know* I'm going to make ace." He of course did; Houston got three credits.[29]

McConnell returned to the United States a hero. He and Pete Fernandez met with President Eisenhower before the top American ace returned to California, where he was assigned to test pilot duties at Edwards AFB. On 25 August 1954, he took an F-86H, an upgraded Sabre, up for an aerobatic test flight. About twenty minutes into the flight, McConnell radioed that he was having problems with his elevators but was using trim to control the aircraft and would attempt to land the aircraft on the dry lakebed. In Korea, he had practiced landing without hydraulic controls, using only throttle and trim. There were a few more garbled transmissions, and then about a minute later ground observers noted a plume of smoke on the desert floor. McConnell got the fighter close to the ground but then at three hundred feet ejected from the aircraft. He cleared the seat but was too low for the parachute to deploy, landing and dying about three-quarters of mile from where the jet crashed. Although many believe that the F-86H suffered hydraulic failure, accident investigators found that two bolts had not been properly secured after the fighter's control stick was repositioned. The aircraft had flown six flights before the bolts worked free. McConnell misdiagnosed the problem as hydraulic failure when in fact his ailerons were disconnected, a much more unstable and dangerous condition. What enemy pilots had not been able to do was done by a careless mechanic.[30]

Pete Fernandez: The Contender

Manuel "Pete" Fernandez was born in Key West, Florida, in April 1925. Because his father was in the Air Corps, it is understandable that the son built model airplanes and sold newspapers to pay for flying lessons through which he learned to fly at age fifteen. Fernandez joined the aviation cadet program shortly after graduating from high school in 1943 and earned his wings in November 1944, but he did not see combat in World War II. Although he was assigned to fighters after the war, he flew C-47s in the Berlin Airlift, as did his father. When the Korean War erupted, he was a gunnery instructor at Nellis AFB, where he instructed Joe McConnell, among others. In late 1952, the USAF assigned him to the 4th's 334th Fighter Squadron.[31]

Fernandez got his first credit on 4 October 1952 and his fifth and sixth on 18 February 1953. On the latter mission, he was flying as an element leader when he spotted thirty-two MiGs. He singled out one, closed, and fired a long burst that hit the Red fighter's fuselage. It was last seen descending in a vertical dive. Another MiG latched onto Fernandez's tail. The Sabre pilot pulled into a hard break to the left; the MiG followed and attempted to turn inside the American, but instead snapped into a spin and crashed. It was one of two MiGs that spun out and were credited as kills on this mission. The 4th Group claimed seven victories on 18 February.[32]

On 21 March, Fernandez was leading a flight of four when Cho-do radar issued a warning that the MiGs were in the area. At this point, the number three man, the squadron commander, was forced to abort because of a mechanical malfunction, taking his wingman with him. Fernandez should have aborted, as one of his drop tanks would not jettison; but he instead headed for the MiGs, or as he put it, he found himself beneath thirty to forty Red fighters. He turned into them, got behind the last two, closed to twelve hundred feet, and fired a burst that scored hits on the enemy's wings and fuselage. The MiG began to smoke and slow as Fernandez continued to fire and get hits. The American ace shifted fire to the wingman, who took hits on the nose and then bailed out. Fernandez closed to two hundred feet on the leader and fired a long burst. He saw flames trailing from the fuselage, and the pilot slumped over the controls. The MiG then went into a vertical dive and crashed.[33] This double ran Fernandez's score up to ten. He scored one victory in April and added 3.5 credits in May, making him the top American scorer until McConnell scored three victories two days later to end the war as the top American ace.[34]

The USAF sent Fernandez home after he had flown 125 missions. He received a hero's welcome, including a meeting with President Eisenhower, a parade down his hometown's (Miami) main street, and a key from the city's mayor. A few months later, with his Korean War rival, Joe McConnell, at his side, he married an airline stewardess. He went back to fighters and in 1956 won the Bendix Trophy for setting a speed record in an F-100C. The Air Force sent him to test pilot school and then in 1960 to South America to advise the Argentineans on how to fly the F-86. Fernandez retired in 1963 as a major.[35]

Then his life began to fall apart, turning a "onetime exuberant flyboy and model citizen to an embittered, abruptly-aged, for-hire pilot."[36] Too old for the commercial airlines, he became a "freelance pilot," flying a hodge-podge of aircraft on a variety of jobs: beef cattle to Mexico City, appliances to Caracas, and Christmas trees to Aruba. On a 1980 flight in an old DC-6, the ace lost an engine and was forced to return to Colombia where he was arrested, apparently on bogus charges. He was imprisoned for forty-nine days until he paid a $25,000 fine. Broke and bitter, on 17 October 1980, Fernandez flew a twin-engine light plane from Florida without a flight plan to a lonely road on the Grand Bahama Island. There he crashed and burned along with a cargo of marijuana. Both his friends and family rejected the notion that Fernandez was a drug runner and instead believed that he was working undercover for the DEA. He was buried at Arlington National Cemetery ten days later.[37]

Some of Fernandez's bitterness arose from his belief that the USAF discriminated against him because of his Hispanic roots. He believed that the USAF pulled him out of combat and sent him home to allow McConnell, with the less ethnic sounding name, to eclipse him. This overlooks the facts that McConnell only surpassed Fernandez's score two days later and that McConnell flew 106 missions while Fernandez flew 125. In addition, the Air Force allowed James Jabara, with a clearly ethnic name, to return to Korea late in the war on a second tour that almost eclipsed McConnell. For whatever reason, Fernandez only rose one grade above his Korean War rank of captain in the next ten years of USAF service.[38]

Few of the Korean War aces have written memoirs or put their experiences on paper. Fernandez wrote a short forward to a 4th Group tactical manual during the war that laid out some advice for F-86 pilots. He began by noting that "the ideal situation in combat for fighter versus fighter is . . . to maintain a higher altitude than the enemy, giving him the opportunity to engage or break off at will."[39] As the MiG-15 had a higher service ceiling than the F-86, the Sabre pilot had to compensate by outsmarting the enemy or forcing him to make a mistake. He asserted that the F-86s should maintain the highest speed that allowed formation integrity because he considered speed next in importance. Fernandez reminded the formation leaders to maneuver gently to allow the wingmen to stick with him. The ace noted that because the Reds used the metric system of measurement, the Americans should fly 1,500 feet above round metric numbers. For example, because 14,000 meters converts to 42,000 feet, the Sabres should fly at 43,500. The F-86 pilots should use surprise. Once within range, Fernandez advised firing a "good healthy burst that would assure you of getting more hits and slowing the enemy."[40]

Fellow pilots thought well of Fernandez. He was a low-key individual and considered a great guy.[41] Known as a good shot, Fernandez had obviously profited from his tenure as a gunnery instructor at Nellis where he learned how to use the gunsight and get long-range hits. As one secondary source put it, "Most pilots of the Korean War speak in awe and admiration of the marksmanship of one particular pilot, Capt. Manuel Fernandez."[42] Unlike a number of other pilots and some aces, he took care of his wingmen. One RCAF exchange pilot summed it up, "Pete was the best there was—no argument."[43]

James Jabara: First Jet Ace and Second Highest Scorer

A third pilot in the race to be the top American ace of the war was James Jabara. Born in Muskogee, Oklahoma, in October 1923, he read about the exploits of Eddie Rickenbacker in World War I and from the sixth grade wanted to be a fighter pilot. Thus it was natural for him to join the aviation cadets upon his graduation from high school in May 1942. After earning his pilot wings in October 1943, he flew two tours in P-51s in Europe, completing 108 combat missions and claiming 1.5 aerial victories.[44] Jabara transitioned to jets in 1948 and flew Sabres for about a year before he arrived in Japan in mid-December 1950. On 3 April 1951, he got his first jet victory and then on 20 May, his fifth and sixth credits, making him the first American ace of the Korean War.[45]

This was not an accident. The USAF was pushing to get an ace. The junior service was very conscious of public relations and knew the impact that an aerial ace had on both the public's and decision makers' minds. Maj. Gen. Earle Partridge, the Fifth Air Force commander, ordered the 4th Wing commander, World War II ace (24 credits) Col. John Meyer, to pick someone for that role and position him to achieve it. Meyer named three or so pilots, including Jabara, who at this point had downed two MiGs and was seen as a good flyer with both combat and jet experience.[46] As a result, Jabara did not fly on missions that were not expected to encounter MiGs, and he only flew as a leader to increase his chances of success. Jabara stayed in Korea when his squadron (334FS) rotated back to Japan and went on temporary duty with its replacement. After racking up two more credits in two missions, he had a dry spell for almost a month. The mission of 20 May 1951 would change all that.[47]

Lt. Col. Bruce Hinton was leading the American formation that day, with Jabara leading an element with 1st Lt. Salvadore Kemp on his wing. About fifteen miles southeast of Sinuiju the Americans spotted MiGs and dropped their tanks. One of Jabara's failed to jettison, but he ignored policy to return by continuing the mission. The fifty MiGs were about three thousand feet above the fourteen Sabres, which were flying at twenty-seven thousand feet. The opposing fighters made a head-on pass, fired, but inflicted no damage. Jabara attempted to reverse and get on the tail of a MiG but failed to do so because of the hung tank. "I couldn't get into any kind of position," Jabara recalled in his after-action report: "That tank really screwed me on that pass."[48] The American formation quickly broke down into elements, with Jabara and Kemp facing off against about a dozen MiGs. Three attacked the pair of F-86s and overshot. Jabara maneuvered behind a MiG and, after going around about three times, got within range (about fifteen hundred feet) and opened fire. His second burst hit the Red fighter below the cockpit and on the left wing. The MiG burst into flames, did two snap rolls, and fell into a spin, trailing heavy black smoke. At about ten thousand feet, the stricken fighter leveled out for a moment, at which time the pilot ejected—none too soon, since the MiG then exploded.[49]

The two F-86s started to climb back to altitude but became separated. In a post-flight interview, Jabara attributed this to his wingman's slow aircraft; other accounts state that Kemp got jumped by MiGs. At twenty thousand feet, Jabara spied six MiGs and pulled in behind the trailing Red fighter. The lone F-86 pursued the Red pilot as he attempted to climb away and probably would have made good his escape except that he foolishly dove off to the left. Jabara had no trouble catching him in a dive and began firing as soon as he was within range. He got strikes on the MiG's wings and tail and saw white smoke poring out of the MiG's tailpipe. Jabara overshot but extended his speed brakes and positioned himself behind the damaged MiG, which was probably on fire, certainly smoking, and definitely flamed out as it was only going about 170 kts.

Jabara was at 6,500 feet when he heard a sound he described as a "popcorn machine right in the cockpit" as two other MiGs attacked him. Jabara retracted his speed brakes and applied full power as he observed the damaged MiG in flames and an uncontrollable spin. Although the Sabre was only traveling at about 500 kts, it was hard to control, forcing the American to use both hands on the control stick. The MiGs were on Jabara's tail firing away every time he straightened out. Tracers from the cannon shells seemed to be getting closer and closer to the evading Sabre as the fighters frantically maneuvered for about two minutes. Two F-86s heading home, flown by Morris Pitts and Gene Holley, spotted the engagement and radioed that there was a Sabre in trouble. Jabara relied "Roger, I know it only too damned well."[50] They responded, "Call me if you need help," an offer that Jabara quickly accepted. When asked who he was, he replied, in a high "g" turn: "Jaaabbbaaarraa!" The pair of Sabres entered the fray, one MiG disengaged, and the other four fighters continued to maneuver, with a MiG firing at Jabara, Holley firing at the MiG, and Pitts covering Holley. Holley fired six bursts and drove off the smoking MiG that he was credited with damaging. The F-86s returned home on minimum fuel; in fact Jabara shut down his engine and then restarted it to land.

Soon after Jabara emerged from his cockpit, Colonel Meyer awarded him the Distinguished Flying Cross. Later, in his office, he reprimanded the new ace for violating the hung tank policy. That evening Jabara told his comrades in an excited victory celebration that he had made a bad mistake that day and warned them not to continue the fight without a wingman. On 22 May, the USAF sent Jabara home. He had scored six victories on sixty-three missions.[51] However, Russian records cast doubt on Jabara's claim of being the first American ace in the Korean War. They deny losing any MiGs on 10 April (his second credit) and acknowledge losing only one on 20 May.[52]

James Jabara was short, measuring five feet five inches tall. He smoked cigars and drank beer, probably too much of both. He had weak eyes, unusual for a successful fighter pilot, and required glasses, prompting some to call him "cousin weak eyes." One pilot commented that Jabara relied on his wingman to "talk" him into the intercepts, similar to the procedures used in GCI (radar controlled, ground controlled intercept). Hyperbole perhaps, but indicative.[53]

Compared to other top aces, for which there are either positive comments or few if any critical comments on personality, Jabara drew some unfavorable memories. Although Jabara was recognized as a great pilot, he was not popular with his comrades, especially those who flew on his wing. On one occasion, Jabara grounded a wingman for firing his guns instead of strictly protecting his leader. Bruno Giordano flew on Jabara's wing on several of the ace's kills. He recently wrote that Jabara seemed "to care less about what happened to his wingman and more than once put them in harm's way."[54] He also relates an incident when Jabara attacked a flight of four MiGs that were landing. The opposing fighters crossed at a 90-degree angle; Jabara fired and missed, and Giordano just avoided a collision. The lieutenant looked back to see the MiG crash, either from the Sabre's jet wash or sheer panic. Giordano called out the crash, believed he was responsible for the MiG's destruction if anyone was, and thus claimed one MiG destroyed. Jabara, however, refuted this claim, insisting that because he initiated the attack, he deserved the credit. Giordano and Jabara "had a little discussion, but he, being the Major and Executive Officer and me being a punk second lieutenant, I lost the argument."[55]

An RCAF officer noted that Jabara always flew the fastest fighter available and then chewed out his wingman for not keeping up with him.[56] On the other hand, Lon Walter, who also flew with Jabara and shared a tent with him, had positive comments. He recalls the ace as a pleasant and quiet tent mate, considerate, and well liked.[57] The 4th's wing commander, John Meyer, relates that Jabara was a discipline problem, with bad characteristics, and that some described him as an "aggressive scrapper" and "arrogant little bastard." The 4th's commander saw the ace as a "hot shot Charlie type," cocky, aggressive, bold, "the guy who sang the loudest in the club and made more noise than the other people and dressed on the extreme side for the military." Meyer noted, however, that Jabara became more stable and mature after becoming an ace.[58]

As he had done in World War II, Jabara returned to Korea to fly a second combat tour. Arriving in the theater in January 1953, he downed his seventh MiG on 16 May, and rapidly added other credits, including pairs on 16 and 26 May and 30 June. He was in tight pursuit of McConnell's record as the war wound down. He got his fifteenth and last victory on 15 July 1953, two weeks before the war's end, and became America's second highest scoring fighter pilot of the Korean War. Jabara flew a total of 163 combat missions on his two tours and was never hit. After the war, the ace flew fighters as well as the supersonic B-58 bomber. He was killed in an automobile accident in November 1966.[59]

George Davis: Daring Ace of Two Wars

The fourth ranking Korean War ace was George Davis. He is notable not just for his high victory scores, but also as one of seven American aces in both World War II and Korea and the lone F-86 pilot of four USAF personnel in the Korean War to earn the Medal of Honor. Along with James Jabara, he scored the most doubles during one mission, on four occasions, and was the only pilot to score more than two victories on a mission, with four on 30 November 1951. He was also the only American ace to be killed in action during the Korean War.

Davis was born in Texas in 1920 and attended Harding College before enlisting in the Army in March 1942. He pinned on his wings in February 1943 and went on to fly P-47s in the Pacific Theater (348FG) where he shot down seven Japanese aircraft. Besides being an ace, two aspects distinguished his World War II record: he scored two doubles and became very adept at deflection shooting. In September 1946, the AAF assigned him to its demonstration team, the predecessor of the Thunderbirds, and then sent him to be among the first to check out in jets. In October 1951, Davis arrived in Korea to command the Fourth's 334th Fighter Squadron. He was highly experienced when he joined the unit; in addition to his seven kills and 266 missions during World War II, he had logged over 2,200 hours of fighter time.[60]

Davis flew his first combat mission on 1 November 1951 and downed his first two MiGs on the 27 November. He achieved ace status with four victories on 30 November. He added two victories on 5 December, four more on 13 December (two on a morning mission and two on an afternoon one) to push his credits to twelve. His success was probably due to his shooting skill; very good fliers are more common than very good marksmen. Some consider him to have been the best deflection shooter of the war, an opinion seemingly confirmed by his multiple successes on one mission.[61] Davis's second outstanding trait was his aggressiveness.

He was an absolute daredevil in the air, in sharp contrast to his subdued on-the-ground behavior where, contrary to that expected of the stereotypical fighter pilot, he rarely drank, did not smoke, and was not rowdy. His conduct in combat went beyond the bounds of what most fighter pilots considered reasonable. He "became more brazen, more aggressive, and more willing to take risks in Korea than he was during World War II."[62] His fellow pilots noted that Davis increased his distain for the ability of the MiG pilots as the war continued; as one pilot put it, "George just didn't respect the MiG pilots."[63] Another stated that this attitude encouraged Davis to take bigger and bigger risks as he "considered himself immortal." He wanted to run up his score and exhibited what a number have called "MiG madness."[64] After his success on 13 December, Davis did not score again for almost two months. This dry spell, coupled with his desire to kill MiGs, helps account for the events of 10 February 1952.

Flying as flight leader, Davis, on his sixtieth mission, headed toward MiG Alley to screen a fighter-bomber strike. The element leader in Davis's flight had to abort because of an oxygen malfunction; Davis's wingman also aborted because of cockpit pressurization problems. William Littlefield, who had been flying in the number four position, now took over as the leader's wingman. According to one secondary source, "Apparently bored with the patrol, Davis left his squadron's formation and took his wingman up to the Yalu to look for action. Leaving formation, especially when he was the leader, was highly unorthodox and incredibly dangerous."[65] Littlefield provides no explanation of how the pair of F-86s were separated from the other Sabres but relates that the two were patrolling along the south side of the Yalu at thirty-eight thousand feet when they saw a dozen MiGs in three flights, well below them and heading southward toward a formation of F-84s. Davis dove on the Red fighters, fired, hit, and set the last MiG in the last flight on fire. The stricken aircraft fell smoking earthward, a kill confirmed by Littlefield. Davis then made a second pass and overshot the second and third Communist flights, leaving seven MiGs behind him. Nevertheless, he deployed his speed brakes, slowed, and attacked the last fighter in the lead flight. It fell out of the formation smoking in a vertical dive. At the same time, a Red fighter closed on the F-86, fired, and hit the Sabre in the fuselage just below the canopy. The Sabre's landing gear came down; the fighter rolled over, did a split "S," and went downward, out of control, spinning in a "falling-leaf" manner. Littlefield called Davis several times but got no response. The fighter crashed thirty miles south of the Yalu. No one sighted a parachute. America's leading ace was dead. For this action, the government awarded Davis its highest decoration, the Medal of Honor.[66]

Davis was a superb fighter pilot who pushed the situation too far. One Sabre ace commented that Davis "had more guts than the law allows."[67] Benjamin Preston, the 4th Group commander, remarked that Davis was overconfident, believing that MiG pilots were incompetent and that none could touch him. Double ace "Boots" Blesse put it in more analytical terms. "what really got George Davis shot down was that he failed to realize that in every group of people there are lousy pilots and there are good pilots. He had been in contact with so many lousy ones that he lost respect for the opponent, but that day he made contact with a good fighter pilot."[68]

Understandably, the Communists attempted to learn who had downed America's leading Korean War ace. The Chinese made their claim first, but the details they offer did not match up well with what we know from the American side. More recently, the Russians have made a similar claim for one of their pilots; again, the details inspire no confidence in their claim. That being said, clearly a Red pilot downed the top USAF pilot of the day, even if the Red pilot cannot be specifically identified.[69]

It was bad enough that Davis was killed and the USAF lost its leading ace, but matters got worse. Davis's widow, mother of his two children and six months pregnant with a third, published a number of the ace's letters that embarrassed the Air Force. She told the press that her husband had written her that he wanted and expected to come home after he got his fifth credit and that he would come home at the first opportunity. Davis also made a number of pessimistic comments about the war, criticized Air Force maintenance, and declared that the F-86 was inferior to the MiG. "Things can't go on like they are," he wrote his wife. "We lose so many planes and so many men. The MiGs are so much better than the Sabres that something must be done."[70] She also complained that Davis should have been sent home, as had the first three U.S. aces. The controversy got to the point that the Fifth Air Force commander, Lt. Gen. Frank Everest, canceled a press conference scheduled with the pilots of the 4th, and those fliers were instructed not to talk to reporters about the story. There were also calls for an Air Force investigation of the situation, but it did not take place. At first, the USAF stated that Davis had volunteered to stay on in Korea. It later retracted that statement, which would have branded Davis a liar, and issued a statement that Davis and two other aces were kept in Korea "because they were needed." Internal USAF messages note that on several occasions Davis indicated that he wanted to complete his tour.[71] The Air Force also publicly stated that its ace policy had changed: initially pilots went home after becoming aces; the new policy required that everyone fly one hundred missions and permitted pilots to volunteer for an additional twenty-five.[72]

Royal Baker: Group Commander and High Scorer

Royal Baker was one of the oldest of the Korean War aces, having been born in Texas in November 1918. He graduated from college in 1941 and shortly thereafter entered the aviation cadet program. After Baker earned his wings in January 1942, the AAF assigned him to the 31st Fighter Group, which went to Great Britain in June 1942. He flew 160 missions there and in North Africa and then returned for a second tour with the 48th Fighter Bomber Group in March 1944, flying 112 missions. He scored 3.5 victories on these tours, flying Spitfires and Thunderbolts. After a twenty-month separation from the service, Baker received a regular commission in June 1947. He was a group commander (52FGp) before his assignment to the 4th in May 1952. At this point Baker had logged about twenty-three hundred flying hours.[73]

In June 1952, Baker took over as the 4th Group commander and got his first Korean War victory on 20 June 1952. Baker destroyed his fifth Communist aircraft on 25 October and his tenth on 14 February 1953. He went on to score three more victories, the last on 13 March. That same month, Baker transferred out of the unit, having flown 127 missions.[74] Baker had three advantages over most other Sabre pilots. First, he was a very experienced combat pilot. Second, due to his position as group commander, he could fly on missions on which they could expect to encounter MiGs. Third, he flew in lead positions and thus was a shooter.

Baker inspired mixed reactions from his subordinates. While some liked him, called him an excellent pilot and a great or good leader, and could recall hearing nothing bad about him, others had a contrary opinion. One stated that he was unlikable but a good combat leader. Another saw nothing spectacular in him. One of his pilots thought that he was too young for the position, was immature, and wanted to be a "big shot," a leading ace rather than a combat leader. This officer also insists that Baker discouraged his subordinates rather than encouraging them. Wherever the truth lies, the facts remain that Baker was one of the USAF's top Korean War aces; the 4th Fighter Group did well under his command, whether because of, or in spite of, his leadership.[75]

Baker went on to more success in the Air Force. He flew 140 combat missions in Vietnam, raising his overall total to almost 540 combat missions in three wars—surely among the highest number flown by an American fighter pilot. After the war, the Korean War ace served in a variety of positions and rose in rank to lieutenant general by the time he retired from the Air Force in 1975.[76]

TWELVE

Double Aces

Many pilots took the fight to MiG Alley and triumphed. But in contrast to the top aces, most of the others who scored victories have gotten lost in the endless sands of history. Three credits separate the top five American aces, those who scored thirteen or more victories, from the next highest group, six men who scored ten victories.

"Boots" Blesse: West Point, Double Ace, and Tactician

Frederick "Boots" Blesse, Leonard Lilley, and Dolph Overton were the only West Pointers who were aces in the Korean War. Blesse was born in the Panama Canal Zone in September 1921; his father was an Army doctor who later rose to flag grade. He entered West Point in July 1942 and graduated with his second lieutenant bars and AAF wings in June 1945 from the wartime compressed three-year course of instruction and nearby flight instruction. Blesse went into fighter training, flying the obsolete P-40, but was too late to fight in the war. He then flew P-47s in Okinawa and survived an over-water bailout. When the Korean War erupted, Blesse was flying F-86s with the famous 56th Fighter Group, which had scored the highest number of aerial victories of any AAF group in the war. There he flew with a number of aces, including three of the top AAF aces of the European war, Francis Gabreski, William Whisner, and David Schilling.

When he volunteered for Korea, Blesse had logged 2,300 flying hours, over 1,300 of them in jet fighters. After surviving a landing accident on his first mission in November 1950 when he hit a truck that turned his Mustang on its back and sent fuel dripping on him, he flew ground support missions, sixty-seven in F-51s and another thirty-five in F-80s. Returning from Korea, he was assigned to an F-86 outfit, Eddie Rickenbacker's famous "Hat-in-the-Ring" 94th Fighter Squadron. When Walker Mahurin, the new group commander, arrived, Blesse was assigned by the luck of the draw to check him out in the Sabre. Mahurin was less than three years older than Blesse, but while the former had demonstrated his combat skills in the European war, claiming 20.8 enemy aircraft and rising to the rank of lieutenant colonel, Blesse had been at West Point. Blesse learned much from the experienced combat veteran. He later wrote that in comparison to his air-to-air tussles with Mahurin, "combat flying was never as challenging."[1]

Blesse returned to Korea for a second combat tour in March 1952, to fly F-86s with the 4th Group. He was assigned to the 334th Fighter Squadron, initially as the engineering officer. Mahurin took over as group commander on 18 March; as many new leaders have done, he shook things up. The 334th had been in a slump since its commander and the leading U.S. ace, George Davis, was killed in action on 10 February. In the three months prior to Davis's death, the unit had claimed twenty-two aircraft destroyed—twelve of them by Davis—27 percent of the totals for the two Sabre groups; in the three months following that event, the squadron claimed only four victories, or 4 percent. Blesse recalled that the goal for many 334th pilots was to log one hundred missions and go home. Another pilot recalled that the unit would only fly to the Chong-chong River, about seventy-five to eighty miles south of the Yalu River, and thus became known as the "Chong-chong Kids." Mahurin fired the squadron commander and replaced the operations officer with Blesse.[2]

Mahurin made clear that if the new team did not produce results, defined in terms of MiGs downed, they too would be history. Blesse, who moved into Davis's quarters and took his bunk, convinced the squadron commander that the unit needed additional training that would require it to stand down from operations for a week. This was a difficult request to approve for a unit heavily engaged in combat; however, Blesse got his week. He flew with each flight commander and instituted new standardized tactics that called for tighter formations and a more aggressive attitude. The flight commanders were to train their flights in the new arrangement. Blesse replaced two flight commanders, telling one, "I'm sorry as hell, but you've [flown] sixty-five missions without a fight. You either don't want to fight or are the unluckiest guy I've ever known. Either way, I can't afford you." In Blesse's words, "It is difficult to tell the difference sometimes between bad luck and no guts."[3] Later, undoubtedly reflecting on that incident, Blesse wrote that, "unfortunately, [there] are frequently highly experienced personnel [who] have the capacity to poison your young pilots just beginning their tour of combat. These 'pseudo leaders' are people you must weed out. To 'tide' [them] along is the greatest mistake a Commander can make. . . . Warn them, remove them, and get a man who wants to do the job. You owe that much to your people who are willing to fight."[4] Blesse also instituted a policy that mandated that a pilot had to fly simulated dogfights if he had not engaged in three dogfights in a week. This kept the unit's edge keen, and morale climbed. In the next three months, the 334th claimed thirteen aircraft destroyed or 16 percent of the Sabre victories.[5]

Blesse demonstrated that opportunities to engage the MiGs varied. He spotted a MiG on his second mission but did not see another until his forty-eighth. In that engagement on 25 May 1952, the opposing fighters made a head-on pass, and then a MiG tried to out-turn the American and failed, allowing Blesse to get behind him. Blesse fired and scored hits; but the MiG moved away, trailing smoke, and headed for China. Just after a frustrated Blesse turned for home, his wingman radioed that the Red pilot had ejected: victory number one.

Less than a month later, he was involved in a different kind of dogfight. On 20 June he heard over the radio that sixteen Sabres led by Royal Baker were battling two World War II piston-powered La-9s without success. The jets would swoop down very fast and take a few shots; then, after the Russian fighters outmaneuvered them, they would then chandelle back to five thousand feet and repeat the process. Blesse ordered his wingman and his second element to provide top cover as he pealed off from eighteen thousand feet and dove to the deck. Unlike the other American attackers, as he approached the enemy fighter he deployed his speed brakes and throttled back to the idle. The Lavochkin pilot maneuvered as he had successfully done before, but this time the F-86 rolled and leveled out about four hundred feet behind him. Blesse had to fire accurately or he would quickly overtake and overshoot the Red fighter and be vulnerable before he could accelerate out of harm's way. The prop fighter blew up about two hundred feet ahead of the F-86, spraying its windshield with oil and blinding Blesse for the moment. The American pilots got three La-9s that day. Blesse knew the risks involved, especially of slowing down in combat, but had simulated such actions in stateside "attacks" on F-51s. He later wrote, "In my book, it was a calculated risk which I reasoned was worth taking. At best it was a fine line between something dumb and an act that characterized you as an outstanding pilot."[6] Success determined where that line was drawn, after the fact.

Blesse did take risks, and some might question the wisdom of some of these actions. Before his third victory, in his words, he got "too aggressive." On this occasion, after seeing MiGs, Blesse attempted to drop his tanks, but one did not depart the aircraft. The policy in this situation was to abort, as hung tanks "slowed the airplane down quite a bit and [asymmetric drag] made it stall in some pretty funny attitudes."[7] However, the lure was too much for "a hungry fighter pilot," in Blesse's words, and would only require one pass. The hungry fighter pilot started his "one pass," when he was jumped by two other MiGs. Then Blesse made a second bad decision: he ordered his wingman, whose F-86 was in a clean condition, to head home. Blesse dove for the deck and then led his pursuers on a chase that took them through the middle of Antung, a large city north of the Yalu. Blesse got over water, where the MiGs gave up the chase.[8]

Blesse, with four victories, put in for a twenty-five-mission extension as he approached one hundred missions and rotation. Four days later he got a double. On 17 September, Blesse scored his ninth victory but almost lost his wingman, Norman Smith. Blesse's .50s tore up the MiG and knocked pieces off of the fighter, some of which were sucked up by his wingman's intake. The engine was ruined, but the Sabre pilot made it over water, ejected, and was rescued by a chopper.[9] This was a precursor for Blesse's final mission, two weeks later.

Blesse was flying his 123rd mission on 3 October 1952. After cruising about for a time without seeing any enemy fighters, the number four man developed fuel problem, so he and his element leader returned home. Blesse and his wingman continued patrolling over China until they reached the minimum fuel when they turned south to return to base. As they approached the water, Blesse spotted four MiGs a mile or two behind them. Because of their fuel state, Blesse nosed down to pick up speed and continued flying toward the sea. The lead MiG opened fire, sending 37 mm shells past the two Sabres. The wingman, a new man with less than ten missions, turned and gave the Red fighter an opportunity to close the range. Blesse radioed him to put the F-86 in a spiral and hold four "g"s while he flew to the rescue. Two

MiGs pursued the wingman, with Blesse behind them and another pair of Communist fighters trailing him. Blesse fired at the second Red fighter and got hits, causing pieces to fall off the MiG. Both that MiG and his leader broke off their attack, as Blesse radioed his wingman, "Keep that thing at [Mach] .9, get it over the water, and head for home. Don't worry about me."[10] The wingman made it home safely.

The third MiG fired on Blesse, who outmaneuvered him. At this point, the American ace found himself alone in the sky with a low but sufficient amount of fuel remaining. He had climbed for altitude to save fuel when he spotted a MiG coming down on him from his left front. Calculating that he might not make it back anyway, he later recalled thinking, "Hell, it's a toss-up anyway. Why not?"[11] The MiG did not see the American, allowing Blesse to slide in behind and underneath him. He closed to six hundred feet, fired, and saw the MiG explode and the pilot eject. This gave Blesse victory number ten. He had one potential problem, however; unless he got home with use-able gun camera film, there would be no way to confirm the credit.

Blesse contacted Cho-do and requested that rescue aircraft orbit Paengnyong-do, where he considered landing if he could not make it back to base. But by this time the F-86 was too low on altitude, fuel, and luck. There was no tailwind; worse, there was a quartering headwind. Realizing the situation, Blesse headed for Cho-do and radioed his intentions to the rescue people. He was still over land when he drew enemy flak as he headed seaward. He crossed the coast at three thousand feet; about a half-mile further he radioed the rescue aircraft, which he had in sight, that he was about to bail out. Blesse disconnected his seatbelt to ensure that he quickly cleared the seat and then successfully ejected at twelve hundred feet, hitting the water almost immediately after his chute opened. He got into his one-man dinghy as the SA-16 landed and taxied toward him. The rescue crew pulled Blesse aboard; although he wanted to recover the raft with his helmet and other equipment in it, the rescue pilot vetoed that idea in no uncertain terms: "They're shooting at me and we're getting the hell out of here!"[12] One story has it that when the SA-16 neared Blesse, he was swimming around the sinking Sabre trying to get the gun camera film; this was undoubtedly hyperbole. In the end, Robinson Risner, another pilot who was in the air that day, confirmed Blesse's victory.[13]

The USAF did not want a repeat of the Davis case and ordered Blesse, who had ten credits on 123 missions and was the top living American jet ace, to return home immediately. After an extended speaking tour, Blesse served in the gunnery school at Nellis. There he produced a tactical manual he entitled "No Guts, No Glory," which standardized the way tactics were taught at Nellis and found its way throughout the USAF fighter community. Blesse retained a hand on the stick as well as on the pen. In a 1955 gunnery competition, Blesse flew with the winning team and also won all six individual events, a truly outstanding feat. He went on to fly two tours in Vietnam and retired as a major general in 1975. He had logged 6,500 flying hours, 3,400 hours in the F-86, and more than 650 in combat.[14]

In many ways Blesse fit the mold of a successful fighter pilot. He was an excellent athlete, a "ferocious competitor" who excelled in golf from his high school days and at ping-pong against fellow Sabre pilots during the Korean War. One of his wingmen later noted that Blesse was the best pilot in the 334th and probably the best in the Wing. He flew the Sabre to its limits and clearly was daring and had a desire for combat. Blesse maintains that, "the key ingredient, I think, to a successful air to air pilot is some previous experience in tactics, and the aggressiveness and the desire to want to mix it up."[15] At the same time he acknowledges that there was "a lot of luck" involved. In other ways he was atypical. Blesse neither smoked, as did many fighter pilots, nor got drunk every night, as did some. He was articulate and a decent writer. He not only wrote a contemporary tactics manual, but he is one of the few aces to write his memoirs.[16]

Vermont Garrison: "The Grey Eagle," the Oldest Ace

The oldest of the aces was Vermont Garrison, born in Kentucky in October 1915. He went to college for two and one-half years and taught school before entering the Army flight-training program. In 1941 he washed out of advanced training. This did not thwart his desire to fly; he joined the Royal Air Force, trained in California, and earned his wings. He arrived in Great Britain and, because of his gunnery skills, was assigned as a gunnery instructor. When the Eighth Air Force absorbed the famous Eagle Squadrons and their American personnel, Garrison joined the new American unit that was designated 4th Fighter Group. In the next months, he claimed seven German fighters and partial credit for a bomber. One of his fellow 4th Group pilots, James Goodson, writes that Garrison was one of the best shots in the unit. But this did not help the Kentuckian on 3 March 1944 when he was brought down by flak. He was confined as a prisoner of war until liberated by the Russians in May 1945. After the war, he again served with the 4th, flying

F-80s and leading the USAF aerobatic team. During this time period, Garrison was on the 4th's gunnery team that took top honors at a USAF-wide gunnery competition where, according to one source, he took top individual honors. In 1950, he was stationed at Nellis AFB as a gunnery instructor and an instructor of pilots deploying to Korea. Garrison got his orders for Korea when Col. James Johnson, commander of the 4th Fighter Interceptor Wing, requested him by name.[17]

"The Grey Eagle," as he was called, started out as operations officer of the 335th Fighter Squadron until he took command of that unit in January 1953. He claimed his first credit on 21 February 1953 and by the end of May had increased his victory count to four. On 5 June, he was leading a flight that saw no activity south of the Yalu, so, after turning off their IFFs, the pilots crossed into China. They flew toward Feng Cheng airfield at forty-five thousand feet and saw thirty to forty MiGs taking off. Garrison led the F-86s as they swooped down on the Red fighters at what he described as slightly over Mach 1, barreling through a formation of fifteen to twenty MiGs orbiting at twenty thousand feet, attempting to provide top cover for the airfield. Garrison pulled behind two MiGs and fired on the closest fighter. After it exploded, Garrison quickly took a second MiG under fire and he observed as it "rolled over, crashed and exploded about five hundred feet below me." Fearing he was almost out of ammunition, he had his wingman, Harry Jones, take over the lead. The lieutenant took advantage of this opportunity to fire and down a third MiG. The other two members of the flight also scored, making this an unusual mission, for seldom did all members of a flight fire, much less claim victories. Garrison's flight claimed five of the nine F-86 victories that day.

At this point, the orbiting MiGs joined the fight as Garrison radioed his troops to "break for home." With a full head of steam, the F-86s were able to shake off the MiGs before they crossed the Yalu again. The Sabres were untouched except for some MiG debris from Garrison's first kill that hit his aircraft. Garrison's two victories made him an ace—at thirty-seven, the oldest in the Korean War. He was also one of only seven Americans to down five or more aircraft in both World War II and Korea. He went on to score four more victories running his final total up to ten.[18]

In October 1953, Garrison led a 4th Group team in the Far East Air Forces gunnery meet. The team, including another double ace, Ralph Parr, lost the team event by a narrow margin, but Garrison took the top individual honors. After a number of other assignments, the USAF posted Garrison to the 8th Tactical Fighter Wing as Vice Commander in late 1966. He flew an F-4 on his fifty-second Vietnam mission on his fifty-second birthday. In all, Garrison completed ninety-seven missions in Vietnam, his third war. Garrison retired as a colonel in March 1973 and died of natural causes in February 1994.[19]

There are a number of ironies and unique elements in Garrison's career: failing AAF flight school, flying with the British, and fighting against the Soviets who liberated him from a POW camp. But he is best remembered for being a fine shot and an excellent flyer who proved his ability in fighter combat in three wars and in jets.

James Johnson: Wing Commander and Double Ace

James Johnson was nearly the same age as Garrison. Born in Phoenix in May 1916, he joined the Aviation Cadet program in December 1939 after graduating from the University of Arizona. He earned his wings and commission in August 1940 and was posted to the Panama Canal Zone where he was serving when the Japanese struck Pearl Harbor. He arrived in Britain in April 1944, rose to full colonel in February 1945, and shot down one German fighter on ninety-two missions.[20]

In November 1952, he took over command of the 4th Fighter Interceptor Wing, a position he held through August 1953. Johnson had combat experience and seniority that allowed him to pick the missions that were more promising for action, and to fly in the lead position where he could do the shooting. Johnson scored his first half-victory on 13 January 1953 and notched his fifth credit on 28 February. On that day, Johnson spotted two MiGs below him and, after dropping his tanks, chased after them. He closed on one and opened fire at two hundred feet, scoring hits on the wing, canopy, and tailpipe. Pieces flew off the Red fighter as it began to burn, and then the pilot ejected. Having fired out, Johnson took the number two position while his wingman began firing on another MiG. But Johnson was in trouble, radioing that he had suffered cockpit depressurization and the effects of hypoxia. This was evident as his Sabre went through a series of wild gyrations. His wingman, Robert Carter, screamed over the radio at him to pull out as the F-86 dove from thirty-eight thousand feet. Johnson recovered consciousness and leveled the aircraft off at five thousand feet, but the lack of oxygen had affected his eyesight; he could not read the flight instruments. Carter thought that his leader should eject over Cho-do, but after Johnson insisted on flying back to home base, Carter talked him down to a safe landing. Johnson went on to get his tenth and last MiG credit on 30 June.

After the war, Johnson served in Strategic Air Command where he first commanded an RB-47 unit and then a B-58 unit between 1957 and 1961. Johnson retired from the Air Force as a colonel in November 1963.[21]

Lonnie Moore: Bomber Pilot to Double Ace

Of all of the double aces, the least has been written about Lonnie Moore. Born in Texas in 1920, he joined the Army after graduating from high school. He entered the Aviation Cadets in 1942 and pinned on his silver wings and gold bars in September 1942. Moore piloted B-26s on fifty-four missions in the war, was shot down twice, and evaded capture on both occasions. In December 1952, he reported to the 335th Fighter Squadron. On 13 March, he got his first half-credit and then a full credit on 12 April. On 30 April, engine failure from non-operational causes forced Moore to eject. He was rescued by helicopter.

Moore hit his stride as the war closed down, downing 4.5 MiGs in June and 4 in July. On 18 July, Moore was leading a flight of four, screening a fighter-bomber strike, when radar controllers warned the Americans of approaching MiGs. Moore attacked and lost contact with his flight during his dive, but he nevertheless continued. He eluded three Red fighters that attacked him and Moore hit one, who abandoned his aircraft. This was his tenth and last victory. There are rumors that Moore was caught crossing the Yalu, threatened with a court martial, and sent home. He died in an F-101 accident at Eglin AFB in January 1956.[22]

Harold Fischer: Double Ace and Prisoner of War

Of the eleven F-86 pilots who scored ten or more victories, four were forced to abandon their machines. As we have seen, three of these pilots were rescued. Harold Fischer was the fourth to bail out; he survived but had to endure captivity that lasted beyond the end of the Korean War. He was an Iowa farm boy, born in May 1925, who built model airplanes, read about the World War I aces, overcame polio, and took his first flight at age eight. Shortly after graduating from high school in 1944, Fischer joined the Navy flying program. He soloed and logged fifty-six flying hours; however, as the war was ending, he accepted the Navy's offer to return home in July 1945.

Fischer spent two years in college and then applied for Air Force flight training and a direct commission in the Army. He received the latter and had completed infantry training at Fort Benning when his acceptance into the USAF flight school came through. Fischer used fancy footwork, paper shuffling, and initiative to transfer into the USAF. He earned his wings in December 1950. The USAF sent him to Japan to join the 8th Fighter Bomber Wing, with which he flew 105 missions, mostly in F-80s. Shipped to Japan, he manipulated a transfer to the 51st Fighter Wing in September 1952 with the encouragement of World War II and Korean War ace William Whisner. The unit was stationed on one side of the airfield at Suwon, Korea, while on the other side was Fischer's former outfit, the 8th Fighter Bomber Wing.[23]

The unit assigned Fischer to a flight that in short order was commanded by Squadron Leader Douglas Lindsay, an RCAF exchange pilot. The soon-to-be ace remembers him with great respect as "one of those extremely rare individuals, truly dedicated to getting the job done" and as the man who taught him to fly combat.[24] Lindsay was a World War II ace who pushed to maximum, leading Fischer on one mission across the Yalu, downing a MiG, and almost running out of fuel. Fischer's Sabre flamed out shortly after landing. Fischer recalled that mission: "As frightening as the consequences could have been, it was the finest indoctrination experience that a pilot could have had so early in his career. After this experience, I was no longer afraid of low fuel."[25]

On 26 November 1952, Fischer was flying the number two position on Lindsay's wing when he spotted MiGs. As Lindsay engaged two others, the Iowan dove on one in a chase that took him into Chinese territory. At approximately a two-thousand-foot altitude and one-thousand-foot range, Fischer opened fire. He got hits and overtook the slowing fighter. As he rolled around his prey, he noted that the canopy and pilot were missing and then saw the fighter crash into the barren Chinese hills. As he climbed to altitude, at about twenty thousand feet, he saw a man and parachute floating earthward. Aiming his guns to one side, he fired in order to get a photograph. Although the gun camera film revealed hits on the MiG's tail, the film ran out before the fighter crashed or the chute was seen; nevertheless the USAF awarded Fischer a destroyed credit.[26] He had scored his first victory.

Fischer added two more credits in December and another two in January to become an ace. The mission on 24 January 1953 was Fischer's forty-seventh mission. The flight was scrambled on search mission and received very precise directions from a radar controller, prompting Fischer to later write, "It was a perfect vector and the only one I received while active in the

Korean air war."[27] The four F-86s lined up behind a MiG flight of four, but just as the Sabres were about to fire, the Communist aircraft bolted. Three climbed for altitude, a favorite tactic because the MiG could outclimb the F-86, but one Red fighter broke formation and dove. As one Sabre element chased the three, Fischer pursued the diving MiG. His wingman Biffle Pittman covered him from a distance and at altitude. Fischer started about four thousand feet behind the MiG, opened fire, and scored a few hits as he slowly narrowed the distance in a chase that took him once more over China. As the F-86 drew closer, a light appeared on the MiG's tail that grew into a flame that enveloped the entire tail. By the time Fischer was within ideal range there was no need to continue firing: the MiG was fatally damaged. Fischer's rate of closure took him alongside the Communist fighter, something that he was to regret, for the American saw the MiG "pilot beating on the canopy, trying to escape. The heat must have been intolerable for the canopy was changing color and the smoke was intense."

The incident changed Fischer, for "up to that moment the enemy had been impersonal, each aircraft a target that had little meaning and not associated with flesh and blood. But the sight of another man trapped in the cockpit of a burning aircraft with no power and with no place to land was impossible for me to forget."[28] But the dogfight was not over. The trapped Communist saw Fischer and attempted to ram him. The American easily evaded the dying MiG pilot and slid back to put him out of his misery. After firing a few shots, the sound of the guns changed, three guns stopped firing, the left rudder pedal went to the firewall, and Fischer lost pressurization. The new ace had an uncomfortable flight back to base but landed safely despite concerns about the fighter's brakes. The F-86 had not been hit by hostile fire; a bullet had exploded in one of the Sabre's guns.[29] Fischer was now an ace.

On 16 February, Fischer was seating on alert when the buzzer went off, prompting a scramble. Fisher took off with Dick Knowland, who was just out of flight school and flying his first mission on his wing. Fischer's flight joined the melee and pounced on three flights of MiGs flying beneath them. Fischer went one-on-one with the number four man in the last flight. He momentarily popped his speed brakes, maneuvering the F-86 to slip six hundred feet behind the MiG. His radar gunsight worked "marvelously," allowing the .50s to pepper the Red fighter, lighting it up from wing tip to wing tip. The Communist pilot ejected. Knowland also was firing at another MiG, but the Americans had to break because a single MiG was lining up on them fifteen hundred feet to their rear. Fischer maneuvered rapidly, losing his wingman in his tight maneuvers. Both headed for home. Fischer saw what turned out to be Knowland heading south with a lone MiG about three thousand feet behind him. The Iowa ace in turn trailed the Communist fighter by about a thousand feet. Fischer radioed Knowland of the MiG's presence and told him to level off, build up speed, and run for home. Fischer also noted that another MiG was following him at a distance. The MiG trailing Knowland began to fire and then turned, but Fischer closed the space to three hundred feet and fired. The American bullets hit behind the cockpit and lit up the Red fighter. The MiG then snapped into a spin that continued all the way into the ground. Fischer then turned into the MiG following him, but the Communist fighter was going too fast and rapidly pulled away, about four thousand feet ahead of the American ace. Fischer fired out the rest of his ammunition as the MiG scampered back into China. The Sabres claimed three destroyed that day: one by McConnell and two by Fischer. Fischer now had eight credits.[30] He added one on 25 February and another on 21 March to become one of the rare double aces.

On 7 April, he was flying his seventieth mission, with Knowland again flying on his wing. In accordance with the briefing, the flight broke into elements in the patrol area, and Fischer spotted a flight of MiGs crossing the Yalu about two thousand feet below. He engaged them, closed to one thousand feet, and fired; however, the Sabre's guns were off target since its previous mission and had not been bore sighted, and the F-86's bullets went two hundred feet to the right. At this point, four MiGs jumped Fischer, forcing him to break off his attack. Since Knowland was having fuel problems, Fischer ordered him to return home. The double ace, now alone, attacked three MiGs that crossed his paths. With his guns not operating as designed, he got behind the formation and fired a long burst at the number two fighter, stopping its engine. Fischer then fired at the leader from about twelve hundred feet and tore the MiG to pieces. As he flew through the debris, the Sabre's engine stopped. Fischer turned toward the ocean and hoped to make it over water, although it would be a reach. When he smelled smoke in the cockpit, he ejected from the Sabre at two thousand feet.[31]

The cause of Fischer's shoot down is in dispute. Fischer assumed he had been downed by debris from the disintegrating MiG. As might be expected, the Communists claimed one of their pilots got the American double ace. Maj. Dimitiri Yermakov, a Soviet World War II ace with twenty-six victories, claims he downed Fischer. Another Soviet account credits Grigoriy Berelidze with shooting down Fischer. The Chinese also claimed the victory, recognizing

Han Dechai as responsible, a pilot who at that time had less than three hundred hours in the MiG.[32]

Fischer was quickly captured. Because he landed in China, he was not released in the prisoner of war exchange that marked the truce that ended the war; instead, he was confined along with some other UN aircrew until May 1955. It goes without saying that his confinement was harsh. The USAF did not give Fischer credit for any victories on 7 April and the Communists assert that Fischer damaged, but did not down, the two MiGs.[33] He stayed in the USAF after repatriation, earned a master's degree, served in an ROTC and intelligence position, and then flew helicopters, prop fighters, and jet fighters in Vietnam. He retired from the service as a colonel in May 1978.[34]

Fischer was regarded as a very aggressive pilot. There was a rumor that he was so aggressive, such a "tiger," that some did not want to fly as his wingman. Like McConnell, he believed you had to coax the MiGs down to the Sabre's altitude, which meant putting yourself at risk. He was also seen as a pilot who tended to get in too close to his victims.[35]

Ralph Parr: America's Last Double Ace

Ralph Parr blazed a remarkable record in his short F-86 combat career. In less than fifty missions over two months, he downed ten enemy aircraft, the last of which was the most controversial kill of the war.[36]

Parr was born in July 1924 and joined the Aviation Cadet program in November 1942 after graduating from high school in Bethesda, Maryland. In February 1944, the AAF commissioned him a second lieutenant with pilot wings. The service then assigned Parr as an instructor in multi-engine aircraft before sending him to transition into P-38s. In 1945, he deployed to the Pacific Theater where he flew with the 49th Fighter Group but claimed no victories. Parr left the AAF in 1946, joined the National Guard, and later in the decade went back on active duty. He flew 165 missions in F-80s in Korea with his old outfit, the 49th Fighter Group. Returning stateside, he was assigned to the 1st Fighter Group at George AFB where he served with "Boots" Blesse and Joe McConnell, honing his flying and fighting skills. Parr wanted to get back to Korea, and his former wing commander and former commander of the 4th Wing, Harrison Thyng, told Parr that if he could get assigned to Japan, Thyng would get him into the 4th. Parr landed in Korea in mid-May 1953. He had almost 2,300 first-pilot hours.[37]

Parr took over as operations officer in the 334th and engaged his first MiGs on 3 June 1953. He was flying as a wingman, as all new pilots did, but got an unusual chance to shoot when an attacking Red fighter overshot and pulled up about 6,500 to 7,000 feet ahead of the F-86. Parr fired, and remarkably at that range, got some hits although he was pulling so much lead that the MiG did not appear on his gun camera film. Parr resolved in the future not to fire until he was within range and was good to his word, not missing any of the subsequent aircraft he fired at. His gun camera film confirmed all of his credits, an unusual occurrence.

On his sixteenth mission on 7 June 1953, he got his first victories, a double. Patrolling along the Yalu, Parr was flying in the number four position when MiGs attacked Parr's flight, breaking it into two elements. As the two F-86s continued their patrol at forty-one thousand feet, Parr spotted some movement below. He radioed his element leader 2nd Lt. Al Cox, who did not see anything. As he had briefed on the ground, Cox told Parr to engage and he would take up a covering position. In his vertical power dive to the deck, Parr lost Cox and leveled off at about five hundred feet above the ground behind what Parr had believed from altitude were two MiGs. They turned out to be two flights of eight MiGs each, flying side by side.

Parr later wrote that he thought "this may be my last chance with the war winding down . . . I'm going to do it. I [might] as well 'take the leader and turn the peasants loose.'"[38] Parr had throttled back and closed to within two thousand feet when the Communists pilots spotted him and scattered. Parr admits he then made a mistake by deploying his speed brakes, but he throttled back to the idle and began firing at their leader. He pulled 9.5 "g"s and in a 70-degree deflection shot, got hits but couldn't stay with the MiG. The gun vibration blew the gunsight fuse; Parr also knew the guns would jam if he continued to fire while pulling over 7.5 "g"s. Tight maneuvering near the stall so close to the ground with so many bullets flying about made the flying extremely dangerous. Every time Parr fired, the recoil slowed the Sabre, and the F-86 flirted with a stall. The two fighters maneuvered at the low level, sometimes canopy to canopy, but Parr got slightly behind the MiG, he says ten to fifty feet, where he certainly did not need an operative gunsight. He hit the Red fighter several times, and on the fourth or fifth burst it began to lose fuel. After the next burst, the MiG erupted into flames, leaving soot on the Sabre, and then crashed.

Meanwhile, five MiGs were pursuing and firing at the lone F-86. Parr outmaneuvered the MiGs, and as each one overshot him, he got some hits on his attackers; one MiG crashed, either from the Sabre's bullets or by stalling out. The remaining Red fighters then broke off the action. Cox called Parr several times to try to join him during the fight and claims that Parr replied, "Don't bother me. I'm busy." Cox's observations and gun camera film allowed the USAF to credit Parr with two MiGs destroyed and one damaged.[39]

Parr quickly followed with a credit on 10 June and a double on 18 June that made him an ace. On the latter mission, he spotted a number of aircraft heading northward toward the Yalu at low altitude. Parr made a high-speed dive through scattered clouds and got some hits on a MiG, which hit the ground and "splashed like a raw egg." He then lined up on a second MiG, held down the trigger for two to three seconds, and got hits that sawed off the enemy's wing. He attempted to nail a third MiG, but it eluded him in the clouds.[40] On 30 June, Parr engaged more than a dozen MiGs and again downed two. As he lined up on a third, his wing commander called for help: his engine had stalled after ingesting MiG debris, and other MiGs were going in for the kill. So Parr broke off his attack to chase off these fighters. The commander was able to restart his engine, and Parr escorted him home.[41]

His last credit was probably the most controversial shoot down of the war on a mission that almost did not happen. On 27 July, Parr was scheduled to lead three flights of Sabres to escort a photoreconnaissance flight, but his aircraft was out of commission. He took the squadron commander's F-86 but was unable to retract the landing gear after takeoff. Parr made several attempts but only managed to have the gear handle come off in his hand. He then played around with the wires, upon which the gear retracted. Parr caught up with the formation; as it approached the Yalu, he spotted a twin-engine transport flying north of the river at about ten thousand feet and watched it cross the Yalu into North Korea. When the recce aircraft aborted his mission because of cloud cover, Parr got permission from the mission leader to investigate the transport. He throttled back and dove down on the unidentified aircraft. He got five hundred feet above it and observed markings such as those that appeared on the MiGs. He made two identification passes, each of which he recorded on film. Parr then checked his map to ensure he was south of the Yalu. He attacked, aiming and hitting the transport's left engine, which burst into flame, and he then shifted his fire to the craft's right engine, which also started burning. The right wing folded and the aircraft exploded.

The Soviets protested that this was a civilian aircraft carrying a truce team and was sixty miles north of the Yalu. Secondary sources claim the transport was carrying seventeen flag rank officers from Port Arthur to a Soviet intelligence conference at Vladivostok. Two days later, the Soviets shot down an RB-50 over international waters, apparently in retaliation. But the story didn't end there. The Soviets sued the U.S. government and Parr in the World Court. The charges were refuted and then withdrawn. The Il-12 was the last aircraft downed in the Korean War, only hours before the truce went into effect at midnight, 27 July 1953.[42]

Parr flew F-4s on two tours in Vietnam, logging 226 missions on the first tour and 201 on the second when he was the commander of the 12th Tactical Fighter Wing. He ended his career with six thousand flying hours in fighters and a total of 641 combat missions in three wars. Parr retired from the USAF in 1976.[43]

THIRTEEN

Other Aces

O nly a single victory credit separated the double aces from the next high-scoring American aces in the Korean War. The USAF credited two Sabre pilots with nine victories.

Cecil Foster

Cecil Foster was born on a Michigan farm in August 1925. He survived a tough childhood, losing his mother at age five and living in poverty. He joined the Army Air Forces (AAF) in 1943, went into navigation training, and served as an instructor; he thus saw no overseas service. He reported for pilot training in early 1947 and graduated in February 1948; after a brief assignment in Alaska, he was released from the USAF in a cutback. He had a struggle in civilian life and was not unhappy to be recalled to active duty as a navigator after the Korean War exploded. Foster worked his way back into an Air Force fighter cockpit, and when he arrived in the Far East, he had a total of 770 flying hours, 126 in jets, 35 of which were in F-86s.[1]

Foster arrived in Korea in late May 1952 and flew his first mission with the 51st Fighter Group the next month. He completed twenty-nine missions by the end of August, and in September checked out as an element leader. He got his chance to score in short order. He just happened to be near the operations area on 7 September, wearing his service blues and carrying his camera, just as the flight on alert was looking for a fourth pilot who was a qualified element leader. The unit had just launched the alert flight and was forming another for that duty. Foster volunteered even though he had not yet flown as an element leader. The flight leader attempted to find someone else since it was Foster's day off. Before another pilot could be found, the operations officer told Foster to suit up, and the flight was scrambled.

Foster grabbed his gear and while one pilot did a quick preflight and another started the engine, the crew chief helped strap Foster into the Sabre. Shortly after takeoff, the flight leader aborted because his landing gear would not retract, leaving Foster on an unplanned mission with two new pilots he did not know on his wing. As per procedure, one pilot was sent to orbit Cho-do as a spare while Foster and his wingman flew north. Foster spotted MiGs as he approached the Yalu and attempted to engage eight of them when more Communist fighters entered the fray. The two F-86s covered each other as they dueled with the two dozen MiGs in a giant Lufbery circle at about thirty-eight thousand feet. This went on for some time, with the Americans scoring some hits. When the F-86s reached the minimum fuel for a safe return to base (bingo fuel), Foster broke off the engagement with a steep dive at maximum power. Each of the Sabre pilots claimed one damaged MiG, but the claims board upgraded Foster's claim to a "destroyed," his first victory. Two weeks later, the unit appointed him a flight commander.[2]

On 26 September, Foster was flying as an element leader at thirty-five thousand feet along the south side of the Yalu when the flight commander spotted and pursued two MiGs. As Foster began to climb to provide cover, he encountered six Red fighters. After some maneuvers, Foster got behind the MiG leader and fired a one-second burst. The tracers just missed the target's tail but "stitched a row of hits along the fuselage of his wingman."[3] Almost immediately, the leading MiG exploded in a large black and orange fireball, while at the same time the second MiG started to burn, emitting brown and black smoke. Foster trailed the burning Red fighter as it inverted and began falling like a leaf. He continued to fire at the MiG and almost rammed the falling fighter. Then he saw a man with no helmet suspended from a parachute at thirty-five thousand, who could not possibly survive the cold or lack of oxygen at that altitude. Foster noted that this action only took seconds, perhaps six in all, compared with his earlier marathon dogfight. The explanation for the strange results was that Foster's F-86 had just been accepted by the 51st and had not been bore sighted, and one gun was shooting considerably to the left of the other five. Clearly it was a freak occurrence to hit two aircraft with one burst, and highly unusual to have one gun destroy the rugged MiG.[4]

On 22 November, Foster flew as the mission leader for four flights of Sabres escorting an RF-80 that was to photograph the famous Sui-ho Reservoir dam. After the F-86s consumed their external fuel, Foster ordered the formation to drop their tanks. Neither of his left the aircraft. Therefore, Foster and his wingman headed south as he made repeated efforts to jettison the reluctant tanks. Finally he pulled out and reset the circuit breakers, and when he toggled the tank release, the tanks fell away. Foster flew back to rejoin the escorting formation but spotted four MiGs head on that fired and missed the Americans. During the ensuing air battle, both the F-86s and MiGs fired. Foster later wrote that, "we could tell by the movements of the MiG aircraft that they were not amateurs; they were experienced pilots and they were ready and willing to fight."[5]

With fuel running low, Foster broke off the action and headed home. But the Communist pilots were not done. Two Red fighters followed the Americans and were gaining on them, closing to two thousand to three thousand feet behind Ed Hepner, Foster's wingman. He took some hits just before Foster drove off the MiG. Foster's third burst struck the Red fighter, which appeared to stop in midair, forcing the American to deploy his speed brakes, pull back his throttle, and turn in both directions to avoid overrunning the wounded MiG. The Communist pilot ejected. Meanwhile, Hepner was in deep trouble, his instrument panel shot out and canopy gone. He ejected near Cho-do and was picked up by a rescue helicopter. He was lucky to be alive because the MiG's shells had smashed his instrument panel and a piece of shrapnel had passed through his helmet, only striking him a glancing blow. Foster was relieved that his wingman had survived but disappointed that his wingman could not verify his kill. Four days later, however, the unit's intelligence officer confirmed the kill, probably from radio intercepts. Foster was now an ace.[6]

On 7 December, he added one more. First, he allowed Hepner to fly as flight leader and bag a MiG as payback for being shot down. Then Foster scored an unusual victory. Foster observed a friendly-fire incident, "red on red," as one MiG shot and hit another MiG about fifteen hundred feet ahead of him. The new ace got behind the first Red fighter as it began to spiral down. He fired, got hits, and then flew close enough to the damaged fighter to see that the pilot was wearing a cloth helmet. Foster continued to pursue the falling aircraft until his wingman, Wilton "Bing" Crosby, yelled for him to pull out. Foster had been so intent on downing the MiG that he misjudged his altitude, forcing him to pull about eight "g"s to make his recovery at about one thousand feet above the terrain.[7]

Foster did not score another victory for five weeks, and it was a difficult one. On the mission of 22 January 1953, the Americans encountered a massive number of MiGs crossing the Yalu. While the mission leader attacked the MiGs at the end of the formation, Foster swung into the middle of the MiG stream. He fired on one MiG, but the maneuver put him in front of another, who opened fire on the F-86. Foster got out of trouble and claimed a damaged MiG. Despite a lack of proof from either his gun camera film or wingman, the USAF granted a victory credit based on confirmation from other pilots in the formation. This was victory number seven.[8]

Two days later, things went better. In the morning, he flew as an element leader and engaged the MiGs. After some inconclusive maneuvering, Foster slid behind a MiG, fired a long burst from two thousand feet, and got some hits. Although he thought he had only damaged the Red fighter that got back across the Yalu, other pilots saw its flaming descent and crash. On the afternoon mission, Foster was flying in the number four slot, checking out another pilot as an element leader. Again the Sabres engaged MiGs near the Yalu. In the midst of the action, the would-be element leader did not react as Foster thought he should, so in frustration he took over the lead. Foster lined up behind a MiG at two thousand feet, got a lock on with his radar ranging sight, fired, and scored some hits before he was forced to break off the action. Again Foster claimed a damaged MiG, and again other pilots confirmed that it had flamed and crashed. Thus, Foster downed two aircraft on one day, albeit on two different missions. This ran his score up to nine MiGs destroyed.[9]

Remarkably, Foster got all his MiGs south of the Yalu, unlike many, if not most, of the other aces. So he was shocked when the acting group commander called him and five other pilots into his office and accused them of crossing the Yalu. The colonel reasoned that the six must have crossed the river because they were getting kills while others flying over North Korea were not. As this was a violation of policy, the commander asserted he was going to send them all to fly T-6s as forward air controllers with the Army. The only alternative was a court-martial. No one said a word until Foster looked the colonel squarely in the eyes and forcefully explained that he had not gone across the river; members of the headquarters staff who had flown with him knew this, and therefore he would take the court-martial. The colonel was stunned, and after a brief exchange and a long silence with the two men staring at each other, the colonel dismissed the six. There were no transfers or courts-martial. That night the squadron (16FS) was grounded. Foster was disgusted and no longer wanted to fly under that colonel. He had officially flown 98 missions, although the true number was closer to 110.[10]

Foster flew fighters throughout the rest of his career. He commanded an F-4 squadron in Vietnam during 1968–69, flying 168 missions and surviving one bailout. He retired in 1975 having flown over five thousand hours.[11]

James Low: Junior Pilot, High Scoring Ace

James Low made a name for himself both for his tactics and also for the fact that he was the only second lieutenant to become an ace in the Korean War. He was born in California in September 1925 and served in the Navy during World War II. He joined the USAF and did well in training, out-shooting his instructor in gunnery and graduating from flying school in December 1951, the oldest in his class. In April 1952 he joined the 4th's 335th Fighter Squadron.[12]

The 335th was doing very well at this time, the highest scoring F-86 squadron between 1 March and 1 August 1952, downing twice as many MiGs as the next highest scoring squadron. Low joined a flight that included Philip Colman, a World War II ace who added four victories in Korea; James Kasler, who got his fifth kill in mid-May 1952; and Robert Love, who became an ace in late April. Low had excellent vision (20/10) and was considered a good pilot, eager, and aggressive. While he writes that the leader would allow him to lead the attack when he saw the MiGs first, others state that he would just break away from his leader in lone wolf style. The flight he joined had a unique policy that allowed anyone to shoot, rather than limiting the wingman to protecting the leader as a matter of standard policy. At one point, his commander was about to ground him for breaking away from the formation. However, as double ace "Boots" Blesse notes, it is "difficult to discipline a guy that comes back with a kill, even though he's broken the rules."[13] And that was the case with Low.

On 8 May 1952, Low was flying one of his first missions, when four MiGs jumped the F-86s. The American leader, James Kasler, made a number of sharp breaks with Low maintaining his wingman's position through several of these. But Low still had his tanks attached and lost Kasler on the fourth break as three MiGs attacked him. The second lieutenant dropped his tanks, jammed his throttle to full power, and maneuvered behind a Red fighter and downed him. Kasler was understandably very steamed because, fighting without a wingman, he was almost shot down. Harrison Thyng, the 4th's Wing commander, questioned the new pilot about losing his leader, but wanting results—MiGs destroyed—he went to bat for him. Low responded, "I got lost and I got screwed up. I knocked an airplane down; I guess that vindicated me, but it wasn't my choice."[14]

Low earned the reputation of a pilot who left his leader, a reputation he never shook. James Horowitz, another pilot in his flight, wrote, under a pen name, a novel of the MiG Alley story entitled *The Hunters*.[15] Hollywood made it into a movie. The book's bad boy was turned into a more appealing, "pretty swell guy," and Robert Wagner, who in his youth never played a bad guy, was cast in the Low role. Low thought Horowitz was a good writer but had a low opinion of him as a fighter pilot, describing him as a "Hudson High [West Point, class of 1945] boy" who didn't want to fight. Low also observed that Horowitz "didn't particularly like me, obviously."[16]

Low quickly racked up more scores. On 11 June, he was sitting alert when radar detected MiGs taking off. The Sabres scrambled, but at forty-five thousand feet, the American pilots could not spot the MiGs, which were flying at fifty-five thousand feet, until they let down a bit and pulled some contrails. One MiG dove down and attacked Low's element, but Low out-maneuvered him, and got a few hits. The MiG then flipped over and spun out, encouraging the pilot to bail out. Another Red fighter came by and Low shot out his engine, giving Low a double. Four days later, he got his fifth victory. He had only been out of flight school six months.[17] After he claimed his sixth credit in July, the USAF sent him back to the States to lecture on the F-86, especially the much maligned and mistrusted radar gunsight. He had flown forty-four missions.

The young ace returned to the action in October as a first lieutenant. He did not receive a very positive reception; in his words, "the new regime kind of sat on my ass, and I was a wingman for forty more missions before I got a chance to lead again."[18] But his superior vision again allowed him to see MiGs the others could not. He got three more victories in December. One of these was his most difficult engagement. Low sighted two MiGs about five miles away and gave chase with his wingman. The two Communist fighters split up. As Low's wingman was in a better position, Low allowed him to take the lead. In any case, the MiG pilot was very good, for while Low's wingman got within five hundred feet, he could not pull enough lead to hit the MiG. Instead, his bullets were falling harmlessly behind the Red fighter. Low radioed him to stop firing until he had more lead, but the wingman had target fixation and instead fired out. Low then slid into the lead position and had the same problem: not enough lead against the maneuvering MiG. The dogfight ended up one hundred feet off the deck and on the Mach, maneuvering around the hills and mountains until Low scored some hits in the tail. A second burst hit the engine and wing root. The canopy flew off, but the pilot didn't eject. He continued to battle Low, at one point pulling straight up with a dead engine and firing at his attacker. But the Sabre's .50s caught him dead center, and he didn't pull out of the dive and crashed. On his last victory on 18 December, Low used the radar gunsight to good use and hit the MiG with his first shot at almost maximum range, forty-eight hundred feet. He finished his tour with nine victories.[19]

There are some who assert Low was sent home after losing his wingman. One pilot claims that the 335th Squadron commander, Carrol McElroy, said that, if he could prove what he knew, he would court-martial Low for using his wingman as bait. No 4th Group pilot was lost during any of the three days on which Low scored victories in December, although Donald Reitsma of the 335th was listed as missing in action on 22 December 1952.

Low did show more eagerness for destroying MiGs than for the well-being of his wingman. On one mission, Low led his element across the Yalu and chased a MiG that was flying between Mukden and Port Arthur. The F-86s closed on the Communist fighter; however, the wingman declared "bingo" fuel, indicating he had fifteen hundred pounds remaining, the amount calculated to get a Sabre home from MiG Alley. The wingman also knew that the Sabre pair was at least fifty miles north of the Yalu and flying farther away from their base in the chase. Low responded that they were gaining on the MiG and would get him shortly. When his fuel dropped to twelve hundred pounds, the wingman again radioed his fuel state and got the same reply. The chase was now down at fifteen thousand feet where fuel consumption increased and where the Sabre left a black smoke trail that would attract MiGs. In due course, the wingman announced nine hundred pounds remaining and Low responded as before. When his fuel gauge read eight hundred pounds, the wingman declared he was heading for home. He climbed to altitude, where fuel consumption was less and tail winds possible, and crossed the Yalu with four hundred pounds of fuel.

Low joined up with his wingman in a loose formation. One hundred miles from home base the wingman had one hundred pounds of fuel; he therefore shut down his engine and set up an optimum glide speed. When he reached one thousand feet, he restarted the engine and landed. His engine ran out of fuel as he taxied in from the runway. What saved the wingman was his coolness, skill, and a two hundred mile per hour tail wind. After filling out the required paperwork on his F-86E, the wingman went over to Low's aircraft (F-86F) and saw that his fuel gauge read six hundred pounds. This revealed much about Low.[20]

Low returned to the States and flew for a while with the Sabre Knights aerobatic team. The Korean War ace went on to fly fighters in Vietnam and was shot down and captured in December 1967. The North Vietnamese released Low in August 1968 although they held almost all the other prisoners until 1973. He retired as major in January 1973.[21]

Aces in Two Wars

Twenty of the AAF's 683 World War II aces added additional victory credits in Korea. Six World War II AAF aces (two of whom—George Davis and Vermont Garrison—have already been discussed) shot down five or more enemy aircraft in Korea. In addition, one Marine shares the distinction of being an ace in two wars.

James Hagerstrom: F-86 Ace Not with the 4th or 51st

Of the remaining World War II aces, James Hagerstrom had the highest score in Korea. Born in Cedar Falls, Iowa in January 1921, at age five Hagerstrom got to sit in a Jenny biplane and had his first flight eight years later in a Ford tri-motor. Hagerstrom attended college for two years, during which time he participated in both an infantry ROTC program and a flying-training program, logging thirty-five flying hours. In January 1942 he entered the AAF and, because of his previous training, was able to earn his wings and commission in just six months. He flew 170 missions in P-40s in the southwest Pacific and downed six Japanese aircraft, four in one morning.

After separating from the AAF, the ace returned to college and earned a degree in economics. He joined the Texas Air National Guard and flew P-51s. Hagerstrom advanced in rank to major and took command of the 11th Fighter Squadron, which was federalized shortly after the start of the Korean War. Assigned to Tactical Air Command headquarters, he checked out in jets and convinced the commander that some staff officers should fly a combat tour in F-86s. The USAF sent Hagerstrom to gunnery school at Nellis, where his instructor was William Whisner. Hagerstrom was then posted to the 4th

Fighter Group as the operations officer. He arrived in September 1952 with about twenty-five hundred flying hours, mostly in fighters.[22]

On 21 November Hagerstrom was returning to base from a patrol, having reached bingo fuel, when he spotted two MiGs about fifty miles south of the Yalu. The Communist fighters split, as did Hagerstrom's element. The World War II ace got behind a MiG and fired. The MiG pilot ejected just before his fighter exploded. After Hagerstrom returned to base and shut down the engine, the group commander, Col. Royal Baker, drove up in a staff car. After getting out and observing the blackened Sabre nose (from the guns' discharge), Baker asked Hagerstrom if he had gotten a MiG. The major answered "yes," but when asked who would confirm the kill, Hagerstrom had to admit he did not know, unless the gun camera film captured the shoot down. At this point, the crew chief came over and asked the Colonel to look at a chunk of MiG-15 debris lodged in the leading edge of the left wing. With that, Baker said he would confirm the kill. In any event, the gun camera film did show the MiG pilot departing the stricken fighter.[23]

His next credit was on Christmas day, when radar controllers directed an F-86 flight toward six MiGs. Hagerstrom was leading the second element and got one thousand feet behind a MiG at nearly fifty thousand feet. He was about to fire when the Red pilot overcontrolled and snapped into an inverted spin. Because stability is reduced at high altitudes, a gentle touch is required; moreover, the MiG was noted for its tendency to snap into a spin. Hagerstrom popped his speed brakes, cut the power, and rolled over to follow the MiG downward. He was about to open fire at the spinning MiG when the pilot ejected. His parachute opened at about forty-four thousand feet, a jump altitude not conducive to long life. Number two.[24]

After he had completed fifty to sixty missions with the 4th, the USAF sent Hagerstrom to the Eighteenth Fighter Bomber Wing in early 1953 to help it transition into the fighter-bomber version of the F-86. The Air Force concept was that the F-86, fitted with four stores stations for tanks, bombs, or both, could serve as a fighter-bomber as well as function as an air-superiority fighter. One problem, however, was that some fighter pilots focused more on getting MiGs than on dropping bombs. As Hagerstrom later admitted, "I was interested in shooting down MiG-15s. That was the name of the game."[25]

On 25 February he attacked a MiG that was after another Sabre and pursued him at low level, literally over the smoke stacks of Mukden, 120 miles north of the Yalu. The Communist pilot bailed out and Hagerstrom returned with minimum fuel; his wingman flamed out on the runway.[26]

Hagerstrom downed two MiGs on 27 March and another on 13 April, and then in May was ordered to return home. As he was waiting in the flight operations office in his blue uniform for transportation from Korea to Japan, he learned that the unit was looking for pilots to immediately scramble four F-86s. Hagerstrom quickly found three pilots, strapped a parachute over his blues, and made for the flight line. A radar controller guided the Sabres northward into a formation of two dozen MiGs which Hagerstrom attacked as it headed back across the Yalu. He engaged a MiG that began to smoke and then went into a dive. Hagerstrom's wingman confirmed the kill, increasing his credits to 8.5 MiGs. During his debriefing he was told to get on an awaiting transport to fly to Japan and then on home. He had flown about twenty-five air-to-ground missions and seventy-five air-to-air missions.[27]

Hagerstrom later commanded a fighter squadron, and then a group. The ace held various staff positions and in his off time earned a law degree. In 1965 the USAF sent him to Vietnam, where he flew thirty combat missions. In late 1966 he passed the California bar examination; less than two years later he retired from the Air Force. He went on to practice law before retiring from that profession in 1980. He died in June 1994.[28]

Hagerstrom was a successful fighter pilot and leader. He focused on getting MiGs and did that very well. He was unusual in a number of ways. He did not drink, as did most fighter pilots, because he did not want to square off against the MiGs at less than 100 percent capability. Instead, he spent his spare time building HO gauge model railroads. One of his fellow pilots noted that he was a good leader with strong religious beliefs and was a fanatic at killing the enemy. He remembers Hagerstrom as an intense fighter pilot who was very aggressive; he was fighting a crusade, not a war.[29] Hagerstrom went to great lengths to ensure his success and safety. Some pilots used binoculars or monoculars to spot the MiGs. Hagerstrom went one step further: before he went overseas he had an optometrist make him a pair of glasses to enhance his distance vision. In addition, he had them mirrored on the top so that he could detect an aircraft flying in front of the sun. He claimed that he could look at a 500-watt light bulb with these glasses and read the writing on the bulb.[30]

Francis "Gabby" Gabreski: Top U.S. European Ace, Ace Again

Most likely the best known of the aces of the two wars was Francis "Gabby" Gabreski. Born in Oil City, Pennsylvania, in January 1919, he showed little interest in aviation until he had attended Notre Dame for two years. He took some flying lessons and logged six hours of flying time while in college but did not solo. Gabreski entered the Army Air Corps in July 1940. In training, he proved to be only a marginal pilot, a slow learner who was almost eliminated from the program, passing an "elimination" check ride before graduating with a commission and wings in March 1941. The Army assigned him to a fighter squadron in Hawaii where he flew P-36s and P-40s. He got airborne on the day of the Pearl Harbor attack but did not engage any Japanese aircraft. Because he could speak Polish, he was assigned as a liaison officer to a Polish squadron based in Britain and flew approximately twenty-five missions in Spitfires.

In February 1943, the AAF assigned him to the 56th Fighter Group where he downed twenty-eight German fighters in P-47s to become the highest scoring American fighter pilot in the European theater. Having flown 166 missions, he was ordered home but had the chance to fly one more mission and took it. Unlike Hagerstrom's experience in Korea, this did not turn out well. Gabreski did not encounter any German aircraft but did strafe a German airfield. On a second pass, not a good decision either, his prop clipped the ground, forcing the Thunderbolt down. The Polish-speaking ace was able to evade the Germans for five days before being taken prisoner.

After the war, he briefly served as a test pilot before separating from the service in April 1947. He flew with the California Air National Guard and worked for Douglas Aircraft for a year before the Air Force recalled him as a lieutenant colonel, one grade below his highest wartime rank. For a short period, he commanded the 55th Fighter Squadron, and then the service sent him to Columbia University where he earned an undergraduate degree in Political Science. In August 1949 the USAF assigned him to his old unit, the 56th, then flying F-80s. As commander of the unit, he oversaw its transition to F-86s. In June 1951, the Air Force posted him to Korea to join the 4th Fighter Wing in Korea, the 56th's World War II rival.[31]

On 8 July 1951 he flew his fifth mission, leading a flight of four F-86s escorting fighter-bombers striking railroad targets. Alerted by radar that MiGs were heading across the Yalu, Gabreski's flight spotted a number of MiGs but was unable to engage them. Then, as the Americans were about to break off the escort and return home, they spotted a Red fighter below them at ten thousand feet. Gabreski dove at full power to get behind the lone MiG, closed to nine hundred feet, and fired a long burst. He got hits over the entire aircraft and lit up the trailing edge of the right wing, as pieces shredded off into the slipstream. The MiG rapidly slowed and pulled up as Gabreski overshot before reversing for a second pass. At this point, the damaged fighter was going down in a smoking, flaming, vertical dive. Gabreski fired again and hit again, and then the Communist fighter entered an inverted spin. Gabreski and his wingman saw the fighter crash. This was his first Korean War credit.[32]

In November, Gabreski took over the 51st Fighter Wing. The first order of business was to transition the unit from F-80s into F-86s, a feat the Wing did in just ten days without the loss of a man or machine.[33] Gabreski led the 51st on its first mission on 1 December 1951 but did not get his fourth victory until 11 January. On 20 February the 51st Wing commander fired six short bursts at a MiG he was chasing toward the Yalu and had gotten hits on its fuselage and wings when a piece fell off the Red fighter and cracked his windshield. He therefore broke off the action. Bill Whisner, who was leading another flight that day, observed the dogfight from a distance and watched as it spiraled down toward his altitude. He saw a half dozen MiGs being hunted by a flight of Sabres, which he overtook and identified as Gabreski's. When Gabreski broke off the action, Whisner continued to trail the damaged MiG and confirmed the kill for his commander, a most noble sentiment in view of the race between the two pilots to be the first jet ace in the 51st.

Fifty miles inside China, and with his fighter at bingo fuel, Whisner realized he had no more time. He then fired three bursts at the damaged MiG and watched as the fighter dove into the ground. Returning to base, Whisner found that Gabreski had claimed a "probable destroyed" for that MiG. Whisner filed a report confirming the incident as a "destroyed" claim for Gabreski and submitted no claims for himself. That evening Gabreski called Whisner and told him not to lie about the incident and asked if Wisner had fired and hit the MiG. They argued rather heatedly about how the incident should be reported, with the conversation ending with Gabreski slamming down the phone. Ten minutes later, the Wing Commander told the Squadron Commander that they would share the honors, bringing both of their totals to 4.5 MiGs.[34] Three days later, Whisner won the distinction of being the first ace in the 51st. Gabreski went on to fly 123 official missions in Korea—he did not count all of his missions—and add two more victories before he was grounded in mid-May and ordered home early the next month.[35] He did not fly that "extra" mission as he had in World War II.

Gabreski went on to the Air War College, staff assignments, and command of various fighter wings. He retired in November 1967 as a full colonel with over five thousand total flying hours, four thousand in jets. He worked for Grumman aviation and then the Long Island railroad before he died in

January 2002.[36] He is best known as America's leading ace in Europe during World War II and for the five decades until his death as the leading living U.S. ace.

There were two views of Gabreski. To the public, and to some, if not many, of his pilots, he was more than just a good fighter pilot; he was flamboyant, heroic, a "fighter pilot's fighter pilot." Certainly in terms of destroying enemy aircraft, he was extraordinarily successful. There is, however, another side of Gabreski that is not as complementary, not as well known, and seldom — if ever — talked or written about. He had a poor reputation with wingmen. He flew the fastest aircraft available and, in action, did not recognize that his wingmen could not keep up in their slower aircraft, a factor that put them in peril. As a result, some pilots were afraid to fly with him. To several pilots, Gabreski seemed more interested in personal glory than in his wingmen or in running an F-86 wing. There is a thin line between leading from the front and being a hot dog, or perhaps better put, a "MiG mad" pilot.

In addition, Gabreski may have originated, or certainly participated in and tolerated, the Sabre penetrations of Chinese territory. The tactic of remaining in the combat area as long as possible despite minimal fuel was a two-edged sword: risky and costly but aggressive and successful in downing MiGs. He also pushed his troops to top its rival, the 4th Fighter Wing, in destroying MiGs; in so doing, he directly encouraged exaggerated, if not false, claims. He also tolerated, although he did not directly engage in, the rowdy, drunken behavior of his flying officers. One pilot believed that Gabreski, in his efforts to be a popular leader, was afraid to confront and discipline his troops. Another explanation is that Gabreski fostered this conduct as conducive to achieving the mission: kill MiGs.[37]

William Whisner

William Whisner was the youngest of the seven who were aces in two wars. Born in Shreveport, Louisiana, in October 1923, Whisner was active in scouting and was a member of the Junior ROTC in high school. He enlisted in the AAF after graduating from high school, joined the AAF cadet program in April 1942, and won his wings and commission in February 1943. He went to Britain with the 352nd Fighter Group, which flew its first combat mission in September 1943. The Air Force credited Whisner with destroying 15.5 German fighters, six on one day and four on another. Discharged in August 1945, he was recalled one year later. He joined the 4th Group in Korea in 1951.[38]

He got his first two credits on two successive days in November 1951 before he transferred to the 51st as it converted to F-86s. He took command of the 25th Fighter Squadron and added two victories in January, tying him with Gabby Gabreski as the highest scorer in the group. He posted a half credit on 20 February, splitting that victory with Gabreski. Three days later, Whisner joined a dogfight in which a number of MiGs were attacking Don Adams, who soon would be an ace. Whisner forced the Red fighters to break off their attack and pursued one. He closed to nine hundred feet and fired, further decreased the range and fired again. The Communist pilot bailed out just before his fighter exploded. Thus Whisner became the first ace in the 51st Fighter Group. This was his last Korean War victory credit.[39]

Whisner returned to the States, took up an assignment at Nellis Air Force Base, and won the Bendix Trophy in 1953. Whisner commanded a number of squadrons, served in staff positions, and ended his Air Force career as the Chief of Staff of the Seventeenth Air Force. He retired as a full colonel in August 1972. In July 1989, a pilot who had flown and fought in two wars and claimed twenty-one enemy aircraft destroyed, died from a yellow jacket sting.[40]

Harrison Thyng

Harrison Thyng has the distinction of flying in three wars, downing fighters of at least three nations, and being the only ace of two wars to achieve flag rank. He was born in Laconia, New Hampshire, in April 1918 and attended a one-room school before he went on to graduate from the University of New Hampshire in 1939. He participated in Army ROTC and received an officer's commission but quickly applied for flight training. Thyng was awarded his wings in March 1940.

Shortly after America entered the war, he was commanding a fighter squadron in the 31st Fighter Group, the first AAF fighter unit to move to Britain where it transitioned to Spitfires. Thyng led the first American fighter mission over Europe and then was part of the covering force for the invasion of North Africa. During the first day's operations on 8 November 1942, Vichy French fighters attacked and downed one of the 31st's fighters, upon which Thyng's flight destroyed three of the Dewoitine 520s, one credited to him. The war continued across North Africa, where Thyng was downed behind enemy lines and walked out and then was hit by British antiaircraft artillery and forced to bail out. Before leaving the Mediterranean theater, he flew 162 missions, rose to command the 31st, and destroyed four German fighters.

The ace went on to command the 413th Fighter Group that flew P-47N long-range fighters operating out of Iwo Jima against Japan. There he flew twenty-two missions and logged one Japanese aircraft as a probable kill. After the war, the USAF assigned him to the Air National Guard in New England for three years, during which time he checked out in the F-80. In 1951 he commanded the 33rd Fighter Wing, flying F-86s for a half year before he was ordered to Korea as the commander of the 4th.[41]

On 24 October, while leading a flight of Sabres, he attacked eleven MiGs, hit the leader, and forced him to eject from his fighter. The Wing commander slowly built up his tally with three victories over the next five months. On 20 May, Thyng and his wingman were pursuing two MiGs at a lower altitude when they in turn were bounced. Thyng turned into the attacking Communist fighters, who responded with a tight maneuver. One of the fighters fell into a tight spiral and dive from which it did not recover. Thyng was now an ace. In all, he flew 114 missions in Korea.[42]

Thyng left the 4th in October 1952 for a number of assignments in Air Defense Command. He later served in the Pentagon and Federal Aviation Agency; then, in May 1963, the USAF promoted him to brigadier general. He spent a brief time in Vietnam in 1966, testing air-to-air missiles, during which time he flew several combat missions. He finished his Air Force career in Air Defense Command before retiring in March 1966, having flown 650 combat hours. He ran a close but unsuccessful campaign for the U.S. Senate that same year and then served as the president of a junior college until 1973. Thyng died in September 1983.[43]

Thyng certainly achieved a number of distinctions as an ace and leader. A few additional points are in order. His score in Korea may not reflect his abilities because some sources claim that after he got his fifth victory there, he did not claim any further credits—which is certainly true—but instead gave these victories to his wingmen. More clearly, Thyng exhibited not only physical skill and courage, but also moral strength and integrity as well. In December 1951, he sent a personal message to the Chief of Staff of the Air Force, forcefully explaining the dire situation in Korea, specifically that the supply situation was inadequate and that his Sabres were greatly outnumbered. He emphatically warned that air superiority might be lost with the words, "I can no longer be responsible for air superiority in north-west Korea."[44] Bosses normally do not like to hear bad news, so Thyng was putting his career on the line with this message as well as by going over the heads of his immediate superiors at Fifth Air Force and Far East Air Forces. His chief clerk, Staff Sergeant Gordon Beem, realized the possible consequences of sending the message and asked Thyng if he really wanted to send it. Thyng replied, "Yes, there are too many lives at stake not to."[45] The message was sent. Gen. Hoyt Vandenberg took quick action to alleviate the situation.

John Bolt: The Last Marine Ace

John Bolt was the only non-USAF pilot to become an ace in the F-86.[46] He was born in Lauren, South Carolina, in May 1921, and attended the University of Florida for two years before entering the Marine Corps in July 1941 to pay for further college. Bolt earned his wings and commission in July 1942. After a stint as an instructor, he joined and flew three tours with Pappy Boyington's famous Black Sheep Squadron, flying the F4U on ninety-two missions and downing six Japanese fighters. He returned for a brief stint aboard a carrier in 1945.[47] In 1951, he flew an exchange tour in USAF F-94 night fighters before transferring to another Air Force unit and logging one hundred hours in the F-86. He then was sent to Korea to fly F9Fs in the ground attack role. On a recreational leave from the unit, he visited George Ruddell, whom he had met a few years earlier and who was the squadron commander of the 39th Fighter Squadron in the 51st Fighter Group, the only unit in Korea flying the F-86F. Bolt explained that he not only had combat experience, but he had also flown the F-86F. Bolt was able to fly the F-86 in Korea after a USAF general requested that the Marines detach Bolt to fly with the Air Force. Ruddell detailed Joe McConnell, who had been taken out of combat, apparently for crossing the Yalu, to fly two or three flights to show Bolt combat tactics being used at the time. Bolt later said McConnell "really taught me lots of things." Bolt had received an assignment he had been told was impossible for him to get, as he already had a "gravy tour."[48]

In March 1953, he began a ninety-day exchange tour with the USAF in the 51st Fighter Group. Ruddell assigned the Marine to the flight under McConnell's command, "D" flight, known as the "hot dog" flight, where he flew the USAF ace's wing on a number of missions. After McConnell rotated home, Bolt took over the flight. He downed four MiGs on thirty-four missions and then got a ninety-day extension, obviously to enable him to achieve acedom.[49]

Bolt was flying his thirty-seventh Sabre mission on 11 July 1953, a mission escorting reconnaissance aircraft. The war was coming to a close, and the 51st pilots had not seen a MiG in ten days. The Marine led his element across the Yalu, and from twenty thousand feet Bolt saw four MiGs that had just taken off. He bounced the Red fighters that were at about five hundred feet and going full speed. Bolt overtook them, but blacked out in a high "g" pull out and ended up about fifteen hundred feet behind the MiGs. He opened fire and was almost hit by his wingman, who also opened fire but should not have. Bolt closed to six hundred feet and fired four bursts at the trailing MiG, which began to smoke and then rolled over and crashed. He closed to within five hundred feet of the other Communist fighter, scored hits, and watched as the MiG began to burn—so close that the dense smoke almost blinded him. The pilot ejected. These were his fifth and sixth—and last—credits.[50]

Bolt consistently crossed the Yalu. He writes of attempting to provoke the Red aviators by hitting their airfields with sonic booms and making low-level, high-speed passes across their airfield. The Americans joked that they were setting their watches from the control tower on Antung airfield.[51] Bolt stayed in the Marine Corps after the war and went on to earn an undergraduate degree from the University of Maryland in 1956. He also commanded his old outfit, the "Black Sheep Squadron," and served in a number of instructor assignments.

Bolt retired from the service as a lieutenant colonel in April 1962 and worked for private industry. When he was passed over to be the company's CEO, he entered the University of Florida law school and earned a law degree in 1969. The Marine ace taught there for two years, and then went into private practice in Florida until he retired on his seventieth birthday in 1991.[52]

FOURTEEN

Other Groups of Pilots
Who Flew F-86s in Korea

lthough John Bolt was the most famous and most successful of the
non-USAF pilots who flew F-86s, there were others, the largest con-
tingent coming from the marines.

Exchange Pilots: RAF, RCAF, Navy, and Marines

There were a number of reasons why other air forces sent their pilots to fly F-
86s in Korea. The Sabre was the best fighter in the West in the late 1940s and
early 1950s, adopted by a host of countries and, quite unusually, by both the
Navy and Marine Corps.[1] Another factor that attracted non-USAF pilots to
the two F-86 units was that the Korean War was the first large-scale air conflict since World War II and the first to use jets. Because the UN forces faced
Soviet equipment and Soviet and Soviet-trained pilots, it was also a primer for
a conflict that the West feared would engulf Europe.

American airmen, both as individuals and in units, had close contacts
with Commonwealth airmen beginning in World War I. Americans served in
both the RAF and RCAF, and American and Commonwealth units served
side by side (or perhaps better put, wing to wing) in World War II. The Commonwealth air forces played a small role in the Korean air war. The Royal Air
Force committed only one unit, a maritime reconnaissance squadron; the
Canadians, no units; and the Australians and South Africans, one fighter unit

each. Probably the most important Commonwealth air contribution was made by the Royal Navy.[2]

The Royal Air Force sent at least seventeen pilots on exchange duty. Five of these accounted for six MiGs, two by Graham Hulse. He was killed, as was another British pilot; a third was shot down and survived captivity, and a fourth was rescued after a mechanical failure.[3] Canada sent twenty-two pilots, all but one of whom flew in combat, logging a total of 1,036 sorties with S. B. Fleming flying the most, 82 sorties. Six RCAF pilots notched nine victories—three by Ernest Glover, who had flown Hurricanes and Typhoons in World War II and was captured by the enemy, and two by James Lindsay, a World War II ace. John McKay was another World War II ace that added 1 MiG to his 11.2 credits, which included an Me 262. Two RCAF pilots were forced to eject, one was downed by friendly fire and captured, and another was rescued after his Sabre suffered mechanical failure.[4]

The U.S. Navy sent as many as six pilots, two of whom scored one credit each, without a loss. But the most famous Navy exchange pilot was a pilot who neither scored a victory nor was lost: Walter Schirra went on to become an astronaut.[5] The Marines made more use of the opportunity to exchange than did the Navy. They had two exchange pilots with each of the two F-86 wings and, based on their victory totals, probably had more pilots cycling through those units than any of the other air forces. Eleven Marines scored 21.5 victories. Bolt downed six MiGs, two other pilots had three victories each, and another two pilots had two each. One Marine exchange pilot was killed in action and another was shot down and rescued.[6] Two of these pilots deserve further treatment.

John Glenn: Pilot and Astronaut

Probably the most famous Marine pilot to fly in F-86s, and for that matter in the Korean War, was John Glenn. (Vying for this distinction, Ted Williams, the outstanding Boston Red Sox hitter, flew Panthers in the war. As fate would have it, the ballplayer and the future astronaut were in the same unit and flew together on occasion.) Glenn left college in his junior year in 1942 to enter Naval flight school and earned his wings and a Marine Corps commission the next year. Based in the Marshall Islands, he flew fifty-nine ground support missions. After the war, he served for two years on the North China Patrol and then as a flight instructor. In February 1953 the Marines sent

Glenn to Korea where he completed sixty-three ground attack missions in Panthers. On two occasions his F9F was damaged by antiaircraft fire.[7]

The Marines posted Glenn to exchange duty with the 51st Fighter Group in the waning days of the war. An Air Force enlisted man accurately summed up Glenn's attitude when he painted "MiG Mad Marine" on his assigned Sabre. The Marine pilot recognized that this was correct: "I flew with a focus on the target, and if it meant flying on the edge, that's what I did."[8] On 12 July 1953 Glenn and his wingman, Sam Young, chased one Red fighter miles into China, claiming "hot pursuit"; Glenn nailed it as it attempted to land. Glenn was fifty feet off the ground as he watched the Red fighter splatter at the edge of the Chinese airfield at Antung. Glenn then shot up the Chinese control tower as he blazed down the field.[9]

A week later, Glenn was leading a flight of four when a fuel feed problem forced one pilot, John Boyd, to abort. In violation of policy, Boyd's element leader, Henry Buttlemann, who had just become an ace, continued the mission.[10] Glenn spotted four MiGs, and as he closed on them, another dozen or more MiGs and four F-86s joined the battle. Glenn got into trouble when he lost his wingman, Jerry Parker, as well as Buttlemann and then overshot his target, allowing the MiG to fire at him. Glenn's wingman came to the rescue and hit the Communist fighter; it fell into a spin and crashed. Parker's fighter was damaged in turn, however, probably by ingesting parts of the disintegrating MiG. Parker headed home with only partial power and, subsequently, lower speed, covered by Glenn. When they neared the Chong-chong River, six Red fighters attacked the pair. Glenn turned into the MiGs and, although well out of range, "lit up the nose." The six .50s were very visible and had the desired effect because the MiGs broke off their attack. But Glenn did not let this end the day; he tacked onto the trailing MiG and shot it down. The remaining five engaged him in uncoordinated attacks and then broke off from the dogfight. Glenn commented, "The MiGs' tactics were so poor I could only imagine it was a training flight, or they were low on fuel, but we were unbelievably lucky."[11] The F-86 pilots had done well on 19 July, claiming ten MiGs, with Glenn, Parker, and Buttlemann each scoring a victory.

Three days later Glenn led a flight into MiG Alley, saw two Communist fighters, and attacked. He fired a long burst, got hits, and watched as the wounded fighter dove and crashed. This action gave Glenn his third credit; Henry Buttlemann his seventh; and Glenn's wingman, Sam Young, his one and only MiG. These were the last MiGs downed in the war. Three MiGs in ten days was quite an accomplishment, highlighted by the fact that Glenn had flown only sixty-seven missions in F-86s.[12]

After the war, the Marines sent Glenn to Navy test pilot school at Patuxent River. In 1958, he joined the original seven Mercury astronauts and in February 1962 made the third American space flight, becoming the first American to orbit the earth. Glenn retired from the Marine Corps as a full colonel in January 1965, having logged almost fifty-five hundred flying hours, nineteen hundred in jets. He went on to the U.S. Senate, made an abortive run for the presidency in 1984, and enjoyed a space shuttle ride in 1998, the same year he retired from the senate.[13]

Tom Sellers: Another Marine Exchange Pilot

It would be great if all stories of American airmen turned out as well as Glenn's. Unfortunately, this is not the case; not all of the F-86 activities were marked with success. The USAF listed 118 F-86 pilots as casualties in the Korean War: 47 killed, 65 missing, and 6 wounded.[14] One of these casualties was Tom Sellers.

Sellers was born in Dallas, Texas, in August 1924, entered pilot training in September 1942, and graduated with wings and a commission in the Marine Corps in August 1943. He remained stateside during the war. The Marines released him from active duty for most of 1946 and then again in December 1947 until he was recalled in February 1951 for the Korean War. Between November 1952 and April 1953, Sellers completed one hundred combat missions in the F9F. The young Marine applied for exchange duty with the USAF and arrived in late April at the 4th Fighter Group.[15]

Sellers demonstrated great persistence in getting the exchange assignment. As a Marine Corps reserve officer, he was not technically eligible for the slot, yet he kept applying until a new commander saw fit to violate Marine policy and approve his application. Sellers wanted to make the Corps his career and sought the F-86 experience because it would enhance his bid to obtain a regular commission. He knew that the Corps was getting Sabres; therefore, pilots with F-86 flying experience, and especially those with MiG credits, would be very valuable. He wrote his wife on 5 April that this duty "will be the biggest opportunity I've ever had, and I intend to make the most of it: to learn as much as I can and to get as much F-86 time as I can, not to be a hero but, if the opportunity affords itself, to test my talents against a MiG."[16]

Sellers believed that if he could get a MiG, "I could write my own ticket in the Marine Corps." He quickly added, "but I'm not sticking my neck out for anything."[17]

The USAF welcomed Sellers, and he fit right in, due to shared interests and his personality and that of his fellow pilots. His initial impression was that "these guys eat, sleep and drink flying, that is, chasing MiGs; they never talk about anything else. . . . That's the way it should be. They have a darn good record and they know it. . . . I think it is going to be fun instead of work, like it was [flying F9Fs]."[18] Sellers was enthusiastic about the F-86, which he thought flew even better than it looked. He attempted to reassure his wife, writing that "my promise still holds that I'll not take any unnecessary chances, such as going north of the Yalu and jumping MiGs in their traffic patterns, as some of the boys have done."[19] Two weeks later, he wrote his wife that she shouldn't worry because "my first ambition is to get home; my second is to get a MiG."[20] Sellers also correctly noted that flying an F-86 was safer than what he had been doing. In his words, "This flying is so much more tame than what we did at K-3 [the F9F base]."[21]

Sellers was irritated by the poor weather that hindered operations, and he was frustrated that the MiGs were hard to find, even on good weather days. From the outset, he counted the days until he would return home, complained about the slow mail service, and emphasized the importance of letters from home. On 22 June, he mentioned how Bolt, a friend of his, was overshadowing him, having downed two MiGs, while he had none. Sellers then wrote that he would do his best, and if that wasn't good enough, that was too bad. "I refuse to go north of the river to look for MiGs." Then, to reassure his wife, he added, "It isn't worth the risk; however, if I've got one in my sights, I'm not going to turn him loose."[22] The next week he changed his mind. Certainly some of this was due to Bolt, who was getting kills (he got his third credit on 24 June), for Sellers wrote his wife that he was just as good a pilot as Bolt, but that Bolt seemed to be at the right place at the right time. This was his self-confidence, ambition, and frustration colliding.

On 25 June, Sellers had his first chance, but just as he was about to fire, the MiGs spotted his Sabre, made a violent maneuver, and flew into a cloud, not to be seen again. On 29 June, he wrote his wife that, "I'm determined to get a MiG, as are most of the boys around here, and it seems there is only one positive way of doing it, and that is to go north of the Yalu. I did it for the second time today but no luck." After writing that he had taken his flight sixty miles north of the river, he commented that, "Practically everyone makes the venture and 50 percent of the time it pays dividends. I've just got to get one; after that I'll be satisfied. Jack Bolt has three now, and I know he got all of them across the river."[23]

Sellers finally got to fire on 1 July and in his words "muffed it." Flying over the city of Antung, Sellers's wingman called a break as four MiGs made a diving firing pass on the Sabres that were at forty-two thousand feet. The fighters went round and round, Sellers remarking that, "they were beautiful; I've never seen a more beautiful sight; I felt like I was in a movie."[24] Sellers got behind the third MiG, fired and missed, and then got behind the fourth MiG. He opened fire at one thousand feet; although he thought his tracers hit the Red fighter, his gun camera film indicated otherwise. At this point, a flight of Sabres intervened and shot down two of the MiGs. Then four MiGs painted jet black flew by and Sellers latched onto the trailing fighter. The MiG dove for the field at Antung with Sellers in trail. At fifteen thousand feet the Marine broke off the pursuit and headed home because he could not close the five-thousand-foot gap and because of his fuel situation. He landed with one hundred pounds of fuel remaining. It was both an exhilarating and frustrating experience.

Sellers's envy of Bolt grew when the latter got his fifth and sixth kills on 11 July. Sellers noted that he was not getting the same breaks in the 4th as Bolt was getting in the 51st, the only hint that Sellers was having any problems with the USAF. He wrote his wife that he would tell her the details when he got home. Meanwhile, the combatants realized that the war would be over shortly. Sellers was frustrated and depressed by the poor weather and his lack of success, writing, "My nerves have taken about all they can, but only fourteen more shooting days left [until the end of his ninety-day tour with the Air Force]. If I could only get a MiG, I'm certain I could snap out of it. I just can't tell you how disgusted I am with myself."[25]

His situation was not helped when he ended up flying on the squadron commander's wing on his fortieth mission, after the number two and four men aborted. Sellers was not in a shooting position and classified his leader as "'P' poor: he can't see a thing."[26] He was understandably upset as he called out MiGs, but before the leader reacted, the Red fighters flew right through their formation, firing as they did. Two others got on the leader's tail and opened fire but missed. Sellers got off a few rounds and believed he scored some hits. He could not confirm this, however, because his gun camera film did not come out. When the pair of F-86s departed the scene, two other MiGs made one pass. In Sellers's view, his leader was the cause of the lack of success. "If he had seen them in time we could have been on the offensive, but these are the breaks I've been having."[27] He finished his letter with this reassurance. "You can stop worrying about our going across the fence [Yalu] into Manchuria: the Fifth Air Force has put a stop to it, threatening to court martial the next man to shoot MiGs trying to land at their own field."[28] Three days later Sellers was over China, as ordered, attacking MiGs that had just taken off from their airfield.

On 20 July 1953, Sellers was leading a flight of four Sabres on an airfield reconnaissance sweep that entailed overflying a number of Communist airfields at least thirty miles inside China. Sellers brought his formation below twenty thousand feet due to an overcast sky and encountered enemy flak. This disrupted the F-86 formation; unknown to Sellers, the two elements split apart. Sellers observed fourteen MiGs taking off and immediately called a bounce. Sellers dove on the Communist fighters and focused on two MiGs in the middle of this gaggle at about one thousand feet. He deployed his speed brakes and retarded his throttle as he closed on the MiGs and then gave his first target a short burst; it started burning. Seller then shifted his attack with a quick burst on the second MiG, which exploded. The Marine's wingman, Albert Dickey, radioed that they were being attacked by two MiGs and called for a left break. Sellers acknowledged and started to turn. About one-quarter way through the break a MiG opened fire from a distance usually considered out of range for the Soviet fighter and its first shots hit Sellers's F-86 in the fuselage near, or on, the canopy. The Sabre exploded, its wings fell off, and the flaming wreckage fell to the ground. Dickey saw three fires on the ground, presumably the two MiGs and one F-86, but did not observe a parachute.[29]

The Marine Corps listed Sellers as missing in action for a year before declaring him killed in action. The USAF credited Sellers with two MiGs destroyed and awarded him the Silver Star for this action. No further information surfaced about his fate, except that the Air Force had falsified the dogfight's location to conceal the intrusion into Chinese air space. There is no report that Sellers's aircraft or remains were discovered. The marine major left a wife without a husband and two young daughters without a father.[30]

Felix Asla: Another Downed Eagle

Sellers was not the only F-86 pilot killed in action. During the war, about seventy pilots who flew Sabres died in combat, accidents, and Communist prison camps.[31] Felix Asla was born in February 1924, and was awarded his wings and commission in June 1944. He flew P-47s and P-51s in World War II, but earned no victory credits. Asla was briefly separated from the service in 1947 before he received a regular commission. He flew F-80s and F-86s prior to joining the 4th in Korea in October 1951. In March 1952, Asla took over as squadron commander of the 336th. At that point, he had one victory credit; he added two more in March and one in June.[32]

On 1 August 1952, he was flying his ninety-seventh mission, leading a formation into MiG Alley. Six F-86s attacked a formation of two dozen MiGs. The first indication the Communist pilots had of the immediate presence of the Americans was the sight of drop tanks falling from the sky above them. Asla got behind a MiG, closed for the kill, and opened fire. Unbeknownst to him, he had lost his wingman in the maneuvering. He probably saw a fighter moving up on him as if to join up and apparently assumed it was his wingman because he took no evasive action and continued to fire at his target. Nikolai Ivanov pulled the trigger and his cannon shells struck home, ripping off the Sabre's left wing. The F-86 entered a spin; no parachute was observed. The 4th Fighter Group claimed four fighters that day, as did the Russians. Americans admit losing one F-86 and one pilot; the Russians admit losing three MiGs and two pilots.[33]

Walker "Bud" Mahurin: World War II Ace, Korean War POW

Walker Mahurin was another casualty of the Korean air war. He was born in Michigan in December 1918 and first flew at age seven. After graduation from high school in Indiana, he attended Purdue University for two years and joined the aviation cadet program in August 1941. Mahurin received his wings and commission in April 1942 and was sent to the Fifty-sixth Fighter Group. He was with the group when it deployed to Britain and earned 19.75 victory credits before a German bomber gunner downed him in March 1944. He evaded capture and then was sent to the Pacific theater as commander of the Third Commando Squadron, where he downed one Japanese aircraft and survived an ocean ditching. He ended up as the AAF's fifteenth highest scoring ace of the war. After the war, Mahurin earned an Aeronautical Engineering undergraduate degree from Purdue and served as Assistant Executive Officer for the Secretary of the Air Force. In December 1951, he went to Korea for ninety days of temporary duty.[34]

His old friend from the World War II Fifty-sixth, Gabby Gabreski, got him into the 51st Fighter Wing, and there he very quickly added to his victory credits. On his first combat sortie on 6 January 1952, Mahurin flew as Gabreski's wingman. Cho-do radar alerted the Americans to the presence of MiGs, and soon the jet fighters were engaged in a dogfight. Mahurin spotted a MiG below and got Gabby's permission to attack. He opened fire at long range without apparent effect; as he closed, the light in his gunsight went out, rendering it useless. Understandably frustrated, he continued to fire but was forced to break off his attack when other MiGs zeroed in on him. He saw three Red fighters hit the ground within five miles of the Communist airfield at Antung but did not think he had damaged his target. However, another pilot who picked up the pursuit of that MiG after Mahurin had broken off his attack confirmed the kill for him.[35]

He earned his second MiG credit on 17 February after jumping a MiG at forty-three thousand feet. Mahurin dueled with the Communist pilot for some time in a fight that ended up about one hundred feet off the ground. The World War II ace slowly gained on the Red fighter and began to get hits that knocked out the MiG's engine. When the Red fighter quickly lost air speed, Mahurin overran his victim, passing twenty feet off of MiG's wing, and observed that the torn up fighter was trailing fuel and fire and the pilot was slumped over his instruments. Mahurin then saw the fighter roll over and dive into the ground.[36]

Mahurin's ninety days were up, but Fifth Air Force changed his orders and sent him to command the 4th Fighter Group, which he took over on 18 March 1952.[37] Mahurin writes that when he learned that one of his pilots, Capt. Jack Owens (334FS), was shooting off all his unexpended ammunition in strafing attacks as he returned from MiG Alley, he jumped on the idea. This was a tactic used by Eighth Air Force fighters in World War II to beat up German targets, although it was costly in lost fighters and downed pilots. However, a pilot in the 51st states that Mahurin discussed the strafing idea with him in January. Mahurin writes that his purpose was to provoke the Communists so they would rise to engage the Sabres. He flew these missions, destroying a train on one of them, but also got his Sabre shot up. Mahurin then took this concept one step further. He obtained enough bomb shackles and associated equipment to outfit twenty-five F-86s with a bombing capability. Mahurin concluded that the Communists would be most sensitive to attacks near the Yalu; however, the distance would require the F-86s to carry one external fuel tank under one wing and one bomb under the other. (North

American mounted two pylons on the F-86A, -E, and early -Fs.) The 4th flew its first bombing mission on 8 May against targets in Sinuiju, just across from the Antung airfield, but with little bombing and no aerial success. In the following days the 4th engaged in more bombing and strafing attacks.[38]

On 13 May 1952, Mahurin pursued the fighter-bomber idea with a vengeance. On his first mission of the day, he led a squadron of Sabres to bomb the Uiju airfield in North Korea and to strafe various targets. Several Red fighters took off in China, but none crossed the Yalu. That afternoon, Mahurin led a flight of four F-86s each carrying two 1,000-pound bombs against rail targets in Kunuri a short (150 mile) distance from the Sabre base. The F-86s began their attack from twelve thousand feet and encountered anti-aircraft fire that Mahurin described as "intense." Nevertheless, they achieved good accuracy. The MiGs came up and were met by escorting F-86s. The Sabres returned home and rearmed for another bombing mission. Mahurin told Harrison Thyng, the 4th Wing commander, that this would be his last bombing mission. In their conversation, Thyng mentioned that in a few days Mahurin would be replacing Gabreski as wing commander of the 51st.

The target for this third mission was again the railroad targets at Kunuri. After Mahurin completed his attack, he circled the target observing the impact of the rest of the flight's bombs. He then saw a truck moving down a road and lined up for a strafing run. He later admitted he got carried away and got hit in the process without hitting the truck. On fire and too low to bail out, he headed for the Yellow Sea, sixty miles away. He flew over more Communist antiaircraft positions and was hit again. He was flying with partial power at only about 150 mph when the fire warning light illuminated and the main hydraulic system went out. Mahurin throttled back to reduce the temperature but soon felt the controls stiffening as the emergency hydraulic system began to fail. One mile from the sea, the Sabre hit the ground hard, broke off the wings, rolled over twice, and reversed direction. Close, but not close enough. He was quickly captured. The Americans abandoned the F-86 fighter-bomber tactics the next day. Despite this experience, the Air Force revived the concept in 1953, converting the 8th and 18th Fighter Bomber Wings to the later versions of the F-86F that mounted four pylons.[39] They too suffered heavy losses.

Mahurin was subjected to extreme pressure from his Communist captors, who were in the midst of a propaganda campaign accusing the UN airmen of conducting germ warfare. Mahurin, along with a number of other captives, "confessed" to this crime. After sixteen months of captivity, Mahurin was released. Some believe his confession ruined his career. In March 1956, he left the regular Air Force and served in the reserves, flying C-119s and C-124s, quite a comedown for a fighter pilot with 20.75 World War II and 3.5 Korean War victories. He went on to work for a number of aviation companies, including Northrop and McDonnell.[40]

Edwin Heller: World War II Ace, Chinese Captive

Ed Heller was born in Philadelphia in December 1918 into an affluent family, whose lifestyle dramatically changed after the 1929 stock market crash. When war came to America, he was working as a state policeman. He quickly enlisted and, with the college requirement dropped, entered the aviation cadet program, graduating in March 1943 with wings and an officer's commission. He flew two tours in Europe, logging 520 combat flying hours with 5.5 aerial credits and at least fourteen ground credits. Heller stayed in uniform after the war as an instructor with the West Virginia National Guard and went on to command the 62nd Fighter Squadron. He arrived in Korea in September 1952 and took over the 26th Fighter Squadron.[41]

Heller scored his first victory in November, downing the last of four MiGs that flew through his formation. The Communist pilot bailed out. Three weeks later he split a kill credit with his wingman. Heller writes that after scoring hits, he could not complete the victory because of a hung up fuel tank that restricted the Sabre's performance. According to the official account, the MiG spun out and crashed trying to elude the Americans.[42] Three days after being notified of his spot promotion to lieutenant colonel, he scored two victories on 22 January 1953, both over China.

The next day he led a flight with the squadron's new operations officer, Harold Herrick, as his element leader with soon-to-be ace Dolph Overton on Herrick's wing. This was Heller's fifty-seventh F-86 mission. Cho-do radar alerted the Americans to a number of MiG formations that were airborne. The flight split into elements to meet Red fighters that swooped down on them. Herrick and Overton each downed a MiG. Meanwhile, Heller lost his wingman; some say he fled the scene. In any case, Heller dove on a Red fighter below him although he spotted a MiG climbing to attack him. That MiG opened fired with a split-second, large-deflection angle shot and cannon shells, which streamed over his cockpit, in Heller's words, looking like "burning golf balls." One or more hit the F-86, exploding in the cockpit—a case of remarkably good shooting or good luck for the MiG pilot.

The American was lucky as well, for the aircraft's armor plate saved his life. Heller was wounded in the arm and in a vertical dive, the control stick useless; the cockpit was in shambles. The canopy was smashed, blood or hydraulic fluid covered the smashed right console, and the instrument panel was completely shot away. Heller locked his shoulder harness, pulled his feet under his seat, and squeezed the ejection seat trigger. Nothing happened: Heller was trapped in the rapidly diving F-86. He actuated the lever several more times with an equal lack of results. However, when the Sabre reached the thicker air at lower altitude, it began to recover from the dive, and pulled so many "g"s that the wounded pilot blacked out. When he recovered he was close to the ground. Heller released his seat belt and harness, stood up in the seat, and was sucked out of the fighter. He survived the bailout and was quickly captured about 60 km north of the Yalu River.[43]

Heller joined a number of other American aviators in captivity. A later captive was Harold Fischer, who may have gotten the MiG that downed Heller. The USAF credited him with a victory that day for a Red fighter that Fischer reported was climbing and firing on an F-86.[44] I. I. Karpova was the Soviet pilot that got Heller, his one and only victory credit. Shortly after Karpova fired a long burst that nailed the Sabre, he in turn was shot up. In his words, "My aircraft was hit and rattled like an empty can, beaten on by peas."[45] His aircraft uncontrollable, the Russian ejected from the faltering MiG.[46] Fischer and Heller were not released with most of the prisoners when the war ended in July. Instead, the Chinese held them and a few others until May 1955. Heller resumed his flying career and went on to retire from the Air Force in 1967 as a lieutenant colonel.[47]

Other Aces, Known for Other Deeds

Robinson Risner: Korean War Ace, Vietnam War Prisoner

Some of the aces were to gain greater fame after the Korean War. John Glenn is obviously one of these; Robinson "Robby" Risner is another. Born in Arkansas in January 1925, he enlisted in the AAF in April 1943 and in May 1944 was awarded his wings and commission. Risner flew P-38s and P-39s in Panama during the war. The AAF discharged him in January 1946, and the former fighter pilot went on to a number of limited, dead-end jobs. In 1947 he joined a fighter unit in the Oklahoma Air National Guard that was activated in February 1951. His effort to get into combat was almost thwarted, for on his last night at home he was thrown from a horse, breaking his hand and wrist. This would have grounded most others, but not Risner. He concealed his injury until he convinced a doctor that it was healed and took his hand out of a cast to fly his first combat mission. He used a connection, a former guardsman he knew, to wrangle his way from the reconnaissance unit to which he was initially assigned, into the 4th Fighter Group in June 1952. This was not outright favoritism; the unit was seeking experienced pilots, and Risner had almost sixteen hundred flying hours.[48]

Risner was not successful at first. One factor was that the MiGs were not consistent in opposing the UN airmen; they flew in cycles. In early August, Risner went to Japan for three days of "rest and recuperation." The second day he was there, he learned that the MiGs were flying and immediately flew back to his unit, arriving there at three in the morning. In short order he joined his flight, which was on alert. The flight launched and spied eight MiGs below them just after leveling off at thirty-five thousand feet. Before the Americans could attack, the number three man spotted six other MiGs diving and firing on the F-86s. Two overshot and Risner pulled about one thousand feet behind them and fired a long burst at one of the enemy fighters. "He lit up like a Christmas tree" from the .50s that struck home, Risner noted, and then "seemed to stop in the air."[49] The American pilot threw out his speed brakes and pulled his throttle back to stay behind the MiG. The Red fighter went into a spin and Risner's Sabre stalled as he attempted to stay with the Communist aircraft. The American regained control, fired again, and closed to about three hundred feet. His bullets severed the MiG's tail from the fuselage. The pilot ejected, but because he was at thirty-two thousand feet when he opened his chute, he probably did not survive. Despite a lack of sleep, Risner had posted his first victory credit.[50]

Risner got two more credits in September, the second of which was perhaps his most memorable. On 15 September 1952, Risner was leading a flight escorting fighter-bombers attacking a chemical plant near the mouth of the Yalu. The Americans flew over China and across the Red airfield at Antung. As the Sabres made a second sweep across the area, four MiGs attempted to attack the F-84s. The Sabre flight broke into elements with Risner and his wingman, Joe Logan, engaging in a dogfight that raged from thirty thousand feet down to the deck. Risner pursued a MiG, at times at nearly the speed of sound, at one point momentarily flying in wing tip formation with the Communist pilot who shook his fist at Risner. The chase led down a dry streambed, across wooded hills, with the MiG flying inverted for a time at very low level. Despite the Communist pilot's superb flying, Risner scored hits on his canopy and tail and started a fire. As the trio of jets crossed a Chinese airfield thirty-five miles inside China, flak gunners let fly. The fighters flew between the hangars and down the runway, and Risner thought the Communist pilot was attempting to crash-land. But then about four feet of the MiG's wing blew off just before the MiG exploded and set some parked fighters afire.

During the overflight of the airfield, flak hit Logan's Sabre, puncturing his fuel tanks and making it impossible for him to reach his home base. But the closer the pilot could get to Cho-do, the greater his chances of rescue. Risner then tried an unprecedented maneuver; he had his wingman shut down his engine and attempted to push him toward safety. But after two attempts Risner had to back off, as the venting fuel and hydraulic fluid covered his canopy.[51] Logan bailed out near Cho-do as Risner, short of fuel, shut down his engine for a time and glided toward home. He restarted the engine, but it flamed out, forcing Risner to make a dead-stick landing. Risner was safe and had notched his third victory. However, his wingman did not survive, for although Joe Logan was a good swimmer, he got entangled in his parachute risers and drowned.[52]

Six days later, Risner bagged two MiGs to become an ace. He added three later, to end the war with eight victories. On one of these kills, the Communist pilot ejected and he and his seat hit Risner's Sabre. Plexiglas flew into his eyes and temporally blinded him. However the ace was able to regain enough sight in his eyes to successfully land. Risner went on to fly 108 or more missions.[53]

After the war Risner commanded a succession of fighter squadrons before taking over an F-105 outfit in August 1964. He led this unit to Thailand and, while flying from there, was shot down twice by flak. He was rescued the first time but was captured the second time. Risner was the ranking U.S. prisoner of war and as such provided leadership and an example to his fellow captives. He also suffered great punishment before his release in February 1973. The USAF promoted him to brigadier general in 1974. He retired from the service in 1976.[54]

James Kasler: World War II B-29 Gunner and Korean War Ace

Risner was not the only Korean War ace who went on to fly in Vietnam, get shot down, and survive captivity. As already noted, James Low shared that distinction, as did Jim Kasler. Born in South Bend, Indiana, in May 1926, Kasler enlisted in the AAF in September 1944 and served in combat as a B-29 gunner.[55] He left the service in 1946 but then joined the aviation cadet program in January 1950 following three years of college. After earning his commission and wings in March 1951, the USAF sent him to Korea in November 1951 where he joined the 4th Group.

On 15 May 1952, flying as an element leader with three victory credits, Kasler was scrambled because of reports of MiGs airborne. The flight of Sabres flew north toward the Yalu. Before they made contact, however, Cho-do radar lost contact with the MiGs. Kasler then broke off his element from the flight and with his wingman, Albert Smiley, punched off his drop tanks and dove toward the Communist airfield at Antung. He caught a formation of MiGs just as they were pitching out to land. Kasler popped his speed brakes, executed a split-S, and got behind the MiG leader. He opened fire at a range of twelve hundred feet and scored hits; as he closed to one hundred feet, the MiG began to flame and fall apart. Kasler pulled alongside the stricken fighter and saw "the pilot sitting in a pool of fire." He crashed and "scorched a wide, fiery trail across the air base."[56]

Kasler then saw his wingman hammering a MiG that was on fire. However, another Red fighter was in turn attacking him. Kasler radioed Smiley to break, as he maneuvered to get that MiG into his sights. The dogfight was at ground level, with flak darkening the sky. Kasler chased the MiG for fifty miles toward the sea. He claims that during the chase, his flight commander, Philip "Casey" Colman, pulled between the MiG and the F-86 and then pulled out of the way as he radioed, "Come on, Kas, you have your five." Kasler replied, "Negative. Smiley got one of them."[57] By this time, the fighters had reached the sea; after the Red pilot executed an Immelmann, Kasler fired, scored again, and closed the gap to five hundred feet. The two were diving at what Kasler later described as about a 60 degree angle at five hundred knots over the mud flats in poor visibility when the MiG crashed—or perhaps better put, splashed—into the mud. Kasler jerked the throttle back, deployed his speed brakes, and pulled hard back on the control stick with both hands, expecting to feel the impact of collision with the ground. He barely avoided joining his victim in the mud. The USAF credited Kasler with two victories, making him an ace, and credited Smiley with one, the only Air Force credits on 15 May. The ace later learned that Mao Tse-tung's son was shot down that day.[58] He got one more MiG credit and completed one hundred missions.

In August 1966, ground fire downed his F-105 on his ninety-first mission in Vietnam. In March 1973, the North Vietnamese released him. Kasler went on to serve as Vice Commander of the 366th Tactical Fighter Wing until his retirement in May 1975.[59]

Iven Kincheloe: Ace and Test Pilot

Iven Kincheloe was another Korean War ace who gained greater fame after the war than in it. Born in Detroit in July 1928, he first flew before his fifth birthday and soloed on his sixteenth. He graduated from Purdue in 1949 with a degree in aeronautical engineering, a desire to be a test pilot, and a second lieutenant's commission through ROTC. The USAF awarded him his pilot's wings in August 1950 and assigned him to fly F-86s. Kincheloe arrived in Korea in September 1951 and flew sixteen missions with the 4th Fighter Group. In mid-November, he transferred to the 51st Fighter Group, which was commanded by his former (56FGp) skipper, "Gabby" Gabreski.[60]

Kincheloe was an eager and inquisitive fighter pilot. He also was in a position to bag MiGs because his squadron commander, Bill Whisner, appointed him a flight commander. Nevertheless, he was not getting any MiGs. The first lieutenant asked Col. "Bud" Mahurin the reason for this. Mahurin answered that he was pressing too hard and firing when he was out of range. Perhaps it was this advice that made the difference.

On 19 January 1952, Kincheloe shot down his first MiG in a classic attack. Kincheloe was leading his flight when his element leader spotted three MiGs ahead and below them. The Americans dove out of the sun with Kincheloe closing to within eight hundred feet before the Communist pilot detected him. The F-86's bullets racked the Red fighter, and it began to fall apart as it fell out of control.[61] He did not score again for two and a half months but then caught fire, probably because he was crossing the Yalu. On 1 April, he got a double and the next day scored another victory. Kincheloe posted his fifth and last aerial victory on 6 April, on his eighty-fourth mission. He downed one of these MiGs near Mukden, 120 miles north of the Yalu.[62]

Kincheloe also registered some kills on the ground. The USAF awarded forty-two air-to-ground victory credits during the Korean War, all but eleven during 1950.[63] During the remainder of the war, there were only three days on which Air Force pilots made ground kills, one in 1951 and two in 1952. The number of ground kills was small because the American airmen could only attack the Communists on the ground in North Korea. Such attacks were off limits in China. On the few occasions the Communists brought aircraft into North Korea, they met stiff opposition and destruction from B-29 strikes and marauding Sabres. On 22 April 1952, Kincheloe and Elmer Harris each destroyed a Yak-9 on the ground. Two weeks later the pair attacked two dozen Yaks on the same North Korean airfield; Kincheloe claimed three and Harris another two on the ground. These were the ace's last victories. In all, Kincheloe flew 101 F-86 missions and 30 F-80 missions (with the 51st, prior to its conversion to Sabres).[64]

Kincheloe went from Korea to Nellis AFB where he served as a gunnery instructor. The USAF then sent him to Britain to attend the Empire Test Pilots' School, which he completed in December 1954 to fulfill his lifelong dream. He went on to fly the X-2 over 2,000 mph and 126,000 feet and was awarded the Mackay Trophy in 1956 for the latter feat. Kincheloe was one of three pilots selected to fly the X-15, the next and newest American experimental aircraft. Unfortunately, he was killed in an F-104 takeoff accident in July 1958 before he could fly the X-15.[65]

In his superb book on flying, test flying in particular, Tom Wolfe has high praise for Kincheloe. He writes that he "was a combat hero and test pilot from out of a dream: blond, handsome, powerful, bright, supremely ambitious and yet popular with all who worked with him, including other pilots. There was absolutely no ceiling on his future in the Air Force."[66] His fellow pilots confirm this assessment and noted that he looked out for the enlisted men and probably could have become Chief of Staff of the Air Force. In 1959, the USAF named one of its bases in Michigan after him.[67]

African-American Sabre Pilots

African-Americans were not permitted to fly in the U.S. military until well into World War II. Then, segregated units were organized using pilots trained at Tuskegee Institute. The Tuskegee airmen of the 332nd Fighter Group flew and fought well in the Mediterranean theater, seventy-one Tuskegee pilots claiming 108 aerial victories. Segregation in the military continued after the war until President Harry Truman issued an executive order in July 1948 that ordered the military to integrate. The USAF disbanded its segregated units and dispersed their personnel to various Air Force units prior to the Korean War.[68]

Despite the number of African-American fighter pilots with World War II experience, none of these veterans flew F-86s in Korea. Instead, they served in a variety of stateside assignments and in other aircraft in Korea. There is no official explanation for this situation, but it may have been to deny blacks this prestigious assignment or perhaps to prevent them from excelling in this very visible position. The war ended before Benjamin Davis, the ranking African-American USAF pilot, took command of the 51st Fighter Wing in November 1953.[69] At least four black pilots, all recently out of pilot training, flew F-86s during the Korean air war. The most prominent of these was Earl Brown. He graduated from Penn State in 1949 and entered aviation cadets in late 1950, pinning on his wings in December 1951. He arrived in Korea in mid-1952 with 103 jet flying hours and flew as wingman for three of the 4th's most successful aces, James Jabara, Pete Fernandez, and "Boots" Blesse. Brown completed 125 missions and damaged one MiG. After Korea, he stayed in fighters and flew 100 missions during two tours in Vietnam, surviving one bailout forced by antiaircraft fire. He retired as a lieutenant general in 1985, having flown over five thousand hours.[70]

Dayton Ragland also flew with the 4th. Born in Kansas City, Missouri, in December 1927, Ragland was involved in the one strafing attack of 1951. On 7 November, the North Koreans moved a number of MiGs onto the airfield of Uiju, in North Korea close to the Yalu River, and flew several missions from there. After American reconnaissance noted twenty-six fighters on the airfield on the tenth of the month, the Fifth Air Force staff proposed a coordinated attack by B-29s, B-26s, and fighters. But as the staffers and decision makers debated the concept, on 18 November Capt. Kenneth Chandler (336FS), with Ragland flying his wing, spotted eight MiGs on the field and pounced. Chandler sprayed the ramp and his gun camera film recorded numerous hits. He claimed four destroyed, one probably destroyed, and three damaged. There is no explanation, but Ragland did not claim any Communist aircraft. Although the USAF credited Chandler with four aircraft destroyed on the ground, a North Korean pilot who was on the field during the attack states that the strafing destroyed one MiG, damaged another, and killed one pilot.[71]

Ten days later, Ragland claimed a MiG, which was the only victory credit posted to an African-American in the Korean War. He was shot down on that same day, 28 November 1951. Ragland survived captivity and continued to serve in the Air Force, advancing to the rank of lieutenant colonel. He flew ninety-seven missions in Vietnam and was shot down flying an F-4 in May 1966 and was listed as missing in action.[72]

Other World War II Veterans Who Scored in the Korean War

A number of veterans of World War II flew Sabres during the Korean air war. We do not know the total number of pilots but we do know those who scored victories in both wars. As already noted, there were seven pilots who scored more than five victories in both World War II and Korea. Six Korean War aces also registered victories in World War II, albeit less than 5. Three of these who have not been discussed were Stephen Bettinger, with 1 credit in World War II and 5 credits in Korea; Richard Creighton, with 2 World War II credits and 5 Korean War credits; and George Ruddell, with 2.5 and 8. Twenty-five pilots registered less than 5 kills in each war. Ten aces in World War II not already discussed also scored in Korea, including Lowell Brueland (12.5 in World War II and 2 in Korea), Van Chandler (5 and 3), Philip Colman (5 and 4), Benjamin Emmert (6 and 1), John Hockery (7 and 1), William Hovde (10.5 and 1), John Mitchell (11 and 4), and Herman Visscher (5 and 1).

John Meyer was the 4th Fighter Group commander between August 1950 and June 1951. He had scored 24 aerial victories in Europe, including 4 kills on one day, and 3 on two others, to rank as the seventh highest scoring AAF fighter pilot of the war. In Korea, Meyer added two more credits to his totals.[73]

Glenn Eagleston replaced Meyer as commander of the 4th Group, a position he held from May until July 1951. He claimed 18.5 German aircraft in the big war and 2 in Korea. Despite his experience, Eagleston almost became a credit for a Communist pilot.[74] In late June 1951, Bruce Hinton was leading the 334th Squadron and Glenn Eagleston was leading the 336th on a MiG sweep near the mouth of the Yalu. The MiGs came up and the Sabres broke into elements in the ensuing dogfight. Hinton latched onto a lone Red fighter and closed to under fifteen hundred feet. As he was about to open fire on what he considered a sure kill, a lone Sabre followed by a MiG firing away five hundred feet behind, crossed at 90 degrees between Hinton's F-86 and his intended target. The Red fighter was moving in for the kill, hitting the American fighter, which was shredding pieces and spouting flame. Hinton yanked his fighter around to engage the MiG that had overshot his prey and was swinging around to complete the kill. At this point, the MiG spotted Hinton and the two engaged in a maneuvering air battle. The American slowly improved his position enough to get off some shots at the MiG, which broke off the action and scurried across the Yalu. Hinton credited the enemy pilot with being very good and perhaps the legendary "Casey Jones," who the Americans believed was an exceptional non-Asian pilot, perhaps a former *Luftwaffe* pilot, who attacked lone F-86s in a MiG painted with a red nose and fuselage stripes.[75] (This story has all the markings of what later became known as an "urban legend.")

Hinton then joined up with the battered Sabre and commenced to escort it home. Because the damaged F-86's radio was knocked out, Hinton used hand signals to suggest the Sabre pilot fly toward the Yellow Sea for a bailout. The pilot emphatically rejected that notion, continued south toward home as he lost altitude, and made a successful wheels-up landing. The Sabre was a wreck and was written off, having been hit by two 23-mm shells in the aft fuselage and a 37 mm in the left gun bay. The cannon fire damaged the engine, knocked out the hydraulic system, and smashed the cockpit. The pilot was unharmed because the three left-side guns had absorbed the impact of the cannon shell that exploded just under the cockpit. Glenn Eagleston, triple ace in World War II, was very lucky and the Sabre proved to be very rugged.[76]

FIFTEEN

Red Aces

The fall of the Soviet Union brought hope that Soviet records would open and provide new information on a wide range of topics, including the air war in Korea. Regrettably, in the decade and a half since that event, the yield has been at best disappointing and certainly much more frustrating than illuminating. Information—or perhaps better put, statements and assertions—from the Communist side does not match up well with American sources, and on a number of important points the information is in terrible disagreement. With this in mind, what follows is a discussion of the top Red pilots based on Communist materials and sources that have appeared in English. Clearly it is unsatisfactory, but it is the best we have at this time. Perhaps it will stimulate scholarly work that is undoubtedly needed in this neglected area.

The Communist aviators claim to have downed 1,337 UN aircraft in aerial combat, including at least 650 F-86s. On its part, the USAF registered 757 losses to enemy action, 139 in air-to-air action.[1] While that overall number is not far off for all UN aircraft losses (including those to antiaircraft fire), the number of Sabres claimed is many times actual combat losses. The USAF admits 78 F-86s were lost in air-to-air action, with another 26 listed as unknown or missing.[2] (My estimate is that about 100 Sabres were lost in air-to-air battle.) We would expect the combatants to know their own losses and thus have numbers that reflect reality, absent a vast conspiracy. Some fifty years after the war, there is no evidence of an American effort to cover up losses, at worst, only some poor bookkeeping around the margins.

Secondary sources state that there were about forty-three to sixty Soviet aces, six to nine Chinese aces, and two to four North Korean aces.[3] This compares with forty U.S. aces, all but one flying F-86s. Sources credit fifteen to eighteen of the Soviet aces with ten or more victories,[4] compared with eleven U.S. aces with ten or more victories. The top two Chinese aces had nine credits, and the top two North Korean aces eight or nine.[5]

There are considerable problems with Communist claims. The Soviet system of claims awards is unclear, and unlike the USAF, there is no official Soviet victory credit listing. It is little wonder that the secondary sources, which do not cite their sources, conflict. Certainly some of this information is recycled from source to source. Therefore, what follows is of questionable reliability, although at present it is the best view we have from "the other side of the hill."

Although the Soviets sent their top World War II ace, Ivan Kozhedub (sixty-two victories), to the Korean War, he was not allowed to fly in combat. The most successful Soviet fighter pilot in the Korean War was Nikolai Sutyagin. He was born in May 1923, joined the army in 1941, and earned his wings the next year. The Soviets stationed Sutyagin in the Far East during the war, where he did not score any aerial victories. His unit was posted into the Korean War in the spring of 1951. Sutyagin claimed his first victory in June and went on to score twenty-one individual victories and two undefined shared victories, including fifteen Sabres. He flew 149 sorties and engaged in 66 dogfights before he returned to the Soviet Union in February 1952. Sutyagin went on to serve as an advisor to North Vietnam in 1970, retired from the military in 1978 as a general major, and died in November 1986.[6]

Evgeny Pepelyaev closely pursued Sutyagin in the race to be the top-scoring Soviet fighter pilot in Korea. Much more has appeared in print, at least in English, about Pepelyaev. He was born in March 1918 and worked in railroad construction and aviation repair before attending a Soviet aviation school. He graduated in 1938 and served mostly in the Far East. He flew twelve combat missions against the Germans and engaged in three air battles, but made no claims. He also flew thirty ground support missions in the brief operations against the Japanese in Manchuria. In April 1951 he took his unit to Antung airfield. Pepelyaev scored his first victory in May and his last in mid-January 1952, flying 108 missions and fighting in 38 aerial duels. His victory record is variously stated between fifteen and twenty victories, mostly

F-86s. Pepelyaev asserts that he downed twenty-three, including twelve F-86s, but "gave" three credits to his wingman. He retired from the air force in 1973.[7]

Pepelyaev admits that the Soviet pilots were not as experienced or as well trained as the Americans, even though 90 percent of his unit's pilots had fought in World War II and had scored victories against the *Luftwaffe*. His men were not ready for combat because they had "lost their combat awareness." He noted, however, that the Chinese were at an even worse disadvantage and suffered heavy losses. Pepelyaev states that the Sabre could outturn and outdive the MiGbis but was inferior in climb and armament. The Soviet ace conceded the advantages of the American gunsight but went on to laud the MiG for its "fantastic" survivability.[8]

A number of sources credit two Soviet aces with fifteen victories. Lev Shchukin was born in October 1923 and joined the army in 1941, but it was not until 1944 that he earned his wings. In the spring of 1951 he was sent to the Korean conflict, where he flew 212 sorties, was shot down two or three times, and claimed fifteen victories. He retired from the air force as a colonel in 1977.[9]

Born in November 1919, Alexandr Smorchkov entered the army in 1939. He saw action in World War II, during which he claimed five victories. In the spring of 1951, his unit entered the Korean War. Between May 1951 and February 1952, Smorchkov flew 191 sorties and claimed twelve to fifteen victories. He retired as a colonel in 1975. Smorchkov thought American pilots and the F-86 were very good. He also highly praised the MiG-15. However, he noted one major flaw: the fighter's engine would stop during sharp turns.[10]

Three sources also credit Dmitrii Oskin with fifteen victories, other sources use fourteen, and three imply the true number may be eleven. In any event, he was born in October 1919, joined the army in 1938, and graduated from military school in 1940. Although he served in World War II, there is no record of his accomplishments. In Korea he scored eight victories in just over three weeks in October and November 1951. According to one source, Oskin flew 122 sorties on which he engaged UN aircraft 86 times, while another source states that he fought 62 combats on 150 missions. He was one of the longest serving officers who had flown fighters in Korea, retiring in 1987 as a general lieutenant.[11]

In a similar way, Mikhail Ponomarev is credited with ten to fourteen victories. He was born in December 1920, joined the army in 1940, and earned his wings in 1942. He served in World War II and scored two victories. The

Soviets sent him to the Korean War in spring 1951 where he flew 140 sorties. He retired from the air force in 1968.[12]

Sergei Kramarenko may have been a double ace in World War II and an ace in Korea, one of only four Soviet pilots who were aces in both wars. But again, there are conflicts between the sources, which are undocumented. Born in April 1923, he completed pilot training in August 1942. Kramarenko was shot down once but went on to log somewhere between three and fourteen victories in World War II. He was also shot down once in Korea. Nevertheless, he racked up twelve or thirteen victories (nine F-86s) on 149 missions. Kramrenko retired as a major general in 1981.[13]

Kramarenko states that the F-86 was superior to the MiG in maneuverability especially at low levels, but the MiG had an advantage in rate of climb. He describes two actions in which he was at a disadvantage, the second of which ended up with Kramarenko ejecting from his damaged fighter. He claims that the Sabres then made a firing pass on him as he floated earthward. Some Sabre pilots did fly toward parachuting MiG pilots and fire to one side in order to capture the event on their gun camera film.[14]

Konstantin Sheberstov claimed twelve victories between the spring of 1951 and February 1952. His total is in question, however, because of a disputed claim between him and Pepelyaev regarding events on 6 October 1951. According to the latter, Sheberstov made a false claim that was exposed and he was disgraced. Pepelyaev asserts that this is why Sheberstov was not awarded the highest Soviet decoration, Hero of the Soviet Union, as were the other top aces and a few others. He later observed "it is dangerous to lead the leadership, especially those in Moscow, into error and, besides, to be caught red-handed. Such things are not forgiven."[15] This incident may explain why even less is known about this pilot than the other Soviet aces already discussed.

In all, the Soviets awarded twenty-two airmen the Hero of the Soviet Union decoration. All of the airmen mentioned above, with the notable exception of Sheberstov, received this honor. One other who was so decorated deserves mention. Serafim Subbotin was born in January 1921, joined the army in 1938, and earned his wings in 1942 after transferring into the air force. There is no record of his World War II experience. Like so many of the other Soviet aces, he arrived in the theater in Spring 1951. On 18 June 1951 he downed two Sabres. Subbotin was with a formation of eight MiGs that bounced sixteen F-86s. He shot down one Sabre, which exploded, and then rushed to the aid of another Communist pilot who was being shot up by a pair of F-86s. At this point, he was hit, his engine began to make grinding noises, and smoke filled the cockpit. The Red pilot jettisoned the canopy and went into a spiraling dive, closely followed by two Sabres. He then deployed his speed brakes and slowed so suddenly and rapidly that the lead F-86 collided with the damaged MiG. Subbotin then successfully bailed out; the American pilot was not as fortunate. Capt. William Crone (334FS) did not survive the collision.[16] Subbotin is credited with nine to fifteen victories, although most of the secondary sources use the lower number. He retired in 1973.[17]

At least one other top Soviet ace of the Korean War was an ace in World War II. Grigorii Okhai was born in January 1917, joined the army in 1937, and flew bombers in the 1939–40 Finnish War. He later transitioned into fighters during World War II, first serving as an instructor before getting into combat in 1943, during which he claimed six or eight German aircraft destroyed. In Korea, he flew 122 missions and engaged in 86 dogfights. He claims three Sabres among his eleven victories. Okhai writes that in Korea, his MiG was only hit once with one .50-caliber bullet in the aileron. He confirms that the F-86 was more maneuverable than the MiG, especially at lower altitudes. Okhai also notes that the MiG was better in the vertical plane but had less range than the Sabre. He retired from the air force in 1960.[18]

Grigorii Ges was born in April 1916, joined the army in 1937, and won his wings in 1941. He served mainly as an instructor until posted to a combat unit in October 1944. He flew twenty-one sorties, engaged in twenty dogfights, and claimed five German aircraft destroyed. The Soviets sent him to the Korean War in 1951, where he flew 120 or more missions and claimed eight or ten UN aircraft. Ges retired as a major in 1957 and died in January 1968.[19]

It is difficult to compare the American and Communist aces of the Korean War. Both groups were an elite subgroup of the much greater number of fighter pilots engaged in that conflict. We can assume that they were perhaps better fliers, surely more aggressive, and probably luckier than their fellow pilots. Three other aspects can be noted. First, the overwhelming number of the top aces had World War II experience, some in combat. Fourteen of the top eighteen or so Soviet aces flew in World War II; we do not have clear information on the remaining four. On the American side, all but three of the top eleven American aces had a similar opportunity. Second, as already noted, four of the top American aces were downed in combat, three were shot down, and one ran out of fuel. One was killed and another captured, with the remaining two rescued. Eight Soviet aces were shot down, one of these twice. Four of these pilots were killed, the rest recovered. A third aspect derived from the relatively sparse data we have is that the Soviet pilots had a much greater chance of engaging in aerial combat than did the American pilots. While many Sabre pilots complained of few engagements on their one mission tour, four Red aces had dogfights between 35 and 70 percent of their sorties. These aces also flew more missions than their American counterparts with nine averaging almost 150 missions, 10 percent more than any American ace.[20]

Conclusion

Although the air war over MiG Alley is best remembered for the glory of fighter pilots engaged in the first jet-versus-jet aerial combat, there was far more to their exploits. Regardless of the widespread discrepancies between U.S. and Communist accounts regarding victory credits, it is clear that the F-86 pilots won an important victory: Red aircraft did not venture far south of the Yalu River. Some may claim that this stemmed from the Communist prohibition against such flights, prompted by their desire not to expose Soviet airmen to capture, possibly widening the conflict. But if the Russians restricted their operations for political purposes, the newly formed North Korean and Chinese air forces may have done so for practical ones: their airmen were less trained and experienced and would have been badly defeated by the Americans. An alternative explanation is that the Communists knew that the American advantage increased the farther south the air battle was waged; as it was, they were defeated over their airfields in China.

Whether the Reds conceded air superiority or the Americans won it, the clear fact is that UN forces essentially had air superiority over all of Korea during the war.

Air superiority was important from the outset and throughout the war. It was especially significant in the initial weeks of the conflict. Airlift got American forces quickly into action, albeit in a piecemeal fashion. These American air and ground units could not stop but did delay and batter the North Korean advance. The elimination of the North Korean air force had a psychological impact, but, more importantly, it allowed air power to operate and gave the UN defenders added reach and firepower. The Communists came close to winning the war in that first month of the conflict, and air power provided what may very well have been the decisive edge to UN forces.

Throughout the war, the UN maintained air superiority over the immediate battle zone, UN rear areas, and arguably over all of North Korea. UN air superiority was there for the long haul. Consequently, with the exception of nighttime nuisance raids, UN ground forces and installations were free from air attack, as were UN movements and supply efforts. This was not so for their foes. Air power pummeled Communist ground forces, restricted most Red operations, and confined most enemy movements to the night. Air superiority also allowed widespread interdiction operations that hindered Communist resupply efforts. While air power could not defeat the massive, dug-in, tough Communist ground forces, it could greatly hinder their operations, as well as make them more costly. Surely air power increased the burden on the Communist ground soldier and lessened the burden on their UN counterparts. As in World War II, the Korean War demonstrated that conventional forces would be hard pressed to fight under unfriendly skies. Certainly such operations would be expensive.

The Communists challenged UN air power with the introduction of the MiG-15. The United States countered with the Sabre, which won and maintained air superiority. The F-86 defeated the MiG, although it is true that the Soviet fighter proved an unpleasant surprise for the West and a worthy opponent for the Sabre. In fact, the MiG initially had a number of performance advantages over the American fighter. However, North American upgraded its fighter so that by the end of the war the F-86 was essentially the equivalent of the MiG. The American pilots also had the advantages of a better gunsight and of "g" suits that permitted them to endure more stressful maneuvers than their opponents without blacking out. The F-86's .50s proved superior to the MiG's mixed cannon armament in the close-in highly maneuvering air battles. Another factor was that the MiG was a more dangerous aircraft to fly than the Sabre and was infamous for its tendency to get into uncontrollable spins. Considering all these factors, the F-86 was a superior fighting machine.

Ironically, American airmen, who have always pushed superior technology, won this fight without it. Just as American airmen in World War II began the conflict with fighters inferior to the enemy, American airmen in the Korean War found themselves in the same predicament in late 1950. But while the United States was able in the "Big War" to produce a greater number of superior piston-powered fighters, the USAF fought the battle in Korea with inferior numbers of an—at best—equivalent aircraft. In both wars, the key to winning air superiority was a better-trained pilot.

If the Sabre was at best equal to the MiG, the same cannot be said of the opposing pilots. Certainly there were good Chinese, North Korean, and Soviet pilots, but overall the Americans had a decisive edge in pilot quality. The USAF put into action numbers of experienced fighter pilots with high flying time, some of whom were World War II combat veterans. In addition, newly trained U.S. pilots proved to be more skillful than newly trained Communist pilots. Although Russian pilots were of a higher quality than their Chinese and North Korean allies, they were less able than the Americans. Most of all, the Sabre pilots were much more aggressive than their foes, a key to success in air-to-air combat.

In World War II, Allied air forces won the air campaign by destroying enemy air forces in the air, on their airfields, and in their factories. In contrast, the battle for air superiority over Korea was limited. Specifically, neither Soviet aircraft factories nor Communist aircraft on the ground in China were hit. The air war was fought and won in the skies over North Korea and China.

A small number of Sabre pilots won and maintained air superiority. On the order of 1,000 to 1,200 pilots flew the F-86 in combat in the Korean War. It was a long battle, a clear American victory, and important to the outcome of the war. The '86s claimed 810 enemy aircraft destroyed in aerial combat, all but 18 of which were MiG-15s. Yet this was not without losses. The official USAF records list a total of 224 Sabres lost to all causes. A further breakdown of the data indicates that approximately 100 F-86s fell in air-to-air combat, and seventy-one pilots died; forty-two were rescued from behind enemy lines or out of the sea, while another twenty-eight survived captivity. The Korean War remains the largest jet fighter action to date, despite the longer duration, greater number of sorties, and heavier tonnage of bombs dropped during the Vietnam War. Thus, the North American F-86 Sabre remains the most successful air-to-air jet fighter of all time.

Victory in the battle for air superiority was important to the overall action and helps explain the war's outcome. Air superiority was one of the few advantages the UN had in the war, and it allowed the UN to apply air power to make the war much more costly for the enemy. The Sabre and its pilots were key to UN air superiority. The F-86 looked good and performed well, but most of all, it was a superlative air-to-air fighter. The Sabre's outstanding success in Korea won it and its pilots a well-deserved place in the history of the Korean War and the annals of aviation history.

Epilogue

While the Korean War was the high point in the history of the F-86, the Sabre soldiered on for some time afterwards. It formed the core of the USAF fighter force in the mid-1950s, equipping more fighter wings than any other fighter type from 1953 until supplanted by North American's F-100 in 1957. Beginning in 1954, F-86s flew more than half a million flying hours each year for five consecutive years, a feat unmatched by any other post–World War II American fighter. In the half-century since 1950, only the F-4 and F-16 have logged more total flying time.[1] Other measures of its importance are the facts that it equipped so many air forces (thirty-seven) throughout the world for so long and that factories in the United States and four other countries turned out almost ten thousand Sabres, a record for a western jet fighter.[2] In these ways, it dominated the air forces of the non-Communist countries in the 1950s.

While our story has been of the Korean War and the three Sabre models that flew there (A, E, and F), the F-86's saga does not end with those models or with the Korean War. Other versions of the fighter took to the air in much larger numbers than those seen over Korea. And although Korea was the largest demonstration of jet aerial combat, the Sabre fought in other places as well.

USAF Sabres: The H

The linear descendent of the Korean War F-86 was the F-86H. Although it was not next in either alphabetical or chronological order, it was more akin to the A, E, and F models than either the Air Force's D or the Navy's FJ series. North American began development of a fighter-bomber version of the Sabre in March 1951. Built around a new General Electric J73 engine that generated 8,920 pounds of thrust, it had a considerable increase over the 6,000 pounds of thrust generated by the F-86F's J47engine.[3] The new engine's requirement for more air flow necessitated a redesign to deepen the fighter's fuselage, thereby creating more volume and allowing an increase of internal fuel from 435 gallons to 562 gallons. (The J73 had higher fuel consumption than the J47, but with the added fuel the H had the same range as the earlier versions.) The aircraft retained the original F-86F wing with slats, along with its landing gear, which was strengthened. Thus it had the same general look as the A, E, and F. The new Sabre was to be armed with four 20-mm cannon; however, the first 115 off the production line mounted the tried and true six .50s. North American fitted four pylons to the H, as in the later F models, and borrowed the clamshell canopy, ejection seat, and single-slab horizontal flying tail without dihedral from the F-86D. Beginning with the fifteenth aircraft, the builder installed the 6-3 wing, without slats, and extended the wingspan to increase wing area. The last ten production F-86Hs added slats, a change retrofitted into the series. From the outset of production models, North American equipped the fighter to carry a 1,200-pound Mk 12 nuclear bomb.[4]

The prototype F-86H made its initial flight in April 1953 and soon encountered problems. First, a shortage of engines delayed delivery of the planes; however, a rash of accidents created more serious difficulties.[5] The first major accident occurred in May 1954, but it was the crash and death of the top American Korean War ace, Joseph McConnell, in August 1954 that focused attention on the program. This high-visibility accident was followed a few days later by another accident when Maj. John Armstrong, who had just set a world speed record for a 500 km distance at the September National Air Races (649 mph) with the F-86H, died attempting to set another record. In 1954, thirty-three major F-86H accidents killed nine pilots and wrecked sixteen aircraft.[6] There were difficulties with both the pilots and the aircraft. One factor was the rapid buildup of Air Force fighter units during the mid-1950s that flooded the H outfits with an influx of brand new pilots. Their lack of experience, combined with limited training in the F-86H, created problems and caused accidents. In addition to difficulties with pilots, another factor was that the aircraft was beset by inadvertent ejections, engine failures, and fires. Firing the guns cracked parts of the structure, and the fighter had a tendency to shed nose wheel doors.

All of these problems did not happen at once; in fairness, all new aircraft are subject to teething difficulties. Nevertheless, it can be argued that the H was hardly a new aircraft, since North American had considerable experience with the Sabre by this time. Therefore, the introduction of the new model should have gone more smoothly. On the other hand, one study states "the F-86H in mid-1956 already encountered fewer operational problems than the F-84F."[7] While this may be true, the F-84F was a troublesome aircraft, hardly a paradigm of success.

The F-86H went into service in November 1954 and garnered a mixed reputation. It was considered inferior to the F in the air-to-air role because it could not sustain tight turns at altitude and because, despite the added power, it was no faster since the aircraft's speed was limited by its airframe. The H was, however, better than the F in the fighter-bomber mode, as it had a shorter takeoff run and higher rate of climb, among other characteristics. In any case, the F-86H served only briefly in the regular Air Force when the better performing F-100 began to arrive on the scene in 1956.[8]

As had been the practice, USAF sent the H to the Air National Guard beginning in the summer of 1957. The last Guard squadron converted from the F-86H in 1970–71.[9] Coming after the fabulously successful Korean War Sabres, the H was anticlimactic, overshadowed by other American and foreign fighters of the day. The F-86H never fired a shot in combat.

USAF Sabres: The D and L Models

The F-86D was much different than the air superiority and ground attack versions of the Sabre, even though it shared the designation, manufacturer, and some outward similarities. The D was a trailblazer, one of the first jets powered by an engine fitted with an afterburner, a fighter without guns, and an interceptor with a one-man crew. More F-86Ds were built than any other version of the Sabre and it, along with the L model developed from it, was the last Sabre variant to retire from the regular Air Force in June 1960.[10]

North American began work on turning the Sabre into an interceptor with strictly missile armament and a second crewmember in March 1949. The Air Force approved the project that July. But the promise of electronics that would enable one man to function as both pilot and radar operator and the cost of accommodating a second crewmember led to the one-man crew concept. In addition, North American and General Electric worked together to simplify flying the plane by developing an afterburning engine that could be more easily controlled by a single throttle. Undoubtedly the Soviet explosion of a nuclear device in 1949 and delays with the Northrop F-89 interceptor pushed the project. George Welch made the first flight in December 1949. Testing was delayed when the aircraft suffered landing-gear damage, a problem shared by the early Sabres.[11]

There were major differences between the F-86D and its siblings. The fighter's fuselage was almost completely redesigned to fit the radar and the more powerful engine. (In all, the D had only about 25 percent in common with the other Sabre variants.) The 18-inch diameter radar antenna with its 30-inch diameter radome mounted in the nose above the air intake gave the F-86D its distinctive protruding snout and ugly appearance.[12] North American also beefed up the wing, enlarged the fuselage and the vertical tail, and fitted it with a single horizontal slab stabilizer without dihedral. The D was approximately four feet longer than the A model to accommodate the afterburner, had a wider fuselage, and weighed one ton more. But powered by a J47-GE-17 engine that produced 5,700 pounds of thrust (dry) and 7,630 pounds with afterburner, it had a maximum speed about 25 mph faster than the A model. The F-86D went on to capture a number of speed records, one of 700 mph in November 1952 (3 km course) that was broken the following July by another F-86D flying 716 mph. On the same day in September 1953, it set records of 708 mph over a 15 km course and 690 mph over a 100 km course.[13]

One of the unique features of the F-86D was its armament. Instead of guns, it mounted twenty-four 2.75-inch diameter unguided air-to-air rockets in a tray beneath the belly. The unguided rockets were chosen over more accurate, heavier, and complex Falcon-guided air-to-air rockets or a package of 20-mm guns. However, the effectiveness of the rockets was questionable, for test photos reveal the erratic pattern they flew. (Therefore the system called for launch at five hundred yards, although the theoretical maximum effective range was fifteen hundred yards.) Although the rockets were not fired in combat, in August 1952 an F-86D downed a DB-17 mother ship instead of the target drone it was directing.[14]

It is not surprising that the more complex F-86D suffered a number of developmental problems. Slow deliveries of electronics for both the radar and engine impeded Air Force acceptances. (At one point in 1953, there were 320 airframes awaiting equipment.) The new equipment, rocket armament, fire control system, radar, and engine controls all proved troublesome. Because the modified airframe increased drag, the manufacturer had to fit vortex generators to deal with boundary control problems. In addition to air-craft difficulties, the increased workload of the one-man crew concept demanded more extensive pilot training. These woes put the project about two and a half years behind schedule.[15]

Despite all of this, the new interceptor became operational in April 1953; by the end of the year, six hundred were in service. In mid-1955, over a thousand F-86s made up almost three-fourths of Air Defense Command's (ADC) inventory. The fighter's service life was short, as ADC began phasing it out of service in April 1958. It equipped the first Air National Guard squadron in May 1957 and served with the Guard until June 1961.[16]

The D was upgraded. Project Pullout, which began in March 1954, involved almost three hundred modifications. The most important changes were the addition of a sixteen-foot diameter drag chute that reduced landing roll, an improved engine, and better electronics for both the autopilot and fire control systems.[17] The USAF went further: beginning in 1956 the Air Force began converting F-86Ds to a newer configuration, designated F-86L. The initial plan was to convert all of the D's to the L standard, but in the end approximately one-half were refurbished. The modifications included a 6-3 wing with slats that had a two-foot longer wingspan. In addition to these aerodynamic improvements, North American upgraded the electronics to allow the aircraft to operate with the SAGE (semi-automated ground environment) equipment.[18] The first L went into operations with the regular Air Force in 1956, and the last was phased out in June 1960. The Guard started flying it in 1959 and kept it in service until mid-1965. Despite its complexity, the F-86D (and L) had the best safety record of the F-86 models flying in the USAF.[19]

The Sabre and the Sea Services

Since 1945 the Air Force has utilized a number of Navy aircraft. In contrast, the Navy and Marines have employed only one Air Force fighter—the F-86, which had its origins as a Navy aircraft (FJ-1).[20] It should be emphasized that the operating conditions of the two services are not parallel, and therefore their aircraft must vary. Certainly operations are more difficult from an air-craft carrier than from a land base, requiring more robust (and thus heavier) aircraft to withstand the higher stresses of carrier takeoffs and landings. Folding wings, catapult points, and arrestor gear also add weight to the aircraft. Good low-speed flying and short takeoff and landing characteristics have always been more important to the Navy than to the Air Force. Nevertheless, the Navy fielded straight-winged jet fighters that had comparable performance to their Air Force contemporaries, the F-80s and F-84s. However, the sea service's transition to swept-wing aircraft was slow. While the first Air Force swept-wing fighter (the F-86) initially flew in October 1947, the first Navy swept-winged aircraft (the Vought F7U Cutlass) did not fly until March 1950. Even if it and other Navy swept-wing fighters that took to the air shortly thereafter could have been ready for Korea, none could compete with the Sabre in air-to-air combat.[21] The appearance of the MiG-15 and operations in Korea made clear that the Navy needed a first-rate jet fighter, and needed it as soon as possible.

The FJ-2

Adapting the F-86 for naval duty seemed the quickest way to get a high performance jet fighter out to the fleet. In January 1951, North American began studying how to accomplish that task. The Navy bought two F-86E models with some modest modifications that included an extended nose-wheel leg (to allow a greater angle of attack for catapult launch), tail hook, and catapult points, along with the strengthening of the landing gear and airframe. It was designated XFJ-2 and first flew in December 1951.[22]

The production FJ-2 incorporated folding wings and four 20-mm cannon. The designers also mounted a slab tail without dihedral, modified the cockpit to improve takeoff visibility, and installed a British Martin-Baker ejection seat, all of which distinguished the XFJ-2 from the F-86F model, which it otherwise closely resembled. The naval equipment modifications added one-half ton to the weight of the aircraft. Despite the Navy's needs, production was slow because the manufacture of the F-86F took precedence. In January 1954, the Navy had only twenty-five FJ-2s. Moreover, the fighter's suitability for carrier operations was at issue because the FJ-2 had a weak nose gear and arrestor hook and a questionable approach and landing performance. Consequently, the Navy preferred the lighter swept-wing F9F-6 Cougar that had better low-speed performance. Therefore, the entire FJ-2 run, which ended in September 1954, went to the Marines for land-based duties, although some of these did deploy onto carriers. (This parallels the history of the F4U Corsair that at first was deemed unsafe for carrier operations and was initially flown by the Marine Corps from land bases.) In any case, the aircraft's service was brief; the FJ-2s were withdrawn from the regular forces by the end of 1956 and then served in naval reserve units until 1957.[23]

North American tried a number of wing changes to improve the fighter's low-speed handling. These included using the 6-3 wing without slats and a full chord wing fence. A larger span wing was also tried, albeit unsuccessfully. A number of wing fences were tried until in October 1954 the manufacturer hit on the solution, not for the FJ-2 but for its successor.[24]

FJ-3

The next Navy version of the F-86 was somewhat different. In the words of a prominent aviation historian, "the Navy finally tore itself free from the shackles of the land-based F-86 Sabre design with which it had been stuck, somewhat reluctantly. Now, the Navy could take the superb features of the swept-wing fighter and improve upon them for its very dangerous business of flying to, from, and around aircraft carriers."[25] A British Armstrong Siddeley Sapphire engine, built under license by Wright and designated as the J65, powered the fighter. That engine produced a maximum thrust of 7,800 pounds—a considerable boost from the 6,000-pound thrust J47 in the FJ-2 and the Korean War F-86Fs. Thus the FJ-3, which first flew in July 1953, had higher performance than its sire. The FJ-3 did encounter some engine problems that forced the Navy to levee certain operating restrictions on the fighter.[26]

The FJ-3 went into service in September 1954 and out for sea duty in May 1955. In 1955, the Navy added a 6-3 wing with wing fences and increased camber but without slats, which increased wing area and provided space in the leading edge for an additional 124 gallons of fuel. This change was retrofitted into the other FJ-3s. The stores stations were increased from two to six. In 1955, the FJ-3 was retrofitted with probe and drogue air-to-air refueling equipment, enabling the fighter to be refueled by another FJ (the "buddy system" introduced in June 1957) or by an AJ-2 Savage tanker. The Navy later modified the fighter to employ the heat-seeking Sidewinder air-to-air guided missile in a version designated FJ-3M.[27]

FJ-4

The final naval version of the Sabre series also varied somewhat from its predecessors. It was designed to meet the requirements of the recently canceled McDonnell F3H Demon that called for a top speed of Mach .95, carrier suitability, availability within two years, and a two-hour patrol time without drop tanks. The last requirement was the tough one because it mandated a 50 percent increase in internal fuel. The fighter retained the Wright J65-W-4 that could produce 7,650 pounds of thrust but essentially had a completely redesigned fuselage that was deepened to accommodate the additional fuel and a spine that extended from the cockpit to the vertical tail. The latter distorted the Sabre's classic good looks. North American attached a new wing with the same 35-degree sweep but thinner profile, as the thickness to chord ratio decreased from 10 percent to 6 percent. The wing had greater camber, carried fuel in the leading edge, had an increased span, and its tail was thinner and taller.[28]

The FJ-4 first took to the air in October 1954. Beginning with production aircraft number 33, North American used the Wright J65-W-16, and the earlier aircraft were modified to this standard. The company also provided the fighter with air-to-air refueling capability. However the aircraft's oil capacity limited flight time to five hours. Later in the production run, the oil capacity was increased from three to four gallons, raising maximum flight time to seven hours.[29]

North American built an attack version of the FJ-4, designated FJ-4B. This Fury featured a strengthened wing that enabled the fighter to carry up to three tons, another pair of speed brakes under the tail, and equipment that permitted delivery of nuclear weapons and the new Bullpup guided air-to-ground missile. It first flew in December 1954, and deliveries began in July 1957. More of these were built than the earlier FJ-4 version. In the early 1960s, the Navy began to phase the aircraft out of service, with the fighter's last cruise ending in August 1962. The reserves received the aircraft and flew them into 1964. The sea services accepted 1,115 Furies.[30]

Foreign Manufacture

One of the unique aspects about the F-86 was that it was manufactured in four countries outside of the United States. In 1949, Canada picked the Sabre to replace its obsolete Vampires. Instead of merely buying the aircraft from the United States, the Canadians decided to build it under license. The original concept of turning out 100 aircraft evolved into manufacturing 1,815 before the line at Canadair shut down in 1958. And while the first Canadian Sabres contained only 10 percent Canadian content, at the end of the production run that proportion evolved to 85 percent. Although these aircraft looked like the original from North American, later models powered by Canadian-built engines were among the best performers in the Sabre family.[31]

After building one example of the F-86A (Mk.1 in the Canadian system), Canadair began in 1951 to turn out the first of 350 Mk.2s, which were essentially the F-86E. Beginning in mid-1952, sixty Canadian-built fighters served in USAF colors in Korea as F-86E-6s, a dramatic statement about the gravity of the situation in Korea and inadequacy of North American production. The Canadians added their flavor to the Sabre beginning with the sole Mk.3, a fighter powered by a Canadian Orenda 3 engine that produced 6,000 pounds of thrust. This engine was only slightly larger in diameter than the J47, thus requiring minor changes to fit into the airframe. Jacqueline Cochrane flew this aircraft to two world women's speed records in May and June 1953. The fighter was mass-produced as the Mk.4 (similar to the F-86E-10) with over four hundred going to the RAF.[32]

The next Sabres that rolled out of the Canadian plant were built like the F-86F. Because they were powered by the Orenda engine, which produced more thrust than the J47 in the American original yet weighed the same, they performed much better. The Mk.5's Orenda 10 produced 6,355 pounds of thrust and like its sibling, the F-86F-30, mounted a 6-3 wing without slats. All 370 of the Mk.5 version went to the RCAF.[33]

The Mk.6 was the best of the lot, powered by the Orenda 14, which generated 7,275 pounds of thrust. It was originally fitted with the slatless wing, but it was soon replaced by one with slats. The plane made its initial flight in November 1954 and Canadair built 655 before it went out of production in October 1958. They went to the Canadians and Germans in large numbers (390 and 225 respectively) and to the Colombians and South Africans in small numbers (6 and 34). The Luftwaffe fighters were later modified to employ Sidewinder missiles. The Canadians phased the Sabre out of service in 1963.[34]

Australian, Japanese, and Italian Sabres

In 1949 the Australians sought a jet fighter to replace their De Haviland Vampires and considered an indigenous design, the Grumman F9F Panther, and two Hawker aircraft. But the F-86 won out in February 1951 in a decision greatly influenced by Commonwealth Aircraft Corporation's (CAC) positive

World War II experience with North American (building the Wirraway and P-51) and doubts concerning the timely availability of the Hunter.[35]

CAC made two major changes to the American design. The first was to use the Rolls Royce Avon engine, forcing a redesign of the fuselage because that engine was shorter, lighter, larger in diameter, and required more airflow than the J47. The substitution of two 30 mm Aden cannons for the six .50s also required rework of the fuselage. Therefore, the Australians redesigned about 60 percent of the structure. Otherwise built to the F standard with slatted wings, the prototype first flew in August 1953.[36]

Although the CAC had to work through engine surge problems, the first (Mk.30) entered service in April 1955. The next batch of twenty fighters (Mk.31) mounted a 6-3 wing without slats (two of this series, and later models carried additional fuel in the wing's leading edge), modifications used on all subsequent aircraft and retrofitted into those already built. The Australians built sixty-nine of the final version, Mk.32, with the last delivered in December 1961. It had a locally built 7,500-pound thrust Avon 26 engine and the ability to employ a pair of Sidewinder missiles. To combat the engine surge problem, the fuel pump was programmed to decrease fuel flow to the engine when the guns fired. The Australians retired the last Sabre in July 1971. All 112 built went to the RAAF, although like other Sabres, they eventually found their way to other countries.[37]

Mitsubishi of Japan turned out 282 F-86Fs and 18 RF-86Fs for the Japanese Air Self Defense Force (JASDF) without change from the American version. These were built between 1956 and 1961, with the first flying in August 1956. The last JASDF Sabre flew in 1982.[38]

Fiat was the fourth foreign manufacturer. The air forces of the North Atlantic Treaty Organization (NATO) were seeking an all-weather interceptor, but rejected the De Havilland Venom because of its limited performance. In January 1953, the USAF notified North American that the Italians would be building a fighter based on the F-86D but with a number of modifications, most notably a simplified fire control system, 20-mm armament, and a two-man crew. The company responded that they had experience with licensing the Sabre but warned that a two-seat version would require considerable redesign. A simpler fire control system was a more practical concept because it would not only protect American secrets from possible compromise, but it would also spare the NATO air forces maintenance problems associated with the advanced avionics. North American proposed a radar system that would guide the fighter to a lead-pursuit

interception of hostile bombers, giving the pilot both firing range and suggested breakaway time.[39]

North American built the first 120 of this new version, designated F-86K.
The aircraft looked like the D but differed in armament, fire control system,
and an additional six inches of length. Later the K was equipped to carry
Sidewinder missiles and fitted with the extended leading edge and longer
wingspan. The first U.S.–built K flew in July 1954 while the first of 221 Fiat-
built fighters took to the air in May 1955. The F-86K entered service with the
Italian Air Force in mid-1955 and was not replaced until 1964. It served with
four other NATO air forces as well.[40]

Post–Korean War Combat

Although the Korean War was the shining moment for the F-86, the Sabre
saw additional action in the next couple of decades. In January 1954, for
example, eight MiGs attacked an RB-45 flying over the Yellow Sea. F-86s
escorting the reconnaissance aircraft downed one MiG-15. In a similar incident in February 1955, a dozen Sabres (335FS) tangled with eight or more
MiGs and destroyed two. In a third encounter in May 1955, twelve MiG-15s
jumped eight F-86s (35FS) over the Yellow Sea, resulting in one Communist
pilot bailing out. None of these American victories were officially credited.[41]

The Sabres also fought for other nations. The Chinese Nationalists
received massive American military aid in the 1950s that permitted them to
field three F-86F and two F-84G fighter wings. In 1958, the Chinese Communists made threatening moves that provoked a crisis in the Taiwan Straits. On
24 September, a large dogfight ensued, during which the Chinese Nationalists
later claimed that their F-86s destroyed ten MiG-15s and MiG-17s. Four of
these fell to Sidewinders in the first combat use of guided air-to-air missiles.
During a six-week period, the Nationalists destroyed thirty-one MiGs at the cost
of two F-86s. In July 1959, Chinese Nationalist F-86s downed five MiG-17s.[42]

Pakistan also received a sizeable number of Sabres. When war broke out
in south Asia in September 1965, Pakistan faced about five hundred Indian
combat aircraft with a small air force built around one hundred F-86s, one-
quarter of which were armed with Sidewinders. The Indians had more modern aircraft than the Pakistanis, but the latter had the advantage of a decade's
experience with the Sabre and many pilots with one thousand or so flying
hours in the aircraft. The claims and admissions by the two sides in the con-

flict are terribly frustrating. The Pakistanis credit one of their pilots, Squadron Leader M. M. Alam, with downing five Hunters on one sortie and nine Indian aircraft in the war.[43] If correct, this makes him the only Sabre ace since the Korean War. The Pakistanis claim that the F-86s destroyed at least thirty-five Indian aircraft in air-to-air combat at a loss of eight fighters, seven of which were F-86s.[44] Whatever the reality, the Pakistani Air Force did well in the conflict and probably had the edge.

Another war engulfed the region in 1971. By this time, the military balance had swung even more sharply in favor of India, with its air force numbering 735 combat aircraft opposed to 240 Pakistani combat aircraft. Again there was frequent air action, and again conflicting claims; in the end, the air battle seems to have been more even. One secondary source puts the losses at probably 65 Indian and 40 Pakistani aircraft.[45]

Today the Sabre is a memory of aviation a half century ago. The magnificent fighter is certainly well regarded by those associated with it for its looks, performance, and combat record. Only a few of the thousands built remain. Some still fly, one appearing with its archrival, the MiG-15, in air shows across the United States. The F-86 is remembered as a magnificent aircraft and most especially for its epic air battles and striking victories over MiG Alley. It clearly was a beautiful aircraft and a significant one as well, for it fought and won the battle for air superiority in the Korean War and dominated the air for almost a decade, thus winning a place in history. The F-86 was truly a great aircraft and a classic fighter. Hail to the Sabre!

Notes

In citing works in the notes, short titles have generally been used. Sources frequently cited have been identified by the following abbreviations:

AFMC   Air Force Materiel Command (Dayton, Ohio)
BOE   Boeing Archives (Seattle, Washington)
DTIC   Defense Technical Information Center (Fort Belvoir, Virginia)
FRCSL   Federal Records Center (St. Louis, Missouri)
HRA   USAF Historical Research Agency (Montgomery, Alabama)
NARA   National Archives and Records Administration (College Park, Maryland)
NASM   National Air and Space Museum (Silver Hill, Maryland)
USAFA   USAF Academy (Colorado Springs, Colorado)

Introduction

1. Far East Air Forces, General Order No. 349, Official Credit for Destruction of Enemy Aircraft, 26 July 1951, HRA K720.193; Robert Futrell, *The United States Air Force in Korea, 1950–1953* (New York: Duell, Sloan and Pearce, 1961), 211. Perhaps fittingly, the 51st Fighter Interceptor Wing later converted to F-86s and became the second of only two USAF air superiority units in the Korean War.

2. Futrell, *The USAF in Korea*, 216.

3. General Order No. 190, 29 April 1951; USAF Credits for the Destruction of Enemy Aircraft Korean War, USAF Historical Study No. 81, 1975 (hereafter cited as USAF Korean War Victory Credits); and Futrell, *USAF in Korea*, 215.

4. Malcolm Cagle and Frank Manson, *The Sea War in Korea* (Annapolis, Md.: Naval Institute, 1957), 526; Richard Hallion, *The Naval Air War in Korea* (Baltimore: Nautical and Aviation, 1986), 74–75.

5. Hinton was a World War II veteran who served in the Panama Canal Zone and thus had no combat experience. Therefore, the 4th Fighter Group commander, Lt. Col. J. C. Meyers, detailed Hinton to fly with the 51st Fighter Group to gain some experience and prove himself. Hinton flew ten missions with the F-80 unit. Bruce Hinton to author, 3 July 2002.

6. Lt. Col. C. S. Demonbrun, Director of Intelligence Evaluation, Operational Intelligence, Memorandum for Deputy for Intelligence, sub: "Follow-up on Enemy Aerial Encounter, 17 December 1950," in Jarred Crabb Journal, frame 0482 USAFA MS-2; "Enemy Air Activity, 17 December 1950," HRA K730.310-5. The materials cited above provided all the quoted material in this paragraph and served as the basic sources for the information cited.

7. USAF Korean War Victory Credits, 46; Leonid Krylov and Yuriy Tepsurkayev, "Combat Episodes of the Korean War: Three Out of One Thousand," *Mir Aviatsiya*, 1-97. Available at www.kimsoft.com/2000/nk-af2.htm. The Russians, who were flying the MiGs in these early battles, claimed to have downed an F-80 on 1 November 1950, although the Americans assert that no Shooting Star was lost in air-to-air combat that day. For their part, the Russians deny that a MiG was lost on 8 November but do admit a loss in combat against the Navy on 9 November.

8. Robert Futrell, William H. Greenhalgh, Carl Grubb, Gerard E. Hasselwander, Robert F. Jakob, and Charles A. Ravenstein, *Aces and Aerial Victories: The United States Air Force in Southeast Asia 1965–1973* (Maxwell AFB, Ala.: The Albert F. Simpson Historical Research Center, Air University and Office of Air Force History, Headquarters USAF, 1976), 157; Rene Francillon, *Vietnam: The War in the Air* (New York: Arch Cape, 1987), 208; Roy A. Grossnick, *United States Naval Aviation, 1910–1995* (Washington, D.C.: Department of the Navy, Naval Historical Center, 1997), 767–69. Available at http://www.history.navy.mil/branches/usna1910.htm; and United States Air Force Statistical Digest: Fiscal Year 1953, 20 HRA K134.11-6. During the Korean War the USAF lost 139 aircraft to enemy aircraft and claimed 962 aerial credits. In Vietnam, American air-to-air losses totaled 79 and victory claims, 199.

9. USAF Statistical Digest: Fiscal Year 1953, 20, 28. The F-86 pilots claimed to have destroyed 810 aircraft in air-to-air combat, including 792 of 823 MiG15s claimed destroyed. B-29s were awarded credit for sixteen MiGs; F-94s, one; F-84s, eight; and F-80s, six. USAF Korean War Victory Credits; and Far East Air Forces, Korean Air War Summary: 25 June 1950–27 July 1953, 12 HRA K720.04D-1. This source credits the UN airmen with a total of 841 MiG-15s and a total of 900 aircraft destroyed in air-to-air combat; Malcolm Cagle and Frank Manson, *The Sea War in Korea* (Anapolis, Md.: Naval Institute, 1957), 526–27. Marine and Navy pilots (aside from those flying exchange tours in F-86s) claimed another ten MiG-15s.

Chapter 1

1. Air Materiel Command, "F-86 Background," June 1955, 1 AFMC R1-205.6; "The North American F-86 Sabre: Description and Brief History," AFMC A1

F-86/his; Short History of the Sabrejet; "The F-86 Sabre" AFMC R1-205.6-1; Air Materiel Command, "XF-86 Abstract," 1–2; and "History of Air Materiel Command," 1946, vol. 1, 96–97.

2. Air Technical Service Command, Research and Development Projects of the Engineering Division, 7th edition, 1 July 1945, XP-86 Airplane, AFMC; Ray Rice, "The Sabre Story," *Skyline* (Feb 1953). The AAF canceled the static article to save money.

3. AMC, "XF-86 Abstract," 16; Norm Avery, *North American Aircraft, 1934–1998*, vol. 1 (Santa Ana, Cal.: Narkiewicz/Thompson, 1998), 162–65, 168; Morgan Blair, "Evolution of the F-86," in *The Evolution of Aircraft Wing Design*, (AIAA Dayton-Cincinnati Section, March 1980), 77. This was the last navy fighter to be armed with 0.50s. North American considered using either .50 or .60 machine guns under development. In late 1946, the Department of Ordnance terminated the .60-caliber program.

4. "XP-86," revision 15 August 1945 AFMC A1 (X)F-86/char; "NAA F-86 Sabre: Description and Brief History," 2, 5; Ray Wagner, *Mustang Designer: Edgar Schmued and the P-51* (Washington, D.C.: Smithsonian, 1990), 170.

5. John Anderson, *A History of Aerodynamics* (Cambridge, UK: Cambridge University, 1998), 403, 423; Ray Wagner, *The North American Sabre* (Garden City, N.Y.: Doubleday, 1963), 13; T. F. Walkowicz, "Birth of Sweepback," 30–32; Ray Wagner, *Mustang Designer* (Washington, D.C.: Smithsonian, 1990), 170.

6. Walter Boyne, *Messerschmitt Me 262: Arrow to the Fume* (London: Jane's, 1980), 25, 107; William Green, *Warplanes of the Third Reich* (Garden City, N.Y.: Doubleday, 1979), 592, 597. The Me 262 used the concept to move the center of gravity rearward while the Me 163 used it to deal with stability and yaw-roll problems.

7. Ray Wagner, *American Combat Planes* (Garden City, N.Y.: Doubleday, 1982), 288–89. In November 1939, the airmen issued a specification for radical pusher-type aircraft. Two of the three aircraft that resulted, the Curtiss XP-55 and Northrop XP-56, featured swept-back wings, although their pusher propellers and lack of a rear horizontal stabilizer were more noticeable. Both flew; both had problems and crashes. (The third was a twin boom, pusher-type with a straight wing, the Vultee XP-54.) None of these aircraft were practical or instrumental in advancing aviation; in brief, they were aeronautical curiosities.

8. Anderson, *A History of Aerodynamics*, 427–28; Blair, "Evolution of the F-86," 77; Col. Carl Green, Materiel Command Liaison Officer NACA to Commanding General, AAF, sub: "Wing Sweep Back and Wing Sweep Forward Pressure Distribution Models," 20 July 1944, FRCSL 324-57-B-1254 121/182.

9. "[Harrison] Storms Comments Cont'd," NAA "F-86 History/General Description," BOE, 11. Also see Blair, "Evolution of the F-86," 77–79; Wagner, *Mustang Designer*, 171; Wagner, *North American Sabre*, 13. Concurrently, Boeing used German data to modify its XB-47 to a swept-back wing configuration by September 1945. The six-engine jet bomber first flew in December 1947, two and a half months after the first XP-86 flight. Curiously, a contemporary design of the XB-86 and XB-47,

North American's four engine jet bomber, the B-45, first flew in March 1947 with a straight wing.

10. Blair, "Evolution of the F-86," 79, 80–81. Blair's March 1945 date for this final change is clearly a typographical error. To be precise, the F-86 wing had a 4.79:1 aspect ratio. Duncan Curtis, *North American F-86 Sabre* (Ramsbury, UK: Crowood, 2004), 9; Wagner, *North American Sabre*, 14. Later (see below) North American adopted the higher ratio wing. The horizontal tail retained its position (on the line of the top of the rear fuselage) and dihedral. The change increased the fuselage length by 2 feet, reduced the horizontal tail span by 2.5 feet, and increased the tail height 1.3 feet. Blair, "Evolution of the F-86," 81, 83. The wing area increased from 255 to 274 square feet. AMC, "XF-86 Abstract," 7.

11. Avery, *North American Aircraft, 1934–1998*, vol. 1. (Santa Ana, Cal.: Narkiewicz/Thompson, 1998), 168–69; Blair, "Evolution of the F-86," 78; and Wagner, *Mustang Designer*, 171.

12. Rice, "Sabre Story"; Stewart Wilson, *F-86 Sabre, MiG-15 'Fagot,' and Hawker Hunter* (Weston Creek, Australia: Aerospace, 1995), 10; and Wagner, *North American Sabre*, 12.

13. The AAF designation system used "P" for pursuit (fighters). In June 1948, the newly founded USAF (September 1947) changed its aircraft designation system, redesignating pursuit aircraft ("P") to fighters, and using the prefix "F." I've attempted to use the correct designation for the appropriate time periods but have referred generically to the fighter as the F-86 for simplicity's sake.

14. Wagner, *North American Sabre*, 13. There is a connection between looks and performance. The more streamlined the airframe, usually the better looking and better performing. One notable exception to this rule was the McDonnell-Douglas F-4 Phantom.

15. AMC, "XF-86 Abstract," 7, 10–11. In October 1945, North American estimated that the top speed of the straight wing version was 582 mph at 10,000 feet while that of the swept-wing version would be 633 mph at 18,500 feet. However, rate of climb and range would be less in the latter. There was concern over the 26-inch wheels, and some consideration given to replacing them with 30-inch tires. But as this would have necessitated a wider fuselage, it was dropped. Instead, Bendix increased the load capacity of the tires and developed a new brake system; AMC, "F-86 Background," 2.

16. Blair, "Evolution of the F-86," 78–79; Wagner, *Mustang Designer*, 170; Green, *Warplanes of the Third Reich*, 534–25, 628, 630–31. Slats were not a new idea; they dated back to the 1923 Hadley Page 21 and were employed on the World War II Me 109.

17. Blair, "Evolution of the F-86," 81; Rice, "Sabre Story."

18. Col. Ben Funk, Chief Aircraft and Missiles Section, Procurement Division to Lt. Col. Fleming, sub: "Request for pilots to fly latest configuration of the F-86," 4 January 1949 item number 7 in F-86 Correspondence, vol. 1 HRA K202.1-57. The removal of the locks and the new slat configuration gave insufficient stall warning. Therefore North American installed a "stick shaker" to warn the pilot of oncoming stall; Flight Operating Instructions, USAF Model P-86A Airplane, 20 Apr 1948,

13 (hereafter cited as Pilot's Manual [aircraft model], [date]). Pilot's Manual F-86A-1, -5, 20 January 1949, revised 30 May 1949, 15; and Blair, "Evolution of the F-86," 84.

19. Kris Hughes and Walter Dranem, *North American F-86 Sabre Jet Day Fighters* (North Branch, Minn.: Speciality, 1996), 18.

20. The nickname came from his appearance on the box of that cereal brand celebrating his Pearl Harbor experience.

21. The U.S. government awarded fifteen Medals of Honor for action at Pearl Harbor, all to naval personnel.

22. Al Blackburn, *Aces Wild* (Wilmington, Del.: SR Books, 1998), 103–4, 130, 261; Curtis, *North American F-86 Sabre*, 13; USAF Credits for the Destruction of Enemy Aircraft, World War II, USAF Historical Study No. 85, 1978, 197. (Hereafter cited as USAF World War II Victory Credits.)

23. Kris Hughes and Walter Dranem, *North American F-86 Sabre Jet Day Fighters*. (North Branch, Minn.: Speciality, 1996), 18, 20, citing the account of Ed Hockey; Al Blackburn, *Aces Wild* (Wilmington, Del.: SR Books, 1998), 144.

24. North American Aviation, Flight Logs, XP-86: 45-59597 NAA F-86/FJ, BOE.

25. Hughes and Dranem, *North American F-86*, 20; AMC, "XF-86 Abstract," 21. This source states that a rod in the landing gear valve was broken, probably due to retracting the gear at too high an air speed; Wagner, *American Combat Planes*, 463. Welch was killed in October 1954 test flying an F-100A.

26. Larry Davis, "North American F-86 Sabre," *Wings of Fame*, vol.10, (1998), 42; Hughes and Dranem, *North American F-86*, 21–22, 25–26; Curtis, *North American F-86*, 13; and Blackburn, *Aces Wild*, 220. Two secondary sources, each citing Ed Horkey, have conflicting dates for this flight, which clocked Mach 1.02 and Mach 1.03 in dives. The earlier date is cited by Davis and the later date by Hughes and Dranem.

27. Davis, "North American F-86 Sabre," 42; Hughes and Dranem, *North American F-86*, 22.

28. Blackburn, *Aces Wild*, 143–44, 152, 154, 162, 164, 249, and 253. Blackburn quotes Palmer and cites Bob Chilton, Welch's wife, his brother-in-law, and another test pilot, Bud Poage.

29. Jerry Scutts, "The Upper Reaches," in *Faster, Further and Higher*, Philip Jarrett, ed., (London: Putnam, 2002), 80.

30. USAF XP-86: 45-59597, 45-59599 BOE. The USAF record cards show it was tested to destruction in September 1952 at Kirtland and dropped from the inventory the following month. The second test plane (serial number 45-59598) first flew in February 1948 and was turned over to the Air Force in May 1950 with almost 96 flying hours on 180 flights. It served at Edwards and Norton Air Force Bases before being transferred to the 6570th Calibration and Ordinance Test Group (ARDC), Phillips Field, Aberdeen Proving Grounds in March 1953. It was dropped from the USAF inventory the next month and picked up by the Army Field Forces. The third test article, serial number 45-59599, first flew in May 1948 and accumulated just over nine hours flying time on fourteen flights before North American turned it over to the USAF, which accepted delivery on 17 December 1948. The third XF-86 had two

major accidents, one in February 1949 when Chuck Yeager had a nose wheel problem and another when Maj. Robert Johnson had an engine fire as he taxied in after a
flight on 26 June 1950.

31. North American Aviation, "The North American F-86 Sabre Description
and Brief History," 7 BOE A1 F-86/his [55MCP-31074]; "North American Aviation,"
Aircraft, Jet, F-86A, 'Sabre,' Fighter, mfr: North American. S/N USAF 47-605 BOE
A1 F-86A/his [D52.1/966]; Wagner, *Mustang Designer*, 173–74.

32. TWX Commanding General, Far East Air Forces to Headquarters Air Force,
Attention Directorate, Maintenance, Supply Services, 19 January 1951, sub: "Operational Deficiencies of the F-84 and F-86 Type Aircraft" in FEAF in History Directorate Procurement and Industrial Planning, 1 July–31 December 1950," AFMC
RI-644.1c. The "V" shaped glass was better for sighting. Eventually the E model
changed to a flat glass; AMC, "XF-86 Abstract," 15, 19. North American considered
and tested a light-green tinted cockpit glass to lower temperatures in the cockpit. The
scheme was dropped because of reduced visibility at night.

33. Air Proving Ground Report, "Operational Suitability Test of Open Gun Ports
for F-86 Aircraft," Project No. 24913-5, 31 August 1949, 5, 8 DTIC AD B971411.
During earlier tests with the gun doors, pilots reported "excessive 'cook offs.'" In later
Eglin Tests of the open gun port panels, there were 82 "cook offs" on sixty thousand
rounds fired, indicating a gun-cooling problem; AMC, "XF-86 Abstract," 18; APG,
Operational Suitability Test of Open Gun Ports, 5, 8; NAA, "North American F-86
Sabre Description and Brief History," 7; Donald Lopez, *Fighter Pilot's Heaven: Flight
Testing the Early Jets* (Washington, D.C.: Smithsonian, 1995), 210.

34. North American Aviation, "Improved F-86F," report No. NA-53-96 DTIC
AD 003153. These opened to 50 degrees in two seconds and closed in one second at
medium and high engine speeds, and opened in six seconds and closed in three seconds at idle speeds. In 1953, North American proposed to double the area of the side
speed brakes and add a third surface beneath the cockpit. It was not adopted. Maurice Allward, *F-86 Sabre* (London: Allan, 1978), 20; Larry Davis, "SabreJet: XP-86
Swept-wing Development," *Sabre Jet Classics* (vol. 5, no. 3), 1997, available at http:
//sabre-pilots.org/classics/v53sabre.htm; "Sabre: A Study of a Renowned Fighter,"
Flight (30 January 1953), 140; Curtis, *North American F-86 Sabre*, 10; Davis, "North
American F-86 Sabre," 43.

35. Allward, *F-86 Sabre*, 22, 24; Curtis, *North American F-86 Sabre*, 15–18;
John Taylor, Michael Taylor, and David Mondey, eds., *Air Facts and Feats* (New
York: Two Continents, 1974), 258–59.

36. Lindsay Peacock, *North American F-86 Sabre* (New York: Gallery, 1991), 13.
There are some that refer to the fighter as "Sabrejet."

Chapter 2

1. "The Sabre and the MiG—A Comparison of Ability," ASTIA *Technical Data
Digest* (April 1952), 6; Robert Futrell, "United States Air Force Operations in the
Korean Conflict: 1 November 1950–30 June 1952" (USAF Historical Study No.72, 1

July 1955), 121; Curtis, *North American F-86 Sabre*, 74; and Marcelle Knaack, *Encyclopedia of U.S. Air Force Aircraft and Missile Systems*, vol. 1, *Post–World War II Fighters, 1945–1973* (Washington, D.C.: Office of Air Force History, 1978), 55.

2. Futrell, Historical Study No. 72, 121; Gordon Swanborough and Peter Bowers, *United States Military Aircraft since 1908* (London: Putnam, 1971), 426.

3. William Dailey, "War Emergency Thrust Augmentation for the J47 Engine in the F-86 Aircraft," (August 1956, iii , viii, 1, 13–21, DTIC AD-095757). The Air Force considered two other possibilities: liquid nitrogen injection and overspeed. Liquid nitrogen injection was tested with fourteen static runs. While the scheme showed a 28 percent thrust augmentation, the testers concluded that problems with nitrogen storage and weight of equipment aboard the aircraft made the arrangement impractical; Robert Futrell, "United States Air Force Operations in the Korean Conflict: 1 July 1952–27 July 1953" (USAF Historical Study No. 127, 1 July 1956), 67.

4. Guy Shafer and V. L. Lemon, "Trip Report: Far Eastern Theater of Operations, 27 Apr–28 May [1953]," 14–15 FRCSL 342-66-G-2680 12/12. The "rats" were pieces of metal (some sources say steel, others titanium) approximately six to eight inches long inserted into the tailpipe and protruding about one-quarter inch into the exhaust, while "mice" were about three and one-half inches long pieces that also protruded about one-quarter inch into the exhaust. About six to eight rats and one mouse were used. The engine was adjusted to get maximum tailpipe temperature on the ground at 96 to 97 percent power, permitting the F-86s to get 100 percent power up to forty-five thousand feet when the pilot moved the throttle pass the stop; USAF Oral History Interview, Maj. Gen. John Giraudo, 8–12 January 1985, 91-92 HRA K239.0512 -1630.

5. WCSWF-1 to WCS, sub: "Weekly Report No. 17," 3 September 1952, item no. 238 in F-86 Correspondence, vol 3, HRA K202.1-57. Rate of climb increased by 1,800 fpm at altitudes between thirty thousand to forty-five thousand feet, nearly twice that of a standard engine (at military power) at thirty-five thousand feet, nearly triple that at forty thousand feet, and four times as great at forty-five thousand feet. Air speed increased 10 kts at fifteen thousand feet and 15 kts at forty-five thousand feet. There was also an increase of 4 to 8 percent in range; Headquarters USAF to Commanding General, Far East Air Forces, sub: "Projects for Improvement of Performance, F-86E and F-86F Airplanes," n.d.; appendix 160 in Fifth Air Force History: 1 July–31 December 1952, vol. 3, app. 2, 160 HRA K730.01; William Dailey, "War Emergency Thrust Augmentation for the J47 Engine in the F-86 Aircraft," AD-095757. Fort Belvoir, Virginia: Defense Technical Information Center, August 1956, 3–12; History of Air Research and Development Command: 1 July 1951–31 December 1952, vol.2, 61 AFMC.

6. Dailey, "War Emergency Thrust Augmentation," 27, 29, 32; Otha Clark, "Altitude Thrust Augmentation Using Water-Alcohol Injection," AF Technical Report No. AFFTC 53-8, Mar 1953 FRCSL 342-66-G-2680 12/12. The water-alcohol mixture more than doubled rate of climb at forty thousand feet, increased top speed 10 kts at twenty thousand feet and almost 15 kts at forty-five thousand feet; "Projects for Improvement of Performance, 158–59."

7. Swanborough and Bowers, *U.S. Military Aircraft since 1908*, 426. GE did some testing on an afterburner for the J47 in February 1948. The F-86D was powered by an afterburning J47-GE-17 engine that boosted its thrust from 5,700 pounds to 7,630 pounds. See Epilogue.

8. Knaack, *Post–World War II Fighters*, 70. Speed increased 15 kts at 20,000 and 35,000 feet, and 60 kts at 50,000 feet. Rate of climb increased by a factor of 2 to 3. Ceiling increased to 52,500 feet an increase of 5,000 feet. The cost was 140 pounds for the system (versus 655 pounds for the J47-17 afterburner in the F-86D) and a decrease of 38 nm in range.

9. North American Aviation, Summary Report, F-86F Airplane with Pre-turbine Injection (PTI) Thrust Augmentation, NA-54-664, 7 September 1954, 2 FRCSL 342-66-J-2680 1/3; Dailey, "War Emergency Thrust Augmentation," 33–34, 43, 45, 47; Donald Wooley and Stuart Childs, "Phase II Performance and Service-ability Tests of the F-86F Airplane USAF No. 51-13506 with Pre-Turbine Modifications," AF Technical Report No. AFFTC 54-16, June 1954, (DTIC AD 037710), 4, ii, 1, Appendix IV, 4, 6; Maj. Gen. Mark Bradley, Director of Procurement and Production to MCP, sub: "Increased Thrust for F-86F Airplane," 15 April 1952, no. 203 F-86 Correspondence; and D. C. Runge, Contracts Operation, Aircraft Gas Turbine Division, GE to Commanding General, Air Materiel Command, 3 September 1952, item no. 239 F-86 Correspondence.

10. Robert Jackson, "Flight Tests of an F-86F with Solid Fuel Rockets for In-Flight Thrust Augmentation," AF Technical Report No. AFFTC 52-36, 1, 6 FRCSL 342-66-G-2680 12/12; "Projects for Improvement of Performance," 159.

11. CG FEAF to CG 5AF, teletype message 24 November 1952, appendix 168 in 5AF History: July-December 1952, vol. 3, app. 2, 177; 5AF History: July-December 1952, vol. 1, 196n17; Headquarters Fifth Air Force to Commanding General Far East Air Forces, sub: "In-flight Thrust Augmentation," 28 December 1952, appendix 169 in 5AF History: July–December 1952, vol. 3, app. 2, 178–79; Headquarters USAF to Commanding General ARDC, 6 November 1952 in Far East Air Forces History: July-December 1952, vol. 2, item no. 18 HRA K720.01; Headquarters Far East Air Forces to Commanding General Fifth Air Force, sub: "Projects for Improvement of Performance, F-86E and F-86F Airplanes," 5 August 1952, Appendix 161 in 5AF History: July-December 1952, vol. 3, app. 2, 163–64; Barbara Stahura, ed., *The F-86 Sabre Jet and Pilots* (Paducah, Ky.: Turner, 1997), 25; and Larry Davis, *The 4th Fighter Wing in the Korean War* (Atglen, Pa.: Schiffer, 2001), 122.

12. Col. D. L. Anderson, Chief Analysis Branch, Weapons Systems Division [WADC] to WCSWF, sub: "F-86F Performance with Rocket," 21 Apr 1952 item no. 183 in F-86 Correspondence. With one thousand pounds boost the F-86 gained an additional 13 kts; with three thousand pounds, 32 kts; and with five thousand pounds, 46 kts.

13. Capt. Norris Hanks and 1st Lt. Duane Baker, "Air Force Evaluation of the F-86F with AR 2 Rocket Augmentation," AFFTC-TR-60-39, October 1960 in History of the Air Force Flight Test Center: 1 July–31 December 1960, vol. 3 HRA K286.69; Capts. Norris Hanks and L. W. Davis, "F-86E Thrust Augmentation Evaluation,"

Mar 1957, 1-2 DTIC AD 118703; correspondence from Maj. Gen. Mark Bradley, Director of Procurement and Production [WADC] to MCF, sub: "Increased Thrust for F-86F Airplane," 15 April 1952 item no. 203 in F-86 Correspondence.

14. Robert Shaw, *Fighter Combat: Tactics and Maneuvering* (Annapolis, Md.: Naval Institute, 1985), 6. These were improved guns. The M2 .50-caliber, which became operational in 1933, had a rate of fire of eight hundred shots per minute and a muzzle velocity of 2,810 feet per second. The M3 .50-caliber machine gun became operational in 1947 and had a rate of fire of 1,200 spm and a muzzle velocity of 2,840 fps. According to one authority, this gave it a lethality (weight of projectile × rate of fire × muzzle velocity squared) that was 50 percent greater.

15. George Davis downed four on 13 December, one MiG and three prop-driven Tu-2s. Credits for the Destruction of Enemy Aircraft, World War II, USAF Historical Study, No. 85, 1978 (hereafter cited as USAF World War II Victory Credits); Far East Air Forces, General Orders. I compared the multiple credits of the eight hundred Korean War victory claims with the first eight hundred AAF World War II victory credits (7 December 1941–28 January 1943) and last eight hundred (7 April 1945–14 August 1945). There were forty-six instances of two credits on one sortie in Korea, while the first World War II sample revealed ninety double credits (plus fifteen more with three and four credits), and the last World War II sample with sixty-eight doubles and an additional eighteen with three, four, and five credits. This 16,000-credit sample represented 10 percent of the 15,800 AAF World War II air-to-air fighter credits. Statistical Summary of Eighth Air Force Operations, European Theater: 17 Aug 1942–8 May 1945, 23 HRA 520.308A; The Statistical Story of the Fifteenth Air Force, 8 HRA 670.308D; "Korean Air War Summary: June 1950–27 July 1953," 13 HRA K720.04D-1; USAF World War II Victory Credits.

16. Yefim Gordon and Vladimir Rigmant, *MiG-15: Design, Development, and Korean War Combat History* (Osceola, Wisc.: Motorbooks, 1993), 136.

17. Ralph Wetterhahn, "The Russians of MiG Alley," *Retired Officer* (August 2000), 71; Squadron Leader W. Harbison, "A Critique on the F-86E versus the MiG-15 Aircraft in the Korean Theater," February–May 1952, 21; Harrison Thyng, End of Tour Report, 1952, 7 HRA K720.131.

18. "The Relationship Between Sortie Ratios and Loss Rates for Air-to-Air Battle Engagements During World War II and Korea," Saber Measures (Charlie), September 1970, 9 HRA 143.044-42; Harbison, "Critique on the F-86E," 22; Thyng, End of Tour Report, 7.

19. Bruce Hinton and Elmer Wingo, "An Analysis of Operations at Kimpo Air Base: Performed by Detachment 'A' 336th Fighter-Interceptor Squadron, 4th Fighter-Interceptor Group" [15 December 1950–2 January 1951], 27 HRA K-Sq-Fi-336-Hi (Kimpo) Det A (December 1950–January 1951); Central Fighter Establishment, Tactical Trials: F-86A-5, Report No. 173, Trial No. 103, May 1951, 20.

20. Jack Lind, "Analysis of F-86 Fighter Encounters with MiG-15s in Korea: March through June 1951," Operations Analysis Office Memo No. 47, 21 HRA K720.301-47.

21. Brig. Gen. Jarred Crabb Journal, 8 January 1951 and 13 March 1951, frames 0594,0700 USAFA MS-2; Col. Gordon Gould, Chief, Armament Laboratory, Directorate of Laboratories to WCOWF-1, sub: "T-130/T-160 Guns," 21 January 1953 item no. 303 in F-86 Correspondence.

22. W. T. G., "Guns for Fighters," *Flight* (28 January 1955), 108–10.

23. Shaw, *Fighter Combat*, 6. Shaw states that the M39 (the gun's later designation) had a lethality (rate of fire × projectile weight × muzzle velocity square) about 3.8 times that of the M3. Adjusting for the number of guns (six .50s versus four 20-mm) yields a factor of 2.5; USAF, "Interim Gun-Val Study: An Analysis of Available Data on Selected Aircraft Weapons," 15 April 1952, 2a DTIC 007221. Shaw's figures differ from those of the USAF documents. Using Shaw's formula and the USAF figures, the difference between the two configurations is about 3.3.

24. Walter Boyne, *Aces in Command: Pilots As Combat Leader* (Dulles, Va.: Brassey's, 2001), 126. Firing the 0.50s slowed the F-86 by 3 or more kts.

25. Commanding General Far East Air Forces to Headquarters USAF, 20 Nov 1952 in FEAF History, July-December 1952, vol. 2; Commanding General Far East Air Forces to Headquarters USAF, 13 November 1952 in FEAF History: July-December 1952, vol. 2. This study states the weight penalty at five hundred pounds translating to a decrease of one thousand feet in ceiling, 140 fpm in rate of climb at thirty-five thousand feet and increasing radius of turn by three hundred feet; Army Biological Labs, "Combat Suitability Test of F-86F-2 Aircraft with T-160 Guns," August 1953, 7, 11, 12, DTIC AD 019725; USAF, Interim Gun-Val Study, 2a; and Headquarters Air Proving Ground Command, "Final Report on Combat Suitability Test of F-86F-2 Aircraft with T-160 Guns," Project No. APG/ADA/43-F-1, 11 FRCSL 342-66-G-2680 10/12.

26. Maj. Gen. Patrick Timberlake, letter 29 April 1954 in Air Proving Ground Command, Final Report, Project No. APG/ADA/43-A-1, sub: "Operational Suitability Test of T-160 20mm Gun Installation in F-86F-1 Aircraft," 29 April 1954 DTIC AD 031528.

27. "Cannon-Armed F-86Fs," available at http://home.att.net/~jbaugher1/p86_25.html; Commanding General Far East Air Forces to Commanding General Fifth Air Force, appendix 180 in 5AF History: July-December 1952, vol. 3, app 2, 199; Hughes and Dranem, *North American F-86 Sabre Jet*, 82; and Curtis, *North American F-86 Sabre*, 85.

28. Army Biological Labs, "Combat Suitability Test," 9, 49–50, 111–12, 179–258; USAF Korean War Victory Credits; USAF World War II Victory Credits. All had earned their wings during World War II, the most junior in November 1944.

29. Army Biological Labs, "Combat Suitability Test," 12, 111–12; 4FG History, May 1951–January 1952, July–December 1952. During the period May 1951 through January 1952, and July 1952 through June 1953, the Fourth Fighter Group expended almost 2.5 million rounds and suffered 422 malfunctions; 4FW History, January–June 1953.

30. Army Biological Labs, "Combat Suitability Test," 13; Lori Tagg, *On the Front Line of R & D: Wright-Patterson Air Force Base in the Korean War, 1950–1953* (Wright-Patterson AFB, Ohio: History Office, Aeronautical Systems Center, 2001), 54.

31. Tagg, *On the Front Line of R & D*, 54; "Cannon Armed F-86Fs."

32. Air Proving Ground Command, "Final Report: Operational Suitability Test of the T-160 20-mm Gun Installation in F-86F-2 Aircraft," 29 April 1954 DTIC AD 031528; Maj. Gen. Patrick Timberlake, Commander Air Proving Ground Command, "Combat Suitability Test of F-86F-2 Aircraft with T-160 Guns," Project No. APG/ADA/43-F-1 in Army Biological Labs, "Combat Suitability Test."

33. Headquarters Air Proving Ground Command, Termination Report on the Operational Suitability Test of the T-130 Caliber .60 Gun Installation in the F-86F-2 Aircraft, Project No. APG/ADA/43-A-4, 2 September 1954, 4–7 FRCSL 342-66-G-2680 12/12. Two other guns tested in the F-86 should be mentioned. Two F-86F-2s were armed with four 0.60-caliber T-130 guns. The .60-caliber had the same rate of fire and carried the same number of rounds of ammunition as did the T-160 but did have an 8 percent higher muzzle velocity. While its accuracy was comparable to the T-160, it had unacceptable reliability, short barrel life (136 rounds per barrel), and defective gun gas seals; Air Force Armament Center, Air Research and Development Command, "Evaluation of Aircraft Armament Installation (F-86F with 206RK Guns) Operation Gun-Val," February 1955, iv, 1, 21 HRA K243.805-103. The Air Force also tested 20-mm Oerlikon 206 RK guns that claimed to have a higher rate of fire and muzzle velocity than the T-160. In Air Force tests they demonstrated poor reliability (considered marginally satisfactory), accuracy, and barrel life (250 rounds per barrel).

34. Curtis, *North American F-86 Sabre*, 37–38; Knaack, *Post–World War II Fighters*, 56, 69, 74, 79. The F-86B design used the wing and tail of the "A" model with a deeper fuselage, different engine, and larger tires. It was never built. The F-86C was intended to be a long-range escort fighter. It later was known as the YC-93A, a design with side air intakes and a different engine. North American built and flew two of these, but the Air Force canceled the June 1948 production order for 118. The F-86D is discussed in the Epilogue.

35. The slats now closed at 180 kts and opened at 115 kts and only operated below Mach .65. Pilot's Manual F-86A-1, -5, 30 January 1949, revised 30 May 1949, 15–16. Pilot's Manual F-86A, 30 June 1950, 1, 11, 39, 42, 77; Standard Aircraft Characteristics: F-86A Sabre North American, 27 April 54, 3 HRA K243.861-1 1949–56 vol. 5; North American Aviation, Air Force Fighter Airplane Projects Chart, May 1953 FRCSL 342-66-G-2680 11/12; Knaack, *Post–World War II Fighters*, 54–55.

36. NAA Air Force Fighter Airplane Projects Chart; Pilot's Manual P-86A, April 1948, 6; Pilot's Manual F-86E, October 1950–March 1951, 2, 13, 17; Air Materiel Command, "Summary of F-86E Flying Tail Investigation," 22 March 1951, 7 AFMC; Curtis, *North American F-86 Sabre*, 61–62; Knaack, *Post–World War II Fighters*, 56–57, 59. The A model had a normal and emergency hydraulic system; the

E had four separate hydraulic systems, one for the flight controls, another for the rest of the hydraulic systems, and a separate backup for each system.

37. Directorate, Procurement and Industrial Planning: January–June 1951, Aircraft Section R1-645.1a AFMC; Lt. Gen. K. B. Wolfe to Commanding General Air Materiel Command, sub: "Configuration of the F-86F," 28 May 1951, enclosure no. 6, ibid; NAA, Air Force Fighter Airplane Projects Chart; Curtis, *North American F-86 Sabre*, 72; Knaack, *Post–World War II Fighters*, 61.

38. Col. Victor Hauger, Chief, Weapons Systems Division, Deputy for Operations to Commanding General, Air Research and Development Command, sub: "Extended Wing Leading-Edge for F-86E and F Aircraft," 18 September 1952, item no. 250 in F-86 Correspondence; Tagg, *On the Front Line of R & D*, 37; Robert Jackson, *F-86 Sabre* (Washington, D.C.: Smithsonian, 1994), 36; Wagner, *North American Sabre*, 57–58; R. H. Rice, Vice President and Chief Engineer, North American Aviation to Commanding General, Air Materiel Command, sub: "Contract AF-6517, F-86F Airplanes Wing Leading Edge—Installation 6-3 Extension MCR 191-52-1, ECP NA-F86F-69," 9 July 1952, item no. 214 in F-86 Correspondence; Harry Guett, Chief Full-Scale and Flight Research Division, Memo for Director, sub: "Visit of Lt. Col. J. W. Lillard of WADC on April 21, 1954," 22 April 1954, item no. 496 in F-86 Correspondence; Futrell, Historical Study No. 127, 68; William Coughlin, "F-86 'Gimmick': Improved Wing," *Aviation Week* (7 September 1953), 15–16.

39. Col. D. D. McKee, Acting Chief, Aircraft Laboratory, Directorate of Laboratories to WCSWF, sub: "Extended Wing Leading Edge Installation on F-86 Aircraft," 15 September 1952, item no. 247 in F-86 Correspondence. Although the 51st Group pilots didn't report adverse handling problems, early on the USAF noted yaw when the aircraft approached the stall (not present with the slatted wing), poor stall warning, and more severe roll-off at the stall; North American Aviation, Development of the F-86F Extended Leading Edge Wing Slats, Report no. NA-54-658, 21 June 1954, fig. 2 FRCSL 342-66-G-2680 10/12. Later, both North American and USAF tests concluded that in stalls, the solid 6 × 3 wing had unsatisfactory yaw and roll-off. This encouraged the Air Force to investigate putting slats on the 6 × 3 wing; Air Force Flight Test Center, AF Technical Report No. AFFTC 54-10, "Phase IV Performance Tests of the F-86F Airplane, USAF No. 52-4349," May 1954, 2 FRCSL 342-66-H-2680 5/8; Maj. R. E. Grote to Commanding General Fifth Air Force (Forward), sub: "Report on Modified Aircraft," 28 August 1952 Appendix 164, 171 5AF History: July-December 1952, vol. 3, app 2.

40. Futrell, Historical Study No. 127, 68; Lt. Col. Benjamin Long, Commander 51st Fighter Interceptor Group to Commanding Officer 51st Fighter Interceptor Wing, sub: "Extended Leading Edge Modification on F-86 Aircraft," 24 August 1952 Appendix 163, 5AF History: July-December 1952, vol. 3, appendix 2; Wagner, *North American Sabre*, 58.

41. Attachment to correspondence of Col. Victor Haugen to Commanding General Air Research and Development Command, sub: "Extended Wing Leading-Edge for F-86E and F Aircraft," 18 September 1952 item no. 250 in F-86 Correspondence. The first 50 cost $4,000 each; at the 250-piece mark, the price had fallen to $3,000.

42. Futrell, Historical Study No. 127, 68. North American looked into using the extended leading edge to carry 120 gallons of fuel, fitting the extended leading edge with slats, extending the wingspan by a foot, and using an inflatable rubber boot on the leading edge. None of these saw action in Korea although all four were being investigated as late as February 1955. Knaack, *Post–World War II Fighters*, 62; Projects for the Improvement of Performance, 158; Col. H. A. Boushey, Assistant Director of Weapon Systems Operations to Commander, Headquarters Air Materiel Command, 27 September 1954, item no. 554 in F-86 Correspondence; Col. Charles Allen, Chief, Fighter Aircraft Division to Commander Air Research and Development Command, sub: "Wing Configurations, F-86F Aircraft," February 1955 item no. 597 in F-86 Correspondence.

43. Hauger to CG ARDC, 18 September 1952 item no. 250 in F-86 Correspondence; AFFTC Technical Report No. AFFTC 54-10, May 1954. After the war the USAF tested a wing with a two foot longer wingspan (that increased wing area from 302 square feet to 313 square feet) with slats that further improved performance for both high performance and takeoff and landing phases. The latter scheme was incorporated in the F-86F-40; Avery, *North American Aircraft 1934-1998*, 182; Curtis, *North American F-86 Sabre*, 83.

44. Joint Commission Support Branch, Research and Analysis Division, DPMO, "The Transfer of U.S. Korean War POWs to the Soviet Union," 26 August 1993, 10, available at www.aiipowmia.com/reports/trnsfr.html. Gen. Georgii Lobov, the initial commander of Soviet MiG units committed in the Korean War, writes, "We wanted the F-86 gun sight at all costs."

45. R. Wallace Clarke, "Armament Diversifies," in *Aircraft of the Second World War: The Development of the Warplane 1939–45*, Philip Jarrett, ed. (London: Putnam, 1997), 201–5; Alfred Price, *World War II Fighter Conflict* (London: Macdonald's and Jane's, 1975), 89–93.

46. "New Computing Sights Vastly Improve Aerial Gunnery," *Impact* (June 1945), 44–45; Price, *World War II Fighter Conflict*, 92–94.

47. Charles Webster and Noble Frankland, *The Strategic Air Offensive against Germany 1939–1945*, vol. 3, *Victory* (London: HMSO, 1961), 147n2; Kenneth Werrell, *Blankets of Fire: U.S. Bombers over Japan during World War II* (Washington, D.C.: Smithsonian, 1996), 199–200.

48. Lopez, *Fighter Pilot's Heaven*, 104–7.

49. History 4th Fighter Interceptor Group: February, March, April 1951, 7 HRA K-Gp-4-Hi. For other problems of the Mk 18 sight, see Futrell, Historical Study no. 72, 119; Commanding General, Far East Air Forces to Headquarters USAF, Attention Directorate, Maintenance, Supply and Services, sub: "Operational Deficiencies of the F-84 and F-86 type Aircraft in FEAF," 19 January 1951 in Directorate, Procurement and Industrial Planning: 1 July–31 December 1950 AFMC R1-644.1c; History 4th Fighter Interceptor Wing, June 1951, 2 HRA K-Wg-Hi; Pilot's Manual, F-86A-1, -5, January 1949, rev. May 1949, 48 NASM.

50. Central Fighter Establishment, Report No. 173, Trial No. 103. Tactical Trials, F.86A-5, May 1951, 12. Meanwhile the RAF flatly stated that the Mk 18 fitted to the F-86A was unsatisfactory.

51. Directorate, Procurement and Industrial Planning, Aircraft Section: January-June 1951 AFMC R1-645.1a; 4th Fighter Interceptor Wing to Commanding General Eastern Air Defense Force, sub: "Operations of the 4th Fighter-Interceptor Wing in Korea," 11 June 1951, 2, in 4th Fighter Wing History, June 1951; John Wester, "The Pattern of Operations in Korea" in Institute for Air Weapons Research, F-86 vs. MiG-15: A Digest of the Briefing on the Analysis of the Korean Air War," 19 May 1954, AUL M34822-14a.

52. Cover letter from Gen Patrick Timberlake, and "Relative Combat Effectiveness of J-2 and K-14," 4, both in Air Proving Command, Final Report Project No. APG/ADB/59-A, sub: "Accelerated Comparison Test of K-14 Sight and J-2 Fire Control System in F-86E for Fighter to Fighter Combat," 26 September 1952 DTIC AD004359; 4th Fighter Interceptor Group, "Operations in MiG Alley, F-86E versus MiG-15 in Korea," 20 HRA K-Wg-4-Hi January 52.

53. Futrell, Historical Study no. 72, 119; "Report on Evaluation of K-14 and J-2 Sighting Systems by the Project Test Team," 1 in APGC, Accelerated Comparison K-14 and J-2; Far East Air Forces, FEAF Report on Korea, draft 15 February 1954, book 2/3, 18, 37, 40 HRA K720.04d; Far East Air Forces, "The Fight for Air Superiority," FEAF Report on the Korean War, vol. 1, 7 HRA 168.7104-53; 4FW "Operations in MiG Alley," 20.

54. Air Materiel Command History, January–June 1952, vol. 1, 205-07 AFMC; FEAF draft Report on the Korean War, book 2/3, 37; Wester, "Pattern of Operations in Korea," 2; Tagg, On the Front Line of R & D, 35.

55. FEAF draft Report on the Korean War, book 2/3, 38; Historical Summary of the Directorate of Requirements, Deputy Chief of Staff, Development for the period 1 January 1952 to 30 June 1952, 59, 60 HRA K140.01, July 51–June 52, vol. 3, part 2.

56. Fifth Air Force History: January–June 1952, 212–13 HRA K730.01.

57. The 51st Fighter Interceptor Wing, "Monthly Analysis for October" in Fifth Air Force Wings, Monthly Analyses, October 1952 HRA K730.310A; 5AF History: July–December 1952, vol. 1, 201–2; Pilot's Manual F-86[F], March 1952, 58; Pilot's Manual F-86[F], February 1953, 95; "Report on Evaluation of K-14 and J-2," 3.

58. Headquarters Fifth Air Force to Commanding General Far East Air Forces, sub: "Evaluation of the A1CM Gun Sight," 23 July 1952, Appendix 170, 180–83 in 5AF History: July–December 1952, vol. 3, app. 2. The five pilots were Felix Asla (four credits by the end of the war), Clifford Jolley (seven credits) and James Low (nine credits) of the 4th, and Elmer Harris (six credits) and William Wescott (five credits) from the 51st; FEAF Report on Korea, draft, book 2/3, 39–41; CG FEAF to CG AF FIVE, Personal from Smart to Barcus, 10 September 1952, Appendix 171, 184 in 5AF History: July–December 1952, vol. 3, app. 2.

59. Smart to Barcus, 10 September 1952.

60. "Day Fighter Aircraft Development Program," chap. 25 in History Air Research and Development Command, 1953, vol.1, 494 AFMC.

61. Bruce Hinton to author, 18 May 2002; Sam Jackson interview with author, 9 February 2002; Smart to Barcus, 10 September 1952; FEAF draft Report on the Korean War, book 2/3, 39.

62. The testers used the J-2 system, consisting of the A-4 gunsight with the APG-30 radar, as the J-1 system with the A-1CM was out of production, replaced by the J-2. "Report on the Evaluation of the K-14 and J-2," 1.

63. Accelerated Comparison K-14 and J-2, "Report on Evaluation of K-14 and J-2," 1; "Relative Combat Effectiveness," 2, 12. The two APGC pilots were Johnston and Green, who respectively flew twenty-two and thirty passes. Francis Gabreski (6.5 Korean and 28 World War II credits) flew forty passes; James Jabara (15 and 1.5), forty-eight; John Meyer (2 and 24), thirty-eight; and William Whisner (5.5 and 15.5), thirteen. James Kasler (6) and Iven Kincheloe (5) were not involved in the flying phase.

64. "Report on the Evaluation of the K-14 and J-2," 3.

65. "Report on the Evaluation of the K-14 and J-2," 1. The J-1 fire control system consisted of the A-1CM gunsight and the APG-30 radar and the J-2 the newer A-4 sight and the APG-30.

66. "Report on the Evaluation of the K-14 and J-2," 5–7.

67. "Report on the Evaluation of the K-14 and J-2," 6–8. The six Korean War veterans signed the report that was based primarily on their opinions; Timberlake cover letter. Neither of the two APGC pilots signed the report, although one (Johnston) wrote comments consistent with the others.

68. Table 4, "Relative Combat Effectiveness of J-2 and K-14," 12. The project used 198 of the 307 APGC passes (or bursts) and 449 of the 616 Korean War bursts.

69. "Relative Combat Effectiveness of J-2 and K-14," 4.

70. Ibid., 1–2, 5–6, 8, 15–16.

71. Timberlake cover letter.

72. Headquarters Fifth Air Force to Commanding General Far East Air Forces, sub: "A1CM Gunsight," 17 September 1952 Appendix 172, 185 in 5AF History: July–December 1952, vol. 3, app. 2. Neither the new commander of the 25th fighter Squadron, Maj. Lewis Andre, nor the 4th Fighter Interceptor Wing Gunsight Maintenance Officer, 1st Lt. Warren Morgan, had flown any missions. The other seven included Royal Baker (13 credits by the end of the Korean War and 3.5 World War II victories), Frederick Blesse (10 credits), Elmer Harris (6 credits), Francis Humphreys (3 credits), Clifford Jolley (7 credits), Albert Kelly (2.5 credits), and Harrison Thyng (5 and 5 credits). Both Harris and Jolley had participated in the July Fifth Air Force response on the A-1CM.

73. Cecil Foster, *MiG Alley to Mu Ghia Pass: Memoirs of a Korean War Ace* (Jefferson, N.C.: McFarland, 2001), 46. Four pilots who contributed to the July 1952 FEAF report had both training with the sight and more positive views of its value. First Lt. James Low (nine credits) had stateside training with the sight and expressed his "complete satisfaction" with the A-1CM gunsight. Capt. Clifford Jolley (seven credits), who had taken an instructor's course at Nellis AFB and was also somewhat familiar with the gunsight, although the radar ranging device was relatively new to him, was also more positive about the sight than the other aces who assessed the gunsight. Two other aces Maj. Elmer Harris (six credits) and Capt. Cecil Foster (nine credits) also had stateside training with the sight; APGC, "Evaluation of the A1CM Gun Sight," 181–83; Air Proving Ground Command, "Operational Suitability Test of

the A-4 G.B.R. Sight with AN/APG-30 Radar Ranging in the F-86E Aircraft," Project No. APG/ADB/18-A-1, 23 October 1952, 10 FRCSL 342-66-G-2680 10/12. An October 1952 report asserted that pilots without stateside training with the A-1CM sight would require ten to fifteen missions "before consistent scoring can be accomplished"; and Smart to Barcus, 10 September 1952.

74. "A1CM Gunsight," 17 September 1952.

75. Royal Baker, "Report on F-86 Operations in Korea," 1 April 1953, 6 HRA K-Gp-Su-Op; Air Proving Ground Command, "Final Report on Combat Suitability Test of F-86F-2 Aircraft with T-160 Guns," Project No. APG/ADA/43-F-1, 3 August 1953, 13 FRCSL 342-66-G-2680 10/12; John Wester, "Effectiveness of the Gunsight," 67 in Institute for Air Weapons Research, "F-86 vs. MiG-15."

76. USAF Oral History Interview, Gen. John Meyer, July 1975, 5 HRA K239.0512-894; Wester, "Effectiveness of the Gunsight," 68; Allen Butterworth, "Operational Interpretation," 19 in Institute for Air Weapons Research, "F-86 vs. MiG-15."

Chapter 3

1. Statistical Summary of Eighth Air Force Operations, European Theater, 17 August 1942–8 May 1945 HRA 520.308A. During this same period (January 1951 through June 1953) the F-80 averaged a 59.5 percent in-commission rate, and the F-84, 58.4 percent. The F-51 had a 50.7 percent in-commission rate from July 1950 through the end of 1952, after which the average number of F-51s fell below one hundred. Fighters in the Eighth Air Force in World War II had an in-commission rate of 65 percent; Far East Air Forces, Korean Air War Summary HRA K720.04D-1, 38, 41–42.

2. Walker Mahurin, *Honest John: The Autobiography of Walker M. Mahurin* (New York: Putnam's Sons, 1962), 76–77.

3. Fifth Air Force Wings, Monthly Analyses [for these months] HRA K730.310A. The 4th averaged an 80.7 percent in-commission rate, the 51st, 76.8 percent.

4. Mahurin, *Honest John*, 78–79. The overall figures for ten months were AOCP rates of 5.8 percent for the Fourth and 5.1 percent for the Fifty-first. 5AF Wing, Monthly Analyses [1952–53]; History of 4th Fighter Interceptor Wing: January through June 1953, 18–19 HRA K-Wg-4-Hi.

5. History of the 4th Fighter Interceptor Group, May 1951–January 1952 HRA; 4FWg History July–December 1952, HRA; 4FWg History, January–December 1953. This data is drawn from the 4th Wing and Group histories. Unfortunately, four full months and four half months of data are unavailable of the thirty-two months the F-86 was in combat. At the wing/group level we only have figures for combat versus test firings for May and June 1952, during which 44 percent of the ammunition was fired in combat.

6. Statement, Capt. Max S. Weill in CO, 4th Fighter Interceptor Wing to Directorate of Flight Safety Research, Office of the Deputy Inspector General for Technical Inspection and Flight Safety, et al., 15 June 1951, 2 HRA (hereafter cited

as Weill Accident Report, 20 May 1951). Accident reports hereafter cited as [name] Accident Report, [date].

7. Weill Accident Report, 20 May 1951, 2; Unsatisfactory Report, 4th Fighter Interceptor Group, sub: "01M Tube assy Gun Barrel Blast," 21 May 1951 in Weill Accident Report, 20 May 1951; CO, 4th Fighter-Interceptor Wing to Directorate of Flight Safety Research, Office of the Deputy Inspector General for Technical Inspection and Flight Safety, et al., 15 June 1951, 1–3, Nelson Accident Report, 20 May 1951 HRA.

8. UR, 21 May 1951 in Weill Accident Report, 20 May 1951; CO, 4th Ftr-Intep Wing to Directorate of Flight Safety Research, Office of the Deputy Inspector General for Technical Inspection and Flight Safety Research, et al., 15 June 1951, 1–3, Nelson Accident Report, 20 May 1951 and Capt. James O. Roberts statement therein.

9. Weill Accident Report, 20 May 1951, 2–4.

10. 4FG History, January 1951; 4FG History: February–April 1951, 6–7; Management Analysis Study of Air and Ground Aborts of F-86 Aircraft Assigned to Units of the 4th Fighter Interceptor Wing during the Period 1 April 1952 through 30 June 1952 in 5AF Monthly Analyses, July 1952; 336th Fighter Squadron History: July–December 1952, 104–5 in 4FW History: July–December 1952; 334th Fighter Squadron History, March and April 1952 HRA K-Sq-Fi-334-Hi; 4FGp History: July–September 1951.

11. Management Analysis Study of 4FW F-86 Aborts.

12. The French apparently were the first to use a droppable tank. They fitted their Breguet bomber with both a fixed and a droppable tank. The former was well protected, and the latter could be dropped in case of fire.

13. Oscar Westover, later chief of the Air Corps, quoted in Wesley Craven and James Cate, eds., *The Army Air Forces in World War II*, vol. 1, *Plans and Early Operations, January 1939 to August 1942* (Chicago: University of Chicago, 1948), 65. Hap Arnold, later chief of the Army Air Forces, shared this view in the early 1930s. Bernard Boylan, "The Development of the American Long Range Escort Fighter," Ph.D. dissertation, University of Missouri, 1955, 17, 54, 57–61.

14. Swanborough and Bowers, *U.S. Military Aircraft since 1908*, 537. The 18,000-pound aircraft had a five-man crew and first flew in September 1937. Bell built a dozen of these exotic aircraft; see Bernard Boylan, *The Development of the Long-Range Escort Fighter*, reprint of USAF Historical Studies No. 136 (Manhattan, Kan.: Sunflower University Press, 1955), for other evidence of the airmen's interest in multi-place aircraft for escort duties.

15. Boylan, *Development of the American Long Range Escort Fighter*, 66–70.

16. Eighth Air Force, "Tactical Development: August 1942–May 1945," 97 HRA; See Boylan, *Development of the American Long-Range Escort Fighter*, chap 3; Roger Freeman, *Mighty Eighth War Manual* (London: Jane's, 1984), 218–21; and Kenneth Werrell, "The Tactical Development of the Eighth Air Force in World War II," Ph.D. dissertation, Duke University, 1969, 116, for other figures; Elke Weal, John Weal, and Richard Barker, *Combat Aircraft of World War Two* (New York: Macmillan,

1977), 170. The Japanese "Zeke" (commonly known as "Zero") A6M2 had even greater range (1,930 miles) than it demonstrated much earlier in the war.

17. Swanborough and Bowers, *U.S. Military Aircraft Since 1908*, 93–94. During World War II the AAF converted a B-17 into an escort role (designated YB-40) by adding an additional dorsal turret, a chin turret, and one extra gun at each waist position. The Eighth Air Force combat tested the aircraft on nine missions; Werrell, *Blankets of Fire*, 182.

18. History of Air Materiel Command, January–June 1952, vol. 1, 203 HRA; History of Far East Air Forces, July–December 1951, vol. 1, 166–67 HRA.

19. W. Harbison, "Critique on the F-86E," Central Fighter Establishment, February–May 1952, 10; 4FIW History: January 1952, 25.

20. FEAF History: January–June 1952, vol. 1, 151–52; Robert Futrell, "United States Air Force Operations in the Korean Conflict, 1 November 1950–30 June 1952," USAF Historical Study No. 72, 1 July 1955, 124; 4FG History: May 1952 in 4FW History, May 1952; 4FWg History, January 1953, 5; 4FW History, March 1953.

21. Fifth Air Force, Directorate of Operations Monthly Historical Report, April 1953, Inclosure No. 20 in 5AF History, January–June 1953, vol. 2, app. 32; and FEAF Report on the Korean War, 13 HRA 168.7104-53.

22. Air Research and Development Command, "External Stores, Armament Servicing Equipment and Facilities: 27 April 1953 to 20 July 1953," 20 July 1953, 8 HRA K243.85-4; E.C. Phillips, Chief, Operations Office Power Plant Laboratory to WDSP, sub: "F86F 200 Gallon Drop Tanks," 13 January 1954 item no. 447, F-86 Correspondence, HRA K202.1-57. This later Air Force report was more critical of the 200-gallon North American tank specifically noting release, leakage, storage, transportation, and cost issues.

23. Victor Pastushin, President and General Manager, Pastushin Aviation Corp to Commanding General Air Materiel Command, sub: "Jettisonable Fuel Tanks. Resume of Inspection Tour of Air Bases in Korea and Japan," 27 June 1953, 3–5 FRCSL 342-66-G-2680 10/12; "Jettisonable Fuel Tanks," 4 tab 18 in FEAF Report on Korea, book 3 of 3 [draft] HRA K720.04D; "External Fuel Tanks," 1 tab A in ARDC, "External Stores and Armament Servicing Equipment and Facilities."

24. Pastushin to AMC, 27 June 1953, 5. Also see pp. 4, 6–7. 5AF History, January–June 1953, vol. 2, 147–48; correspondence from Lt. Col. D. M. Ross, Chief, Installations Branch, Power Plant Laboratory to WCOWF-1, sub: "F-86 Drop Tank Difficulties," 14 March 1953, item no. 322 in F-86 Correspondence; History Directorate Procurement and Industrial Planning: July–December 1950, AFMC R1-644.1c.

25. Pastushin to AMC, 27 June 1953, 5–6; 5AF History, January–June 1953, vol. 2, 151.

26. 5AF History, January–June 1951, vol. 2, 237; 4FG History: July 1951–February 1952; 51FW History: January–June 1953, 17.

27. 5AF History: January–June 1951, vol. 2, 238; 4FW History: May 1951, 23; 4FW History: June 1951, 31; 4FW History: July 1951, 95; 51FW History: January–June 1953, 19.

28. ARDC, "External Stores and Armament Servicing Equipment and Facilities," tab A, 2. The shackles cost the 1948 series F-86 5 kts in level flight, 8 kts in a climb, and 20–25 kts in a steep dive. Therefore the airmen decided to jettison both the drop tanks and the shackles. The 1949 series Sabre suffered less degradation of performance, respectively 3–4 kts, 1–2 kts, and 8–10 kts. Louis Ford, Group Materiel Officer, 4th Fighter Interceptor Group to Col. Meyer, sub: "F-86 'Fletcher' Tank Test Project," 6 January 1951 in [4FIW] Test Data and Combat Reports Relative to Vulnerability and Limitations of F-86 Aircraft, January–July 1951 HRA K-Gp-4-SU-Op.

29. History Directorate, Procurement and Industrial Planning: July–December 1951, 1 AFMC R1-644.1c; 5AF History: July–December 1952, vol. 2, 216.

30. ARDC, "External Stores and Armament Servicing Equipment and Facilities," tab A, 2.

31. Freeman, *Mighty Eighth War Manual,* 219; 5AF History: January–June 1953, vol. 1, 110–11. The Eighth Air Force used such a device during World War II, although there are no documents that link the two; 5AF History: January–June 1953, vol. 2. 149; 51FWg History: January–June 1953, 20.

32. 4FWg History: January–June 1953, 36; 4FG History: Feb 1953.

33. See chart, "Percentage of Cost of Wing Tanks to Operating Cost," in FEAF Draft Report on Korea, book 3; 5AF Wings Monthly Analyses, January–May 1952.

34. See chart, "Average Cost per Wing Tank by Month," in FEAF Draft Report on Korea, book 3; 5AF History: July–December 1952, vol. 2, 20–21; FEAF Draft Report on Korea, book 3, 7.

35. ARDC, "External Stores and Armament Servicing Equipment and Facilities," tab A, 7–8,11–12, 14; 4FIW History: January–June 1953, 35; 4FW History: February 1952, 28; 51FW History: July–December 1952, 42; Harbison, "Critique on the F-86E," 10.

36. 5AF History: January–June 1953, vol. 1, 111–12, 333; ARDC, "External Stores and Armament Servicing Equipment and Facilities," tab A, 14. The airmen believed the large influx of new pilots was the other major factor.

37. Handbook Flight Operating Instructions, USAF Series F-86A Aircraft, 30 June 1950, 5 NASM; Ibid., F-86F, 20 Mar 1952, 12; Ibid., F-86[F] 20 February 1953, 100; correspondence from R. H. Rice, Vice President and Chief Engineer [NAA] to Commanding General, Air Materiel Command, sub: "F-86F Structural Demonstration Results with 200 Gallon Tanks, and Recommended Airspeed and Load Factor Limits . . ." 5 August 1952, item no. 225 in F-86 Correspondence; [Lt. Col. Louis Andre] CG 5AF to CO 51st Fighter Interceptor Wing Korea, Appendix 186 in 5AF History: July–December 1952, vol. 2, app. 2, 206; FEAF draft Report on Korea, book 3, tab 18, 2; Chronology of the 4th Tactical Fighter Wing from 1942, 24 HRA K-Wg-4-Hi (September 1942–December 1980); Larry Davis, *Walk Around: F-86 Sabre* (Carrollton, Tex.: Squadron/Signal, 2000), 24, 26.

38. Correspondence from W. E. Stit to R. G. Ruegg, Chief Aircraft Laboratory to WCSWF, sub: "F-86F Airplanes, Fuel Tank and Bomb Rack Station Additions," 18 August 1952, item no. 229 in F-86 Correspondence.

39. Air Materiel Command, Memorandum Report, sub: "In-flight Refueling of the T-33, F-84, and F-86 Type Aircraft Using the Drogue-Probe Method," 25 May 1951, 1, 6–7, 9 NASM.

40. Melvin Shorr, Assistant Chief, Aerodynamics Branch to WCOWF-1, sub: "(Rest) Development of Probe Kits for F-86F External Tanks," 10 July 1953, item no. 380 in F-86 Correspondence.

41. Transland Company, Fuel-Wing, 15 November 1950 FRCSL 342-62-A-16 62/80. In 1950, the Transland Company proposed a fuel wing to extend the range of the F-86. It consisted of a straight wing with tip tanks attached above the Sabre. Although a January 1953 AMC document requested the device be built, there is no further USAF record of the project; Shorr, "(Rest) Development of Probe Kits"; Larry Davis, "North American F-86 Sabre," 42, 49; Richard Smith, *Seventy-Five Years of In-flight Refueling: Highlights, 1923–1998* (Washington, D.C.: Air Force History and Museums Program, 1998), 34–36; R. Cargill Hall and Clayton Laurie, eds., *Early Cold War Overflights, 1950–1956: Symposium Proceedings*, vol. 1, *Memoirs* (Washington, D.C.: Office of the Historian, National Reconnaissance Office, 2003), 61.

Chapter 4

1. History AAF Training Command, July–December 1946, 157–58, 258 HRA K220.01.

2. AAF/USAF Statistical Digest, 1946–53. I have used the F-51 and F-80 as surrogates for prop and jet fighters. Unlike other fighters of this period, 1949–53, both were in large-scale service throughout the period and flew a comparable number of flying hours: between January 1947 and August 1953 the F-51 logged 1.5 million flying hours and the F-80, 1.2 million flying hours. The other jets (F-84 and F-86) came into service later and flew fewer hours (F-84 just under 1 million flying hours and the F-86, .6 million flying hours). By August 1953 the F-80 had flown 70 percent of its total life (cumulative flying hours); the F-84, 25 percent; and the F-86, 10 percent. "F-80 History," "F-84 History," "F-86 History" www. AFSC.SAIA.af.mil/AF/RDBMS/Flight/Statis/F[80/84/86]MDS.html.

3. Office of the Inspector General [Flying Safety], "Human Factors in Jet Fighter Accidents: Period 1 January 1950–30 June 1952," 8 HRA K259.2. Compared to the 70 to 85 kts touchdown speed of the F-51, jet fighters touchdown speeds were between 110 and 150 kts.

4. "Human Factors in Jet Fighter Accidents," 37–38.

5. "Flight Operating Instructions USAF Model P-86A Airplane," April 1948, 25 NASM. This series hereafter cited as [model] Pilot's Manual, [date].

6. Pilot's Manual F-86A, January 1949, rev. May 1949, 29.

7. Syring Accident Report, 1 September 1953 HRA. An inspection of 153 engine failures in 1953 found that one-third had foreign object damage; Reports of individual accidents can be found at HRA and NARACP. These will be cited as [name] Accident Report, [date]. Information on Individual F-86 Major Accidents up to 1 August 1953 along with all fatal F-80, F-84, and F-86 accidents through 31

December 1953 were entered into a data base cited as Accident Data Base. This does not include F-86D accidents.

8. History AAF Training Command, January–June 1946, 105; Larry Davis, *The 4th Fighter Wing in the Korean War* (Atglen, Pa.: Schiffer, 2001), 21.

9. Christopher Carey, "A Brief History of the Development of Western Aircraft Ejection Seat Systems" available at http://webs.lanset.com/aeolusaero/Articles/seat_history.htm; "Milestones in Ejector Seat History," available at www.ejectorseats.co.uk/milestones_in_ejection_seat_hist.htm; Robert Campbell and Perry Nelson, "Escape Systems Evolution," *Flying Safety* (November 1955), 7; L. F. E. Coombs, "The Well-equipped Warplane," in *Aircraft of the Second World War: The Development of the Warplane, 1939–45*, Philip Jarrett, ed. (London: Putnam, 1997), 245.

10. "Ejection Seat Development" (USAF Museum), available at www.wpafb.af.mil/museum/history/postwwii/esd.htm; Eloise Engle, "Escape Systems," in *Above and Beyond: The Encyclopedia of Aviation and Space Sciences*, vol. 4 (Chicago: New Horizons, 1968), 731, 733.

11. Directorate of Flight Safety Research, "Analysis of Ejection Seat Operation in Jet Fighter Accidents, May 1951," August 1951, 2, 6, 9 HRA K239.163-27; Seven of eleven bailouts below two thousand feet proved fatal. According to the report, the lack of an automatic release from the seat "must be considered as a probable cause of eight of nine deaths." Of these eight deaths, four hit the ground still in the seat and the other four failed to pull the parachute ripcord.

12. C. D. Smiley, "RCAF Ejection Experience, 1952–1961," n.d., 39, 41 DTIC AO-465171. The RCAF was flying F-86s, CF-100s, and T-33s. Of thirty-eight Canadian bailouts below one thousand feet, 55 percent were fatal.

13. Carey, "Brief History of Ejection Seat Systems"; Accident Data Base. At least one of these did not use the ejection seat. There were five cases in which the ejection seat failed to operate; two of these proved fatal. In three other fatal cases there was a question of whether or not the pilots bailed out.

14. David Perry and Lidie Dyer, "Incidence, Nature, and Extent of Injury in Crash Landings and Bailouts," November 1956, 46 HRA K237.163-27.

15. Pilot's Manual P-86A, April 1948, 27.

16. Ambrose Nutt, Chief Special Projects Branch, Aircraft Laboratory to Mr. Carmichael [sub:] "F-86F Pilot Ejection System," 8 November 1957 item no. 809 in F-86 Correspondence, vol. 9 HRA K202.1-57.

17. Pilot's Manual P-86A, April 1948, 3, 15, 28; Pilot's Manual F-86A, January 1949 rev. May 1949, 19; Pilot's Manual F-86A, June 1950; Pilot's Manual F-86F, February 1953, 73; North American Aviation memo to Commanding General Air Materiel Command, sub: "Escape System—F-86A, F-86E, and F-86F Airplanes," 23 April 1953, item no. 346 in F-86 Correspondence; Robert Dorr, *F-86 Sabre: History of the Sabre and FJ Fury* (Osceola, Wisc.: Motorbooks, 1993), 12.

18. Lt. Col. Ralph Switzer, Chief Medical Safety Division to Director of Research and Development, Hq USAF, sub: "Materiel Requirements Directive No. 01-13, Manual Mechanical Canopy Jettison Release," 18 January 1951 in Williams

Accident Report, 31 January 1951 HRA; History Fifth Air Force, January–June 1953, vol. 1, 143 HRA K130.01, vol. 1.

19. "Ejected to Safety," *Flying Safety* (Nov 1949), 8–9.

20. Rebecca Cameron, *Training to Fly: Military Flight Training, 1907–1945* (Washington, D.C.: Air Force History and Museums Program, 1999), 388, 400.

21. USAF Fighter Accident Review, 1 January–31 May 1950 HRA K259.2-13. This study covering the first half of 1950 noted that classes 49A through C had an accident rate three times that of the USAF; Directorate of Flight Safety Research, "Jet Fighter Accidents Related to Pilot Flying Experience" HRA K259.2-13 January–November 1950; Brief History of ATC, 1939–53, 21 HRA K220.01; "A Study of Jet Fighter Accidents and Their Relations to Flying Experience, 1 January 1951–30 June 1953," November 1953, 6 AUL M38368 1953 no. 27.

22. Accident Data Base. Apparently few members of this class were flying F-86s. During this period, four of thirty-seven major Sabre accidents involved members of this class.

23. ATC History, July–December 1949. Training Command's semi-annual history noted that the class of 49C was substandard with problems of morale, motivation, and discipline, a rare criticism for an official history.

24. Fighter Accident Review, 1 January–31 May 1950, 3; [chart] "Major Accident Rates for Classes 49A-C, 1 July 1949–30," April 1950 HRA K259.2-13; Fighter Accident Review, August 1950, 4.

25. Fighter Accident Review, 1 January–31 May 1950, 11; Accident Data Base.

26. Wagner, *North American Sabre*, 22–23.

27. Fighter Accident Review, 1 January–31 May 1950, 132.

28. Fighter Accident Review, August 1950, 5.

29. Fighter Accident Review, 1 January–31 May 1950, 14, 15.

30. Ibid., 16; ATC History, July 1950–June 1951, vol. 1, 185.

31. AAF Training Command, January–June 1946, 95–96, 105; AAF Training Command, July–December 1946, 145, 150.

32. Accident Data Base.

33. Accident Data Base; Swanborough and Bowers, *U.S. Military Aircraft since 1908*, 338.

34. ATC History, July 1950–June 1951, vol. 1, 268.

35. ATC History, July–December 1951, 56; ATC History, January–June 1952, 61–62; ATC History, January–June 1953, 57.

36. First Ind. Maj. John Walker, Maintenance Staff Officer to CG Air Materiel Command, 16 July 1952 in Comey Accident Report, 8 July 1952. The cylinder rod specifications called for a hardness of 140,000 to 160,000 psi, but the older ones were tested and found to be 46,000 psi. USAF inspectors checked seventy-five aircraft and found heat treatment stamps on only thirty-eight rods; of thirty-two rods in stock, only fifteen had been heat-treated.

37. "Nose Gear—F-86," *Flying Safety* (July 1949), 27. For the period December 1947 (the first major accident) through August 1953. This does not include fourteen accidents caused by pilots landing with their landing gear up and some others caused

by a failure of the gear indicator system; "Who Towed That F-86?" *Flying Safety* (July 1950), 9; Fighter Accident Review, January–May 1950, 8; Nash Accident Report, 13 December 1949; 6th Ind. Col. E. L. Tucker, Acting Vice Commander Eastern Defense Force to CG, Continental Air Command, 14 November 1950 in Larsh Accident Report, 14 October 1950; 5th Ind. Brig. Gen. Herbert Thatcher Air Defense Command to Director of Flight Safety Research, 31 January 1951 in Hearin Accident Report, 29 October 1950; Accident Data Base.

38. 3rd Ind. Lt. Col. Harrison Thyng, commander 33rd Fighter Interceptor Group to Commanding Officer 33rd Fighter Interceptor Wing, 4 January 1951 in Cutler Accident Report, 18 December 1950; 2nd Ind. Lt. Col. Norman Christensen, Chief Aircraft Section to Commander Otis AFB, 2 May 1951 in Newell Accident Report, 11 August 1951.

39. Pilot's Manual F-86A, June 1950, 77. However, the early F-86As had a "stick shaker" device to warn the pilot of an approaching stall when the landing gear and flaps were extended, required with the initial slat installation because the pilot got little indication of an oncoming stall. A later modification of the flaps alleviated the need for the stick shaker, which was then removed.

40. George Welch, "Spinning the Sabre," *Flying Safety* (February 1954), 15–16.

41. Pilot's Manual F-86A, January 1949, rev. May 1949, 37. It further noted that the modified (6-3) wing was not a contributor to spins and that the spins were about as frequent in each of the three F-86 versions. WCLSR-4 to WCSE-1, sub: "Major Aircraft Accidents," 20 January 1954, item no. 15 in Reports, Histories, Surveys, Summaries, and Comments 1954-55 HRA K202.1-57.

42. 1st Ind. Lt. Col. Harrison Thyng Cmdr 33rd Fighter Interceptor Group to Commanding Officer 33rd Fighter Interceptor Wing, 7 June 1950 in Scale Accident Report, 14 May 1950.

43. 3rd Ind. Brig. Gen. Hugh Parker, Vice Commander Western Air Defense Force to CG, Air Defense Command, 16 April 1953 in Mitson Accident Report, 8 March 1953; Supplement to Section "O," Description of Accident and Col. Avelin Tacon Commander Nellis AFB to CG Air Training Command, sub: "Report of Major Accident," 18 April 1951 both in Baertsch Accident Report, 3 April 1951.

44. B. H. R. Spicer, Commander Nellis AFB to Office of the Inspector General, Norton AFB, sub: "Report of Major Aircraft Accident Involving F-86A, Serial Number 49-1330, Pilot 2nd Lt. George M. Shields," 23 September 1953 in Shields Accident Report, 24 August 1953.

45. TWX Inspector General Norton to CG Air Materiel Command, 4 February 1953 in Jocylen Accident Report, 20 January 1953.

46. Directorate of Flight Safety Research, OTIG, USAF, Norton AFB, CA, "USAF Ejection Escape Experience: 29 August 1949 through 30 June 1958," table XVII, 10 November 1958 HRA K237.163–27. This 1958 study that listed the cause of ejection from USAF aircraft indicated that the F-86 pilots ejected less than the average for engine failure and loss of control but more than the average for fire, explosion, mid-air collisions, and fuel starvation; Accident Data Base.

47. Pilot's Manual F-86E, October 1950, rev. March 1951, 8.

48. Accident Reports: Christenson, 18 November 1949; Pasqualicchio, 8 February 1950; Ramsby, 15 June 1950; 2nd Ind. 334th Fighter Squadron, Dunton Accident Report, 17 September 1950.

49. George Goertz, UR [unsatisfactory report] no.52-733, 7 October 1952 in Richards Accident Report, 30 September 1952. Also Peterson Accident Report, 15 September 1952.

50. 2nd Ind., Col. Clay Tice, HQ 3595th Flying Training Group, n.d., Campbell Accident Report, 6 February 1953; Gillory Accident Report, 1 February 1953.

51. 2nd Ind., Col. Clay Tice, 3595th Training Group, 27 August 1953; Reed Accident Report, 3 August 1953.

52. Col. Norman Appold, Chief Power Plant Laboratory (WCKPG-2) to WCOWF-1, sub: "Effect of Removing Emergency Fuel Controls from F86A, E, and F, Type Aircraft," 27 April 1953, item no. 348 in F-86 Correspondence; History of Fifth Air Force, January–June 1953, vol. 1, 144 HRA K730.01; 5th Ind., Maj. Gen. Glenn Barcus, Hq Air Training Command, 1 October 1953, Reed Accident Report, 3 August 1953.

53. H. H. Bowe, Chief Aircraft Branch to North American Aviation, sub: "Contract AF33(600)-6517, F-86F Airplanes Deletion of Emergency Fuel System, ECP NA-F86F-140," 20 May 1953, item no. 364 in F-86 Correspondence. This was the recommendation of the Aircraft Branch at AMC. Col.; Pilot's Manual F-86[F], February 1953, 12, 14.

54. Engineering Standards Section, Air Materiel Command to Commander Tactical Air Command, sub: "Power Control Deficiencies on F-86F Aircraft," 1 June 1954, item no. 512 in F-86 Correspondence.

55. I have not considered the D model, which was considerably different from the A, E, and F in that it employed an afterburner, carried an airborne radar, and was fitted with unguided rockets in place of guns. It did not see service in the Korean War. For the F-86D, see Epilogue.

56. Accident Data Base; F-86 Aircraft Cards HRA.

57. Accident Data Base. There were two undetermined incidents connected with the E and one with the F. If these are counted, then the fatality rates would be 32 percent in the E and 33 percent in the F.

58. Accident Data Base. In 367 major accidents with the F-86A, of which 5 were fatal, engines were cited fifty-two times. The figures for the E were 142 major accidents, 7 of which were fatal and 28 of which were attributed to engines. For the F, there were 89 major accidents, 1 involving a fatality and 9 connected with engines.

59. Russell Accident Report, 18 October 1953; Kemp Accident Report, 31 January 1953; Boggs Accident Report, 31 January 1953; Beneke Accident Report, 31 May 1953; Smotherman Accident Report, 31 May 1953; Varble Accident Report, 31 May 1953.

60. USAF Flying Accident Bulletin: 1953, 7 HRA K259.3-3 1953.

61. USAF Statistical Digest, fiscal year 1953, 173 HRA K134.11-6; USAF Flying Accident Bulletin, 1953, 7; James Kitfield, "Flying Safety: The Real Story," *Air Force Magazine* (June 1996), 57; USAF History, FY75-FY00, www.kirtland.af.mil. Army Air

Force Statistical Digest World War II, 310; AAF Statistical Digest 1946; USAF Statistical Digest, 1947 through 1953. The latter two items hereafter cited as AAF/USAF Statistical Digest 1946–53.

62. Eighth Air Force Statistical Summary, 56–58 HRA 520.308A. The Eighth Air Force in World War II included statistics of accidents based on landings.

63. USAF Statistical Digest, 1951–53. In fairness, by this time the F-51 was growing rather long in the tooth.

64. AAF/USAF Statistical Digest, 1946–53.

65 Ibid. The differences in absolute numbers between the F-86 and F-80 and the F-84 at the half-million flying-hour mark were respectively ninety-two and ninety-one major accidents, twenty-one and twenty-five fatal accidents, and forty-nine and eight-six wrecked aircraft. Note one caveat: the F-80 figures include the T-33 for one fiscal year. A more precise breakdown is not possible because the USAF used quarterly, not monthly, statistics, resulting in the rounding that follows. The F-80 logged almost 509,000 flying hours by July 1950; the F-84, almost 516,000 flying hours by the end of 1951; and the F-86, just over 512,000 flying hours by April 1953.

66. Accident Data Base. While 21 of the 256 F-80 fatalities were of students learning to fly (unrated), there were no student pilots killed in the F-86.

67. Individual aircraft histories: www.afsc.saia.af.mil/AFSC/RDBMS/Flight/Statisticalisticals/f86mds.html.

68. USAF Oral History Interview, Lt. Gen. William Campbell, 17, 18, 19 December 1985, 16, 22 HRA K239.0512-1689.

69. James Salter, *Burning the Day: Recollections* (New York: Random House, 1997), 142; Colman Accident Report, 25 January 1952. The USAF accident report paints a different picture, suspecting a faulty gas gauge and noting that the pilot entered the landing pattern with less that the established minimum fuel.

Chapter 5

1. John Taylor, *Combat Aircraft of the World: From 1909 to the Present* (London: Paragon, 1979), 453, 598–99.

2. John Greenwood, "The Great Patriotic War, 1941–1945," in *Soviet Aviation and Air Power: A Historical View*, Robin Higham and Jacob Kipp, eds. (London: Brassey's, 1977), 108, 115, 128; Von Hardesty, *Red Phoenix: The Rise of Soviet Air Power 1941–1945* (Washington, D.C.: Smithsonian, 1982), 97–98; Ray Wagner, ed., *The Soviet Air Force in World War II: The Official History* (Garden City, N.Y.: Doubleday, 1973), 400.

3. Alexander Boyd, *The Soviet Air Force since 1918* (New York: Stein and Day, 1977), 188, 206–8.

4. Boyd, *Soviet Air Force*, 209, 211; C. T. Eriksen, ed., *The Red Air Force, 1913–1963* (Mitcham, UK: Smith, 1963), 35; Taylor, *Combat Aircraft of the World*, 584–85, 629–30.

5. Boyd, *Soviet Air Force*, 210–11; Taylor, *Combat Aircraft of the World*, 585, 629.

6. Gordon and Rigmant, *MiG-15*, 8.

7. Jerry Scutts, "The Jet Revolution," in *The Modern War Machine: Military Aviation Since 1945*, Philip Jarrett, ed., (London: Putnam, 2000), 55, 66; *Jane's All the World's Aircraft, 1952–53* (London: Jane's, 1953), 266.

8. Yefim Gordon, *Miloyan-Gurevich MiG-15: The Soviet Union's Long-lived Korean War Fighter* (Hinckley, UK: Aerofax, 2001), 4.

9. Boyd, *Soviet Air Force*, 212; Gordon and Rigmant, *MiG-15*, 14; Wilson, *Sabre, MiG-15 and Hunter*, 86.

10. Gordon and Rigmant, *MiG-15*, 15; Richard Hallion, "Technology for the Supersonic Era," in *Faster, Further, Higher: Leading-edge Aviation Technology Since 1945*, Philip Jarrett, ed., (London: Putnam, 2002), 49.

11. Gordon, *Mikoyan-Gurevich MiG-15*, 8; Gordon and Rigmant, *MiG-15*, 10–11.

12. Gordon, *Mikoyan-Gurevich MiG-15*, 23; Gordon and Rigmant, *MiG-15*, 20.

13. Gordon and Rigmant, *MiG-15*, 14–15, 18.

14. Gordon, *Mikoyan-Gurevich MiG-15*, 12, 21, 25.

15. Gordon and Rigmant, *MiG-15*, 16; Taylor, *Combat Aircraft of the World*, 586.

16. Gordon, *Mikoyan-Gurevich MiG-15*, 12–13; Gordon and Rigmant, *MiG-15*, 41, 49.

17. Gordon and Rigmant, *MiG-15*, 16–17.

18. Ibid., 17, 19; Wilson, *Sabre, MiG-15 and Hunter*, 89.

19. Gordon and Rigmant, *MiG-15*, 19; Wilson, *Sabre, MiG-15 and Hunter*, 87.

20. Gordon, *Mikoyan-Gurevich MiG-15*, 4.

21. Asher Lee, *The Soviet Air Force* (London: Duckworth, 1961), 118; Alfred Monds, "The Soviet Strategic Air Force and Civil Defense," in Higham and Kipp, *Soviet Aviation*, 223; Robert Kilmarx, *A History of Soviet Air Power* (New York: Praeger, 1962), 227; Gordon, *Mikoyan-Gurevich MiG-15*, 54; Christopher Shores, *Fighter Aces* (London: Hamlyn, 1975), 133. F-86 figures are from aircraft cards, HRA. Soviet fighter numbers are more difficult.

22. Gordon, *Mikoyan-Gurevich MiG-15*, 4, 19, 120–21. The engine service also markedly improved from 100 hours in the RD-45 to 150 to 200 hours in the VK-1A.

23. Gordon and Rigmant, *MiG-15*, 40; Gordon, *Mikoyan-Gurevich MiG-15*, 21. Curiously the same author gives slightly different numbers in this publication, albeit in the same ballpark; Gordon and Rigmant, *MiG-15*, 40. To combat the increased landing roll, the designers tested and then discarded drag chutes for braking.

24 Gordon and Rigmant, *MiG-15*, 37–38.

25. Ibid., 41.

26. Gordon, *Mikoyan-Gurevich MiG-15*, 21–22.

27. Ralph Wetterhahn, "To Snatch a Sabre," *Air and Space* (June/July 2003), 44–45.

28. Gordon, *Mikoyan-Gurevich MiG-15*, 23.

29. Ibid., 9, 19, 21–22.

Chapter 6

1. RoK and North Korean aircraft numbers are taken from Futrell, *USAF in Korea*, 18–20.

2. Two short, readable, and fairly accurate overviews of the war are Stanley Sandler, *The Korean War: No Victors, No Vanquished* (Lexington: University Press of Kentucky, 1999) and James Stokesbury, *A Short History of the Korean War* (New York: William Morrow, 1988). Other works drawn upon for this summary of the war were Vincent Esposito, ed., *The West Point Atlas of American Wars*, vol. 2, 1900–1953 (New York: Praeger, 1960); R. Ernest Dupuy and Trevor Dupuy, *The Encyclopedia of Military History from 3500 B.C. to the Present* (New York: Harper & Row, 1977); Max Hastings, *The Korean War* (New York: Simon and Schuster, 1987); Callum Mac-Donald, *Korea: The War Before Vietnam* (New York: Free Press, 1986).

3. Casualty figures are from Dupuy and Dupuy, *Encyclopedia of Military History*, 1251.

4. Far East Air Forces, Korean Air War Summary, June 1950–27 July 1953, 32 HRA K720.04D-1; William Y'Blood, *MiG Alley: The Fight for Air Superiority* (Washington, D.C.: Air Force History and Museum Program, 2000), 1.

5. Futrell, *USAF in Korea*, 9–13. The official USAF History is still the best account of the Korean air war. Also useful is the more recent A. Timothy Warnock, ed., *The USAF in Korea: A Chronology, 1950–1953* (Washington, D.C.: Air Force History and Museums Program and Air University Press, 2000), 1–3. For USAF victory credits, see USAF Korean War Victory Credits.

6. USAF Korean War Victory Credits; Futrell, *USAF in Korea*, 266–31, 264, 292; D. Clayton James, *The Years of MacArthur*, vol. 2, *Triumph and Disaster, 1945–64* (Boston: Houghton Mifflin, 1985), 425–26.

7. Later in the Korean War the Communists used small, slow biplanes to launch night attacks on American installations, the infamous "Bed Check Charlie."

8. Futrell, *USAF in Korea*, 92–94, 105; Hallion, *Naval Air War in Korea*, 34, 38, 41; James Stewart, ed., *Airpower: The Decisive Force in Korea* (Princeton, N.J.: Nostrand, 1957), 78; William Y'Blood, ed., *The Three Wars of Lt. Gen. George E. Stratemeyer: His Korean War Diary* (Washington, D.C.: Air Force History and Museums Program, 1999), 83, 107.

9. Y'Blood, *The Three Wars of Lt. Gen. George E. Stratemeyer*, 85, 206, 207n28, 280n122.

10. United States Air Force Statistical Digest, fiscal year 1953, 20 HRA K134.11-6.

11. USAF Statistical Digest, fy 1953, 20; Futrell, *USAF in Korea*, 96; Cagle and Manson, *Sea War in Korea*, 526; Otto Weyland, "The Air Campaign in Korea," in *Airpower: The Decisive Force in Korea*, James Stewart, ed. (Princeton, N.J.: Nostrand, 1957), 7.

12. USAF Strategic Digest, fy 1953, 38, 44–45, 60; Futrell, *USAF in Korea*, 131, 152; "Heavyweights Over Korea," 78, 81 in *Airpower: The Decisive Force in Korea*, James Stewart, ed.; Hallion, *Naval Air War in Korea*, 61.

13. Futrell, *USAF in Korea*, 122, 139, 160, 164–65; Weyland, "Air Campaign in Korea," 10.

14. Futrell, *USAF in Korea*, 142; Warnock, *USAF Korea Chronology*, 18–20.

15. USAF Korean War Victory Credits; Cagle and Manson, *Sea War in Korea*, 526; Futrell, *USAF in Korea*, 214–15; Warnock, *USAF Korea Chronology*, 22–23; Y'Blood, *MiG Alley*, 12.

Chapter 7

1. Y'Blood, *Three Wars of Lt. Gen George E. Stratemeyer*, 175.

2. Ibid., 255.

3. Ibid., 267.

4. USAF Korean War Victory Credits. As for the other USAF fighters, 194 of the 351 F-51s that were lost fell to enemy action, 143 of the 373 F-80s, and 110 of the 224 F-86s. In air-to-air combat the F-51 downed twelve Communist aircraft and lost ten, and the F-80 seven for fourteen lost.

5. Roger Freeman, *The Mighty Eighth: Units, Men and Machines* (London: Macdonald, 1970), 238, 242. The 4th claimed 583.5 aerial and 469 ground credits, whereas the 56th Fighter Group claimed 674.5 aerial and 311 ground credits; USAF World War II Victory Credits. The official credits, however, are 548.5 aerial victories for the 4th and 665.5 for the 56th; M. Mauer, ed., *Air Force Combat Units of World War II* (Washington, D.C.: Office of Air Force History, 1983), 35–36; Futrell, *USAF in Korea, 1950–1953*, 232.

6. Davis, *4th Fighter Wing in the Korean War*, 32, 34, 68; Bruce Hinton, "Sabres Used Tankers for Korea Deployment," *Sabre Jet Classics* (Summer 2002), available at http://sabre-pilots.org/classics/v102tankers.htm; Warren Thompson and David McLaren, *MiG Alley: Sabres vs. MiGs Over Korea* (North Branch, Minn.: Specialty, 2002), 2–3.

7. Chronology of the 4th Tactical Fighter Wing: from 1942, 19 HRA K-Wg-4 -Hi (September 1942–December 1980); History of the Fourth Fighter Group, October–December 1950, 5–6, 10–11, HRA K-Gp-4-Hi; Headquarters Air Proving Ground, "Report on Combat Operations of the F-86A during Period 15 December 1950 thru 2 January 1951," 23 January 1951, 270, 275, in History of the Air Proving Ground, January–June 1951, vol. 2 HRA K240.01.

8. History of the Fifth Air Force: November 1950–December 1950, vol. 1, 148, HRA K730.01; APG, "Report on Combat Operations F-86A," 270–71, 274; Futrell, *USAF in Korea*, 235–36.

9. Y'Blood, *The Three Wars of Lt. Gen. George E. Stratemeyer*, 359; 4FGp History, October–December 1950, 6; Bruce Hinton and Elmer Wingo, "An Analysis of Operations at Kimpo Air Base Performed by Detachment 'A,' 336th Fighter-Interceptor Squadron, 4th Fighter-Interceptor Group," 3–5, 29, HRA K-Sq-Fi-336-Hi (Kimpo, Det A); USAF Korean War Victory Credits; Askold Germon, *Red Devils* (Kiev: 1998), 43; Gordon, *Mikoyan-Gurevich MiG-15*, 62; APG, "Report on Combat Operations F-86A," 271, 276, 282.

10. Pilot's Manual, F-86A, June 1950, revised January 1951, 1; Pilot's Manual F-86F, March 1952, 3, both NASM Suitland, Maryland. Hinton and Wingo, "Analy-

sis of Operations at Kimpo," 4–5; APG, "Report on Combat Operations F-86A," 265, 282.

11. Hinton and Wingo, "Analysis of Operations at Kimpo," 26–27; George Smith, Commander 4th Fighter Interceptor Wing, to Commanding General Far East Air Forces, sub: "Combat Evaluation of the MiG-15 vs. the F-86," 26 December 1950 HRA K146.003-140; Maj. Gen. B. L. Boatner, Commander Air Proving Ground to Chief of Staff, Headquarters USAF, sub: "Evaluation of the Combat Operations of the F-86A Aircraft in Combat," 8 February 1951, 265 in APG History: January–June 1951, vol. 2.

12. H. A. Schmid, Commander 4th Fighter Interceptor Wing to Commanding General, Eastern Air Defense Force, sub: "Operations of the 4th Fighter-Interceptor Wing in Korea," 11 June 1951 in History 4th Fighter Interceptor Wing, June 1951 HRA K-Wg-4-Hi (hereafter cited as 4FIW History [date]).

13. USAF Korean War Victory Credits. The official credits are for forty-one MiGs downed. Prior to 29 July the USAF listed five F-86s lost to the MiGs.

14. Bruce Hinton, "MiG-15 versus F-86A in Korea: Prepared by Lt. Col. Bruce H. Hinton 4th Fighter Interceptor Group Compiled from Combat Encounter Reports by Pilots of the 4th Fighter Interceptor Group," 25 July 1951, 24–25, HRA K-Sq-Fi-336-Hi (Kimpo, Det A).

15. Hinton, "MiG-15 versus F-86A," 24–25.

16. USAF Korean War Victory Credits; USAF Statistical Digest, fy 1953, 38, 45–47; Warnock, ed., USAF in Korea; Futrell, USAF in Korea, 271.

17. USAF Statistical Digest, fy 1953, 57–59; Futrell, USAF in Korea, 270–74; Germon, Red Devils on the 38th Parallel, 52, 75; Warnock, USAF Korea Chronology.

18. Futrell, USAF in Korea, 275.

19. USAF Korean War Victory Credits; Futrell, USAF in Korea, 276–77, 279.

20. Futrell, USAF in Korea, 277.

21. Ibid., 279–84.

22. USAF Statistical Digest, fy 1953, 44, 67–68. While interdiction missions accounted for only one-third of air-to-air losses, they accounted for 60 percent of losses to ground fire.

23. FEAF Report on the Korean War, 172–73 HRA 168.7104-53; Futrell, USAF in Korea, 291–95, 298–300, 303; Eduard Mark, Aerial Interdiction in Three Wars (Washington, D.C.: Center for Air Force History, 1994), 278.

24. Futrell, USAF in Korea, 297, 296.

25. Ibid., 413.

26. Ibid., 289, 291–95, 298–300, 303, 310; Mark, Aerial Interdiction, 307, 313, 323, chart 10. Losses and sorties are noted above. On the issue of overclaiming see Futrell, USAF in Korea, 423.

27. Low American production led the Air Force to buy 60 Canadian-built Sabres in mid-1952 that were designated F-86E-6, some of which saw combat in Korea; Wagner, North American Sabre, 113.

28. 4FIW History, August 1951; History 4th Fighter Interceptor Group, August 1951 in 4FIW History, August 1951; Futrell, USAF in Korea, 296–97, 302, 308, 372, 374.

29. USAF Statistical Digest, fy 1953, 56. There were only seven months during the war in which the USAF lost more than five aircraft to enemy aircraft. Four of these were the last four months of 1951; USAF Korean War Victory Credits; Futrell, *USAF in Korea*, 372–73, 378–80.

30. Futrell, *USAF in Korea*, 380–82.

31. 4FIW History, November 1951; USAF Korean War Victory Credits; Futrell, *USAF in Korea*, 383–84.

32. History of 51st Fighter Interceptor Wing: 15 January 1941–31 December 1955, 36–37 HRA K-Wg-51-Hi; USAF World War II Victory Credits; Mauer, *Air Force Combat Units*, 112.

33. USAF Korean War Victory Credits; History 51st Fighter Interceptor Wing, December 1951 (hereafter cited as 51FIW History, [date]); 51FIW History, January 1952; 51FIW History, May 1952; 51FIW History, June 1952; 51FIW History, July 1952; Futrell, *USAF in Korea*, 389; Thompson and McLaren, *MiG Alley*, 31, 41, 51, 54.

34. USAF Korean War Victory Credits. The two units had the exact same number (35) of aircraft destroyed in accidents or by AA; John Sullivan, "51st Tactical Fighter Wing . . . Combat Unit in Two Wars," 31 HRA K-Wg-51-Hi; History Fifth Air Force: January–June 1953, vol. 3, app. 27 HRA K730.01.

35. Y'Blood, *MiG Alley: The Fight for Air Superiority*, 46. Of the thirty-nine Korean War jet aces, ten earned their victories only with the 51st and twenty-four only with the 4th. Four got credits with both units, while one scored with both the 4th and 8th Fighter Bomber Group; USAF Korean War Victory Credits, 44; 51st Tactical Wing . . . in Two Wars, 35.

36. USAF Korean War Victory Credits; Futrell, *USAF in Korea*, 388.

37. 4th Fighter Interceptor Group, "F-86E versus MiG-15 in Korea," 15 January 1952, 22 HRA K-Wg-4-Hi.

38. W. Harbison, "Critique on the F-86E," Central Fighter Establishment, February–May 1952, 13; George Jones, Deputy Commander [4FIG] to Commanding Officer, 4th Fighter Interceptor Wing, sub: "F-86E Combat Evaluation," 1 November 1951, 1–2, HRA 4FIW History, October–December 1951; Harrison Thyng, "The Operation of the 4th Fighter Wing in Korea," 3 HRA K720.131 Thyng; 4FIG, "F-86E versus MiG-15 in Korea," 15 January 1952, 28 in [4FIW], "Operations in MiG-Alley" K-Wg-4-Hi (January 52); Fifth Air Force Intelligence Summary, vol. 2, No. 8, 2 May 1952, 44; "Performance Comparison between F-86 and MiG-15 Aircraft," NA 342-54-7025 5AF-40.

39. William Quinlan, "A Critique on the F-86E versus the MiG-15 Aircraft in the Korean Theater," Operations Analysis Office Memorandum No. 50, 1 Apr 1952, in Sullivan, "51st Tactical Fighter Wing," 93, 86–90; Albert Schinz, [end of tour report], 10 July 1952, 5 HRA K720.131-1; 4FIG, "F-86E versus MiG-15 in Korea," 20.

40. Pilot Manual, F-86A, June 1950, 62–64.

41. USAF Statistical Digest, fy 1953, 32, 45–47.

42. Futrell, *USAF in Korea*, 442–53; "The Attack on Electric Power in North Korea," in *Airpower: The Decisive Force in Korea*, James Stewart, ed. (Princeton, N.J.: Van Norstrand, 1957), 120–21, 126–27; Hallion, *Naval Air War in Korea*, 132–34.

43. Futrell, *USAF in Korea*, 453, 483; "Attack on Electric Power in North Korea," 138–39; Warnock, *USAF Korea Chronology*, 73.

44. USAF Korean War Victory Credits; USAF Statistical Digest, fy 1953, 53; Futrell, *USAF in Korea*, 481–82, 489.

45. USAF Korean War Victory Credits; 5AF History, July–December 1952, vol. 1, 7,183; 4FIW History, Aug 1952; 4FIW History, July–December 1952; Futrell, *USAF in Korea*, 460, 609.

46. Glenn Carus interview with author, 19 February 2002; P. C. Davis to author, 11 February 2002; Futrell, *USAF in Korea*, 609.

47. USAF Korean War Victory Credits; USAF Statistical Digest, fy 1953, 53.

48. Futrell, *USAF in Korea*, 624–28. It is noteworthy that in the Vietnam War dikes were the only major target system the U.S. airmen did not attack.

49. Futrell, *USAF in Korea*, 636–39.

Chapter 8

1. "Operation MiG," History of Fifth Air Force: January–June 1951, vol. 2, 61-62 HRA K730.01.

2. Donald Nichols, *How Many Times Can I Die?* (Brooksville, FL: Brooksville Printing, 1981), 4.

3. Michael Haas, *Apollo's Warriors: United States Air Force Special Operations During the Cold War* (Maxwell AFB, Ala.: Air University, 1997), 54–55.

4. The unit sought documents, nameplates, and identification tags. In addition to focusing on the engine and its component parts, the unit was looking for skin samples, instruments, radios, armament, and tailpipe samples.

5. History of 51st Fighter Interceptor Wing: 15 January 1941–31 December 1955, 33 HRA K-Wg-51-Hi; "Operation MiG," 65.

6. "Operation MiG," 66.

7. C. B. Colby, "The Day We Stole a MiG," *Air Trails* (January 1953), 20–21; Nichols, *How Many Times Can I Die?*, 154; "Operation MiG," 66–67. The H-19 was the largest helicopter in the theater with a four-ton payload and over two-hundred-mile range. Nichols says the crash site was one hundred miles inside communist territory; Colby says it was thirty-five miles behind enemy lines.

8. Nichols, *How Many Times Can I Die?*, 131; "Operation MiG," 67. The official account does not mention any shooting and instead states, "There were indications that the wreck had been under regular guard for a fresh well beaten path was observed surrounding the aircraft."

9. Colby, "The Day We Stole a MiG," 21, 85; "They Snatched a MiG," *American Legion Magazine* (November 1959), 44–46; "Operation MiG," 67–69.

10. "Operation MiG," 70–71.

11. Warnock, ed., *The USAF in Korea*, 45.

12. There was a general policy that the Royal Navy operated off the west coast of Korea while the U.S. Navy operated off the east coast. One reason for this geographic arrangement was that the British had diplomatic relations with the Chinese

Communists, which might be an asset in any unforeseen future incident in Chinese air space or waters.

13. Piotr Butowski and Jay Miller, *OKB MiG: A History of the Design Bureau and Its Aircraft* (Leicester, UK: Specialty, 1991), 69; USAF Oral History Interview, Gen. Earle Partridge, 23–25 April 1974, 637 HRA K239.0512-729; Allison March and Donald McElfresh, *Submarine or Phantom Target?* (Silver Spring, Md.: Edisto, 1999), 26–32. A body on the mud flats was not recovered.

14. 5AF History, July–December 1951, vol. 1, 164.

15. Gordon, *Mikoyan-Gurevich MiG-15*, 68. On 20 May 1953 Lt. Zdzislaw Jazwinski, from the same unit, also defected to Bornholm; USAF Europe, Air Intelligence Information Branch, Airframe, Report No. ATI-880-53, 23 April 1953, 7, 20–22, 46 AUL M37745 1953 no. 880, part.1; Ibid, Summary, 3, 4, 7.

16. "Flight to Freedom" www.mig29.com/features98/mig15/story-defection.html; Kum-Sok No, *A MiG-15 to Freedom: Memoir of a Wartime North Korean Defector Who First Delivered the Secret Fighter Jet to the Americans in 1953* (Jefferson, N.C.: McFarland, 1996), 142.

17. Futrell, *USAF in Korea, 1950–1953*, 610; Rob Young, "ATIC Mig-15bis Exploitation," www.wpafb.af.mil/naic/history/mig15/mig15.html.

18. Tom Collins, "Testing the Russian MiG," in *Test Flying at Old Wright Field*, Ken Chistrom, ed., (Omaha, Neb.: Westchester House, 1991), 42, 44; Columbia University Oral History Interview with Maj. Gen. Albert Boyd, June 1960, 14 HRA K146.34-12; USAF Oral History Interview, Lt. Gen. Kenneth Schulz, 27–31 October 1980, 66 HRA K239.0512-1728; Chuck Yeager and Leo Janos, *Yeager* (Toronto: Bantam, 1985), 207; Headquarters Far East Air Forces, Immediate No. 2829, 16 October 1953 AFM; Wagner, *North American Sabre*, 81.

19. Gordon, *Mikoyan-Gurevich Mig-15*, 68; FEAF, Immediate No. 2829; No, *MiG-15 to Freedom*, 159; Yeager and Janos, *Yeager*, 206.

20. Air Technical Information Center, "MiG-15 Flight Test," Technical Report No. TR-AC 27, 13 October 1953, v AMC; FEAF, Immediate No. 2829; Collins, "Testing the Russian MiG," 46; Yeager and Janos, *Yeager*, 206.

21. Yeager and Janos, *Yeager*, 205–6. Collins agreed with the first Yeager statement. Collins, "Testing the Russian MiG," 46; Boyd Interview, 15; No, *MiG-15 to Freedom*, 159. Gordon, *Mikoyan-Gurevich MiG-15*, 68. One contrary voice, a Russian pilot writes that the MiG-15 was reluctant to spin and could be brought out of a spin if the proper procedures were followed.

22. Boyd Interview, 15; Yeager and Janos, *Yeager*, 207; Collins, "Testing the Russian MiG," 45.

23. Report No. ATI-880-53, 20–21; Yeager and Janos, *Yeager*, 207. The pilot accounts do not explain how they could exceed Mach .94 as reportedly the MiG's speed brakes automatically extended at this speed.

24. Boyd Interview, 14–15; Collins, "Testing the Russian MiG," 45–46; Yeager and Janos, *Yeager*, 208. Both Boyd and Collins claim to have flown Yeager's wing on this maximum speed flight.

25. No, *Mig-15 to Freedom*, 164; ATIC, "MiG-15 Flight Test," iii–v; Boyd Interview, 14; FEAF, Immediate No. 2829; Partridge Interview, 639; Schulz Interview, 66–67; Yeager and Janos, *Yeager*, 206–7.

26. Young, "ATIC Mig-15bis Exploitation," 2–3.

27. William Coughlin, "Reds Fly Captured Sabres in Combat," *Aviation Week* (18 May 1953), 13; 5AF History: July–December 1951, vol. 1, 96; Far East Air Forces Weekly Intelligence Roundup, No. 69 (22–28 December 1951); Ibid, No. 75 (2–8 February 1952); Ibid, No. 78 (23–29 February 1952); Ibid, No. 82 (22–28 March 1952); Fifth Air Force Intelligence Summary, vol. 1, no. 8 (7 November 1951); Ibid, vol. 2, no. 6 (5 April 1952); Ibid, vol. 3, no. 6 (5 October 1952); Ibid, vol. 3, no. 7 (20 October 1952); Ibid, vol. 3, no. 9 (20 November 1952) all at NARACP.

28. Gordon, *Mikoyan-Gurevich MiG-15*, 69; Gordon and Rigmant, *MiG-15*, 113; Paul Cole, POW/MIA Issues, RAND, vol. 1, The Korean War, 167 AUL MU 30352-84 no. 351; Laurence Jolidon, *Last Seen Alive* (Austin, Tex.: Ink-Slinger, 1995), 185; V. A. Zolotarev, ed., *Russia (USSR) in Local Wars and Regional Conflicts in the Second Half of the 20th Century* (Moscow: Kuchkovo Polye Publishing, 2000), part I, chapter 2; Wetterhahn, "To Snatch a Sabre," 42.

29. This was a dangerous rescue as the plane came down just outside a North Korean air base. The SA-16 landed about one-fourth of a mile offshore but could only get within two hundred yards of shore because of the mud. The amphibian came under small arms and mortar fire during the operation. John Freemont, "Third Air Rescue Squadron Saves 100th Downed Pilot," History of Third Air Rescue Squadron, Nov 1951 HRA; Bob Mason to author 8 June 2000 and 13 June 2000.

30. Leonid Krylov and Yuri Tepsurkayev, "The Hunt for the 'Sabre,'" (Mir Aviatsii, 1998) part II. Available at www.aeronautics.ru/nws002/the_hunt_for_the_sabre_ii.htm. The Russians, finding it very difficult to sneak up behind the Sabre, speculated that the aircraft was equipped with a rear-viewing radar. They found instead that the American advantage was the excellent cockpit visibility.

31. Jolidon, *Last Seen Alive*, 183–84. This account claims three F-86s were sent to Russia; Joint Commission Support Branch Research and Analysis Division, DPMO, "Sand in the Fuselage," the section titled "The Transfer of U.S. Korean War POWs to the Soviet Union" indicates that two or three F-86s were brought to the Soviet Union. See www.aiipowmia.com/reports/trnsfr.html; Igor Gordelianow, "Soviet Air Aces of the Korean War," available at http://aeroweb.lucia.it/~agretch/RAFAQ/Soviet Aces.html; Leonid Krylov and Yuriy Tepsurkayev, "Russia's Plan to Seize the Sabre," *Combat Aircraft* (August 2000), 836–43; Gordon, *Mikoyan-Gurevich MiG-15*, 69; Gordon and Rigmant, *MiG-15*, 137; Zolotarev, ed., "Russia (USSR) in Local Wars," part I, chapter 2; "MiG-15 Fagots over Korea," available at http://dzampi.boom.ru/Korea/MiGsoverKorea.htm; Krylov and Tepsurkayev, "The Hunt for the 'Sabre,'" part II.

32. Gordon, *Mikoyan-Gurevich MiG-15*, 69, 71.

33. Gordon and Rigmant, *MiG-15*, 113; Krylov and Tepsurkayev, "The Hunt for the 'Sabre.'" The Soviets also learned that their artificial horizon indicator was far inferior to the American one, a deficiency not corrected in the fighters until 1954.

34. "Sand in the Fuselage."

35. Paul Cole, POW/MIA Issues, vol. 1, The Korean War, RAND, n.d., 17. DoD accounted for the remainder as dead or presumed dead, returned, and currently captured; All POW-MIA Casualties, 2, available at www.aiipowmia.com/koreacw/kwkia_menu.html. Another recent document states that there were 8,200 bodies not identified or not recovered.

36. All POW-MIA Casualties, 2.

37. Cole, POW/MIA Issues, vol. 1, 17, 37, 159; Peter Tosuras, et al., "The Transfer of U.S Korean War POWs to the Soviet Union," 26 August 1993, 1, 2, 6, available at www.aiipowmia.com/reports/trnsfr.html.

38. Hearing Before the Military Personnel Subcommittee of the Committee on National Security House of Representatives, 104th Congress, 2nd Session, 20 June 1996, 2, 8. The other congressman was Representative Robert Dornan.

39. House Hearings of Military Personnel Subcommittee, June 1996, 82.

40. "The Transfer of U.S. Korean War POWs," 21.

41. Ibid., 1.

42. Ibid., 2.

43. Laurence Jolidon, "Soviet Interrogation of U.S. POWs in the Korean War," *Cold War International History Bulletin* (Winter 1995/1996), 6–7.

44. Jolidon, *Last Seen Alive*, 130–31.

45. Cole, POW/MIA Issues, vol. 1, 160. This is in error. My figures agree with those of Thompson and McLaren that twenty-eight F-86 pilots survived captivity; Jolidon, *Last Seen Alive*, 127; Thompson and McLaren, *MiG Alley*, 171–74.

46. "The Transfer of U.S. Korean War POWs," 11–12, 18. One Russian officer and a number of personnel at the design bureaus are the source of this account. This same story is repeated in Jolidon, *Last Seen Alive*, 126, 187.

47. House Hearings of Military Personnel Subcommittee, June 1996, 3.

48. "The Transfer of U.S Korean War POWs," 10; Jolidon, *Last Seen Alive*, 127.

49. House Hearings of Military Personnel Subcommittee, June 1996, 5.

50. "The Transfer of U.S. Korean War POWs," 22–23.

51. Robert Jones, Joint Commission Support Directorate, "The Gulag Study," 7 February 2001.

Chapter 9

1. Fifth Air Force History: July–December 1951, vol. 1, 165 HRA K730.01; Headquarters Fifth Air Force to Commanding Officer FEC Liaison Detachment (Korea), sub: "Defense of Friendly Islands," 10 December 1951, 5AF History, July–December 1951, vol. 3, app. 42, 86–89; "Friendly Islands," Fifth Air Force Intelligence Summary (20 December 1952), vol. 3, no. 11, 53–56 NARACP; [Lawrence

Schuetta], "Guerrilla Warfare and Airpower in Korea, 1950–53," Aerospace Studies Institute, Air University, January 1964, 94–95.

2. United States Air Force Operations in the Korean Conflict: 1 July 1952–27 July 1953, USAF Historical Study no. 127, 1 July 1956, 54, 83.

3. David Hatch and Robert Benson, *United States Cryptologic History*, series V, *The Early Postwar Period, 1945–1952*, vol. 3, *The Korean War: The SIGINT Background* (Center for Cryptologic History, National Security Agency, 2000), 5. Also see pages 3–4.

4. Hatch and Benson, *Korean War SIGINT*, 5–6.

5. Matthew Aid, "American Comint in the Korean War (Part II): From the Chinese Intervention to the Armistice," *Intelligence and National Security* (Spring 2000), 15–19, 27, 34; Hatch and Benson, *Korean War SIGNIT*, 7–8, 11.

6. Aid, "American Comint in the Korean War," 37, 38–39, 41; Hatch and Benson, *Korean War SIGNIT*, 14.

7. Aid, "American Comint in the Korean War," 28–29; Futrell, *USAF in Korea, 1950–1953*, 281; Korean Conflict: Chronological Listing [of victory credits] HRA.

8. Xiaoming Zhang, *Red Wings over the Yalu: China, the Soviet Union, and the Air War in Korea* (College Station, Tex.: Texas A&M, 2002), 156–58. One account states the prop-powered communist fighters were La-11s.; Far East Air Forces Weekly Intelligence Roundup (25 November–1 December 1951), no. 65, II-7 HRA K720.607A; Futrell, *USAF in Korea*, 383–84. Lawrence V. Schuetta, "Guerrilla Warfare and Airpower in Korea, 1950–53." Typescript, Aerospace Studies Institute, Maxwell AFB, 1964, 184. This source states the Chinese landed under close air support on the afternoon of 31 November.

9. Joe Foss and Matthew Brennan, eds., *Top Guns: America's Fighter Aces Tell Their Stories* (New York: Pocket Books, 1991), 270.

10. Douglas Evans, *Sabre Jets over Korea: A Firsthand Account* (Blue Ridge Summit, Pa.: Tab Books, 1984), 155. USAF sources, as do two of the American pilots involved in the fight, state that there were twelve Tu-2s; Foss and Brennan, *Top Guns*, 270; Futrell, *USAF in Korea*, 384. John Bruning, *Crimson Sky: The Air Battle for Korea* (Dulles, Va.: Brassey's, 1999), 169; Zhang, *Red Wings over the Yalu*, 158. Communist sources, however, state that there were only nine Tu-2s.

11. Gene Gurney, *Five Down and Glory* (New York: Ballantine, 1958), 198. Zhang, *Red Wings over the Yalu*, 158, 162. This account states the Chinese prop fighters were La-11s; Foss and Brennan, *Top Guns*, 272.

12. Evans, *Sabre Jets over Korea*, 157.

13. Foss and Brennan, *Top Guns*, 272.

14. During the war, thirty-six U.S. pilots scored two or more victories on one mission. Davis did it four times, as did James Jabara.

15. USAF Korean War Victory Credits. Ralph Parr and William Wescott had two missions on which they claimed two victories.

16. Zhang, *Red Wings over the Yalu*, 162; Fifth Air Force Intelligence Summary (5 December 1951), vol. 1, no. 12, 11 HRA K720.059-73; USAF Korean War Victory Credits; Davis, *4th Fighter Wing in the Korean War*, 99–100; Futrell, *USAF in Korea*, 384.

17. Zhang, *Red Wings over the Yalu*, 161, 185.

18. Far East Air Forces, General Order no. 204, 26 April 1952, "Official Credit for Destruction of Enemy Aircraft," HRA K720.193; General Order no. 208, 29 April 1952. His wingman meanwhile had destroyed a Tu-2.

19. Raymond Barton interview with author, 22 March 2002; General Order no. 3, 4 January 1952; General Order no. 202, 26 April 1952; Bruning, *Crimson Sky*, 174–76.

20. General Order no. 206, 29 April 1952; Foss and Brennan, *Top Guns*, 272–74.

21. Schuetta, "Guerrilla Warfare and Airpower in Korea," 184; Korean War: Chronology of U.S. Pacific Fleet Operations, September–December 1952, available at www.history.navy.mil/wars/kora/chron52c.htm.

22. Air Intelligence Information Report, sub: "Investigation of Bombing Incident on Cho-do Island," 22 October 1952 Fifth Air Force Intelligence Summary, vol. 3, no. 8, 5 November 1952, NARACP.

23. Air Intelligence Information Report, sub: "Investigation of Bombing Incident on Cho-do Island," 9 December 1952; 5AF Intelligence Summary, vol. 3, no. 11, 20 December 1952, NARACP; Futrell, *USAF in Korea*, 620.

24. Richard Muller, *The German Air War in Russia* (Baltimore: Nautical and Aviation, 1992), 130.

25. Jarred Crabb Journal, 17 June 1951, fr 0881 USAFA MS-2; Futrell, *USAF in Korea*, 620–23; USAF Korean War Victory Credits; Cagle and Manson, *Sea War in Korea*, appendix VII.

26. Statistical Summary of Eighth Air Force Operations, European Theater: 17 Aug 1942–8 May 1945, 54–55, 71 HRA 520.308A; Earl Tilford, *Search and Rescue in Southeast Asia* (Washington, D.C.: Office of Air Force History, 1980), 3–8; Werrell, *Blankets of Fire*, 143–45, 305n68.

27. "Guardian Angels," 5AF Intelligence Summary (5 October 1952), vol. 3, no. 6, 49–50; Futrell, *USAF in Korea*, 536–40; Forrest Marion, "'The Dumbo's Will Get Us in No Time': Air Force SA-16 Combat Operations in the Korean War Theater, 1950–1953," *Air Power History* (Summer 1999), 19; Swanborough and Bowers, *U.S. Military Aircraft since 1908*, 299–300, 480–83; Tilford, *Search and Rescue*, 8–9, 12, 14.

28. Schuetta, "Guerrilla Warfare and Airpower in Korea," 151–52. Lt. Gen. Thomas McMullen, videotape interview, April, May, October 1998 HRA K239.0512-2172; Futrell, *USAF in Korea*, 543; Tilford, *Search and Rescue*, 13. Of seventy-seven airmen who made it back from behind Communist lines from July 1950 through January 1952, helicopters rescued thirty-two and SA-16s thirteen.

29. Futrell, *USAF in Korea*, 539–40.

30. Robert McIntosh interview with author, 17 June 2003. The first of these was a deadstick landing, which the pilot attributes its success to "extreme good luck"; Dorr, *F-86 Sabre*, title page.

31. Pilot's Manual F-86A Airplane, 30 June 1950, revised 15 September 1950, 48; Pilot's Manual F-86E Aircraft, 30 March 1950, revised 30 March 1951, 37; Pilot's

Manual F-86F Aircraft, 20 March 1952, 40, all three NASM; Harrison Thyng, "End of Tour Report," 4 HRA K720.131. The 70 nm figure was true for all three models of the F-86.

32. Forrest Marion, "Sabre Pilot Pickup: Unconventional Contributions to Air Superiority in Korea," *Air Power History* (Spring 2002), 23. Two pilots landed on Cho-do after bailing out were picked up by choppers, two were rescued by both SA-16s and choppers, four to unknown agents, leaving twelve to SA-16s and twenty-one to helicopters. Col. Albert Schniz, see below, was the forty-second.

33. Far East Air Forces, Korean Air War Summary, 15 HRA K720.04D-1; United States Air Force Statistical Digest, fy 1953, 28 HRA K134.11-6. The former lists 223, the latter 218.

34. Marion, "Sabre Pilot Pickups," 24–25; Tilford, *Search and Rescue in Southeast Asia*, 19.

35. Robert Dorr, "The Day the Reds Shot Down Our Top Jet Ace," in *Fighting Aces*, Phil Hirsch, ed. (New York: Pyramid, 1965). This most detailed account; unfortunately is not the most accurate.

36. Tomas Polak with Christopher Shores, *Stalin's Falcons: The Aces of the Red Star* (London: Grubb Street, 1999), 116; Igor Gordelianow, "Soviet Air Aces of the Korean War," available at http://aeroweb.lucia.it/~agretch/RAFAQ/SovietAces. html; Al Bowers and David Lednicer, "Fighter Pilot Aces List," available at http://www.csd.uwo.ca/~pettypi/elevon/aces.html. Fedorets had earned his wings during World War II and flew P-39s in that conflict. He flew ninety-eight missions in Korea, engaged in forty combats, and claimed six F-86s and a total of seven or eight UN aircraft.

37. "Captain Joseph McConnell," available at www.acepilots.com/korea_ mcconnell.html; Harold Chitwood to Jack Hilliard, 13 January 1984 AFM MI McConnell.

38. Futrell, *USAF in Korea*, facing 135. For example, in the Newport [Mass.] *Daily News* (16 April 1953) and Larry Davis, *MiG Alley: Air to Air Combat over Korea* (Carrollton, Tex.: Squadron/Signal, 1978), 57.

39. Robert Sullivan to author, 25 August 2002. The rescue commander had the special operations people take the rescue markings off of their choppers; Robert Futrell, *The United States Air Force in Korea* (Washington, D.C.: Office of Air Force History, rev. ed. 1983), 298. The USAF revised Futrell's work in 1983 and published the same photo with the caption: "An H-19 of the 3d Air Rescue Group hoists an airman to safety"; Robert Sullivan to author, 27 August 2002; Marion, "Sabre Pilot Pickup," 26.

40. Robert Sullivan to Maj. Forrest Marion, 24 April 1998.

41. Sullivan to Marion, 25 April 1998.

42. Sullivan to Marion, 25 April 1998; Robert Sullivan to author, 22 August 2002.

43. USAF Korean War Victory Credits.

44. This account is drawn mainly from Clay Blair, *Beyond Courage* (New York: Ballantine, 1955), 7–37. This is the most detailed account, but has some accuracy

problems. Also see Haas, *Apollo's Warriors*, 63–64; Schuetta, "Guerrilla Warfare and Airpower in Korea," 135, 186; Rod Paschall, "Special Operations in Korea," *Conflict*, vol. 8, no. 2 (1987), 167.

45. Joe Clark, "Not Quite a Hero," unpublished manuscript, 290.

46. Blair, *Beyond Courage*, 36–37; Clark, "Not Quite a Hero," 290–91. Schniz rose to the rank of major general in the Air Force and died in January 1985.

47. Wesley Tillis to author, 18 March 2002. On 4 February 1952, a F-86 pilot ejected near Cho-do, but his chute did not open. On 4 July 1952 and 15 September 1952, F-86s pilots drown before rescue crews could reach them.

48. The bulk of this account and the quote are from Marion, "Sabre Pilot Pickup," 27–28; John Lowery to author, 20 June 2003. The USAF credited Spath with one-half MiG kill.

49. Cookie Sewell email to unknown, 4 January 2002; "Enemy's Method of Capturing Helicopters," 5AF Intelligence Summary (5 September 1952), vol. 3, no. 4, 60–62.

Chapter 10

1. This area has not been explored. There are twenty to thirty files on specific air-to-ground incidents at NARACP.

2. Joe Clark, "Not Quite a Hero," unpublished manuscript, 75.

3. As is noted elsewhere, ground sited radar on Cho-do Island gave the pilots some basic information about the MiGs. IFF (Identification Friend or Foe) is a transmitting device from World War II that sent coded signals to ground based radar that helped ground controllers detect and identify friendly aircraft when it was working and when it was turned on.

4. Interview, Bruno Giordano with author, 20 February 2002. Five or six years later, Giordano related this story over drinks at the Officer's Club bar in Tripoli to another F-86 pilot. That pilot, Lonnie Moore, confirmed that he was the pilot of the story; Thompson and McLaren, *MiG Alley*, 152–53; Muhurin, *Honest John*, 74.

5. Harold Fisher with Penny Wilson, *Dream of Aces: The Hal Fischer Story, Korea and Vietnam* (Dallas: Great Impressions, 2001), 107.

6. Fischer, *Dreams of Aces*, 107–8. Joe Clark to author, 11 February 2002; Clark, "Not Quite a Hero," 205; Charles Cleveland interview with author, 3 April 2000; P. C. Davis to author, 15 February 2002; William Dunbar to author, 30 April 2002; Robert McIntosh to author, 6 March 2002; Robert Makinney to author, 11 February 2002; Richard Merian to author, 25 February 2002; Earl Payne to author, 17 April 2002; Wesley Tillis to author, February 2002. Of the sixty or so F-86 pilots I interviewed, nine relate incidents of F-86s firing on other F-86s. Even discounting some of these as rumor or duplication, clearly this indicates a serious problem.

7. In the Eighth Air Force in World War II, about 10 percent of damage on returning bombers was caused by "friendly fire," either self inflicted or by other bombers in the formation.

8. Arthur O'Connor to author, 31 May 2002. Miller was captured but died at the end of the war in a truck accident as the prisoners were being exchanged.

9. Dale Smiley interview with author, 12 March 2002; Clark, "Not Quite a Hero," 232.

10. Frederick Blesse interview with author, 29 August 2002.

11. John Melady, *Korea: Canada's Forgotten War* (Toronto: Macmillan, 1983), 119–21, 130; Fischer, *Dreams of Aces*, 158. The shooter was taken off combat duty and was killed shortly afterwards in an aircraft accident.

12. John Lowery, "MiG Fever," in *The F-86 Sabre Jet and Pilots*, Barbara Stahura, ed. (Paducah, Ky.: Turner, 1997), 49.

13. Robert Windoffer to author, March 2002; Windoffer to author, 17 April 2003.

14. Lowery, "MiG Fever," 49.

15. USAF Korean War Victory Credits. The USAF credits Frailey with one MiG destroyed on 26 May 1953; Dennis Flynn interview with author, 10 Mar 2002; Giordano interview with author; Lowery, "MiG Fever," 49, 52–53; essentially the same account is John Lowery, "MiG Fever," *Air and Space* (April/May 1999), 16.

16. Foster, *MiG Alley to Mu Ghia Pass*, 60; Mahurin, *Honest John*, 66; Zhang, *Red Wings over the Yalu*, 141, 258n69.

17. P. C. Davis to author, 14 February 2002. The downed pilots were Paul Turner and Ed Heller; P. C. Davis to author, 15 February 2002; John Sherwood, *Officers in Flight Suits: The Story of American Air Force Fighter Pilots in the Korean War* (New York: New York University, 1996), 87–88; William Dunbar to author, 30 April 2002; Clark, "Not Quite a Hero," 70–71, 86, 100, 110–11.

18. Francis Gabreski, "[End of Tour] Report by Colonel Francis S. Gabreski," 8 July 1952, 4 HRA K720.131-2.

19. William Borders, MiG Fights in Korea.

20. United States Air Force Statistical Digest: fy 1953, 32 HRA K134.11-6. These were the average number of aircraft possessed by committed units (in action), as contrasted to the much higher number of aircraft present throughout the theater including non-committed units.

21. USAF Report on Korea: A Summary of Combat Operations, 1 July 1951–30 June 1952, 12; USAF Report on Korea: A Summary of Combat Operations: 1 July 1952–27 July 1953, 23 both HRA 134.78-101.

22. USAF Statistical Digest, fy 1953, 26.

23. "Soviet Fliers in the Korean Sky." These translated Soviet materials indicate 60,450 day sorties and 2,779 night sorties. Also see Zhang, *Red Wings over the Yalu*, 138, 201–2 and Wetterhahn, "The Russians of MiG Alley," 72.

24. USAF Report on Korea: June 1950–June 1951, 33. Unfortunately, there is no comparable data available for the period prior to 1 July 1951. However, the Sabres flew only five thousand effective sorties during this period, or about 6 percent of the total combat sorties; USAF Report on Korea: July 1951–June 1952, 12–13, 64; USAF Report on Korea: July 1952–July 1953, 2, 23–24; Korean War Victory Credits; Korean

Air War Summary, 12 HRA K720.04D-1. United States Air Force, Assistant Chief of Staff, Studies and Analysis, The Relationship between Sortie Ratios and Loss Rates for Air-to-Air Battle Engagements during World War II and Korea, Saber Measures (Charlie), September 1970, 11 AUL MU42210-75. A USAF study during the Vietnam War covering the period July 1951 through the end of the war used seventy-seven thousand U.S. sorties (apparently total F-86 sorties) and forty-one thousand MiG sorties (apparently those sighted, a factor which clearly skewed its results.)

25. Quoted in R. Cargill Hall, "Early Cold War Overflight Programs: An Introduction," in R. Cargill Hall and Clayton Laurie, eds., *Early Cold War Overflights, 1950-1956: Symposium Proceedings*, vol. 1, *Memoirs* (Washington, D.C.: Office of the Historian National Reconnaissance Office, 2003).

26. Jared Crabb Journal, 2 November 1950, fr 0430 USAFA MS-2. Partridge repeated the request about a week later. Futrell, *USAF in Korea, 1950–1953*, 209; Y'Blood, *The Three Wars of Lt. Gen. George E. Stratemeyer*, 253.

27. Y'Blood, *The Three Wars of Lt. Gen. George E. Stratemeyer*, 253.

28. Ibid.

29. Dean Acheson, testimony, Hearings on the Military Situation in the Far East, 82nd Congress, 1st Session, part 3, 1723–24 in Balchen papers, part 2 HRA 168.7053-332; D. Clayton James, *The Years of MacArthur*, vol. 2, *Triumph and Disaster, 1945–1964* (Boston: Houghton Mifflin, 1985), 524–52; Futrell, *USAF in Korea*, 211.

30. Acheson and Marshall testimony, Hearings of the Military Situation in the Far East, part 3, 1723–24; part 5, 3583; Futrell, *USAF in Korea*, 211; James, *Triumph and Disaster*, 525.

31. Davis, *The 4th Fighter Wing in the Korean War*, 133. Sixteen of the fifty-four F-86 pilots I interviewed volunteered this view; none expressed a contrary view. Three others took the same position in their published accounts. I have found only one individual that wrote that he would not allow hot pursuit, Col. Ben Preston, 4th Fighter Interceptor Group commander, July 1951 through mid-March 1952.

32. Mele Vojvodich, "Overflights Conducted During the Korean War," 67 and Samuel Dickens, "RF-86 Sabre Overflights in Asia," 77, both in Hall and Laurie, *Early Cold War Overflights*.

33. Vojvodich, "Overflights," 68.

34. Vojvodich, "Overflights," 75. This is based on the fact that one pilot, Mele Vojvodich, flew ten to fifteen such missions during the last year of the war; F-86 pilots relate the escort missions in Raymond Toliver and Trevor Constable, *Fighter Aces of the U.S.A.* (Fallbrook, Cal.: Aero, 1979), 52; Lt. Gen Thomas McMullen, videotaped USAF Oral Interview, Apr, May, October 1998 HRA 239.0512-2172; William Borders to author, February 2002; Earl Brown to author, 17 March 20002; William Thomas interview with author, 26 May 2002; Houston Tuel interview with author, March 2002.

35. Bruce Hinton to author, 2 June 2002.

36. Dolph Overton, "The Air Force."

37. Glenn Carus, interview with author, 19 February 2002; Fischer, *Dreams of Aces*, 135; McMullen Interview.

38. Walker Mahurin interview with author, June 2000; Mahurin, *Honest John*, 84–85.

39. Jon Halliday, "Air Operations in Korea: The Soviet Side of the Story," in *A Revolutionary War: Korea and the Transformation of the Postwar World*, William Williams, ed. (Chicago: Imprint, 1993), 154–55.

40. Gordon, *Mikoyan-Gurevich MiG-15*, 75; Oleg Sarin and Lev Dvoretsky, *Alien Wars: The Soviet Union's Aggressions Against the World, 1919 to 1989* (Novato, Cal.: Presidio, 1996), 76; Zhang, *Red Wings over the Yalu*, 136.

41. Thompson and McLaren, *MiG Alley*, 53.

42. Interview with Colonel James Hagerstrom, by John Sherwood, 3 February 1995, 13.

43. Davis, *4th Fighter Wing in the Korean War*, 139–40.

44. Frederick Blesse interview with author, 29 August 2002.

45. Robinson Risner, *The Passing of the Night: My Seven Years as a Prisoner of the North Vietnamese* (New York: Random House, 1973), 52.

46. U.S. Senate Committee on Foreign Relations Republican Staff, "An Examination of U.S. Policy Toward POW/MIAs," 23 May 1991, 274, 282.

47. Walker Mahurin interview with author, April 2000; Walker Mahurin interview with author, 23 May 2000; Mahurin, *Honest John*, 68–69.

48. Mahurin, *Honest John*, 88–89; Walker Mahurin Interview, 23 May 2000; Bud Mahurin interview for "Secrets of War," 1997, available at www.acepilots.com/korea_mahurin.html.

49. Blesse interview.

50. Charles Cleveland interview with author, 2 March 2000; Charles Cleveland, lecture to SOS instructors, 3 April 2000.

51. Michael DeArmond interview with author, 2 January 2001. Thyng was correct. DeArmond survived a shoot down and a year and a half in a Communist prison camp to rise to flag grade.

52. USAF Interview with Gen. John Roberts, 10 February 1977, 28 HRA K239.0512-1076.

53. Walter Boyne, "The Forgotten War," *Air Force Magazine* (June 2000), 33.

54. Cleveland Interview, 2 March 2000; Sherwood, *Officers in Flight Suits*, 1. Four of the top aces and five of the other aces admit to crossing the Yalu. There is, of course, some conflicting evidence. For example while Chick Cleveland states that Royal Baker, 4th Fighter Interceptor Group commander between June 1952 and March 1953, "was strictly against crossing the Yalu." John Sherwood writes that at least on one occasion in October 1952 Baker gave implicit permission to cross the river by informing his men to turn off their IFFs; Clyde Gilbert, interview with author 10 February 2002; USAF Oral History Interview, Maj. Gen. John Giraudo, 8–12 January 1985, 84 HRA K239.0512-1630; Sam Jackson interview with author, 9 February 2002; John Kumpf to author, February 2002; USAF Oral Interview, Gen. John Roberts, 10 February 1977, 28 HRA K239.0512-1076; Vincent Stacy interview with author, 7 March 2002. A number of pilots state that many if not most of the aces got kills north of the Yalu.

55. Clark, "Not Quite a Hero"; Foster, *MiG Alley to Mu Ghia Pass*, 70; Hinton interview with author, 2 June 2002

56. Thompson and McLaren, *MiG Alley*, 53; McMullen Interview; Cecil Foster interview with author, 25 January 2003. The fracas concerning Dolph Overton also may have played a role in this action.

57. USAF Oral History Interview, Maj. Gen. John Giraudo, 8–12 January 1985, 98; Carus Interview. On the other hand there is a rumor that Mitchell disallowed three kills that McConnell scored across the river.

58. John Lowery interview with author, 4 February 2002.

59. Dolph Overton interview with author, 8 November 2000; Overton, "The Air Force"; "Dolph D. Overton, III" (Maxwell Air Force Base Air University), available at www.au.af.mil/au/goe/eaglebios/99bios/overton99.htm.

60. Overton Interview, 8 November 2000; Dolph Overton interview with author, 18 July 2000; Cleveland Interview, 2 March 2000.

61. Mitchell had led the famous Yamamoto mission and had bagged eleven Japanese aircraft in World War II and four in Korea.

62. Jim Mesko, *Air War over Korea* (Carrollton, Tex.: Squadron/Signal, 2000), 53. Some claim Overton was stripped of his victories; Tucker interview with author, 18 June 2002. This former F-86 pilot says that Mitchell took the victories away but was overturned by the claims board.

63. Mesko, *Air War*, 53; Paul Cole, POW/MIA Archive Research Project: Ukraine, Lithuania, Latvia, Estonia, and Berlin, vol. 1, Moscow Research, rev. February 1995, 243n49.

64. Cleveland interview, 8 November 2000.

65. Robert Orr, "Defense and Strategy," *Fortune* (October 1953), 65; Michael McCarthy, "Uncertain Enemies: Soviet Pilots in the Korean War," *Air Power History* (Spring 1997), 37–38. In one case MiGs strafed a Communist pilot about to be rescued by UN helicopters. In May 1951 a Soviet pilot downed in an UN–controlled area committed suicide when faced with capture.

66. Clark, "The Korean Air War Revisited," 72.

67. A passionate and eloquent critique of the border crossing is in Joe Clark's memoir, "Not Quite a Hero," 163, and "The Korean Air War Revisited," 62, 72

68. Headquarters Fifth Air Force, 5th AF Regulation Number 14-4, May 1952 HRA; USAF Victory Credits Korean War.

69. I entered all of the F-86 MiG claims (from the General Orders) into a database. Two General Orders covering 11 individuals and 10.5 claims are unavailable.

70. I arranged the data by chronology into four essentially equal portions based on credits. In the first quarter, 82 percent of kills were claimed by leads; in the second quarter, 80 percent; and in each of the last two quarters, 84 percent.

71. There were forty aces in the war, all but one flying F-86s. Most of their kills were MiG-15s. I listed the aces by their total kills, although my calculations are for their MiG kills.

72. I did not count engagements that began as head-on passes, and listed engagements that began with Communist fighters attacking UN aircraft, not just the F-86s, as Communist initiative.

73. Cecil Foster interview with author, 25 January 2003. Cecil Foster told me that a MiG he claimed as damaged was reassessed by his intelligence officer as destroyed after returning from Seoul. Foster believes that officer consulted with higher ranking intelligence officers who probably used radio intercept information to reevaluate that claim; W. W. Marshall, "MiG Alley," in *Top Guns: America's Fighter Aces Tell Their Stories,* Joe Foss and Matthew Brennan, eds., (New York: Pocket Books, 1991), 264. Another ace called the radio intelligence "another witness."

74. Glenn Carus stated that the cameras worked only 60 percent of the time, Chick Cleveland said 20 percent of the time, and ace Dolph Overton put the figure at 10 percent. Overton says that the film was left over from World War II. Glenn Carus interview with author, 19 February 2002; Charles Cleveland interview with author, 2 March 2000; Dolph Overton interview with author, 18 July 2000. Because of the characteristics of the gun camera photography, analysts concluded that if film captured thirteen hits on the MiG there was a 100 percent certainty of destruction while four hits on film gave a 50 percent certainty. This begs the question, for this seems to be working backward from aircraft assessed as destroyed to the number of hits on film. James Hall, "Statistical Analysis of the Firing Pass," in Institute for Air Weapons Research, "F-86 vs. MiG-15: A Digest of the Briefing on the Analysis of the Korean Air War," 19 May 1954 AUL M34822-14a, 41.

75. FEAF Report on the Korean War, vol. 1, 12–13 HRA 168.7104-52; Operations Analysis Office, "An Analysis of F-86, MiG-15, Engagements September 1952 through April 1953," Memorandum No. 63, 5 June 1953, 1, 8 HRA K720.3101-63.

76. H. E. Collins, "Testing the Russian MiG," in *Test Flying at Old Wright Field,* Ken Chilstrom, ed. (Omaha, Neb.: Westchester House, 1991), 46.

77. OAO, "Analysis of F-86, MiG-15, Engagements," Memo No. 63, 11–12, 13. HRA K720.3101-63.

78. In addition, four MiG pilots bailed out without being hit, two MiGs collided and were destroyed, and one MiG was shot down by a comrade. All seven of these were credited to American pilots as kills.

79. Only two pilots claimed more than one victory this way: USAF ace Pete Fernandez and Marine ace John Bolt.

80. Martha Olson and Richard Sandborn, "Aircraft Attrition in Korea: An Analysis of MiG-15 Effectiveness," Operations Analysis Technical Memorandum No. 31, 11 Feb 1952, 2n1, 6–7 AUL 31622no.31. This study looked at thirty-one Eighth Air Force missions during 1944; Stephen Rosen, *Winning the Next War: Innovation and the Modern Military* (Ithaca, N.Y.: Cornell, 1991), 143. American submariners had a similar problem during World War II.

81. USAF Korean War Victory Credits. The official USAF totals are 841 MiGs destroyed, 800 by F-86s.

82. Joe Clark to author, 23 February 2003; Clark, "Not Quite a Hero"; Cecil Foster interview with author, 25 January 2003; Dale Smiley interview with author,

12 March 2002; Wesley Tillis interview with author, 18 March 2002; Houston Tuel interview with author, 4 March 2002; Alonzo Walter interview with author, 5 March 2002.

83. Gordon, *Mikoyan-Gurevich MiG-15*, 66; Aleksandr Konlobovskii, "Twenty Years in Combat (Part II): A History of the MiG-15 in Combat," *Aerokhobbi* (March 1994); Krylov and Tepsurkayev, "The Hunt for the 'Sabre'"; Diego Zampun, "MiG-15 Fagots over Korea," http://dzamoububiinry/Korea/MigsoverKorea.html; "Soviet Fliers in the Korean Sky," translations on the Soviet Air Force Operations in Korea; Wetter-hahn, "The Russians of MiG Alley," 75. These two sources give Soviet claims at 1,309.

84. Task Force Russia, "The 1059 Document," in Steven L. Sewell, "Russian Claims from the Korean War 1950–53," available at www.korean-war.com/sovietunion.html. The thirty non-USAF aircraft claimed were two Navy F6F-5s and twenty-eight Meteors.

85. Zhang, *Red Wings over the Yalu*, 201.

86. Vladislav Morozov and Serguy Uskov, "On Guard for Peace and Labor," *Mir Aviatsii* (February 1997); Kotloblovskii, "Twenty Years in Combat"; "Soviet Fliers in the Korean Sky"; Zampini, "Mig-15 Fagots over Korea."

87. Gordon, *Mikoyan-Gurevich Mig-15*, 66–67.

88. Wetterhan, "Russians of MiG Alley," 65. For the various numbers of credits for Pepelyaev see Gordon, *Mikoyan-Gurevich MiG-15*, 66–67 and Gordon and Rig-mant, *Mig-15*, 134, 138.

89. USAF Statistical Digest fy 1953, 28. In addition to the 139 air-to-air losses, the USAF listed 550 losses to antiaircraft fire, 472 to non-enemy action on operational missions and 305 in two categories of unknown and missing. I estimate that about 100 F-86s were lost in air-to-air combat.

Chapter 11

1. USAF Credits for the Destruction of Enemy Aircraft, World War II, USAF Historical Study no. 85, 1978. Hereafter cited as USAF World War II Victory Credits.

2. The thousand pilots are a rough estimate based on Mike Spick, *The Ace Factor: Air Combat and the Role of Situational Awareness* (Annapolis, Md.: Naval Institute Press, 1988), 128 and a small, rough survey of F-86 veterans, the number of F-86 sorties, and the missions flown by F-86 pilots as of the end of July 1953. United States Air Force Statistical Digest, fy 1953, 36, 94 HRA K134.11-6; USAF Credits for the Destruction of Enemy Aircraft, Korean War, USAF Historical Study no. 81, 1975. Hereafter cited as USAF Korean War Victory Credits. Guy Bordelon was the only Navy ace of the war; he downed five Red aircraft at night flying a F4U Corsair. Raymond Toliver and Trevor Constable, *Fighter Aces of the USA* (Fallbrook, Cal.: Aero, 1979), 307.

3. Toliver and Constable, *Fighter Aces of the USA*, 78, 103, 105, 107, 114, 121, 194, 197, 392.

4. Frederick Blesse, *"Check Six": A Fighter Pilot Looks Back* (New York: Ivy, 1987), 74.

5. Futrell, *USAF in Korea*, 652.

6. W. Harbison, "Critique on the F-86E," Central Fighter Establishment, February–March 1952, 5; Futrell, *USAF in Korea*, 652; USAF Korean War Victory Credits; Flint DuPre, *U.S. Air Force Biographical Dictionary* (New York: Watts, 1965), 12, 52, 76, 113, 150.

7. USAF Korean War Victory Credits; USAF World War II Victory Credits.

8. "Yank Triple Ace Had Hard Time Convincing Brass He Was Pilot," AFM; "McConnell, World's Top Jet Ace, is Killed Testing Plane on Coast," *New York Times* (26 Aug 1954), 20; William Head, "McConnell, Joseph C." in *Air Warfare: An International Encyclopedia*, vol. 2, Walter Boyne, ed. (Santa Barbara, Cal.: ABC Clio, 2002), 402; Frank Olynyk, *Stars and Bars: A Tribute to the American Fighter Ace 1920–1973* (London: Grubb Street, 1995), 435; "Captain Joseph McConnell" www.acepilots.com/korea_mcconnell.html; Robert Hucker, "Joe McConnell— Top Korea Ace," *Air Combat* (May 1980), 13; DuPre, *USAF Biographical Dictionary*, 150.

9. Hucker, "Joe McConnell," 13; "Yank Triple Ace."

10. USAF Korean War Victory Credits; History of the 51st Fighter Interceptor Wing, January–June 1953 HRA K-Wg-51-Hi.

11. "Captain Joseph McConnell," Internet. Barcus knew McConnell who had flown as his wingman on at least one occasion. (There was a Fifth Air Force policy that authorized general officers to fly twice a month.) 51st Tactical Fighter Wing . . . A Combat Unit in Two Wars, 35 HRA K-Wg-51-Hi.

12. USAF Korean War Victory Credits; 51FWg History: January–June 1953.

13. Abbott claims that they were authorized by a "hot pursuit" policy. Dean Abbott, "On Mac's Wing," *SabreJet Classics* (Summer 1999).

14. Abbott, "On Mac's Wing."

15. Capt. Joseph McConnell [report] 18 May 1953 in Davis, *MiG Alley*, 62.

16. Davis, *MiG Alley*, 62. Another wingman, Gilbert Lowder, describes how McConnell saved him on 15 May 1953 by shooting a MiG off his tail in a very close-range battle. Gilbert Lowder in Thompson and McLaren, *MiG Alley*, 115.

17. Abbott, "On Mac's Wing."

18. McConnell, "Ace Tells of Battles."

19. Abbott, "On Mac's Wing."

20. McConnell, "Ace Tells of Battles."

21. There were eight days on which the Air Force claimed ten or more victories. USAF Korean War Victory Credits. Some insist McConnell had additional victories. Houston Tuel relates that McConnell downed two MiGs on a test flight, but lacking witnesses, could not get credit for them. Houston Tuel interview with author, 8 February 2002.

22. "McConnell, World's Top Jet Ace," 20.

23. McConnell, "Ace Tells of Battles."

24. Hucker, "Joe McConnell," 14.

25. McConnell, "Ace Tells of Battles." One can only wonder if this was genuine or ghost written by a USAF public relations officer.

26. Abbott was a brand new pilot, having earned his wings less than a year earlier (in September 1952), who joined the 51st that December. Abbott, "On Mac's Wing"; Pilot's Manual F-86[F], 20 February 1953, 76 NASM Suitland.

27. Glenn Carus interview with author, 19 February 2002; Archie Tucker to author, 18 June 2002; USAF Oral History Interview, Lt. Gen. Thomas McMullen, April, May, October 1998 HRA K239.0512-2172.

28. If this is true, then McConnell was lucky or very clear headed when he punched out of his fighter in April. Interview with Colonel James Hagerstrom by John Sherwood, 3 February 1995, 92.

29. Houston Tuel interview with author, 4 March 2002; USAF Korean War Victory Credits.

30. McConnell was not only a superior combat flyer, he was also highly experienced. At the time of his death he had logged 1,800 total flying hours, just over 1,300 in jets, 677 hours in F-86s, including 34 in the "H" model. McConnell Accident Report, 25 August 1954; Adams, "On Mac's Wing." In 1955 McConnell's life was the subject of perhaps the best non-fiction movie made about the Korean air war, *The McConnell Story* starring Alan Ladd and June Allyson. The film had just been completed when McConnell was killed, which required that the ending be reshot. Head, "McConnell."

31. Fernandez was a consultant for the 1955 McConnell movie. DuPre, *USAF Biographical Dictionary*, 76; Jo Thomas, "Korea Jet Ace Recalled as Modest Hero," *New York Times* (27 October 1980), 16; "The USAF Museum Celebrates Hispanic Heritage Month by Recognizing Manuel 'Pete' Fernandez."

32. The USAF awarded Fernandez the Silver Star for this engagement. Far East Air Forces, General Order no. 244, 21 May 1953 HRA K720.193; General Order no. 143, 20 March 1953, fr 205; USAF Korean War Victory Credits.

33. General Order no. 187, 16 April 1953, fr 0271; General Order no. 244, 21 May 1953, fr 0360; Toliver and Constable, *Fighter Aces of the USA*, 295.

34. USAF Korean War Victory Credits.

35. DuPre, *USAF Biographical Dictionary*, 76; "USAF Museum Celebrates Hispanic Heritage Month"; Fritz McAden, "Hero Dies with Honor," *Dayton Daily News* (23 November 1980), 2-F.

36. McAden, "Hero Dies with Honor."

37. McAden, "Hero Dies with Honor"; Thomas, "Korea Jet Ace Recalled as Modest Hero."

38. Boyne, *Aces in Command*, 141; Mesko, *Air War over Korea*, 54.

39. Thomas DeJarnette, 4th Fighter-Interceptor Group, "Operations in MiG Alley," 17 July 1953, iii HRA 4FWg History, January–June 1953.

40. DeJarnette, "4FIG Operations in MiG Alley," iv.

41. Bruno Giordano interview with author, 19 February 2002; John Hoye interview with author, 28 February 2002; James Magill interview with author, 20 April 2003.

42. Toliver and Constable, *Fighter Aces of the USA*, 294; Earl Brown interview with author, 17 March 2002; Magill interview.

43. Larry Milberry, *The Canadair Sabre* (Toronto: CANAV, 1986), 98; Bruno Giordano interview with author 6 March 2002.

44. A number of secondary sources credit Jabara with more World War II aerial victories than does the official USAF victory list. "Lieutenant Colonel James Jabara, USAF," available at www.wpafb.af.mil/museum/afp/jjbio.htm; USAF World War II Victory Credits; William Allmon, "Air Ace of the Korean War" [Jabara], available at www.military.com/Contents/MoreContent?file=Prkorace.

45. "Lt. Col. James Jabara, USAF"; Allmon, "Air Ace of the Korean War."

46. USAF Oral History Interview, Gen. John Meyer, July 1975, 1–2 HRA K239.0512-894; Craig Miner, "James Jabara: Hero," available at www.wingsoverkansas.com/archives/profiles6-2000.html.

47. Meyer interview, 2; USAF Korean War Victory Credits.

48. Lon Walter, "The First Ace is Crowned,'" *SabreJet Classics* (Summer 1998); James Jabara, "First Jet Ace" *The Catholic Digest* (August 1951), 17.

49. James Jabara interview, 21 May 1951 HRA K239.0512-648; Walter, "First Ace is Crowned"; John Dille, "The Jets' First Ace," *Life* (4 June 1951), 136,139.

50. Dille, "Jets' First Ace," 139.

51. Jabara interview, 21 May 1951; Jabara, "First Jet Ace," 17; Allmon, "Air Ace of the Korean War"; Dille, "Jets' First Ace," 139; Walter, "First Ace is Crowned"; Miner, "James Jabara: Hero."

52. Diego Zampini, "Sabre Ace." Available at dzampini.800m.ru/korea/sabreaceng.htm.

53. Sam Jackson interview with author, 9 February 2002; John Lowery interview with author, 4 February 2002; "Maj. James Jabara," available at www.acepilots.com/korea_jabara.html; Dennis Flynn interview with author, 10 March 2002.

54. Giordano interview with author, 6 March 2002; Bruno Giordano interview, 20 February 2002 and 25 October 2004; Flynn interview, 10 March 2002; John Lowery interview with author, 31 January 2002.

55. Bruno Giordano interview with author, Mar 2002; Bruno Giordano interview with author 25 October 2004. Only one of Jabara's fifteen kills was officially listed as not been fired on, the first of two credits he got on 26 May 1953. General Order no. 292, 18 June 1953, fr 0435.

56. Milberry, *Canadair Sabre*, 98.

57. Lon Walter, "Recollections of James Jabara," SabreJet Classics (Summer 1998).

58. Meyer Interview, July 1975, 1.

59. Columbia University Oral Interview with James Jabara, December 1960, 13 HRA K146.24-55; USAF Korean War Victory Credits; Allmon, "Air Ace of the Korean War"; "First Jet versus Jet Aces," available at www.wpafb.af.mil/museum/history/korea/ke17.htm.

60. USAF World War II Victory Credits; 4FIW History: November 1951; DuPre, *USAF Biographical Dictionary*, 52; Brunning, *Crimson Sky*, 180, 183; Bill Hess, "King of MiG Alley," *Air Classics* (February 1965), 15–16; William Oliver, *The Inner Seven: The History of Seven Unique American Combat "Aces" of World War II and Korea* (Paducah, Ky.: Turner, 1999), 25; Olynyk, *Stars and Bars*, 224.

61. USAF Korean War Victory Credits; Bruning, *Crimson Sky*, 183; Foss and Brennan, *Top Guns*, 270.

62. Bruning, *Crimson Sky*, 181,182.

63. Alfred Dymock quoted in Bruning, *Crimson Sky*, 185.

64. Claude Mitson quoted in Bruning, *Crimson Sky*, 185,186; USAF Oral Interview with Maj. Gen. F. C. "Boots" Blesse, 14 February 1977, 29 HRA K239.0512-1077.

65. Blesse, *"Check Six,"* 71; Bruning, *Crimson Sky*, 186; Hess, "King of MiG Alley," 14–15.

66. Littlefield's eyewitness version contrasts with secondary sources and the Medal of Honor citation that claim Davis was shooting at a third MiG when he was hit. William Littlefield quoted in Blesse, *"Check Six,"* 71–72; DuPre, *USAF Biographical Dictionary*, 52–53; Bruning, *Crimson Sky*; 186–88.

67. Richard Creighton quoted in Bruning, *Crimson Sky*; 189.

68. Blesse interview, 14 February 1977, 29; William Littlefield quoted in Davis, *4th Fighter Wing in the Korean War*, 113.

69. Zhang, *Red Wings over the Yalu*, 163–68.

70. "Davis–Air Force"; "Air Force Defends Sabre Jet Record," *Lubbock Evening Journal* (13 Feb 1952); "Davis Hoped War Would Be Last One"; "Mrs. Davis Claims Ace Never Given Chance," all four in HRA reel no. 33776.

71. TWX CG FEAF Tokyo Japan to HQ USAF Washington HRA reel no. 33776.

72. "FEAF Leader Weyland Pays Tribute to Maj. Davis's Deeds." The USAF established the original policy of sending aces home on 1 June 1951, modified it in December 1951 to allow aces to volunteer to stay in the theater. On 4 February 1952 the Fifth Air Force changed the policy to require all pilots to fly one hundred missions. "Policy Providing for the Return of Jet Aces from FEAF to the ZI has been Rescinded"; TWX CG FEAF Tokyo Japan to HQ USAF Washington both in reel no. 33776; "Air Force Defends Sabre Jet Record."

73. Royal Baker, Report on F-86 Operations in Korea, 1 April 1953, 1 HRA K-Gp-4-Su-Op; USAF World War II Victory Credits; DuPre, *USAF Biographical Dictionary*, 12–13; Olynyk, *Stars and Bars*, 125.

74. Chronology of the 4th Tactical Fighter Wing from 1942, 24 HRA K-Wg-4-Hi; USAF Korean War Victory Credits; DuPre, *USAF Biographical Dictionary*, 13; Olynyk, *Stars and Bars*, 125.

75. Frederick Blesse interview with author, 29 August 2002; Flynn interview, 10 March 2002; Jackson interview, 9 February 2002; John Ludwig interview with author, 13 September 2002; John Lowery to author, 5 February 2002; James Magill interview with author, 30 April 2003.

76. Olynyk, *Stars and Bars*, 125.

Chapter 12

1. Blesse, *"Check Six,"* 67, chaps 2–8; USAF Credits for the Destruction of Enemy Aircraft, Korean War, USAF Historical Study No. 81, 1975. Hereafter cited as

USAF Korean War Victory Credits; West Point Alumni Association, 1971 *Register of Graduates and Former Cadets of the United States Military Academy* (Chicago: R. R. Donnelley and Sons, 1971), 542, 557; Boyne, *Aces in Command*, 110–25.

2. USAF Korean War Victory Credits; Blesse, *"Check Six,"* 71, 74–75; Frederick Blesse interview for "Secrets of War," interview no. S3234, 1997, available at www.secretsofwar.com/experts/blesse1.html; Frederick Blesse interview with author, 29 August 2002; Charles Cleveland interview with author, 3 April 2000.

3. Blesse, *"Check Six,"* 77; Rosen, *Winning the Next War*, 141. The navy used a similar policy with submarine commanders during World War II, giving skippers no more than two patrols to prove themselves.

4. Frederick Blesse, "No Guts, No Glory," USAF Fighter Weapons School, no. 1, 64 AUL Ref 358.4 A29833n.

5. Blesse, *"Check Six,"* 80; USAF Korean War Victory Credits.

6. Blesse, *"Check Six,"* 85, 82–84; Blesse interview, 29 August 2002; Earl Brown, "Memories of Great Fighter Pilots: Frederick C. 'Boots' Blesse," *SabreJet Classics* (Spring 2000).

7. Blesse, *"Check Six,"* 85.

8. Ibid., 86.

9. Ibid., 94; Boyne, *Aces in Command*, 138. USAF records do not indicate a loss or a helicopter rescue on 17 September 1952.

10. Blesse, *"Check Six,"* 96, 94–95; Blesse interview "Secrets of War," 1997; Boyne, *Aces in Command*, 138.

11. Blesse, *"Check Six,"* 96.

12. Ibid., 99; Blesse interview "Secrets of War," 1997.

13. Blesse, *"Check Six,"* 97.

14. Ibid., 99–105, 108, 113–14; Maj. Gen. Frederick Blesse, Biography United States Air Force, HRA reel no. 23234; Blesse interview, 29 August 2002; "Jet Ace from West Point, Frederick C. Blesse," available at www.wpafb.af.mil/museum/history/korea/kc15.htm.

15. Blesse interview 1997; Blesse, *"Check Six,"* 9–10, 78–79; Brown, "Memoirs of Great Fighter Pilots"; Boyne, *Aces in Command*, 138.

16. The manual was "No Guts, No Glory" and the book, *"Check Six."* Blesse interview, 14 February 1977, 17; Blesse interview, "Secrets of War," 1997.

17. Headquarters Far East Air Forces, General Order No. 387, fr 0539 HRA K720.193; James Goodson, *Tumult in the Clouds* (New York: St. Martin's, 1983), 129; Oliver, *Inner Seven*, 53–54, 59–61; Art Brewster, "Jet Methuselah," [unknown] (1 August 1953) AFM.

18. The quoted portion is from Davis, *4th Fighter Wing in the Korean War*, 149. Vermont Garrison, [after action report], 5 June 1953 in Davis, *MiG Alley*, 67–68; Oliver, *The Inner Seven*, 62–63; USAF Korean War Victory Credits.

19. Davis, *4th Fighter Wing in the Korean War*, 191; Oliver, *The Inner Seven*, 64–65.

20. Flint DuPre, *U.S. Air Force Biographical Dictionary* (New York: Watts, 1965), 116; Olynyk, *Stars and Bars*, 364.

21. Carter clearly was well thought of as a wingman as he flew that position on eight of Johnson's ten kills, and on some of Baker's thirteen. He is credited with two

half kills. USAF Korean War Victory Credits; Davis, *4th Fighter Wing in the Korean War*, 173–74; Thompson and McLaren, *MiG Alley*, 87–88; Olynyk, *Stars and Bars*, 364.

22. General Order no. 391, 20 October 1953, fr 0484; DuPre, *USAF Biographical Dictionary*, 174; John Lowery to author 4 March 2002; Olynyk, *Stars and Bars*, 461.

23. Harold Fischer, "My Ten MiGs," *SabreJet Classics* (Winter 1998); Fischer, *Dreams of Aces*, chaps. 1–7; Olynyk, *Stars and Bars*, 268.

24. Fischer, *Dreams of Aces*, 89.

25. Ibid., 92, 93.

26. Lindsay claimed a MiG and stated that the pilot had ejected. The USAF awarded one victory credit that day, to Fischer. While there may in fact have been two MiGs downed, with the parachute Fischer observed from Lindsay's claim, it is also possible that there was only one Communist fighter that both Sabre pilots engaged. Fischer, *Dreams of Aces*, 97–100; USAF Korean War Victory Credits.

27. Fischer, *Dreams of Aces*, 114, 115.

28. Ibid.

29. General Order no. 223, 7 May 1953; Fischer, *Dreams of Aces*, 115–17.

30. USAF Korean War Victory Credits; Fischer, *Dreams of Aces*, 125–28.

31. Fischer, *Dreams of Aces*, 137–39.

32. Various sources give different spellings: Decai, De-Cai, Decha. Fischer, "My Ten MiGs"; Fischer, *Dreams of Aces*, [preface], 202; Olynyk, *Stars and Bars*, 268; Thompson and McLaren, *MiG Alley*, 182; Zhang, *Red Wings over the Yalu*, 192.

33. These included F-86 pilots Ed Heller, Andy MacKenzie, and Ronald Parks. Oylynk, *Stars and Bars*, 268; Fischer, *Dreams of Aces*, chaps 17–19.

34. Fischer, *Dreams of Aces*, [preface].

35. Glenn Carus interview with author, 19 February 2002; P. C. Davis to author, 6 March 2001; Archie Tucker interview with author, 18 June 2002.

36. The secondary sources give the mission total as low as 30 missions, Dan Allsup, "Parr for the Cross," *Legion Magazine* vol. 149, no.3; John Lowery, "Captain Ralph S. Parr, Double Jet Ace," in *The F-86 Sabre Jet and Pilots*, Barbara Stahura, ed. (Paducah, Ky.: Turner, 1997), 54; Ross Buckland, "Shooter's Odds," *SabreJet Classics* (Spring 1997); one says 37, Olynyk, *Stars and Bars*, 491; and two others 47, Toliver and Constable, *Fighter Aces of the USA*, 308; John Frisbee, "The Pinnacle of Professionalism," *Air Force Magazine* (February 1987). While the precise number may be in dispute, the basic fact is that Parr downed a lot of MiGs in a short time, at a rate unmatched by all but Dolph Overton.

37. DuPre, *USAF Biographical Dictionary*, 185; Lowery, "Captain Ralph S. Parr Double Jet Ace," 55; Olynyk, *Stars and Bars*, 491.

38. Capt. Ralph Parr [after action report] in Davis, *MiG Alley*, 65.

39. Parr After Action Report, 64–67; Lowery, "Captain Ralph S. Parr Double Jet Ace," 54–56; Buckland, "Shooter's Odds."

40. Lowery, "Captain Ralph S. Parr Double Jet Ace," 56–57.

41. Allsup, "Parr for the Cross."

42. Lowery, "Captain Ralph S. Parr Double Jet Ace," 57–58; Wagner, *North American Sabre*, 76; Davis, *4th Fighter Wing in the Korean War*, 186–87.

43. Frisbee, "Pinnacle of Professionalism"; "Ralph Parr" Maxwell biography.

Chapter 13

1. Foster, *MiG Alley to Mu Ghia Pass*, chaps 1–4; Olynyk, *Stars and Bars*, 278.

2. Foster, *MiG Alley to Mu Ghia Pass*, 34–39; Cecil Foster, "Nine Was Enough: My Favorite Sabre Stories," *SabreJet Classics* (Winter 1993); Cecil Foster quoted in Larry Davis, *MiG Alley*, 49–50.

3. Foster, *MiG Alley to Mu Ghia Pass*, 41, 40.

4. Ibid., 40–42; Foster, "Nine Was Enough."

5. Foster, *MiG Alley to Mu Ghia Pass*, 56, 54–55.

6. Ibid., 56–58; Foster, "Nine Was Enough."

7. Foster, *MiG Alley to Mu Ghia Pass*, 59–61.

8. Ibid., 66–67.

9. Foster, *MiG Alley to Mu Ghia Pass*, 68–70; Foster, "Nine Was Enough."

10. Ibid., 70–72.

11. Ibid., 2, 148.

12. Dorr, *F-86 Sabre*, 113; Robert Dorr and Warren Thompson, *The Korean Air War* (Osceola, Wisc.: Motorbooks, 1994), 131; Olynyk, *Stars and Bars*, 410.

13. Frederick Blesse interview for "Secrets of War," interview no. 3234, 1997; Glenn Carus interview with author, 19 February 2002; Dolphin Overton interview with author, 8 November 2000; USAF Oral History Interview with Gen. John Roberts, 10 February 1977, 60 HRA K239.0512-1076; John Ludwig to author, 13 September 2002; William Thomas interview with author, 26 May 2002; USAF Credits for the Destruction of Enemy Aircraft Korean War, USAF Historical Study No. 81, 1975. Hereafter cited as USAF Korean War Victory Credits.

14. Duncan Curtis, *North American F-86 Sabre* (Wiltshire, UK: Crowood, 2000), 78; USAF Korean War Victory Credits.

15. This gives an interesting view of what it was like in the Fourth Group. James Salter, *The Hunters* (New York: Harper, 1956). Also see Salter's postwar memoir, *Burning the Days: Recollections* (New York: Random House, 1997).

16. The movie resembles the book little except in title and the characters' names. Dorr, *F-86 Sabre*, 114, 116; Curtis, *North American F-86 Sabre*, 78; Davis, *4th Fighter Wing in the Korean War*, 112; Dorr and Thompson, *Korean Air War*, 131.

17. USAF Korean War Victory Credits; Curtis, *North American F-86 Sabre*, 78–79; Dorr, *F-86 Sabre*, 116.

18. Curtis, *North American F-86 Sabre*, 79.

19. Ibid., 79; Dorr, *F-86 Sabre*, 117; Toliver and Constable, *Fighter Aces of the USA*, 305.

20. William Dunbar interview with author, 30 April 2002; Robert Ingalls interview with author, 12 April 2002; James Magill interview with author, 30 April 2003; Houston Tuel interview with author, 4 March 2002.

21. It is unclear if a SAM or a MiG-21 downed Low. James Kasler and Robinson Risner were two other Korean War aces also shot down and captured by the North Vietnamese. Curtis, *North American F-86 Sabre*, 79; Olynyk, *Stars and Bars*, 410.

22. Interview with Col. James Hagerstrom by John Sherwood, 3 February 1995, 1, 9; Oliver, *Inner Seven*, 69–70, 73; Olynyk, *Stars and Bars*, 313.

23. Hagerstrom interview, February 1995, 13–15.

24. Ibid., 15–17.

25. Ibid., 1, 4.

26. Oliver, *Inner Seven*, 75.

27. Hagerstrom interview, February 1995, 85; Oliver, *Inner Seven*, 76–77.

28. Oliver, *Inner Seven*, 77–79.

29. Hagerstrom interview, February 1995, 93–94; Thompson and McLaren, *MiG Alley*, 125.

30. Hagerstrom interview, February 1995, 84–86, 88–92.

31. USAF Korean War Victory Credits; Francis Gabreski, *Gabby: A Fighter Pilot's Life* (New York: Orion, 1991), chaps. 1–12; "Biography: Colonel Francis S. Gabreski, USAF (Ret.)" AFM; Olynyk, *Stars and Bars*, 285–86.

32. There are a number of versions of this action that vary in specific details. General Order no. 388, 13 August 1951 HRA K720.193; Maurice Allward, *F-86 Sabre* (London: Ian Allan, 1978), 35; Gabreski, *Gabby*, 222–23; Oliver, *Inner Seven*, 48; Edward Sims, *Fighter Tactics and Strategy, 1914–1970* (New York: Harper and Row, 1972), 223–25. Gabreski's wingman's account also differs on several minor details. Robert Makinney, "B-29 Escort in Korea," *SabreJet Classics* (Spring 2000).

33. Gabreski, *Gabby*, 227, 229; Gabreski Biography; Oliver, *Inner Seven*, 48.

34. General Order no. 198, 26 April 1952; Gabreski, *Gabby*, 238–39; Oliver, *Inner Seven*, 48; Maj. William Whisner quoted in Davis, *MiG Alley*, 27, states that the pilot ejected, while I have followed the details in the confirmation order.

35. Gabreski, *Gabby*, 244–45; Report by Col. Francis S. Gabreski, 8 July 1952, 2 HRA K720.131-2.

36. Gabreski biography.

37. Clark, "Not Quite a Hero"; William Johnson interview with author, 14 February 2002; Richard Merian interview with author, 25 February 2002; Earl Payne interview with author, 17 April 2002; Dale Smiley interview with author, 12 March 2002; Wesley Tillis interview with author, 18 March 2002.

38. USAF Korean War Victory Credits; Oliver, *Inner Seven*, 97–105; Olynyk, *Stars and Bars*, 631.

39. Oliver, *Inner Seven*, 108.

40. John Frisbee, "A Very Special Ace," *Air Force Magazine* (June 1990); Oliver, *Inner Seven*, 107–9.

41. Oliver, *Inner Seven*, 83–89, 95; Olynyk, *Stars and Bars*, 593.

42. Harrison Thyng, "The Operation of the 4th Fighter Wing in Korea" HRA K720.131; John Frisbee, "A Thyng of Valor," *Air Force Magazine* (January 1989), 111; Oliver, *Inner Seven*, 90–91.

43. Frisbee, "A Thyng of Valor," 111; Oliver, *Inner Seven*, 91–93; Olynyk, *Stars and Bars*, 593.

44. William Thomas interview with author, 26 May 2002; Larry Davis, "The Bloody Great Wheel!: Harrison R. Thyng," *SabreJet Classics* (Winter 2002), 16–17; Stahura, *F-86 Sabre Jet and Pilots*, 22.

45. Dorr, *F-86 Sabre*, 43.

46. The only American ace in the Korean War who did fly an F-86 was Navy Lieutenant Guy Bordelon who earned his five credits flying an F4U at night.

47. Marine Corps Historical Center, Oral Interview, John Bolt, tape number 10668. This interview was published as Bruce Gamble, "Time Flies . . . The Oral History of Lt. Col. John F. Bolt, USMC (Ret.)," [Naval Aviation] *Foundation* (Spring 1993), (Fall 1993) which hereafter is cited as Bolt Interview. Olynyk, *Stars and Bars*, 152; Ed Wright, "An Ace Among Aces," *Naval Aviation News* (May–June 2003), 45.

48. Bolt Interview, 95, 98–99; Bolt quoted in Eric Hammel, *Aces at War* (Pacifica, Cal.: Pacifica, 1997), 222; Philip Kaplan, *Fighter Pilot: A History and a Celebration* (New York: Barnes and Noble, 1999), 245.

49. Bolt Interview, 99; Bolt quoted in Davis, *MiG Alley*, 68; Hammel, *Aces at War*, 222–23; Kaplan, *Fighter Pilot*, 248; Wright, "Ace Among Aces," 45.

50. Bolt Interview, 103–4; Bolt quoted in Davis, *MiG Alley*, 68; Hammel, *Aces at War*, 228–29; Oliver, *Inner Seven*, 20–21; "Two Aces in Korean Air War," *Naval Aviation News* (September 1953), 16.

51. Bolt quoted in Davis, *MiG Alley*, 68.

52. Bolt Interview, 104; Hammel, *Aces at War*, 229; Oliver, *Inner Seven*, 21; Olynyk, *Stars and Bars*, 152.

Chapter 14

1. The reverse was not the case, for in the years since World War II the USAF has fielded a number of Navy aircraft including the A-7, B-66, and of course the F-4.

2. James Paul and Martin Spirit, "Korean War: The Air War," available at www.britains-smallwars.com/korea/air-war.html.

3. USAF Credits for the Destruction of Enemy Aircraft Korean War, USAF Historical Study No. 81, 1975. Hereafter cited as USAF Korean War Victory Credits; King Accident Report, 4 June 1953; Ryan Accident Report, 5 June 1953. Accident reports can be found at HRA. "Korean War: The Air War"; Grant Hammond, *The Mind of War: John Boyd and American Security* (Washington, D.C.: Smithsonian, 2001), 37; W. Harbison, "Critique on the F-86E," Central Fighter Establishment, February–May 1952; Evans, *Sabre Jets Over Korea*, 215; J. H. R. Merifield, "Sabre vs. MiG," *RAF Quarterly* (July 1953), 251.

4. South Africans of Number 2 Squadron flew F-86 fighter-bombers while attached to the 18th Fighter Bomber Wing. USAF Korean War Victory Credits; Curtis, *North American F-86 Sabre*, 75; Jim Hanford, "Sabres in Combat," *Yankee Wings* (November/December 1993), 11; Milberry, *The Canadair Sabre*, 93, 96–97, 102; John

Melady, *Korea: Canada's Forgotten War* (Toronto: Macmillan, 1983), 120; Christopher Shores, *Air Aces* (Novato, Cal.: Presido, 1983), 166.

5. The Navy credits Schirra with one victory, Simpson Evans with one, and Paul Pugh with two. However, the USAF credits Evans and Pugh with one victory each. USAF Korean War Victory Credits; Cagle and Manson, *Sea War in Korea*, 526; D. C. Bennett (National Museum of Naval Aviation) interview with author, 11 February 2001.

6. USAF Korean War Victory Credits; Bruce Gamble, "The Oral History of Lt. Col. John F. Bolt, USMC (Ret.)" [National Museum of Naval Aviation] *Foundation* (Fall 1993), 99.

7. "John Glenn: USMC Sabre Jet Pilot, Astronaut," available at www.acepilots.com/korea_glenn.html; *Above and Beyond: The Encyclopedia of Aviation and Space Sciences* (Chicago: New Horizons, 1968), vol. 6, 983; Richard Hallion, *The Naval Air War in Korea*, 114; Glenn Infield, "The Day John Glenn Almost Died Over Korea," in *Fighting Aces*, Phil Hirsch, ed. (New York: Pyramid, 1965), 117.

8. John Glenn, *John Glenn: A Memoir* (New York: Bantam, 1999), 141–42.

9. Far East Air Forces, General Order no. 356, 17 August 1953 HRA K720.193; Askold Germon, *Red Devils on the 38th Parallel* (Kiev: unknown, 1998, translation 2000), 348; Glenn, *John Glenn*, 144.

10. Boyd flew twenty-two missions in Korea but never got to shoot at a MiG. Later at the Fighter Weapons School he established a reputation as the hottest pilot in the Air Force. He went on to develop the "energy-maneuverability" theory, helped design both the F-15 and F-16, and led the Military Reform Movement. Hammond, *The Mind of War*; Infield, "The Day John Glenn Almost Died," 119.

11. Glenn, *John Glenn*, 146,145; Infield, "The Day John Glenn Almost Died," 119–26.

12. General Order no. 356, 17 August 1953; USAF Korean War Victory Credits; "John Glenn."

13. "John Glenn"; USAF Museum, "Maj. John H. Glenn, Jr., Exchange Pilot," available at www.wpafb.af.mil/museum/history/korea/kc20.htm; *Above and Beyond*, vol. 6, 984.

14. This included accidents, non-combat operational losses, and fighter-bomber losses. It is unclear, but the missing probably includes prisoners of war, some of whom later returned home. United States Air Force Statistical Digest: fy 1953, 28 HRA K134.11-6.

15. Chronological Record of Military Service [Thomas Sellers]; Thomas M. Sellers to Commandant of the Marine Corps, sub: "Integration into the Regular Marine Corps," request for, 18 July 1953; Flight Log, VMF-115 [Thomas Sellers]; Individual Flight Record, Thomas Sellers, 336th Ftr-Intcp Sq.

16. Sellers to wife, 5 April 1953. Sellers wrote his wife on average every other day. Sharon MacDonald, Sellers's daughter graciously made sixty of her father's letters and other documents available to the author.

17. Sellers to wife, 9 April 1953.

18. Sellers to wife, 29 April 1953.

19. Sellers to wife, 4 May 1953.

20. Sellers to wife, 16/17 May 1953.

21. Sellers to wife, 29 May 1953.

22. Sellers to wife, 22 June 1953; USAF Korean War Victor Credits. Bolt not only visited Sellers's widow but he also helped answer questions she and (more recently) her daughter had about Sellers's death.

23. Sellers to wife, 29 June 1953.

24. Sellers to wife, 1 July 1953.

25. Sellers to wife, 14 July 1953.

26. Sellers to wife, 17 July 1953.

27. Ibid.

28. Ibid.

29. James Johnson [commander 4FIW] to Mrs. Thomas M. Sellers, 22 July 1953; F. P. Tatum, Head, Casualty Section [USMC] to Mrs. Thomas M. Sellers, 31 July 1953; John Bolt to Mrs. Sellers [5 August 1953]; Albert Dickey to Mrs. Sellers, 27 August 1953; Dean Pogreba to Mrs. Sellers, 3 September 1953. One aspect of the action that is unexplained is why the MiGs fired on Sellers and not on Dickey who was closer to the Communist fighters.

30. According to a third hand source, Sellers's Sabre crashed on the Antung airfield. USAF documents listed the crash site as off the mouth of the Yalu, however, they conducted a twenty-minute search for Sellers 25 km north of Antung airfield. Jack Bolt to Dorothy [Sellers], 7 January 1954; John Bolt to Sharon MacDonald, 30 November 1997; USAF Korean War Victory Credits; General Order no. 13, 22 January 1954; Headquarters, U.S. Marine Corps, Reviewing Officer to Head, Personal Affairs Branch, sub: "Finding of death in the case of Maj. Thomas M. Sellers, O29118, U.S. Marine Corps Reserve," 20 July 1954; A. Hammers, Assistant Head Casualty Section, Military Personnel Services Branch, Personal and Family Readiness Division [USMC] to Sharon MacDonald, 13 December 2000.

31. This is based on my research into the unit and prisoner records. It includes all causes and all F-86s (fighter-bombers as well). It indicates that thirty-nine pilots were killed, thirty listed as missing in action, twenty-eight returned from captivity, two died in prison, and forty-two rescued from the sea or from behind enemy lines.

32. USAF Korean War Victory Credits; Roy Wenzl, "Son Finds the Father He'd Lost," available at www.iwitnesstohistory.org/Felix/felix5.htm; 336th Fighter Squadron History, March 1952, appendix in 4th Fighter Wing History, March 1952.

33. A Russian account of the action that day adds only confusion to the story. Germon, *Red Devils on the 38th Parallel*, 250. USAF Korean War Victory Credits; 336FS History, August 1952 in 4th Fighter Group History, August 1952; Paul Cole, "POW /MIA Research Project: Ukraine, Lithuania, Latvia, Estonia, and Berlin vol. 1: Moscow," available at www.aiipowmia.com/koreacw/mockbacole03.html; Thompson and McLaren, *MiG Alley*, 45; Zampini, "MiG Fagots over Korea," available at www.dzampini.boom.ru/Korea/MiGsoverKorea.htm; Zhang, *Red Wings over the Yalu*, 135–36.

34. USAF Credits for the Destruction of Enemy Aircraft, World War II, USAF Historical Study no. 85. Hereafter cited as USAF World War II Victory Credits. Flint DuPre, *USAF Biographical Dictionary* (New York: Franklin Watts, 1965), 158;

Walker Mahurin, *Honest John* (New York: Putnam's Sons, 1962), 23; Olynyk, *Stars and Bars*, 420; Shores, *Air Aces*, 167.

35. Mahurin, *Honest John*, 40–43.

36. Ibid., 47–48.

37. Mahurin, *Honest John*, 74–75; Olynyk, *Stars and Bars*, 421.

38. Clark, "Not Quite a Hero"; Mahurin, *Honest John*, 89–90, 93–97.

39. The Sabres claimed five MiGs destroyed on this day, four by the 4th. USAF Korean War Victory Credits; Mahurin, *Honest John*, 98–106; Germon, *Red Devils on the 38th Parallel*, 231.

40. Bruning, *Crimson Sky*, 115; DuPre, *USAF Biographical Dictionary*, 158; Olynyk, *Stars and Bars*, 420; Shores, *Air Aces*, 167.

41. Eric Hammel interview with author, 12 March 2002; Ed Heller, "Out of Control," in *Aces in Combat: The American Aces Speak*, vol. 4, Eric Hammel, ed. (Pacifica, Cal.: Pacifica, 1997), 213; Edwin Heller, "All the Way," draft for "Bluenoser Tales."

42. General Order no. 2, 2 January 1953; USAF Korean War Victory Credits; Heller, "All the Way."

43. USAF Korean War Victory Credits; Dolph Overton interview with author, November 2000; Paul Cole, "POW/MIA Archive Research Project," 243n49; Edwin Heller, "I Thought I'd Never Get Home," in Barbara Stahura, ed., *The F-86 Sabre Jet and Pilots* (Paducah, Ky.: Turner, 1997), 40–41; Heller, "Out of Control," 213, 216, 218–21.

44. These included F-86 pilots Lyle Cameron, Harold Fischer, Roland Parks, and Paul Turner. Heller, "I Thought I'd Never Get Home"; Heller, "All the Way"; Appendix C, "Korean War USAF F-86 Pilots Who Were Captured and Repatriated," available at www.nationalalliance.org/korea08.htm. Of the three USAF MiG shoot downs on this date, Fischer's seems to be the most likely although Heller writes that his attacker came at him from a considerable angle, while Fischer writes that the MiG he bagged was "zooming up behind the lone F-86." Fischer, *Dreams of Aces*, 135. USAF Korean War Victory Credits.

45. Germon, *Red Devils on the 38th Parallel*, 297.

46. Ibid.

47. Heller, "Out of Control," 221.

48. 336th Fighter Squadron History, November 1952 in 4FIG History, November 1952; Risner, *Passing of the Night*, 46; Olynyk, *Stars and Bars*, 523; Sherwood, *Officers in Flight Suits*, 15–16.

49. Risner, *Passing of Night*, 48–49; Sherwood, *Officers in Flight Suits*, 86.

50. Risner, *Passing of Night*, 49; Sherwood, *Officers in Flight Suits*, 86.

51. While some secondary sources claim Risner pushed Logan, I find this extremely unlikely if not impossible. Obstruction of the Sabre's nose intake would have stalled the engine if sucking in the streaming fuel and hydraulic fluid did not. Of course, pushing the fighter makes a much better story.

52. Despite some conflicts (and confusion) in the secondary sources, this mission took place on 15 September. The USAF awarded both Logan and Risner the Silver Star for that mission. General Order no. 653, 29 December 1952; Larry Davis,

MiG Alley: Air to Air Combat Over Korea (Carrollton, Tex.: Squadron/Signal, 1978), 42–43, 46; Dorr, et al., *Korean War Aces*, 63–64; Risner, *Passing of Night*, 51–53; Sherwood, *Officers in Flight Suits*, 2–5. Logan had been Felix Asla's wingman on the day he was lost. Thompson and McLaren, *MiG Alley*, 67–68.

53. USAF Korean War Victory Credits; Interview with James Hagerstrom by John Sherwood, 3 February 1995 [date of transcription]; USAF Oral History Interview, BG Robinson Risner, 1–2 Mar 1983, 17 HRA K239.0512-1370; Risner, *Passing of Night*, 53; Charles Gross, "Turning Point: The Air National Guard and the Korean War," 14.

54. Olynyk, *Stars and Bars*, 523.

55. Ibid., 373.

56. Jim Kasler, "Mudder," in *Aces in Combat: The American Aces Speak*," vol. 5, Eric Hammel, ed. (Pacifica, Calif.: Pacifica, 1998), 225–26, 227; Olynyk, *Stars and Bars*, 373.

57. Kasler, "Mudder," 227.

58. Kasler, "Mudder," 227; Raymond Toliver and Trevor Constable, *Fighter Aces of the USA*, (Fallbrook, Cal.: Aero, 1979), 300.

59. John Frisbee, "Valor in Three Wars," *Air Force Magazine* (November 1986), 119; Olynyk, *Stars and Bars*, 373–74.

60. Curtis Burns, "Kincheloe Air Force Base, 16th Anniversary"; James Hagerty, *First of the Spacemen: Iven C. Kincheloe, Jr.* (New York: Duell, Sloan and Pearce, 1960), 45. The Hagerty book is rich on details but contains errors of chronology and other specifics.

61. Hagerty, *First of the Spacemen*, 50.

62. The secondary sources have considerable difficulty with the dates of Kincheloe's victories. USAF Korean War Victory Credits; Burns, "Kincheloe Air Force Base, 16th Anniversary"; Cole, "POW/MIA Archive Research Project," 274; Mahurin, *Honest John*, 71.

63. USAF Korean War Victory Credits, 43.

64. Harris was a World War II veteran who the USAF recalled from his airline job to active duty. He also bagged three MiGs in the air. USAF Korean War Victory Credits; "Captain Iven Kincheloe, Jr.," available at www.edwards.af.mil/history/docs_html/people/bio_kincheloe.html. Clark, "Not Quite a Hero"; Haggerty, *First of the Spacemen*, 47; Wagner, *North American Sabre*, 67.

65. DuPre, *USAF Biographical Dictionary*, 126; Olynyk, *Stars and Bars*, 378; "Captain Iven Kincheloe, Jr."

66. Tom Wolfe, *The Right Stuff* (New York: Farrar, Straus, Giroux, 1979), 77.

67. Clark, "Not Quite a Hero"; DuPre, *USAF Biographical Dictionary*, 126; Mahurin, *Honest John*, 71; Dale Smiley interview with author, 12 March 2002;

68. AAF World War II Victory Credits.

69. Davis was the son of an Army general, a 1936 graduate of West Point, and commander of the 322nd during and after the war. He retired as a two-star general. DuPre, *USAF Biographical Dictionary*, 52.

70. Dan Allsup, "Wingman," *Legion Magazine*, vol. 149, no. 3; William Brown, "A Fighter Pilot's Story," Charles A. Lindbergh Memorial Lecture, 21 May 1992,

NASM; "William Earl Brown, Jr.," available at www.au.af.mil/au/goe/eaglebios/98/brown98.htm.

71. One month later Chandler downed a MiG in an aerial duel. A B-29 night raid on 24 November left 454 bomb craters on the runway, which grounded the Communist fighters. On 15 December they abandoned the field. USAF Korean War Victory Credits; Jarred Crabb Journal, 10–28 November 1951 USAFA MS-2; General Order no. 24, 11 January 1952; Davis, *4th Fighter Wing in the Korean War*, 95–96; No Kum Sok, A *MiG-15 to Freedom*, 102, 106; "Ragland, Dayton William," available at www.taskforceomegainc.org/r002.html.

72. Two other African-American F-86 pilots in the Korean War who flew with the 4th were Fred Davis and Beverly Dunjill; "Ragland, Dayton William"; Earl Brown interview with author, 17 October 2003.

73. Born in April 1919 in Brooklyn, Meyer had enlisted in the Army in November 1939 and earned his commission and wings in July 1940. He went on to four-star rank, retired in July 1974 and died in December 1975. "Biography, United States Air Force: General John C. Meyer," AUL.

74. As throughout this study, the credits are taken from USAF World War II Victory Credits and USAF Korean War Victory Credits.

75. The name "Casey Jones" came from the fact that American radar controllers warned F-86 pilots of MiGs heading their way by radioing that the train (large numbers of MiGs) had left the station (their home base). Hence the use of the name of the crack train engineer for a crack MiG pilot.

76. Foss and Brennan, eds., *Top Guns*, 291–92; Bruce Hinton, "Casey Jones and the Eagle," *SabreJet Classics* (Fall 1995); Curtis, *North American F-86 Sabre*, 30; Wagner, *North American Sabre*, 51–52.

Chapter 15

1. United States Air Force Statistical Digest, fiscal year 1953, 28 HRA K134.11-6; Hans Seidl, *Stalin's Eagles: An Illustrated Study of the Soviet Aces of World War II and Korea* (Atglen, Pa.: Schiffer, 1998), 245.

2. United States Air Force Statistical Digest, fiscal year 1953, 28 HRA K134.11-6; Seidl, *Stalin's Eagles*, 245.

3. USAF Statistical Digest, fy 1953, 28; Allan Magnus, lists of People's Republic of China, North Korea, and USSR Korean War [victory credits], available at www.users.accesscom.ca/magnusfamily/korprc.htm; Al Bowers and David Lednicer, "Fighter Pilot Aces List," www.au.af.mil/awc/awcgate/aces/aces.htm; Curtis, *North American F-86 Sabre*, 83; Andrew Mikhailov [list of Soviet Korean War Aces], available at aeroweb.lucia.it/~agretch/RAFAQ/SovietAces.html; Polak, *Stalin's Falcons*; Seidl, *Stalin's Eagles*, 245.

4. Bowers and Lednicer, "Fighter Pilot Aces List" (16); Curtis, *North American F-86 Sabre*, 83 (16); Mikhailov, [List of Soviet Korean War Aces] (16); Polak, *Stalin's Falcons* (17); Seidl, *Stalin's Eagles*, 245 (15); Mike Spick, *The Complete Fighter Ace: All The World's Fighter Aces, 1914–2000* (London: Greenhill, 1999), 195 (15).

5. Bowers and Lednicer, "Fighter Pilot Aces List"; Magnus, [victory credit list].

6. Anatoli Dokuchayev, "Aces of Jet Wars," *Krasnaya Avezda* (11 March 1995), 6; Polak, *Stalin's Falcons*, 310.

7. Col. Evgeny Pepelyaev quoted in Gordon and Rigmant, *MiG-15*, 135, 138; Aleksandr Kotlobovskiy, "Aces of the World: Yevgeniy Pepelyaev," *Mir Aviatsii* (February 1993), 25–26; Polak, *Stalin's Falcons*, 248; Spick, *Complete Fighter Ace*, 192. While most secondary sources use twenty credits for Pepelyaev's score, lower figures can be found in Dokuchayev, "Aces of Jet Wars" (19); Seidl, *Stalin's Eagles*, 245 (19); and "Soviet Fliers in the Korean Sky," Translations on the Soviet Air Force Operations in Korea (15).

8. Gordon and Rigmant, *MiG-15*, 134–37.

9. Polak, *Stalin's Falcons*, 284–85.

10. Ibid., 300; Igor Gordelianow, "Soviet Air Aces of the Korean War," available at http://aeroweb.lucia.it/~agretch/RAFAQ/SovietAces.html.

11. Bowers and Lednicer, "Fighter Pilot Aces List" (11 or 14); Curtis, *North American F-86 Sabre*, 83 (14); Mikhailov, [List of Soviet Korean War Aces](11 or 14); Polak, *Stalin's Falcons*, 243 (11–15); Seidl, *Stalin's Eagles*, 245 (15); Spick, *Complete Fighter Ace*, 195 (15).

12. Bowers and Lednicer, "Fighter Pilot Aces List" (11 or 14); Curtis, *North American F-86 Sabre*, 83 (14); Mikhailov, [List of Soviet Korean War Aces](11 or 14); Polak, *Stalin's Falcons*, 257 (12 or 14); Seidl, *Stalin's Eagles*, 245 (14); Spick, *Complete Fighter Ace*, 195 (14).

13. Polak, *Stalin's Falcons*, 181; Seidl, *Stalin's Eagles*, 245; Spick, *Complete Fighter Ace*, 193, 195.

14. Kramarenko quoted in Gordon and Rigmant, *MiG-15*, 127–29.

15. Pepelyaev quoted in Gordon and Rigmant, *MiG-15*, 136. Also see page 135; Polak, *Stalin's Falcon's*, 285.

16. The USAF admits only the loss of Crone on 18 June 1951 and in turn claimed the destruction of five MiGs that day. USAF Korean War, Victory Credits; Polak, *Stalin's Falcons*, 308.

17. Bowers and Lednicer, "Fighter Pilot Aces List" (9); Curtis, *North American F-86 Sabre*, 83 (9); Gordon and Rigmant, *MiG-15*, 118 (15); Mikhailov, [List of Soviet Korean War Aces] (9); Polak, *Stalin's Falcons*, 308 (12 to 15); Seidl, *Stalin's Eagles*, 245 (9); Spick, *Complete Fighter Ace*, 195 (15).

18. Gordon and Rigmant, *MiG-15*, 124–26; Polak, *Stalin's Falcons*, 239.

19. Polak, *Stalin's Falcons*, 124.

20. Olynyk, *Stars and Bars*; Polak, *Stalin's Falcons*.

Epilogue

1. Wagner, *North American Sabre*, 92. The only other USAF fighter that has flown more than a half million flying hours in one year was the F-4, which it did twice. Air Force flying safety statistics available at www.afsc.saia.af.mil/AFSC/RDBMS/Flight/stats/[aircraft type]mds.html.

2. North American built 6,233 F-86s and 1,148 FJs. Canadair built 1,815, Commonwealth (Australia) 112, Fiat (Italy) 221, and Mitsubishi (Japan) 300. Dorr, *F-86 Sabre*, 140–41; Wilson, *Sabre, MiG-15 and Hunter*, 9.

3. Compared with the J47 it was shorter and narrower but weighed almost four thousand pounds, one thousand pounds more that the J47. Curtis, *North American F-86 Sabre*, 92.

4. To employ this weapon, the H would use a "loft" (or "toss") bombing technique that employed the low altitude bombing system (LABS) equipment, first seen on the F model. This computer calculated the path the low flying fighter would take to begin an Immelmann and release the bomb toward the target and then allow the fighter to complete the reversal of direction flying away from the bomb blast. Curtis, *North American F-86 Sabre*, 92–93; Knaack, *Post–World War II Fighters*, 67; Wagner, *North American Sabre*, 86, 88.

5. Maintenance was also a problem due primarily to a shortage of parts and lack of experience with the J73. Knaack, *Post–World War II Fighters*, 67; Wagner, *North American Sabre*, 90.

6. Aircraft Accident Cards, HRA; Curtis, *North American F-86 Sabre*, 93–94.

7. Knaack, *Post–World War II Fighters*, 67; Curtis, *North American F-86 Sabre*, 94, 96–98. Wagner, *North American Sabre*, 92.

8. Curtis, *North American F-86 Sabre*, 94, 96.

9. Curtis, *North American F-86 Sabre*, 99–100, 102; Larry Davis, "North American F-86 Sabre," *Wings of Fame*, vol. 10, 83.

10. North American built 2,506 D models and 2,239 F models. Knaack, *Post–World War II Fighters*, 79. The aircraft was originally designated YF-95A for funding purposes (new aircraft being seen in a different way than developments of older ones), but that designation was short lived (December 1949 to July 1950). Alward, *F-86 Sabre*, 116; Wagner, *North American Sabre*, 29–30.

11. Martin Bowman, *Combat Legend: F-86 Sabre* (Ramsbury, UK: Crowood, 2004), 50–51; Curtis, *North American F-86 Sabre*, 41; Knaack, *Post–World War II Fighters*, 69–70.

12. Davis, "North American F-86 Sabre," 64; Taylor, *Combat Aircraft of the World*, 541; Wagner, *North American Sabre*, 29.

13. Curtis, *North American F-86 Sabre*, 41; Davis, "North American F-86 Sabre," 64; Knaack, *Post–World War II Fighters*, 50–51, 75; Swanborough and Bowers, *United States Military Aircraft since 1908*, 423–24, 426.

14. Six men died and two survived the accident. DeBolt Accident Report, 25 August 1952 HRA. Curtis, *North American F-86 Sabre*, 41; Knaack, *Post–World War II Fighters*, 73; Wagner, *American Combat Planes*, 456; Wagner, *North American Sabre*, 29, 31, 40–41.

15. Alward, *F-86 Sabre*, 53; Bowman, *Combat Legend*, 51; Knaack, *Post–World War II Fighters*, 72; Wagner, *American Combat Planes*, 457.

16. Bowman, *Combat Legend*, 52; Curtis, *North American F-86 Sabre*, 58; Knaack, *Post–World War II Fighters*, 72, 75.

17. Knaack, *Post–World War II Fighters*, 73; Taylor, *Combat Aircraft*, 541; Wagner, *North American Sabre*, 35.

18. SAGE automatically relayed information the ground station received to the interceptor, cutting out the previous communication between the ground radar operator and the aircraft.

19. Curtis, *North American F-86 Sabre*, 55; Knaack, *Post–World War II Fighters*, 78–79; Swanborough and Bowers, *U.S. Military Aircraft since 1908*, 424; Wagner, *North American Sabre*, 132. Beginning in 1955 the USAF broke F-86 accident statistics into three categories: D, H, and "others." For the period starting with fiscal year 1955 and ending in fiscal year 1960 the D had thirty major accidents per one hundred thousand flying hours compared with the H and the "other" F-86s that had thirty-nine per one hundred thousand. During this period the Sabre flew about two thirds of its total flying. For the period calendar year 1950 though 1971 the F-86 had a cumulative major accident rate of forty-four per one hundred thousand flying hours. "F-86 History," available at www-afsc.saia.af.mil/AFSC/RDBMS/Flight/stats/f86mds.html; United States Statistical Digest fiscal years 1955–60 HRA K134.11-6.

20. Besides the F-4, more of which were used by the USAF than either of her sister services, these include the A-7 and B-66.

21. One source attributes the naval problems to its "scandalous commitment to the Westinghouse J40 engine that failed utterly and almost paralyzed naval aviation in the early to mid-1950s." Dorr, *F-86 Sabre*, 48. Gordon Swanborough and Peter Bowers, *United States Navy Aircraft since 1911* (New York: Funk & Wagnall, 1968), 179, 232, 285, 385; Swanborough and Bowers, *U.S. Military Aircraft since 1908*, 420.

22. Curtiss, *North American F-86 Sabre*, 118–19.

23. Ibid., 119–20; Wagner, *North American Sabre*, 97–99.

24. Curtiss, *North American F-86 Sabre*, 121; Wagner, *North American Sabre*, 100–101.

25. Dorr, *F-86 Sabre*, 53.

26. The J65 also powered the Air Force's F-84F which also experienced difficulties with that power plant. Dorr, *F-86 Sabre*, 54–57; Knaack, *Post–World War II Fighters*, 39, 41; Wagner, *North American Sabre*, 102–3.

27. Curtis, *North American F-86 Sabre*, 122, 124–25; Wagner, *North American Sabre*, 103, 108.

28. Alward, *F-86 Sabre*, 123; Curtis, *North American F-86 Sabre*, 126, 128; Wagner, *North American Sabre*, 106.

29. Curtis, *North American F-86 Sabre*, 128–29.

30. The Navy flew a Fury designated FJ-4F with rocket boost in the late 1950s. The throttleable Rocketdyne AR-1 engine pushed the craft to an unofficial speed of Mach 1.4 at seventy-one thousand feet. Curtis, *North American F-86 Sabre*, 129–30, 132; Dorr, *F-86 Sabre*, 140; Wagner, *North American Sabre*, 111.

31. Curtis, *North American F-86 Sabre*, 106; Wagner, *North American Sabre*, 112; Wilson, *Sabre, MiG-15 and Hunter*, 46.

296 Notes to Pages 230–33

32. Curtis, *North American F-86 Sabre*, 109; Wagner, *North American Sabre*, 115; Wilson, *Sabre, MiG-15 and Hunter*, 46–47.

33. Wilson, *Sabre, MiG-15 and Hunter*, 47.

34. Bowman, *Combat Legend*, 63; Wilson, *Sabre, MiG-15 and Hunter*, 46, 49.

35. Curtis, *North American F-86 Sabre*, 112–13; Dorr, *F-86 Sabre*, 66; Wilson, *Sabre, MiG-15 and Hunter*, 49.

36. Wilson, *Sabre, MiG-15 and Hunter*, 49, 51.

37. Curtis, *North American F-86 Sabre*, 115; Dorr, *F-86 Sabre*, 67; Wilson, *Sabre, MiG-15 and Hunter*, 51, 54.

38. Bowman, *Combat Legend*, 82.

39. Wagner, *North American Sabre*, 122–23.

40. Alward, *F-86 Sabre*, 94; Knaack, *Post–World War II Fighters*, 77; Wagner, *North American Sabre*, 123–24.

41. Victor Flintham, *Air Wars and Aircraft: A Detailed Record of Air Combat, 1945 to the Present* (New York: Facts on File, 1990), 28. The second dogfight extended 50 miles into North Korea. Bob Stonestreet, "International Incident over the Yellow Sea, Korea—February 5, 1955," *SabreJet Classics* (Fall 1995). The third incident penetrated into China. Dorr, *F-86 Sabre*, 138–39.

42. Chris Bishop, ed., *The Aerospace Encyclopedia of Air Warfare*, vol. 2, *1945 to the Present* (London: Aerospace, 1997), 101; Flintham, *Air Wars and Aircraft*, 248.

43. Although the first of the five fell to a Sidewinder, the inability of American pilots during the Korean War to down more than two MiGs on a single sortie cast doubt on this claim.

44. Curtis, *North American F-86 Sabre*, 167; Flintham, *Air Wars and Aircraft*, 190–91, 195; Lon Nordeen, *Air Warfare in the Missile Age* (Washington, D.C.: Smithsonian, 1985), 79, 86, 90–91; John Fricker, *Battle for Pakistan: The Air War of 1965* (London: Allan, 1979), 12–13, 58, 183–86.

45. Curtis, *North American F-86 Sabre*, 168; Flintham, *Air Wars and Aircraft*, 196, 200–201; Nordeen, *Air Warfare in the Missile Age*, 93, 103, 106.

Bibliographic Essay

Primary Sources

The official USAF records are located at the Historical Research Agency, Montgomery, Alabama. They have the unit records (Far East Air Forces, Fifth Air Force, 4th and 51st Interceptor Wings), development records of the F-86, accident reports, and various studies and reports on the Korean War. The National Archives has microfilm copies of these materials as well as some additional Fifth Air Force files. Material on the development of the Sabre can also be found in Air Force Material Command files at Dayton, Ohio, the Wright Field development records at the Federal Records Center at St. Louis, and North American records in the Boeing archives at Seattle, Washington. The best collection of pilot's manuals (dash one) is located at the National Air and Space Museum facility at Silver Hill, Maryland. Information on the aces can be found at Air Force Museum at Dayton, Ohio.

Internet

There is a variety of material on the subject on the internet, but as with all else on this medium, it is of greatly varied quality that typically lacks support. Nonetheless, valuable materials from the Air Force Museum, Historical Research Agency, and *SabreJet Classics* can be found here. It also has considerable materials on the aces and items that cannot be found elsewhere from the Communist side, however these should be used with considerable caution.

Magazines

There is considerable material of a mixed nature in magazines. In addition to extensive wartime material, more recently the flood of popular aviation publications has yielded some articles on the Korean air war. Of these many periodicals I would emphasize three. *SabreJet Classics* is the organ of the F-86 Sabre Pilots Association that prints interesting and useful first person accounts; the magazine appears on the Internet. Over the years a number of documented articles of value have appeared in what is now known as *Air Power History*. *Wings of Fame*, now defunct, was a lavishly illustrated, large format magazine that printed extended articles on aviation history, albeit, without documentation. A four part series by Warren Thompson is in essence a book that gives an excellent, readable, and well-illustrated account of the air war that appeared in the periodical's first four issues. Larry Davis also published a lengthy, detailed, excellent, and extensively illustrated study of the F-86 in volumes 10 and 11 of that same publication.

Books

There are numerous books that cover the Korean air war. Like much else in aviation history, the focus of most of these is at the basic level of aircraft and flying, with little on analysis or explanation. Very few of these books are documented.

Bibliography

Abbott, Dean. "On Mac's Wing." *SabreJet Classics* (Summer 1999).

Above and Beyond: The Encyclopedia of Aviation and Space Sciences. Chicago: New Horizons, 1968.

Aid, Matthew. "American Comint in the Korean War (Part II): From the Chinese Intervention to the Armistice." *Intelligence and National Security* (Spring 2000).

"Air Force Defends Sabre Jet Record." *Lubock Evening Journal* (13 February 1952).

Allsup, Dan. "Parr for the Cross." *Legion Magazine* 149, no. 3.

———. "Wingman." *Legion Magazine* 149, no. 3.

Allward, Maurice. *F-86 Sabre.* London: Ian Allan, 1978.

Anderson, John. *A History of Aerodynamics.* Cambridge, UK: Cambridge University, 1998.

"The Attack on Electric Power in North Korea." In *Airpower: The Decisive Force in Korea,* James Stewart, ed. Princeton, N.J.: Nostrand, 1957.

Avery, Norm. *North American Aircraft, 1934–1998,* Vol. 1. Santa Ana, Cal.: Narkiewicz/Thompson, 1998.

Bishop, Chris, ed. *The Aerospace Encyclopedia of Air Warfare.* Vol. 2, *1945 to the Present.* London: Aerospace, 1997.

Blackburn, Al. *Aces Wild.* Wilmington, Del.: SR Books, 1998.

Blair, Clay. *Beyond Courage.* New York: Ballantine, 1955.

Blair, Morgan. "Evolution of the F-86." In *The Evolution of Aircraft Wing Design.* AIAA Dayton-Cincinnati Section, March 1980.

Blesse, Frederick. *"Check Six": A Fighter Pilot Looks Back.* New York: Ivy, 1987.

Bowman, Martin. *Combat Legend: F-86 Sabre.* Ramsbury, UK: Crowood, 2004.

Boyd, Alexander. *The Soviet Air Force since 1918.* New York: Stein and Day, 1977.

Boylan, Bernard. *The Development of the Long-Range Escort Fighter.* (Reprint of USAF Historical Studies No. 136.) Manhattan, Kan.: Sunflower University Press, 1955.

Boyne, Walter. *Aces in Command: Pilots as Combat Leaders*. Dulles, Va.: Brassey's, 2001.

——. "The Forgotten War," *Air Force Magazine* (June 2000).

——. *Messerschmitt Me 262: Arrow to the Future*. London: Jane's, 1980.

Brown, Earl. "Memories of Great Fighter Pilots: Frederick C. 'Boots' Blesse." *Sabre-Jet Classics* (Spring 2000).

Bruning, John. *Crimson Sky: The Air Battle for Korea*. Dulles, Va.: Brassey's, 1999.

Buckland, Ross. "Shooter's Odds." *SabreJet Classics* (Spring 1997).

Butowski, Piotr, and Jay Miller. *OKB MiG: A History of the Design Bureau and Its Aircraft*. Leicester, UK: Specialty, 1991.

Cagle, Malcolm, and Frank Manson. *The Sea War in Korea*. Annapolis, Md.: Naval Institute, 1957.

Cameron, Rebecca. *Training to Fly: Military Flight Training, 1907–1945*. Washington, D.C.: Air Force History and Museums Program, 1999.

Campbell, Robert, and Perry Nelson. "Escape Systems Evolution." *Flying Safety* (November 1955).

Clark, Otha. "Altitude Thrust Augmentation Using Water-Alcohol Injection," AF Technical Report No. AFFTC 53-8, March 1953 (FRCSL 342-66-G-2680 12/12). St. Louis, Mo.: Federal Records Center.

Clarke, R. Wallace. "Armament Diversifies." In *Aircraft of the Second World War: The Development of the Warplane, 1939–45*, Philip Jarrett, ed. London: Putnam, 1997.

Colby, C. B. "The Day We Stole a MiG." *Air Trails* (January 1953).

Collins, H. E. "Testing the Russian MiG." In *Test Flying at Old Wright Field*, Ken Chilstrom, ed. Omaha, Neb.: Westchester House, 1991.

Cooling, Benjamin, ed. *Case Studies in the Achievement of Air Superiority*. Washington, D.C.: Center for Air Force History, 1994.

Coombs, L. F. E. "The Well-equipped Warplane." In *Aircraft of the Second World War: The Development of the Warplane, 1939–45*, Philip Jarrett, ed. London: Putnam, 1997.

Coughlin, William. "F-86 'Gimmick': Improved Wing," *Aviation Week* (7 September 1953).

——. "Reds Fly Captured Sabres in Combat." *Aviator Week* (18 May 1951).

Crane, Conrad. *American Airpower Strategy in Korea, 1950–53*. Lawrence, Kan.: University Press of Kansas, 2000.

Craven, Wesley, and James Cate, eds. *The Army Air Forces in World War II*. Vol. 1, *Plans and Early Operations, January 1939 to August 1942*. Chicago: University of Chicago, 1948.

Curtis, Duncan. *North American F-86 Sabre*. Ramsbury, UK: Crowood, 2000.

Davis, Larry. "The Bloody Great Wheel!: Harrison R. Thyng," *SabreJet Classics* (Winter 2002).

——. *F-86 Sabre in Action*. Carrollton, Tex.: Squadron/Signal, 1992.

——. *The 4th Fighter Wing in the Korean War*. Atglen, Pa.: Schiffer, 2001.

——. *MiG Alley: Air to Air Combat over Korea*. Carrollton, Tex.: Squadron/Signal, 1978.

——. "North American F-86 Sabre," *Wings of Fame*. Vol. 10, 1998. Aerospace Publishing, Ltd., 1998.

——. "SabreJet: XP-86 Swept-wing Development." *Sabre Jet Classics* 5, no. 3 (1997).

——. *Walk Around: F-86 Sabre*. Carrollton, Tex: Squadron/Signal, 2000.

Dickens, Samuel. "RF-86 Sabre Overflight in Asia." In *Early Cold War Overflights, 1910–1956*, Symposium Proceedings, Vol. 1, memoirs edited by R. Cargill Hall and L. Clayton. Washington, D.C.: Office of the Historian National Reconnaissance Office, 2003.

Dille, John. "The Jets' First Ace." *Life* (4 June 1951).

Dokuchayev, Anatoli. "Aces of Jet Wars," *Krasnaya Avezda* (11 March 1995).

Dorr, Robert. "The Day the Reds Shot Down Our Top Jet Ace." In *Fighting Aces*, Phil Hirsch, ed. New York: Pyramid, 1965.

——. *F-86 Sabre: History of the Sabre and FJ Fury*. Osceola, Wisc.: Motorbooks, 1993.

Dorr, Robert, Jon Lake, and Warren Thompson. *Korean War Aces*. London: Osprey, 1995.

Dorr, Robert, and Warren Thompson. *The Korean Air War*. Osceola, Wisc.: Motorbooks, 1994.

DuPre, Flint. *U.S. Air Force Biographical Dictionary*. New York: Watts, 1965.

Dupuy, R. Ernest, and Trevor Dupuy. *The Encyclopedia of Military History from 3500 B.C. to the Present*. New York: Harper & Row, 1977.

"Ejected to Safety." *Flying Safety* (November 1949).

Engle, Eloise. "Escape Systems." In *Above and Beyond: The Encyclopedia of Aviation and Space Sciences*, vol. 4. Chicago: New Horizons, 1968.

Eriksen, C. T., ed. *The Red Air Force, 1913–1963*. Mitcham, UK: Smith, 1963.

Esposito, Vincent, ed. *The West Point Atlas of American Wars*. Vol. 2, *1900–1953*. New York: Praeger, 1960.

Evans, Douglas. *Sabre Jets Over Korea: A Firsthand Account*. Blue Ridge Summit, Pa.: Tab Books, 1984.

Fischer, Harold. *Dreams of Aces: The Hal Fischer Story, Korea and Vietnam*. Dallas: Great Impressions, 2001.

——. "My Ten MiGs." *SabreJet Classics* (Winter 1998).

Flintham, Victor. *Air Wars and Aircraft: A Detailed Record of Air Combat, 1945 to the Present*. New York: Facts on File, 1990.

Foss, Joe, and Matthew Brennan, eds. *Top Guns: America's Fighter Aces Tell Their Stories*. New York: Pocket Books, 1991.

Foster, Cecil. *MiG Alley to Mu Ghia Pass: Memoirs of a Korean War Ace*. Jefferson, N.C.: McFarland, 2001.

——. "Nine Was Enough: My Favorite Sabre Stories." *SabreJet Classics* (Winter 1993).

Francillon, Rene. *Vietnam: The War in the Air*. New York: Arch Cape, 1987.

Freeman, Roger. *The Mighty Eighth: Units, Men and Machines*. London: Macdonald, 1970.

——. *Mighty Eighth War Manual*. London: Jane's, 1984.

Fricker, John. *Battle for Pakistan: The Air War of 1965*. London: Allan, 1979.

Frisbee, John. "The Pinnacle of Professionalism." *Air Force Magazine* (February 1987).

———. "A Thyng of Valor." *Air Force Magazine* (January 1989).

———. "Valor in Three Wars." *Air Force Magazine* (November 1986).

———. "A Very Special Ace." *Air Force Magazine* (June 1990).

Futrell, Robert. *The United States Air Force in Korea,* rev. ed. Washington, D.C.: Office of Air Force History, 1983.

———. *The United States Air Force in Korea, 1950–1953.* New York: Duell, Sloan and Pearce, 1961.

Futrell, Robert, William H. Greenhalgh, Carl Grubb, Gerard E. Hasselwander, Robert F. Jakob, and Charles A. Ravenstein. *Aces and Aerial Victories: The United States Air Force in Southeast Asia 1965–1973.* Maxwell AFB, Ala.: The Albert F. Simpson Historical Research Center, Air University and Office of Air Force History, Headquarters USAF, 1976.

Gabreski, Francis. *Gabby: A Fighter Pilot's Life.* New York: Orion, 1991.

Gamble, Bruce. "Time Flies . . . The Oral History of Lt. Col. John F. Bolt, USMC (Ret.)." [Naval Aviation] Foundation (Spring 1993) (Fall 1993).

Germon, Askold. *Red Devils on the 38th Parallel.* Kiev, 1998.

Glenn, John. *John Glenn: A Memoir.* New York: Bantam, 1999.

Goodson, James. *Tumult in the Clouds.* New York: St. Martin's, 1983.

Gordon, Yefim. *Mikoyan-Gurevich MiG-15: The Soviet Union's Long-lived Korean War Fighter.* Hinckley, UK: Aerofax, 2001.

Gordon, Yefim, and Vladimir Rigmant. *MiG-15: Design, Development, and Korean War Combat History.* Osceola, Wisc.: Motorbooks, 1993.

Green, William. *Warplanes of the Third Reich.* Garden City, N.Y.: Doubleday, 1979.

Greenwood, John. "The Great Patriotic War, 1941–1945." In *Soviet Aviation and Air Power: A Historical View,* Robin Higham and Jacob Kipp, eds. London: Brassey's, 1977.

Grossnick, Roy A. *United States Naval Aviation, 1910–1995.* Washington, D.C.: Department of the Navy, Naval Historical Center, 1997. Available at http://www.history.navy.mil/branches/usna1910.htm.

"Guns for Fighters." *Flight* (28 January 1955).

Gurney, Gene. *Five Down and Glory.* New York: Ballantine, 1958.

Haas, Michael. *Apollo's Warriors: United States Air Force Special Operations During the Cold War.* Maxwell AFB, Ala.: Air University, 1997.

Hagerty, James. *First of the Spacemen: Iven C. Kincheloe, Jr.* New York: Duell, Sloan and Pearce, 1960.

Hall, R. Cargill. "Early Cold War Overflight Programs: An Introduction." In *Early Cold War Overflights, 1950–1956,* Symposium Proceedings, Vol. 1, memoirs edited by R. Cargill Hall and Laurie Clayton. Washington, D.C.: Office of the Historian National Reconnaissance Office, 2003.

Hall, R. Cargill, and Laurie Clayton, eds. *Early Cold War Overflights, 1950–1956: Symposium Proceedings.* Vol. 1, *Memoirs.* Washington, D.C.: Office of the Historian, National Reconnaissance Office, 2003.

Halliday, Jon. "Air Operations in Korea: The Soviet Side of the Story." In *A Revolutionary War: Korea and the Transformation of the Postwar World*, William Williams, ed. Chicago: Imprint, 1993.

Hallion, Richard. *The Naval Air War in Korea*. Baltimore: Nautical and Aviation, 1986.

———. "Technology for the Supersonic Era." In *Faster, Further, Higher: Leading-edge Aviation Technology Since 1945*, Philip Jarrett, ed. London: Putnam, 2002.

Hammond, Grant. *The Mind of War: John Boyd and American Security*. Washington, D.C.: Smithsonian, 2001.

Hanford, Jim. "Sabres in Combat." *Yankee Wings* (November/December 1993).

Hardesty, Von. *Red Phoenix: The Rise of Soviet Air Power 1941–1945*. Washington, D.C.: Smithsonian, 1982.

Hastings, Max. *The Korean War*. New York: Simon and Schuster, 1987.

Head, William. "McConnell, Joseph C." In *Air Warfare: An International Encyclopedia*, Vol. 2, Walter Boyne, ed. Santa Barbara, Cal.: ABC Clio, 2002.

"Heavyweights over Korea." In *Airpower: The Decisive Force in Korea*. James Stewart, ed. Princeton, N.J.: Nostrand, 1957.

Heller, Ed. "Out of Control." In *Aces in Combat: The American Aces Speak*, Eric Hammel, ed., Vol. 5. Pacifica, Cal.: Pacifica, 1998.

———. "I Thought I'd Never Get Home." In *The F-86 SabreJet and Pilots*, Barbara Stahura, ed. Paducah, Ky.: Turner, 1997.

"Hero Dies With Honor." *Dayton Daily News* (23 November 1980).

Hess, Bill. "King of MiG Alley," *Air Classics* (February 1965).

Hinton, Bruce. "Casey Jones and the Eagle." *Sabre Jet Classics* (Fall 1995).

———. "Sabres Used Tankers for Korea Deployment." *Sabre Jet Classics* (Summer 2002).

Hucker, Robert. "Joe McConnell—Top Korea Ace." *Air Combat* (May 1980).

Hughes, Kris, and Walter Dranem. *North American F-86 Sabre Jet Day Fighters*. North Branch, Minn.: Speciality, 1996.

Infield, Glenn. "The Day John Glenn Almost Died Over Korea." In *Fighting Aces*, Phil Hirsch, ed. New York: Pyramid, 1965.

Jabara, James. "First Jet Ace." *The Catholic Digest* (August 1951).

Jackson, Robert. *Air War over Korea*. New York: Scribner's, 1973.

———. *F-86 Sabre*. Washington, D.C.: Smithsonian, 1994.

James, D. Clayton. *The Years of MacArthur*. Vol. 2, *Triumph and Disaster, 1945–64*. Boston: Houghton Mifflin, 1985.

Jolidon, Laurence. *Last Seen Alive*. Austin, Tex.: Ink-Slinger, 1995.

———. "Soviet Interrogation of U.S. POWs in the Korean War." *Cold War International History Bulletin* (Winter 1995/1996).

Kaplan, Philip. *Fighter Pilot: A History and A Celebration*. New York: Barnes & Noble, 1999.

Kasler, Jim. "Mudder." In *Aces in Combat: The American Aces Speak*, Vol. 5, Eric Hamel, ed. Pacifica, Calif.: Pacifica, 1998.

Kilmarx, Robert. *A History of Soviet Air Power.* New York: Praeger, 1962.

Kitfield, James. "Flying Safety: The Real Story." *Air Force Magazine* (June 1996).

Knaack, Marcelle. *Encyclopedia of U.S. Air Force Aircraft and Missile Systems.* Vol. 1, *Post–World War II Fighters, 1945–1973.* Washington, D.C.: Office of Air Force History, 1978.

Konlobovskii, Aleksandr. "Twenty Years in Combat (Part II): A History of the MiG-15 in Combat." *Aerokhobbi* (March 1994).

———. "Aces of the World: Yevgeniy Pepelyaev." *Mir Aviatsii* (February 1993).

Krylov, Leonid, and Yuriy Tepsurkayev. "Combat Episodes of the Korean War: Three Out of One Thousand." *Mir Aviatsiya* (January 1997).

———. "The Hunt for the 'Sabre.'" *Mir Aviatsii* (1998).

———. "Russia's Plan to Seize the Sabre." *Combat Aircraft* (August 2000).

Lee, Asher. *The Soviet Air Force.* London: Duckworth, 1961.

Lopez, Donald. *Fighter Pilot's Heaven: Flight Testing the Early Jets.* Washington, D.C.: Smithsonian, 1995.

Lowery, John. "Captain Ralph S. Parr, Double Jet Ace." In *The F-86 Sabre Jet and Pilots,* Barbara Stahura, ed. Paducah, Ky.: Turner, 1997.

———. "MiG Fever." *Air & Space* (April/May 1999).

———. "MiG Fever." In *The F-86 Sabre Jet and Pilots,* Barbara Stahura, ed. Paducah, Ky.: Turner, 1997.

MacDonald, Callum. *Korea: The War Before Vietnam.* New York: Free Press, 1986.

Mahurin, Walker. *Honest John: The Autobiography of Walker M. Mahurin.* New York: Putnam's Sons, 1962.

Makinney, Robert. "B-29 Escort in Korea." *SabreJet Classics* (Spring 2000).

March, Allison, and Donald McElfresh. *Submarine or Phantom Target?* Silver Spring, Md.: Edisto, 1999.

Marion, Forrest. "'The Dumbo's Will Get Us in No Time': Air Force SA-16 Combat Operations in the Korean War Theater, 1950–1953." *Air Power History* (Summer 1999).

———. "Sabre Pilot Pickup: Unconventional Contributions to Air Superiority in Korea." *Air Power History* (Spring 2002).

Mark, Eduard. *Aerial Interdiction in Three Wars.* Washington, D.C.: Center for Air Force History, 1994.

Marshall, W. W. "MiG Alley." In *Top Guns: America's Fighter Aces Tell Their Stories,* Joe Foss and Matthew Brennan, eds. New York: Pocket Books, 1991.

Mauer, M., ed. *Air Force Combat Units of World War II.* Washington, D.C.: Office of Air Force History, 1983.

McCarthy, Michael. "Uncertain Enemies: Soviet Pilots in the Korean War." *Air Power History* (Spring 1997).

"McConnell, World's Top Jet Ace, Is Killed Testing Plane on Coast." *New York Times* (26 August 1954).

Melady, John. *Korea: Canada's Forgotten War.* Toronto: Macmillan, 1983.

Merifield, J. H. R. "Sabre vs. MiG." *RAF Quarterly* (July 1953).

Mesko, Jim. *Air War Over Korea.* Carrollton, Tex.: Squadron/Signal, 2000.

Milberry, Larry. *The Canadair Sabre.* Toronto: CANAV, 1986.

Monds, Alfred. "The Soviet Strategic Air Force and Civil Defense." In *Soviet Aviation*. Robin Higham and Jacob Kidd. London: Brassey's, 1972.

Morozov, Vladislav, and Serguy Uskov. "On Guard for Peace and Labor." *Mir Aviatsii* (February 1997).

Muller, Richard. *The German Air War in Russia*. Baltimore: Nautical and Aviation, 1992.

"New Computing Sights Vastly Improve Aerial Gunnery." *Impact* (June 1945).

Nichols, Donald. *How Many Times Can I Die?* Brooksville, Fla.: Brooksville Printing, 1981.

No, Kum-Sok. *A MiG-15 to Freedom: Memoir of a Wartime North Korean Defector Who First Delivered the Secret Fighter Jet to the Americans in 1953*. Jefferson, N.C.: McFarland, 1996.

Nordeen, Lon. *Air Warfare in the Missile Age*. Washington, D.C.: Smithsonian, 1985.

"Nose Gear—F-86." *Flying Safety* (July 1949).

Oliver, William. *The Inner Seven: The History of Seven Unique American Combat "Aces" of World War II and Korea*. Paducah, Ky.: Turner, 1999.

Olynyk, Frank. *Stars and Bars: A Tribute to the American Fighter Ace 1920–1973*. London: Grubb Street, 1995.

Orr, Robert. "Defense and Strategy." *Fortune* (October 1953).

Paschall, Rod. "Special Operations in Korea." *Conflict* 8, no. 2, 1987.

Peacock, Lindsay. *North American F-86 Sabre*. New York: Gallery, 1991.

Polak, Tomas, with Christopher Shores. *Stalin's Falcons: The Aces of the Red Star*. London: Grubb Street, 1999.

Price, Alfred. *World War II Fighter Conflict*. London: Macdonald's and Jane's, 1975.

Rice, Ray. "The Sabre Story." *Skyline* (February 1953).

Risner, Robinson. *The Passing of the Night: My Seven Years as a Prisoner of the North Vietnamese*. New York: Random House, 1973.

Rosen, Stephen. *Winning the Next War: Innovation and the Modern Military*. Ithaca, N.Y.: Cornell, 1991.

"Sabre: A Study of a Renowned Fighter." *Flight* (30 January 1953).

Salter, James. *Burning the Day: Recollections*. New York: Random House, 1997.

———. *The Hunters*. New York: Harper, 1956.

Sandler, Stanley. *The Korean War: No Victors, No Vanquished*. Lexington: University Press of Kentucky, 1999.

Sarin, Oleg, and Lev Dvoretsky. *Alien Wars: The Soviet Union's Aggressions Against the World, 1919 to 1989*. Novato, Cal.: Presidio, 1996.

Scutts, Jerry. "The Jet Revolution." In *The Modern War Machine: Military Aviation Since 1945*, Philip Jarrett, ed. London: Putnam, 2000.

———. "The Upper Reaches." In *Faster, Further and Higher*, Philip Jarrett, ed. London: Putnam, 2002.

Seidl, Hans. *Stalin's Eagles: An Illustrated Study of the Soviet Aces of World War II and Korea*. Atglen, Pa.: Schiffer, 1998.

Shacklady, Edward. *The North American F-86A Sabre*. London: Profile, 1965.

Shaw, Robert. *Fighter Combat: Tactics and Maneuvering*. Annapolis, Md.: Naval Institute, 1985.

Sherwood, John. *Officers in Flight Suits: The Story of American Air Force Fighter Pilots in the Korean War.* New York: New York University, 1996.

Shores, Christopher. *Air Aces.* Novato, Cal.: Presido, 1983.

———. *Fighter Aces.* London: Hamlyn, 1975.

Sims, Edward. *Fighter Tactics and Strategy, 1914–1970.* New York: Harper and Row, 1972.

Smith, Richard. *Seventy-Five Years of In-flight Refueling: Highlights, 1923–1998.* Washington, D.C.: Air Force History and Museums Program, 1998.

Spick, Mike. *The Ace Factor: Air Combat and the Role of Situational Awareness.* Annapolis, Md.: Naval Institute Press, 1988.

———. *The Complete Fighter Ace: All The World's Fighter Aces, 1914–2000.* London: Greenhhill, 1999.

Stahura, Barbara, ed. *The F-86 Sabre Jet and Pilots.* Paducah, Ky.: Turner, 1997.

Stewart, James, ed. *Airpower: The Decisive Force in Korea.* Princeton, N.J.: Nostrand, 1957.

Stokesbury, James. *A Short History of the Korean War.* New York: William Morrow, 1988.

Stonestreet, Bob. "International Incident over the Yellow Sea, Korea—February 5, 1955." *SabreJet Classics* (Fall 1995).

Swanborough, Gordon, and Peter Bowers. *United States Military Aircraft since 1908.* London: Putnam, 1971.

———. *United States Navy Aircraft since 1911.* New York: Funk & Wagnall, 1968.

Tagg, Lori. *On the Front Line of R & D: Wright-Patterson Air Force Base in the Korean War, 1950–1953.* Wright-Patterson AFB, Ohio: History Office, Aeronautical Systems Center, 2001.

Taylor, John, ed. *Combat Aircraft of the World: From 1909 to the Present.* London: Paragon, 1979.

Taylor, John, Michael Taylor, and David Mondey, eds. *Air Facts and Feats.* New York: Two Continents, 1974.

"They Snatched a Mig." *American Legion Magazine* (November 1959).

Thomas, J. "Korea Jet Ace Recalled as Modest Hero." *New York Times* (27 October 1980).

Thompson, Warren. *F-86 Sabre Fighter-Bomber Units over Korea.* Oxford, UK: Osprey, 1999.

———. *F-86 Sabres of the 4th Interceptor Wing.* Oxford, UK: Osprey, 2002.

Thompson, Warren, and David McLaren. *MiG Alley: Sabres vs. MiGs Over Korea.* North Branch, Minn.: Specialty, 2002.

Tilford, Earl. *Search and Rescue in Southeast Asia.* Washington, D.C.: Office of Air Force History, 1980.

Toliver, Raymond, and Trevor Constable. *Fighter Aces of the USA.* Fallbrook, Cal.: Aero, 1979.

"Two Aces in Korean Air War." *Naval Aviation News* (September 1953).

Vojvodich, Mele. "Overflights Conducted During the Korean War." In *Cold War Overflights, 1950–1956,* symposium proceedings, vol. 1, memoirs edited by

R. Cargill and L. Clayton. Washington, D.C.: Office of the Historical National Reconnaissance Office, 2003.

Wagner, Ray. *American Combat Planes*. Garden City, N.Y.: Doubleday, 1982.

———. *Mustang Designer: Edgar Schmued and the P-51*. Washington, D.C.: Smithsonian, 1990.

———. *The North American Sabre*. Garden City, N.Y.: Doubleday, 1963.

———, ed. *The Soviet Air Force in World War II: The Official History*. Garden City, N.Y.: Doubleday, 1973.

Walter, Lon. "The First Ace is Crowned." *SabreJet Classics* (Summer 1998).

———. "Recollections of James Jabara." *SabreJet Classics* (Summer 1998).

Warnock, A. Timothy, ed. *The USAF in Korea: A Chronology, 1950–1953*. Washington, D.C.: Air Force History and Museums Program and Air University Press, 2000.

Weal, Elke, John Weal, and Richard Barker. *Combat Aircraft of World War Two*. New York: Macmillan, 1977.

Webster, Charles, and Noble Frankland. *The Strategic Air Offensive against Germany 1939–1945*. Vol. 3, *Victory*. London: HMSO, 1961.

Welch, George. "Spinning the Sabre." *Flying Safety* (February 1954).

Werrell, Kenneth. *Blankets of Fire: U.S. Bombers over Japan during World War II*. Washington, D.C.: Smithsonian, 1996.

———. "The Tactical Development of the Eighth Air Force in World War II," Ph.D. diss., Duke University, 1969.

West Point Alumni Association. *1971 Register of Graduates and Former Cadets of the United States Military Academy*. Chicago: R. R. Donnelley and Sons, 1971.

Wetterhahn, Ralph. "The Russians of MiG Alley." *Retired Officer* (August 2000).

———. "To Snatch a Sabre." *Air and Space* (June/July 2003).

Weyland, Otto. "The Air Campaign in Korea." In *Airpower: The Decisive Force in Korea*, James Stewart, ed. Princeton, N.J.: Nostrand, 1957.

"Who Towed That F-86?" *Flying Safety* (July 1950).

Wilson, Stewart. *F-86 Sabre, MiG-15 Fagot, and Hawker Hunter*. Weston Creek, Australia: Aerospace, 1995.

Wolfe, Tom. *The Right Stuff*. New York: Farrar, Straus, Giroux, 1979.

Wright, Ed. "An Ace Among Aces." *Naval Aviation News* (May–June 2003).

Y'Blood, William. *MiG Alley: The Fight for Air Superiority*. Washington, D.C.: Air Force History and Museums Program, 2000.

———, ed. *The Three Wars of Lt. Gen. George E. Stratemeyer: His Korean War Diary*. Washington, D.C.: Air Force History and Museums Program, 1999.

Yeager, Chuck, and Leo Janos. *Yeager*. Toronto: Bantam, 1985.

Zhang, Xiaoming. *Red Wings over the Yalu: China, the Soviet Union, and the Air War in Korea*. College Station, Tex.: Texas A & M, 2002.

Zolotarev, V. A., ed. *Russia (USSR) in Local Wars and Regional Conflicts in the Second Half of the 20th Century*. Moscow: Kuchkovo Polye Publishing, 2000.

Index

Note: Page numbers followed by the letter *n*, plus a number, refer to endnotes.

performance (*continued*)
boosters, 18–19; water-alcohol injection, 17; weight reduction, 15–16. *See also* maintenance; models, changes in
Peterson, Paul, 22
photographic intelligence, 129
Pickett, Owen, 102
pilots: age, 87, 145; aggressiveness of, 138; Communist, 140, 221; ejection seats, 47; exchange, 139; friendly fire, 122–24; gunsights, 27, 29; personal equipment, 78; personality traits, 145; reluctant warriors, 124–25; safety training, 48–51; shooter position, 137–38. *See also* specific pilots, aces
Pittman, Biffle, 170
Pitts, Morris, 154
Ponomarev, Mikhail, 215–16
Poulton, Gail, 119
Power Plant Laboratory, 17. *See also* Wright Air Development Center (WADC)
Prasccindo, Robert, 95
Preston, Benjamin, 16, 108, 157, 274n31
prisoners of war, 102–3, 202–3, 204, 206
propellers, 45–46
Pullout, Project, 226
Pusan Perimeter, 72
Pyongyang, 84

radar, 27, 32
radio intelligence, 105–7
RAF (Royal Air Force), 193–94
Ragland, Dayton, 210
range, 26, 37, 38–39, 44
rats, 21, 241n4
RB-45s, 232
RB-50Gs, 106
RB-50s, 175
RCAF (Royal Canadian Air Force), 193–94
RD-1s, 60–61
RD-45Fs, 60–61
rearward vision: MiG-15bis, 64
Red aces, 213–18
reflector gunsights, 26–27

refueling, 44
Reitsma, Donald, 182
Republic of Korea (RoK), 66–67, 106
Rhee, Syngman, 70
Rice, Ray, 7, 8
Richtoven, Manfred von, 144
Rickenbacker, Eddie, 14, 144, 152
Ridgway, Matthew, 89, 135
Right Stuff, The, 11
ring and bead gunsights, 26
Risner, Robinson, 131, 164, 204–6, 286n21, 290n51
rivalry, 86
Roach, Paul, 86
Roberts, James, 36
Roberts, John, 275n54
rocket boosters, 18–19
Rocketdyne, 19
Rolls Royce Nene, 60–61
Royal Heater, 43
Ruddell, George, 191, 211

Sabre: origination of name, 14
Sabre Knights, 183
safety: accident records, 55; big picture, 56–58; ejection, 46–48; props to jets, 45–46; training, 48–51
SA-16s, 112, 113
Schilling, David, 133–34, 160
Schmued, Ed, 7
Schniz, Albert, 116–19, 123
Second Air Rescue Squadron, 112
Sellers, Tom, 196–99, 288n16
shackles, 42, 253n28
Shchukin, Lev, 215
Sheberstov, Konstantin, 216
Sherwood, John, 275n54
shooter position, 137–38
Sicily, HMS, 97
signals intelligence (SIGINT), 106
Simmi-do, 107
slats, 7, 8–9, 238n18
Smiley, Albert, 207
Smith, Norman, 163

About the Author

Kenneth P. Werrell graduated from the USAF Academy in 1960 and went on to earn his pilot wings the following year. He was stationed in Japan and flew weather reconnaissance missions over the northwestern Pacific, first as a pilot and later as an aircraft commander of the WB-50. He resigned his commission in 1965, going on to earn master's and doctorate degrees in history from Duke University.

Werrell taught at Radford University, with brief assignments at the Army's Command and General Staff College and the USAF's Air University, until his retirement in 1996. He has published numerous articles in professional journals and six other books on aviation history. He lives with his wife, Jeanne, and cat, Fritz, in Christiansburg, Virginia.

Also by Kenneth P. Werrell

Chasing the Silver Bullet: U.S. Air Force Weapons Development from Vietnam to Desert Storm (2003)
Blankets of Fire: U.S. Bombers over Japan During World War II (1996)
Who Fears? The 301st in War and Peace, 1942–1979 (1991)
Archie, Flak, AAA, and SAM: A Short Operational History of Ground-Based Air Defense (1988) (revised and updated as *Archie to SAM*, 2005)
The Evolution of the Cruise Missile (1985)
Eighth Air Force Bibliography (1981, revised and updated 1996)

The Naval Institute Press is the book-publishing arm of the U.S. Naval Institute, a private, nonprofit membership society for sea service professionals and others who share an interest in naval and maritime affairs. Established in 1873 at the U.S. Naval Academy in Annapolis, Maryland, where its offices remain today, the Naval Institute has members worldwide.

Members of the Naval Institute support the education programs of the society and receive the influential monthly magazine *Proceedings* and discounts on fine nautical prints and on ship and aircraft photos. They also have access to the transcripts of the Institute's Oral History Program and get discounted admission to any of the Institute-sponsored seminars offered around the country. Discounts are also available to the colorful bimonthly magazine *Naval History.*

The Naval Institute's book-publishing program, begun in 1898 with basic guides to naval practices, has broadened its scope to include books of more general interest. Now the Naval Institute Press publishes about one hundred titles each year, ranging from how-to books on boating and navigation to battle histories, biographies, ship and aircraft guides, and novels. Institute members receive significant discounts on the Press's more than eight hundred books in print.

Full-time students are eligible for special half-price membership rates. Life memberships are also available.

For a free catalog describing Naval Institute Press books currently available, and for further information about joining the U.S. Naval Institute, please write to:

Membership Department
U.S. Naval Institute
291 Wood Road
Annapolis, MD 21402-5034
Telephone: (800) 233-8764
Fax: (410) 269-7940
Web address: www.navalinstitute.org